The Book of Revelation

The Book of Revelation

Worship for Life in the Spirit of Prophecy

JOHN PAUL HEIL

CASCADE *Books* • Eugene, Oregon

THE BOOK OF REVELATION
Worship for Life in the Spirit of Prophecy

Copyright © 2014 John Paul Heil. All rights reserved. Except for brief quotations in critical publications or reviews, no part of this book may be reproduced in any manner without prior written permission from the publisher. Write: Permissions, Wipf and Stock Publishers, 199 W. 8th Ave., Suite 3, Eugene, OR 97401.

Cascade Books
An Imprint of Wipf and Stock Publishers
199 W. 8th Ave., Suite 3
Eugene, OR 97401

www.wipfandstock.com

ISBN 13: 978-1-62564-444-2

Cataloging-in-Publication data:

Heil, John Paul

The book of Revelation : worship for life in the spirit of prophecy / John Paul Heil

viii + 366 p. ; 23 cm. Includes bibliographical references and indexes.

ISBN 13: 978-1-62564-444-2

1. Bible. Revelation—Criticism, interpretation, etc. 2. Worship. I. Title.

BS2825 H37 2014

Manufactured in the U.S.A.

Contents

Abbreviations   vii

1   Introduction   1

PART ONE: Grace from John in Spirit to Churches to Be Shown What Must Happen Soon (1:1—3:22)

2   Prologue: John's Authorization to Prophesy to the Seven Churches (1:1-20)   17

3   Prophetic Oracles to the Seven Churches (2:1—3:22)   34

PART TWO: John in Spirit Shown What Must Happen after These Things (4:1—16:21)

4   John's Visions of Lamb Opening Seals and Worship around Throne in Heaven (4:1—7:17)   69

5   John's Visions of the Seven Angels Trumpeting Their Seven Trumpets (8:1—11:19)   112

6   Worship of Dragon and Beasts on Earth and Worship with Lamb in Heaven (12:1—14:20)   159

7   John's Visions of the Seven Angels Pouring out Their Seven Bowls (15:1—16:21)   205

PART THREE: Carried in Spirit to Wilderness, John Shown Prostitute and Wife of Lamb (17:1—21:8)

8   Vision and Downfall of the Idolatrous Prostitute Babylon (17:1—18:24)   235

Abbreviations

    9   Heavenly Worship and Final Judgment (19:1—21:8)   266

PART FOUR: Grace from John Carried in Spirit to Mountain and Shown Holy City (21:9—22:21)

    10   Visions of the Heavenly City's Worship of God and the Lamb for Eternal Life (21:9—22:5)   307

    11   Epilogue: Exhortations about Words of This Prophecy for Worship of God (22:6-21)   322

    12   Conclusion   336

          Bibliography   339

          Author Index   347

          Scripture Index   351

Abbreviations

ABR	*Australian Biblical Review*
AcT	*Acta theologica*
ATJ	*Ashland Theological Journal*
AUSS	*Andrews University Seminary Studies*
BAR	*Biblical Archaeology Review*
BBR	*Bulletin for Biblical Research*
BECNT	Baker Exegetical Commentary on the New Testament
Bib	*Biblica*
BNTC	Black's New Testament Commentaries
BR	*Biblical Research*
BSac	*Bibliotheca sacra*
BTB	*Biblical Theology Bulletin*
BiTS	Biblical Tools and Studies
BZNW	Beihefte zur Zeitschrift für die neutestamentliche Wissenschaft
CBQ	*Catholic Biblical Quarterly*
CBQMS	Catholic Biblical Quarterly Monograph Series
CTR	Criswell Theological Review
CurTM	*Currents in Theology and Mission*
ETL	*Ephemerides theologicae lovanienses*
EvQ	*Evangelical Quarterly*
ExpTim	*Expository Times*
HTR	*Harvard Theological Review*
IBS	*Irish Biblical Studies*
Int	*Interpretation*
JBL	*Journal of Biblical Literature*

Abbreviations

JETS	*Journal of the Evangelical Theological Society*
JSNT	*Journal for the Study of the New Testament*
JSNTSup	Journal for the Study of the New Testament: Supplement Series
JSP	*Journal for the Study of the Pseudepigrapha*
LNTS	Library of New Testament Studies
Neot	*Neotestamentica*
NICNT	New International Commentary on the New Testament
NIGTC	New International Greek Testament Commentary
NovT	*Novum Testamentum*
NTL	New Testament Library
NTM	New Testament Monographs
NTS	*New Testament Studies*
SBLECL	Society of Biblical Literature Early Christianity and Its Literature
SBLSymS	Society of Biblical Literature Symposium Series
ScrB	*Scripture Bulletin*
SP	Sacra pagina
SVTQ	*St. Vladimir's Theological Quarterly*
TJ	*Trinity Journal*
VR	*Vox reformata*
WBC	Word Biblical Commentary
WUNT	Wissenschaftliche Untersuchungen zum Neuen Testament

1

Introduction

THIS BOOK PRESENTS NEW proposals for the structure and the worship theme of the book of Revelation. First, I will illustrate a new comprehensive chiastic structure that attempts, in contrast to previous proposals, to account for all of the textual data.[1] This structure provides a visual guide to the oral presentation of the text as it was heard by its original audience in a context of liturgical worship.[2] I will employ my proposed structure as the organizational basis for the exegetical chapters that follow this introduction.

Secondly, I will demonstrate a new unifying theme by which Revelation functions as a liturgical prophecy to exhort and enable its implied audience to witness against idolatrous worship and for true worship in accord with the eternal life now available as a result of the death and resurrection of Jesus Christ. The subtitle of this book, "Worship for Life in the Spirit of Prophecy," sums up this unifying

---

1. DeSilva ("X Marks the Spot?," 343–71) has noted that several past proposals for chiastic structure have been based on selectivity and manipulation of the textual data. My proposed chiastic structure is based on a close reading of all of the textual data. There is an identifiable textual basis for every chiastic parallel that I will present. On the structure of Revelation, see Beale, *Revelation*, 108–51; Tavo, *Woman*, 25–45; Wilson, *Victor Sayings*, 1–30; Bandy, *Prophetic Lawsuit*, 95–122; Bandy, "Layers of the Apocalypse," 469–99; McNicol, *Conversion*, 112–20.

2. Barr, "Apocalypse of John as Oral Enactment," 243–56. See also Seal, "Aural Elements," 38–51; Skaggs and Doyle, "Audio/Visual Motif," 19–37; Lee and Scott, *Sound Mapping*.

theme. In this introductory chapter I will present an overview of the structure of Revelation followed by a discussion of my presuppositions and preliminary analysis of its main theme of worship.

The Structure of the Book of Revelation

The Four Major Sections

The book of Revelation divides into four major sections, each introduced by a similarly recurring linguistic pattern. This pattern consists of the first four occurrences in Revelation of the verb "to show" (1:1; 4:1; 17:1; 21:9) shortly followed by the only four occurrences in Revelation of the phrase "in Spirit" (1:10; 4:2; 17:3; 21:10). The pattern for the first two sections employs the verb "I was" with "in Spirit," whereas in the final two sections the verb "he carried" occurs with "in Spirit." In addition, the final two sections introduce the verb "to show" with the only two occurrences in Revelation of the adverb "here" (17:1; 21:9).

This recurring linguistic pattern thus indicates that the following are the four major sections of Revelation: First, 1:1—3:22: "I was in Spirit on the Lord's day" (1:10) to be shown what must happen soon (1:1); second, 4:1—16:21: "I will show you what must happen after these things.' Immediately I was in Spirit" (4:1-2); third, 17:1—21:8: "'Here, I will show the judgment' (17:1) . . . then he carried me into the wilderness in Spirit" (17:3); fourth, 21:9—22:21: "'Here, I will show you the bride' (21:9) . . . then he carried me in Spirit to a mountain" (21:10).

The Ten Macrochiastic Subsections

Within the four major sections are ten macrochiastic subsections arranged as follows:
1) Grace from John *in Spirit* to the Churches To Be **Shown** What Must Happen Soon (1:1—3:22)
    a) Prologue: John's Authorization To Prophesy to the Seven Churches (1:1-20)
    b) Prophetic Oracles to the Seven Churches (2:1—3:22)

Introduction

2) John *in Spirit Shown* What Must Happen after These Things (4:1—16:21)

      c) John's Visions of Lamb Opening Seals and Worship around Throne in Heaven (4:1—7:17)

         d) John's Visions of the Seven Angels Trumpeting Their Seven Trumpets (8:1—11:19)

            e) Worship of Dragon and Beasts on Earth and Worship with Lamb in Heaven (12:1—14:20)

            e′) John's Visions of the Seven Angels Pouring Out Their Seven Bowls (15:1—16:21)

3) Carried *in Spirit* to Wilderness John *Shown* Prostitute and Wife of Lamb (17:1—21:8)

         d′) Vision and Downfall of the Idolatrous Prostitute Babylon (17:1—18:24)

      c′) Heavenly Worship and Final Judgment (19:1—21:8)

4) Grace from John Carried *in Spirit* to Mountain and *Shown* Holy City (21:9—22:21)

   b′) Visions of the Heavenly City's Worship of God and the Lamb for Eternal Life (21:9—22:5)

a′) Epilogue: Exhortations about Words of This Prophecy for Worship of God (22:6-21)

The Sixty-Five Microchiastic Units

Within the ten macrochiastic subsections are sixty-five microchiastic units arranged as follows:

1. Grace from John in Spirit to the Churches To Be Shown What Must Happen Soon (1:1—3:22)

A. Prologue: John's Authorization To Prophesy to the Seven Churches (1:1–20)

    1a) John Witnessed to the Prophetic Word of God and Witness of Jesus Christ (1:1–3)

        2b) Opening Greeting of the Letter from John to the Seven Churches (1:4–9)

        3b′) Command for John To Write What He Observes to the Seven Churches (1:10–16)

    4a′) Command for John To Write Things That Are and That Are about To Be (1:17–20)

B. Prophetic Oracles to the Seven Churches (2:1—3:22)

    1a) Oracle to the Angel of the Church in Ephesus (2:1–7)

        2b) Oracle to the Angel of the Church in Smyrna (2:8–11)

            3c) Oracle to the Angel of the Church in Pergamum (2:12–17)

                4d) Oracle to the Angel of the Church in Thyatira (2:18–29)

            5c′) Oracle to the Angel of the Church in Sardis (3:1–6)

        6b′) Oracle to the Angel of the Church in Philadelphia (3:7–13)

    7a′) Oracle to the Angel of the Church in Laodicea (3:14–22)

Introduction

2. John in Spirit Shown What Must Happen after These Things (4:1—16:21)

C. John's Visions of Lamb Opening Seals and Worship around Throne in Heaven (4:1—7:17)

    1a) Vision of the One Sitting on the Throne in Heaven (4:1-5a)

        2b) Worship of the One Sitting on the Throne in Heaven (4:5b-11)

            3c) Vision of the Scroll and the Mighty Angel (5:1-5)

                4d) Vision of and New Song to the Lamb (5:6-10)

                    5e) Vision of Universal Worship of the Lamb and One Sitting on the Throne (5:11-14)

                    6e′) First Four Seals: The Four Horsemen (6:1-8)

                7d′) Fifth Seal: Prayer of the Slaughtered Souls under the Altar (6:9-11)

            8c′) Sixth Seal: The Anger of God and the Lamb (6:12-17)

        9b′) Vision and Audition of 144,000 Who Had Been Sealed (7:1-8)

    10a′) Vision of Great Crowd Standing before the Throne and Worshiping God (7:9-17)

D. John's Visions of the Seven Angels Trumpeting Their Seven Trumpets (8:1—11:19)

    1a) Seventh Seal and Seven Angels Given Seven Trumpets (8:1-5)

        2b) First Four Trumpets and Announcement of Three Woes (8:6-13)

            3c) Vision of Fifth Trumpet: A Fallen Star Given the Key to the Abyss (9:1-12)

                4d) Vision of Sixth Trumpet: Release of the Four Angels/Horses with Riders (9:13-21)

       5c′) Vision of the Mighty Angel with the Small Scroll (10:1–11)

    6b′) Martyrdom and Vindication of the Two Prophetic Witnesses (11:1–14)

  7a′) Seventh Trumpet: Sounds of Worship and Appearance of the Ark in Heaven (11:15–19)

E. WORSHIP OF DRAGON AND BEASTS ON EARTH AND WORSHIP OF LAMB IN HEAVEN (12:1—14:20)

  1a) Appearances in Heaven of Signs of Woman with Child and of Dragon (12:1–6)

    2b) Dragon Thrown Down to Earth and Sound in Heaven (12:7–12a)

      3c) The Devil/Dragon/Serpent and the Woman (12:12b–18)

        4d) Vision of the Beast from the Sea (13:1–10)

          5e) Vision of the Beast from the Earth (13:11–18)

          6e′) Vision of the Lamb with 144,000 (14:1–5)

        7d′) Announcement of God's Judgment and Fall of Babylon (14:6–8)

      8c′) Blessed Are Those Who Die for Not Worshiping the Beast (14:9–13)

    9b′) Vision of Harvesting Earth by One Like a Son of Man for Judgment (14:14–17)

  10a′) Vine of the Earth Thrown into the Winepress of God's Fury (14:18–20)

E′. JOHN'S VISIONS OF THE SEVEN ANGELS POURING OUT THEIR SEVEN BOWLS (15:1—16:21)

    1a) Visions of Angels with Seven Last Plagues and of Those Who Conquered (15:1-4)

        2b) Vision of Seven Angels Given Seven Bowls Filled with the Fury of God (15:5-8)

            3c) First Four Bowls Poured Out and No Repentance (16:1-9)

            4c′) Fifth Bowl Followed by No Repentance and Sixth Bowl (16:10-12)

        5b′) Vision of Three Unclean Spirits Who Assemble Kings for Harmagedon (16:13-16)

    6a′) Seventh Bowl: Great Earthquake and Hail and They Blasphemed God (16:17-21)

3. Carried in Spirit to Wilderness John Shown Prostitute and Wife of Lamb (17:1—21:8)

D′. VISION AND DOWNFALL OF THE IDOLATROUS PROSTITUTE BABYLON (17:1—18:24)

    1a) An Angel Will Show the Judgment of the Great Prostitute (17:1-5)

        2b) Vision of Woman and Angel's Explanation of Marveling at Beast (17:6-8)

            3c) Explanation of Vision of Seven Heads and Ten Horns (17:9-14)

                4d) Explanations of Visions of Waters, Ten Horns and Beast, and Woman (17:15-18)

            5c′) The Fall and Divine Judgment of Babylon the Great (18:1-8)

>> **6b′)** Kings and Merchants Pronounce Woes of Divine Judgment on Babylon (18:9–19)
>
> **7a′)** Babylon Not Found Again as in Her Was Found Blood of Those Slaughtered (18:20–24)

> c′. HEAVENLY WORSHIP AND FINAL JUDGMENT (19:1—21:8)
>
>> **1a)** Hearing Worship of God in Heaven for Judgment of Great Prostitute (19:1–5)
>>
>>> **2b)** The Wedding Feast of the Lamb and Worship of God (19:6–10)
>>>
>>>> **3c)** Vision of the Faithful and True Rider on a White Horse (19:11–16)
>>>>
>>>>> **4d)** Great Supper of God and Beast and False Prophet Thrown into Lake of Fire (19:17–21)
>>>>
>>>> **5c′)** One Thousand Years and Final Defeat of Devil (20:1–10)
>>>
>>> **6b′)** Vision of Judgment and of Death and Hades Thrown into Lake of Fire (20:11–15)
>>
>> **7a′)** Vision of a New Heaven and a New Earth (21:1–8)

4. Grace from John Carried in Spirit to Mountain and Shown Holy City (21:9—22:21)

> B′. VISIONS OF THE HEAVENLY CITY'S WORSHIP OF GOD AND THE LAMB FOR ETERNAL LIFE (21:9—22:5)
>
>> **1a)** Angel Shows Bride of Lamb/Holy City Jerusalem from Heaven (21:9–14)
>>
>>> **2b)** No Temple Seen in the Heavenly City (21:15–22a)
>>>
>>> **3b′)** God and Lamb Are Temple of City for Glory and Honor of Nations (21:22b–27)

> **4a′)** Angel Showed John the Worship for Eternal Life in the Heavenly City (22:1–5)

A′. Epilogue: Exhortations about Words of This Prophecy for Worship of God (22:6–21)

> **1a)** Keep the Faithful and True Words of the Prophecy of This Scroll (22:6–9)
>> **2b)** Do Not Seal the Words of the Prophecy of This Scroll (22:10–15)
>
> **3a′)** Witness to the Words of the Scroll of This Prophecy (22:16–21)

The Role of Chiastic Structures

Ancient documents that were performed orally frequently exhibit chiastic structures. Chiastic patterns serve to organize the content to be heard and not only aid the memory of the one delivering or performing a document but also make it easier for the implied audience to follow, comprehend, and remember the content. Chiastic structures thus serve not only as a way of punctuating and unifying the oral performance, but also as a way of rhetorically emphasizing key points and themes. A chiasm works rhetorically by leading its audience through introductory elements to a central, pivotal point or points, and then reaching its conclusion by recalling and developing, via the chiastic parallels, aspects of the initial elements that led to the central, pivotal point or points. The rhetorical goal of each chiasm is thus a climactic conclusion arrived at after a previous turning point or points.[3]

Since chiasms were apparently very common in ancient oral-auricular and rhetorical cultures, the original audience may and need not necessarily have been consciously identifying or reflecting upon any of these chiastic structures in themselves as they heard them. They merely

---

3. For chiastic structures of other NT documents, see Heil, "Philemon," 178–206; Heil, *Ephesians*; Heil, *Philippians*; Heil, *Colossians*; Heil, *Hebrews*; Heil, *James*; Heil, *1 Peter, 2 Peter, and Jude.*

experienced the chiastic phenomenon, which had an unconscious effect on how they perceived the content. But a discovery, delineation, and bringing to consciousness of the chiastic structures of ancient documents can greatly aid the modern audience to a more proper and precise interpretation of them. Their identification serves as a visual guide to how the original ancient audiences heard the organization of the document. Based on my identification of the chiastic structures comprising Revelation, I will provide an interpretation focused on how the audience implied by the text are to respond to the rhetorical strategies presented by the dynamics of these chiastic structures as they listen to them.[4]

Presuppositions and Preliminary Analysis of Main Theme

The text of Revelation identifies its implied author simply as "John" (1:1, 4, 9; 22:8), designated as a "servant" of God (1:1), who refers to his writing repeatedly as "the words of the prophecy" (1:3; 22:7, 10, 18, 19). The historical author seems to have been an otherwise unknown Christian prophet.[5] Revelation is to be dated sometime in the second half of the first century, probably during the reign of the emperor Domitian around 95 CE.[6] Revelation locates its implied author John on the island of Patmos (1:9). The implied audience are seven churches in the Asian cities of Ephesus, Smyrna, Pergamum, Thyatira, Sardis, Philadelphia, and Laodicea (1:11), a group representative of all of the churches in western Asia Minor. The social and cultural context includes the idolatrous worship of pagan gods and emperors, a major problem addressed throughout Revelation.[7]

---

4. The collective noun "audience" will be used as a plural noun throughout, so that it covers both those cases where the listeners are referred to as a singular, collective entity and those cases where the listeners are conceived of as a group composed of individual members with responsibilities toward one another. Revelation begins by addressing its audience with plural forms—"servants" (1:1), "those who hear" (1:3), and "the seven churches" (1:4).

5. Harrington, *Revelation*, 8–9; Beale, *Revelation*, 34–36; Blount, *Revelation*, 5–8.

6. Beale, *Revelation*, 4–27; Harrington, *Revelation*, 9; Blount, *Revelation*, 8.

7. For recent nuanced discussions regarding the Roman imperial cult or cults, see Brodd and Reed, *Rome and Religion*. See also Voorwinde, "Worship," 3–35.

Introduction

As words of prophecy, Revelation was intended to be read aloud in the context of communal liturgical worship. The many allusions to the OT throughout Revelation serve to demonstrate the continuity of its prophecy with the scriptural prophecy of the past. These scriptural allusions also contribute to the worship character of Revelation, since the audience can be expected to recognize and appreciate them as a result of their use in their liturgical worship.[8]

As liturgical prophecy, Revelation engages its audience in various acts of worship.[9] It begins and concludes with liturgical dialogues (1:4–8; 22:6–21), and contains some dialogue-style content throughout (13:9–10; 14:12–13; 16:15; 19:1–8).[10] Revelation invites its audience to participate in several hymns or songs of worship (4:9–11; 5:9–14; 7:10–17; 11:15–19; 12:10–12; 15:2–4; 16:5–7).[11] It refers to "the prayers of the holy ones" (5:8; 8:3, 4), and contains a key prayer of supplication (6:10).[12] And the oral performance of Revelation may well have been followed, at least at times, by the celebration of the Lord's Supper.[13] In addition, as I will indicate in the following chapters, there are allusions throughout Revelation to different dimensions of the Eucharist—its sacrificial character, its eating and drinking with the risen Lord for eternal life, its foretaste of the eschatological banquet, its anticipation of the final coming of the Lord for judgment, etc.[14]

8. According to Aune (*Revelation 1–5*, 23), "the author intended, even designed, his composition to be read aloud before Christian congregations assembled for worship."

9. Barr (*Tales of the End*, 179) refers to Revelation "as a kind of ritual text." See also Vassiliadis, "Apocalypse and Liturgy," 95–112.

10. Vanni, "Liturgical Dialogue," 348–72. On the liturgical language and setting of Revelation, see Thompson, *Book of Revelation*, 69–73; Barr, *Tales of the End*, 171–75; Ruiz, "Betwixt," 221–41; Ryan, "Heavenly Temple Liturgy," 13–25.

11. Ruiz, "Praise," 70–73; Tonstad, *Saving God's Reputation*, 149–54.

12. Heil, "Fifth Seal," 220–43.

13. Roloff, *Revelation*, 249–54; Aune, *Revelation 17–22*, 1235; Beale, *Revelation*, 1155.

14. Revelation "can be read as a book of eucharistic prophecy" (Koenig, *Feast*, 212). "The Apocalypse can be seen as an elaborate story that explains the rite of the Eucharist . . . Support for the thesis that this story should be connected with the Eucharist can be drawn from the story itself, which is fascinated with the notion of blood, especially the blood of Jesus (1:5; 5:9; 7:14; 12:11; 14:20 etc.)" (Barr, *Tales of the End*, 171–72).

A prologue (1:1–20) and an epilogue (22:6–21) form a literary inclusion that frames the book of Revelation. They give preliminary indications that its main theme, function, and purpose is to exhort and enable its audience to "worship for life in the Spirit of prophecy." The prologue introduces the worship context of Revelation by pronouncing a divine blessing upon the lector who reads it aloud to the audience depicted as a liturgical assembly. They are to hear the words of the prophecy from John and complete their act of worship by keeping the things written in it through their prophetic witness regarding true and false worship (1:3).[15] The prologue then engages the audience in a liturgical dialogue (1:4–9), which contains an act of doxological worship of Jesus Christ (1:5–6). The reference to him as the one who "has released us from our sins by his blood" (1:5b) provides a first allusion to the sacrificial character of the Eucharist.

With regard to "worship for life," the prologue presents John in an act of worship oriented toward the eternal life of the risen Lord. When John had his vision of the risen Jesus, "the firstborn of the dead" (1:5), he fell toward his feet as if dead (1:17). In Revelation this functions as a gesture of worshipful submission (cf. 3:9; 19:10; 22:8). Jesus then identifies himself as "the one who is living, once I was dead, but behold I am living for the ages of the ages and I have the keys of Death and of Hades" (1:18). This implies that the risen Jesus has the power to grant John and his audience a share in his eternal life. And it alludes to the Eucharist as a meal shared with the risen Lord in anticipation of their final attainment of eternal life.

With regard to worship for life "in the Spirit of prophecy," after the epistolary and liturgical greeting from the seven divine Spirits before God's heavenly throne (1:4), the prologue reports that John was "in Spirit" on the Lord's day, the day of worship and a reminder of the Lord's Supper (1:10).[16] While "in Spirit," John received his prophetic commission to write the "words of the prophecy" contained in Revelation (1:3,

---

15. "Since Christian prophets normally prophesied in the context of Christian worship meetings, we must assume that this is what John usually did. The reading of his written prophecy in the worship service (1:3) was therefore a substitute for John's more usual presence and prophesying in person" (Bauckham, *Theology*, 3).

16. Koenig, *Feast*, 205.

19). John exemplifies "worship for life in the Spirit of prophecy" as a servant of God "who witnessed to the word of God and the witness of Jesus Christ" (1:1-2), and who "was on the island called Patmos on account of the word of God and witness of Jesus" (1:9). Revelation thus exhorts its audience, as servants with John (1:1), to worship for eternal life in the divine Spirit of prophecy by not only listening to the words of the prophecy (1:3) during their liturgical worship but by likewise witnessing to the word of God and the witness of Jesus Christ as a consequence of this worship. Indeed, the audience are to "worship God, for the witness of Jesus is the Spirit of prophecy" (19:10).

The epilogue of Revelation (22:6-21) confirms its worship context as John again performs an act of worship by falling down before the feet of the angel, but is told instead to worship God. He is to do this along with his brothers, the audience, as those who keep the "words of this scroll," that is, the words of prophecy regarding true and false worship written in the scroll/book of Revelation (22:8-9; cf. 1:3). With regard to "worship for life," the epilogue pronounces a divine blessing upon the audience as those who metaphorically "wash their robes" by witnessing to the witness of Jesus (cf. 1:2; 22:16, 18, 20), so that their authority will be over the "tree of [eternal] life" (22:14; cf. 22:19; 7:14). The epilogue's liturgical dialogue then announces, "Let the one who thirsts come, let the one who wishes receive water of [eternal] life freely" (22:17), an invitation for every individual in the audience to participate in the eucharistic eating and drinking for eternal life. Indeed, the audience's listening to the words of the prophecy written in Revelation has aptly prepared them for this.

With regard to worship for life "in the Spirit of prophecy," after the notice in the epilogue that the God of the "Spirits of the prophets" sent his angel to show his servants—John and the audience of Revelation—what must happen soon (22:6), this divine Spirit of prophecy joins the audience, depicted as "the bride" in the liturgical dialogue, to invite Jesus to "come!" (22:17). The Spirit of prophecy thus inspires the audience to pray for Jesus to come not only for the final judgment (22:12), but for their celebration of the Lord's Supper, which anticipates this final coming (cf. 1 Cor 11:25-26). The closing references in the epilogue to the divine Spirit of prophecy regarding true and false worship, to various aspects of true and false worship, and to the eternal life of the risen Jesus thus form an inclusion with the opening references in the prologue. The prologue and epilogue together provide preliminary indications that Revelation's main theme, function, and purpose is to exhort and enable its audience in the divine Spirit of prophetic witness against idolatrous worship to worship God and the Lamb for eternal life.

Summary

Revelation comprises sixty-five microchiastic units distributed among ten subsections. There is a chiastic arrangement based on linguistic parallels between these subsections, and the units within each subsection also have a chiastic arrangement based on textual data. The ten subsections are distributed among four major sections (1:1—3:22; 4:1—16:21; 17:1—21:8; 21:9—22:21). The delineation of this comprehensive chiastic structure provides the modern audience with a visual guide for how the original ancient audiences heard the oral performance of Revelation within a context of liturgical worship.

The prologue (1:1-20) and epilogue (22:6-21) provide preliminary indications of the main theme, function, and purpose of the book of the Revelation of Jesus Christ—worship for eternal life in the divine Spirit of prophecy, a prophecy that calls for witnessing to the word of God and the witness of Jesus Christ regarding true and false worship.

PART ONE

Grace from John in Spirit to Churches to Be Shown What Must Happen Soon (1:1—3:22)

2

Prologue: John's Authorization to Prophesy to the Seven Churches

Revelation 1:1–20

1a) John Witnessed to the Prophetic Word of God and Witness of Jesus Christ (1:1–3)

  A ^{1:1a} Revelation of **Jesus Christ** that **God** gave him

    B ^{1b} to show his **servants** the things it is necessary to happen soon,

      C ^{1c} and he signified it, sending it through his angel

    B′ ^{1d} to his **servant** John,

  A′ a) ² who witnessed to the *word* of **God** and the witness of **Jesus Christ**, as many things as he saw.

    b) ^{3a} Blessed is the one who reads aloud

  a′) ^{3b} and those who hear the *words* of the prophecy and keep the things written in it, for the time is near.[1]

---

1. All translations are my own. The words in bold indicate the parallels between the chiastic elements within each unit. The words in bold italics indicate the parallels between the chiastic sub-elements within each sub-unit. Note that words in bold

PART ONE—*Shown What Must Happen Soon (1:1—3:22)*

The opening term, "revelation," begins to establish a worship context for what follows, since speaking a prophetic "revelation" of a previously hidden divine mystery under the inspiration of God's Spirit often formed part of worship services in early Christian communities.[2] The expression "revelation of Jesus Christ" allows the audience to understand it as both a revelation from and about the Jesus Christ they know as now living in heaven, having been raised from the dead by God.[3] Thus, "God gave him" (1:1a) the revelation that is about him when he raised him from the dead, and the revelation that is from him as the Jesus Christ now living with God in heaven.

The grammatically ambiguous expression regarding the purpose of the revelation God gave to Jesus Christ encourages the audience to consider the relationship between God and Jesus Christ as one of dynamic oneness—what is said of and by Jesus is at the same time said of and by God.[4] Thus, God gave the revelation to Jesus Christ for God and/or Jesus Christ to show "his"—God's and/or Jesus Christ's—"servants the things it is necessary to happen soon" (1:1b).[5] The audience are to

---

italics may sometimes indicate the parallels for both the units and the sub-units. Words in italics indicate the chiastic parallels that may occur in a chiastic pattern within a sub-element.

2. In 1 Cor 14:6 speaking with a "revelation" is listed along with knowledge, prophecy, and teaching as gifts of the Spirit (1 Cor 12:1–13) and an element of the worship service. And in 1 Cor 14:26 the assembly for worship includes individuals to whom the Spirit has given a psalm, a teaching, a revelation, a tongue, or an interpretation. See Heil, *Letters of Paul*, 40–41. John is repeatedly said to be "in Spirit" (Rev 1:10; 4:2; 17:3; 21:10) when he is given the contents of what he communicates in this document as the "revelation of Jesus Christ" (1:1), and which later was given the title "revelation of John" (Aune, *Revelation 1–5*, 3–4). As Hurtado ("Worship," 921) notes, "it appears that in gathered worship, believers might convey what were presented as revelations given by the Spirit."

3. "Interpreted in light of the entire prophecy, both are true. That is, the revelation comes from Jesus Christ, and it is a revelation about Jesus Christ" (Brighton, *Revelation*, 33).

4. "As a Christian prophet, he [John] is concerned to communicate the voice of Jesus as the voice of God, and the voice of God as the voice of Jesus" (Boring, "Voice of Jesus," 356).

5. Although most references in Revelation are to the servants of God (7:3; 10:7; 11:18; 15:3; 19:2, 5; 22:6), in 2:20 Jesus refers to "my servants" and in 22:3 "his servants" refers to the servants of God and/or of the Lamb.

Prologue: John's Authorization to Prophesy to the Seven Churches

see themselves as the "servants," literally, "slaves," to whom both God and Jesus Christ show the revelation in the document that is to follow. As servants or slaves, the audience are to be submissively obedient as those entrusted with the privilege and responsibility of acting prophetically on behalf of their divine Lord. They are to be shown the things "it is necessary," in accord with the necessity of the divine plan, to happen soon, that is, the things certainly to take place in the future as a result of God having raised Jesus Christ from the dead.

And "he"—God and/or Jesus Christ—"signified" the revelation, that is, made it known by way of signs or symbols, thus preparing the audience for the symbolic mode of communication to follow. And it was signified by sending it through "his"—God's and/or Jesus Christ's—angel (1:1c).[6] The chiastic progression of parallels from his "servants" who are to be shown the things it is necessary to happen soon (1:1b) to his "servant" John (1:1d), as the one to whom the revelation was sent through the angel, tells the audience that they are closely related to John as fellow prophetic servants of God and/or Jesus Christ.

That John "witnessed" (1:2) means both that he received the revelation as an eyewitness and that he bore witness to it by his words and actions in a public domain with a judicial connotation.[7] In accord with the chiastic progression of parallels, the "revelation of *Jesus Christ* which *God* gave to him" (1:1a) and to which John witnessed is further described as "the word of *God* and the witness of *Jesus Christ*" (1:2). The revelation of Jesus Christ is both the word about and from God and the witness about and from Jesus Christ. The "witness" that Jesus Christ gave by his words and actions was about himself as the one whom God raised from the dead, and it was to this witness from and about Jesus Christ that John himself witnessed. The clause, "as many things as he saw" (1:2), reinforces John's prophetic role as both eyewitness (he *saw*) and fully credible judicial witness who accounts for all of the evidence

---

6. In 22:6 "the God of the Spirits of the prophets sent his angel" and in 22:16 "I, Jesus, sent my angel."

7. With regard to the judicial or legal character of Revelation, Bandy notes, "the lawsuit motif in Revelation encompasses the entire scope of the book, beginning and ending with a solemn oath attesting to its veracity (Rev 1.2; 22.8, 16)" (*Prophetic Lawsuit*, 125).

PART ONE—*Shown What Must Happen Soon (1:1—3:22)*

(*as many things* as he saw). As the revelation of Jesus Christ, the document that follows will enable the audience, as prophetic "servants" with the "servant" John, to do the same.

The beatitude that pronounces "blessed" by the God who gave the revelation to Jesus Christ (1:1a) "the one who reads aloud" (1:3a), that is, the lector of the worship service, further establishes the worship context for what is to follow. In reading aloud this beatitude as performative language, the lector is making the blessing a reality not only for himself but for the audience as the "servants" (1:1b), the liturgical assembly, of those who are to "hear the words of the prophecy" (1:3b) in the document to follow.[8] The "words of the prophecy" further describes the "word of God" as the witness and revelation of Jesus Christ to which John himself witnessed (1:2). Not only are the audience to listen to the words of the prophecy in their worship service, but they are to complete their act of worship by also "keeping"—preserving, obeying, and carrying out—the things written in it, which includes their witnessing as prophetic servants along with the servant John.[9] That "the time is near" (1:3b) echoes "the things it is necessary to happen soon" (1:1b), adding a sense of urgency to this worship.

2b) Opening Greeting of the Letter from John to the Seven Churches (1:4–9)

> **A** [4] **John** to the seven churches in Asia: Grace to you and peace from **the one who is and who was and who is coming** and from the seven Spirits that are before his throne, [5a] and from **Jesus** Christ—the **witness**, the faithful one, the firstborn of the dead, and the ruler of the kings of the earth.
>
> **B** [5b] To the one who loves us and has released us from our sins by **his** blood, [6] and who has made us into a kingdom, priests for **his** God and Father (Exod 19:6; Isa 61:6), to

---

8. "A blessing is a performative utterance, a speech act that effects the very thing it describes . . . the blessing spoken here brings the blessedness of God and of Christ right into the midst of the assembly" (Mangina, *Revelation*, 41).

9. "To 'keep' the message of Revelation's prophecy means 'to worship God' (22:9)" (Koester, *Revelation*, 47).

Prologue: John's Authorization to Prophesy to the Seven Churches

> **him** be the glory and the might for the ages of the ages. **Amen**!
>
> **C** [7a] Behold he is coming with the clouds (Dan 7:13),
>
> **B′** [7b] and every eye will see **him**, even those who pierced **him**, and all the tribes of the earth will lament over **him** (Zech 12:10, 12). Yes! **Amen**!
>
> **A′** [8] "I am the Alpha and the Omega," says the Lord God, "**the one who is and who was and who is coming**, the Almighty." [9] I, **John**, your brother and fellow sharer in the tribulation and kingdom and endurance in **Jesus** was on the island called Patmos on account of the word of God and the **witness** of **Jesus**.

The John who witnessed to the word of God and the witness of Jesus Christ (1:2) begins the epistolary dimension of this document. The servant John (1:1d) addresses the audience of his fellow servants as the sender of the letter which contains the words of the prophecy (1:3) they are to hear in their liturgical assemblies: "John to the seven churches in Asia" (1:4).[10] In accord with the grace of the revelation that God "gave" to Jesus Christ (1:1a) and with the divine blessing already conveyed to the audience (1:3), John pronounces the greeting that initiates the letter as a ritual of worship: "Grace to you and peace" (1:4). This epistolary and liturgical greeting affirms that the audience, as God's and/or Jesus Christ's servants (1:1b), have already received the gift of God's grace in Jesus Christ as well as the peace—the overall well-being with God and with one another—that results from that grace. And as a performative utterance it also assures that, as a consequence of hearing and keeping the words of the prophecy written in this letter, they will continue to experience the blessing of this divine grace and peace.[11]

---

10. "In writing to seven assemblies, John is in fact addressing the whole 'Church', including communities not explicitly mentioned." (Trebilco, *Self-designations*, 204). On the local setting of the churches, see Hemer, *Letters*.

11. "More than a casual greeting, it bestows what it proclaims" (Mounce, *Revelation*, 45). "The result of 'grace' is 'peace' . . . the presence of wholeness or well-being within individuals and social relationships" (Resseguie, *Revelation*, 65).

PART ONE—*Shown What Must Happen Soon (1:1—3:22)*

This blessing of grace and peace has its source in three divine entities. First, it comes from God as "the one who is and who was and who is coming" (1:4). This indicates that God's absolute sovereignty embraces all three temporal dimensions—present, past, and future. But the future completion of his plan of salvation has already begun and is dynamically progressing, as he is the one who is presently and continually "coming."[12] Secondly, it comes from "the seven Spirits which are before his throne," that is, from the totality of the divine Spirit located before God's throne in heaven as the place from which God sovereignly rules and is worshiped. The expression "seven Spirits" suggests a special relevance of this divine Spirit for the "seven churches" which comprise the audience (1:4).

And thirdly, the blessing of grace and peace comes "from Jesus Christ—the witness, the faithful one, the firstborn of the dead, and the ruler of the kings of the earth" (1:5a). Jesus Christ was the faithful "witness" in and through his suffering, death, and resurrection. This is the "witness" from and about Jesus Christ to which John "witnessed" (1:2), the revelation from and about Jesus Christ which God gave to him (1:1a). His faithful witness includes his being the "firstborn" of the dead, the one who inaugurates a new birth into eternal, risen life, with the implication that others are likewise to be (re)born into this life. Because of his heavenly status of eternal life with God as the firstborn of the dead, he is the ruler of the kings of the earth, which indicates his transcendent superiority as one worthy of receiving allegiance and worship from all earthly rulers and their subjects.[13]

Having established the worthiness of Jesus Christ, the climactic third divine source of the epistolary and liturgical greeting of grace and peace, as an object of worship (1:4–5a), John, through the lector reading aloud to the audience as a liturgical assembly (1:3), appropriately leads them in an act of communal doxological worship in the form of a

---

12. "[T]his threefold title of Yahweh is an indeclinable noun that by its very form effectively highlights the unchangeable and eternal character of God" (Harris, *Prepositions*, 67).

13. "Since the primary concern of the text is with the establishment of the rule of God, either a positive or negative stance by 'the kings of the earth' could be well within the realm of possibility" (Herms, *Apocalypse*, 217).

liturgical dialogue: "To the one who loves us and has released us from our sins by his blood, and who has made us into a kingdom, priests for his God and Father, to him be the glory and the might for the ages of the ages. Amen!" (1:5b–6).[14]

This act of communal worship acknowledges Jesus Christ as the one who is presently "loving us" (1:5b)—not only John and the audience of his fellow servants (1:1) but all believers, who may thus join in this act of worship. That he loves us as the one who has released us from our sins by his blood (1:5b) resonates with the eucharistic worship of the audience, their celebration of the Lord's Supper, which centers on the blood of Jesus by which he freed us from our sins to make possible a new covenantal relationship with God (Matt 26:27–28; Mark 14:23–24; Luke 22:20; 1 Cor 11:25). This new covenantal relationship thus establishes "us" believers in Jesus as the new people of God in continuity with the people of Israel (Jer 31:31–34).

Jesus, the ruler of the "kings" of the earth (1:5a), has made "us" believers corporately into a different "kingdom," one comprised individually of "priests" set apart as a holy nation to perform proper sacrificial worship for his God and Father (Exod 19:6; Isa 61:6).[15] This fulfills the prophetic promise made to the chosen people of Israel of old, indicating that we believers are now the new royal and priestly people of God. In response to all that Jesus Christ has done and is doing for us (1:5b-6), the audience appropriately are led to worship him. Through the lector reading aloud (1:3) their part of this liturgical dialogue, they are drawn into the doxological worship of declaring the eternal glory and might

---

14. For an outline of the liturgical dialogue in 1:4–8, see Aune, *Revelation 1–5*, 28. See also Vanni, "Liturgical Dialogue," 348–72. "With this threefold 'us,' the voice of the worshiping assembly is heard for the first time ... This whole section breathes with the language and spirit of the liturgy" (Mangina, *Revelation*, 46, 47).

15. "This foundational identification of Christians with a priesthood in service to God resonates throughout the narrative of Revelation. Both Christian prayer and Christian martyrdom are depicted in cultic terms. The prayers of the saints are a form of incense-offering arising to God from the heavenly altar (5:8; 8:3–4), while in 6:9 martyrdom is described as a form of sacrifice in that the souls are under the altar" (Stevenson, *Power and Place*, 239–40).

of Jesus Christ, the firstborn into eternal life (1:5a), climactically concluded with their resounding liturgical affirmation—"Amen!" (1:6).[16]

As part of this liturgical dialogue, John, through the lector reading it aloud, then pronounces a prophetic promise to the audience about the Jesus Christ they have just worshiped (1:6). Through the lector reading their part, the audience respond by enthusiastically participating in the concluding communal liturgical affirmation. John thus not only initiates the words of the prophecy the audience are to hear and keep to be blessed by God (1:3), but also continues the revelation of Jesus Christ to be shown to the servants who comprise the audience (1:1): "Behold he is coming with the clouds, and every eye will see him, even those who pierced him, and all the tribes of the earth will lament over him. Yes! Amen!" (1:7).[17]

That Jesus Christ "is coming" is one of the ways that God, the one who is and who was, also "is coming" (1:4). That Jesus Christ "is coming with the clouds" (1:7a) alludes to Dan 7:13 and suggests that God has given him, as the "one like a son of man," eternal dominion and sovereignty, so that when he comes for the final time all peoples will offer him worship (Dan 7:14). The additional allusion to Zech 12:10, 12 indicates that when he comes all peoples will see him, even those who "pierced" him and were thus responsible for his death. That all of the tribes of the earth will lament over him means that they will perform a ritualistic act of mourning or lamentation for the death of Jesus Christ, indicating their repentance and participation in the universal worship of Jesus Christ.[18] In response to John's prophetic pronouncement, the

---

16. "The closing 'Amen' corresponds to liturgical usage. This Hebrew word meaning 'so be it' or 'so it is' was the answer of the community in the synagogue worship to the prayer of praise spoken by the prayer leader. This practice was adopted in Christian worship" (Roloff, *Revelation*, 26).

17. "The subject matter or topic of the book is now described in a prophetic annunciation presented in a highly liturgical, even hymnic, format that at one and the same time provides the contents of the 'revelation' of 1:1 as well as a prophecy presented in OT style" (Osborne, *Revelation*, 68).

18. "John does not say whether the mourning has a positive or negative sense, but the allusion to Zechariah suggests that it may be a sign of repentance" (Jauhiainen, *Use of Zechariah*, 106). See also Beale and McDonough, "Revelation," 1090–91; Thompson, "Lamentation," 683–703.

audience proclaim their emphatic liturgical affirmation, "Yes! Amen!" (1:7b), reinforcing and intensifying their previous "Amen!" that concluded their doxological worship of Jesus Christ (1:6).[19]

John's prophetic pronouncement, which is being read aloud by the lector to the audience as a liturgical assembly, continues with an explicit expression of the word of God, proclaimed by God himself, an example of the word from and about God to which John witnessed (1:2): "'I am the Alpha and the Omega,' says the Lord God, 'the one who is and who was and who is coming, the Almighty'" (1:8).[20] The first divine source of the opening epistolary and liturgical greeting of grace and peace—"the one who is and who was and who is coming" (1:4)—is now explicitly identified as "the Lord God." His emphatic proclamation that "I am the Alpha and the Omega," the first and last letters of the Greek alphabet as a rhetorical merism to express totality, as well as the concluding addition, "the Almighty," underline his absolute sovereignty and eternality.[21] The audience are to appreciate that the "coming" of Jesus Christ with the clouds (1:7) climaxes the continual "coming" of the absolutely sovereign and eternal Lord God.

Following the divine self-identification with an emphatic "I"— "*I* am the Alpha and the Omega" (1:8)—John, with his own emphatic "I," further identifies and relates himself to his audience: "*I*, John, your brother and fellow sharer in the tribulation and kingdom and endurance in Jesus was on the island called Patmos on account of the word of God and the witness of Jesus" (1:9).[22] The John who is the sender of the letter (1:4) is not only the John who is a servant along with his audience of servants (1:1), but is their "brother" and fellow sharer in the kingdom into which Jesus has made them (1:6), which involves tribulation that

19. "First John uses the Greek 'so it is to be' (lit. 'yes') and then reinforces it with the Hebrew 'amen'" (Resseguie, *Revelation*, 68).

20. "Finally, as if to confirm what has already been said, the voice of the reader becomes the vehicle for the voice of God" (Boxall, *Revelation*, 35).

21. "Here the emphasis falls not so much on God's transcendence over time as on his perfect life and fullness, exceeding creation even as he embraces it, the way the letters Alpha and Omega bracket the Greek alphabet" (Mangina, *Revelation*, 47).

22. With his use of the first person singular here John conveys to his audience his role as an indispensable link between the divine and human realms, according to Bovon, "John's Self-presentation," 693–700.

PART ONE—*Shown What Must Happen Soon (1:1—3:22)*

calls for their endurance. For John this tribulation and endurance has led him to the island of Patmos. He is in exile, separated from his audience of seven churches in Asia (1:4) on account of the word of God and witness of Jesus, to which he witnessed, "as many things as he saw" (1:2). He thus "witnessed" to the "witness" Jesus gave as *the* "witness," the faithful one, the firstborn of the dead, and the ruler of the kings of the earth (1:5a).[23]

3b′) Command for John to Write What He Observes to the Seven Churches (1:10–16)

> A [10] I was in Spirit on the Lord's day and I heard behind me a great **sound as** a trumpet
>
> > B [11a] saying, "What you **observe**
> >
> > > C [11b] write in a scroll and send it to the seven churches—to Ephesus and to Smyrna and to Pergamum and to Thyatira and to Sardis and to Philadelphia and to Laodicea."
> >
> > B′ [12a] Then I turned to **observe**
>
> A′ a) [12b] the ***sound*** that was speaking with me, and having turned, I saw ***seven*** golden lampstands (Exod 25:31–40; Zech 4:2)
>
> > b) [13] and in the midst of the lampstands one *like* a Son of Man (Dan 7:13) dressed in a robe reaching to the *feet* and girded at the breasts with a golden belt.
> >
> > > c) [14a] His head and hair were ***white***
> > >
> > > c′) [14b] as ***white*** wool, as snow,
> >
> > b′) [14c] and his eyes **as** a flame of fire (Dan 7:9) [15a] and his ***feet like*** burnished bronze, **as** in a furnace of refining,
>
> a′) [15b] and his ***sound* as** the ***sound*** of many waters (Dan 10:5–6), [16] and having in his right hand ***seven*** stars and

---

23. For four possible ways of explaining John's exile on Patmos, see Aune, *Revelation 1–5*, 79–80.

from his mouth a sharp two-edged sword is going out and his countenance appears **as** the sun in its power.

The John who "was" on Patmos (1:9) "was" also in "Spirit," that is, within the realm of the divine Spirit, previously referred to as the seven "Spirits" before God's throne (1:4), on the Lord's day (1:10). This is the day of communal worship, a setting appropriate for John to be shown the prophetic revelation of Jesus Christ (1:1).[24] That John heard behind him "a great sound as a trumpet" (1:10) indicates that a divine revelation is to follow (Exod 19:13, 16, 19; 20:18). The divine "sound" or "voice" directs John to write in a scroll the revelation he is about to observe and send it to the seven churches, listed in clockwise fashion from Ephesus to Laodicea, as representative of all the churches in Asia (1:11).[25] This command to "write" not only provides divine authorization for the letter John has addressed to the seven churches (1:4), but also reinforces the exhortation for the audience—all of those who gather for worship on the Lord's day—to hear and keep the words of the prophecy "written" ultimately by God (divine passive) in it (1:3).

After being told by the great sound to write what "you observe" (1:11), when John turned "to observe" the sound or voice speaking with him, he saw "seven golden lampstands" (1:12).[26] As instruments with a role in heavenly worship (Exod 25:31–40; Zech 4:2), the "seven" lampstands suggest a close relationship with the audience of "seven" churches as worshiping assemblies (1:4, 11).[27] In the midst of the lampstands John saw "one like a Son of Man" (1:13), that is, the exalted Jesus Christ, the one who is coming with the clouds (1:7a) in fulfillment of Dan 7:13.[28] That he is dressed in a "robe reaching to the feet" and girded

---

24. "It is likely that the Jewish–Christian church worshiped in the synagogues on the Jewish Sabbath and in their own assemblies from the earliest times on Sunday, celebrating the Eucharist and worshiping Christ together (cf. Acts 2:42)" (Osborne, *Revelation*, 83–84). See also Boxall, *Revelation*, 40; Llewelyn, "Use of Sunday," 205–23.

25. "The entire scroll including all seven letters was to be read at each church" (Mounce, *Revelation*, 56).

26. "The verb ['to observe'] suggests spiritual perception, as in a vision, rather than physical sight by itself" (Smalley, *Revelation*, 52).

27. "These lampstands are cultic instruments that recall similar lampstands from the Jerusalem Temple" (Stevenson, *Power and Place*, 239).

28. "This 'Voice', the voice of God, can be seen, but when John turns to see the

PART ONE—*Shown What Must Happen Soon (1:1—3:22)*

at the breasts with a "golden" belt (1:13) indicates his royal priestly character (Exod 28:4, 31; 29:5; 1 Macc 10:89; 11:58) as a divine being. This is in accord with his having been worshiped by the audience as the one who has made us into a kingdom, priests for his God and Father (1:6).

That "his head and hair were white as white wool, as snow, and his eyes as a flame of fire" (1:14) likens the exalted Jesus to God himself, described as the "Ancient of Days" in Dan 7:9. That his feet were "like burnished bronze, as in a furnace of refining, and his sound as the sound of many waters" (1:15), like that of God (Ezek 1:23: 43:2), further enhances his status as a divine heavenly being (Dan 10:5–6), a worthy object of worship. In the authoritative grasp of his right hand he has "seven" stars (1:16), further suggesting a relevance for the audience of "seven" churches (1:4, 11).[29] From his mouth is going out a "sharp two-edged sword" (1:16), symbolic of the word of God by which he will execute divine judgment (Isa 11:4; 49:2).[30] And that "his countenance appears as the sun in its power" climaxes this description of his divine majesty (1:16). Central to this revelation is the divine sound of Jesus, as indicated by the progression of chiastic parallels from "a great sound" (1:10) to "the sound which was speaking with me" (1:12) to "his sound as the sound of many waters" (1:15).

4a') Command for John to Write Things That Are and That Are about to Be (1:17–20)

> **A** [17a] And when **I saw** him, I fell toward his feet as if dead, and he placed his **right hand** upon me saying,

---

voice that addresses him, he sees the exalted Christ" (Boring, "Voice of Jesus," 354).

29. "The right hand throughout Scripture symbolizes power and authority . . . Israel is at all times forbidden to worship the 'stars' (Deut 4:19) . . . In the ancient world stars were frequently seen as powers (usually the gods) that could influence the course of history and determine the destiny of humankind" (Osborne, *Revelation*, 91–92).

30. "John graphically illustrates the juridical force of Christ's word as a sharp two-edged sword coming out of his mouth. The sword, his only weapon, denotes his power to execute judgments simply with an utterance" (Bandy, *Prophetic Lawsuit*, 154).

> B ¹⁷ᵇ "Do not fear. I am the first and the last, ¹⁸ᵃ and the one who is **living**,
>
> C ¹⁸ᵇ once I was dead
>
> B′ ¹⁸ᶜ but behold I am **living** for the ages of the ages and I have the keys of Death and of Hades.
>
> A′ ¹⁹ Write then the things **you saw**, that is, the things that are and the things that are about to happen after these things. ²⁰ The mystery of the seven stars which **you saw** upon my **right hand** and the seven golden lampstands: the seven stars are the angels of the seven churches and the seven lampstands are the seven churches."

John reports that "when I saw him," the one whom he saw (1:12) as one like a Son of Man (1:13) with a divine sound or voice (1:10, 12, 15), he fell toward his feet, which were like burnished bronze, as in a furnace of refining (1:15). John thus performs an act suggestive of worship in submissive acknowledgment of Jesus' awesome divine sound and status (1:17a; cf. 19:10; 22:8).[31] The John who led his audience to worship Jesus Christ as the "firstborn of the dead" (1:5) now seems to worship him from a position of himself being "as if dead" (1:17a), a symbolic recognition of the exalted Jesus' sovereignty over life and death.

Then the exalted Jesus placed his powerful, authoritative "right" hand upon John (1:17a), the "right" hand in which he has control of seven stars (1:16).[32] His saying to John, "Do not fear. I am the first and the last" (1:17b), resonates with the divine voice of the Lord God who says, "I am the Alpha and the Omega" (1:8). These are synonymous merisms to express absolute divine sovereignty as well as eternity. As

---

31. "What is lacking is any remonstration of John for what could be understood as a posture of worship. The Jesus who died is appropriately to be worshipped" (Boxall, *Revelation*, 43).

32. "Has Jesus once more illustrated that he is the 'firstborn of the dead' (1:5), and that he has 'the keys of Death and of Hades' (1:18), by placing his right hand on John and, in a sense, restoring him to life, resurrecting him from his deathly, fallen position?" (Resseguie, *Revelation*, 79). "Again, as in verse 16, we hear that it is the 'right' hand of Christ which is laid on John: the side of power, as well as protection; and the entire action at this point is a gesture of blessing, as well as of commissioning" (Smalley, *Revelation*, 55).

PART ONE—*Shown What Must Happen Soon (1:1—3:22)*

the Lord God is "the one who is" (1:8), so the exalted Jesus goes on to say that he is "the one who is living" (1:18a). He tells the "as if dead" John (1:17a), still subject to the power of death, "once I was dead but behold I am living for the ages of the ages" (1:18bc).

After the pivotal notice that "once I was dead" (1:18b), the audience experience a chiastic progression of parallels that emphasizes that the once dead Jesus is now not only living but living eternally. After he says, "I am the first and the last, and the one who is living" (1:17b–18a), he says, "but behold I am living for the ages of the ages" (1:18c). That he is living eternally "for the ages of the ages" resonates with the audience's doxological worship of him—"to him be glory and might for the ages of the ages" (1:6). The Jesus "having" seven stars in the powerful and authoritative grasp of his right hand (1:16) goes on to claim that "I have" the metaphorical "keys," which indicate his sovereignty over the power of Death personified and Hades, the realm of the dead personified (1:18c). His divine power and authority to grant a share in his eternal life to John and the audience, as those who worship Jesus Christ, is thus emphatically confirmed.

The command for John to "write" the things he saw (1:19) reinforces the command for him to "write" what he observes in a scroll and send it to the seven churches (1:11). These include the things "written" in this document as the words of the prophecy the audience are to hear and keep (1:3). The things that "you saw" refer to all of the features of the exalted Jesus, as well as the seven golden lampstands, which "I saw" (1:12, 17). They are included within the many things John "saw" as the basis for his witness to the word of God and the witness of Jesus Christ (1:2). That the things John sees are "the things that are and the things that are about to happen after these things" (1:19) resonates with "the things that must happen soon" (1:1b). These are the things that are to be shown to the audience of servants and that must inevitably—as a divine necessity—take place, in accord with the revelation of Jesus Christ which God gave to him (1:1).

As part of the revelation of Jesus Christ (1:1), the exalted Jesus reveals the mystery of the seven stars which John saw upon his right hand and the seven golden lampstands (1:20). The "right" hand upon which John saw the seven stars that Jesus has in his control (1:16) is the "right" hand that the eternally living Jesus who has the keys that control Death and Hades (1:18) placed on John when he fell toward his feet as if dead (1:17). That the seven stars are the "angels" of the seven churches (1:20) suggests that each of the churches has an "angel" through which the revelation of Jesus Christ will be sent to them (1:1). The exalted Jesus thus has divine authority over both the angels, the stars he has in his right hand, and the churches they represent.[33] And that the seven "lampstands" are the seven churches (1:12, 20) indicates that each of the churches has a heavenly status in association with the one like a Son of Man in the midst of the "lampstands" in heaven (1:13), who, as the eternally living one (1:18), can grant eternal life to those who worship him (1:5, 17–18).

Summary on 1:1–20

A worship context is introduced with the first word, "revelation" (1:1), as prophetic revelations were often elements in early Christian worship services. The worship context is confirmed by the beatitude that concludes the introductory unit. It declares "blessed" by God the lector of the worship service who reads aloud and the audience who hear the words of the prophecy to follow in the document and keep the things written in it (1:3). The audience of prophetic "servants" are invited to keep the things written in the prophecy by witnessing to the word of God and the witness of Jesus Christ (1:2), like their fellow prophetic "servant" John, through whom they are to be shown the revelation of Jesus Christ that God gave to him, signified and sent through an angel (1:1). This already begins to indicate that the audience are to worship God in the divine Spirit of the prophecy involved in the witness of Jesus Christ. That the revelation is to show the audience the things that must happen soon (1:1), for the time is near (1:3), adds a sense of urgency that underlines the importance of this worship.

John indicates that the revelation of Jesus Christ (1:1) will be sent to the audience of the seven churches in Asia in the form of a letter as

---

33. "The angels of the churches most likely represent the heavenly reality, the spiritual condition of the church, the counterpart to its earthly reality" (Resseguie, *Revelation*, 81).

PART ONE—*Shown What Must Happen Soon (1:1—3:22)*

a ritual of worship (1:4). After an epistolary and liturgical greeting of grace and peace from three divine sources, John leads his audience in an act of doxological worship of Jesus Christ (1:4–6). That he is worshiped as the "firstborn of the dead" (1:5a) introduces the theme of worship for life—the eternal life of the risen Jesus Christ. He is worshiped as the one who loves us and has released us from our sins by his blood (1:5b), resonating with the worship of Jesus in the Eucharist with its focus on the significance of his sacrificial blood. That he has made us into a kingdom, priests for his God and Father, points to a priestly dimension of the audience's worship (1:6). The audience add their exuberant liturgical affirmation, "Yes! Amen!," to the prophecy that at his final coming he will be universally worshiped (1:7). The word of the sovereign and eternal God further affirms this worship (1:8), which John initiated on Patmos on account of the word of God and witness of Jesus (1:9).

John experienced his vision of the exalted Jesus Christ when he was within the realm of the divine Spirit that inspires prophecy on the Lord's day, Sunday as the day of Christian worship, further underlining the worship context of the letter the audience of the seven churches are to hear when assembled for their worship (1:10–11). That John sees the exalted Jesus in the midst of seven golden lampstands, cultic instruments of the heavenly liturgy, as one like a Son of Man dressed in a robe reaching to the feet and girded at the breasts with a golden belt indicates his royal priestly character (1:12–13) as the one who made us into a kingdom, priests for his God and Father (1:6). The exalted Jesus displays the dazzling divine features of God himself (1:14–15), including the divine sovereignty to rule and judge (1:16), underlining his worthiness to be an object of worship, emphatically confirmed by his speaking to John with a divine sound or voice (1:10, 12, 15).

As an appropriate response to the exalted Jesus' worthiness to be an object of worship, John performed a dramatic act of worship by falling toward the feet of the risen Jesus as if dead. Jesus then placed his divinely authoritative right hand upon John as a gesture of both comforting and commissioning him (1:17). He comforts the "as if dead" John by identifying himself as the one who, although once actually dead, is now living eternally with divine sovereignty over the power of death, so that he can bestow a share in his eternal life on those who worship him (1:18). He then commissions John to write the things he saw, that is, the things that are and the things that are about to happen after these things (1:19), the things that must happen soon (1:1), as the inevitable outcome of his resurrection in accord with divine necessity. That the seven stars in his authoritative right hand are the angels of the seven churches and the seven lampstands are the seven churches (1:20) reveals that the worship of the churches on earth has its counterpart in the heavenly liturgy.

In sum, the prologue of Revelation (1:1–20) begins to indicate its major theme of worship for life, the eternal life offered by the risen Jesus, in the divine Spirit that inspires prophecy, the prophecy written in Revelation as the basis for the audience of servants to witness to the word of God and the witness of Jesus Christ together with their fellow prophetic servant, John.

3

Prophetic Oracles to the Seven Churches

Revelation 2:1—3:22

1a) Oracle to the Angel of the Church in Ephesus (2:1–7)

    A ²:¹ᵃ To the angel of the **church** in Ephesus write: "These things **is saying**

        B ¹ᵇ the one holding the seven stars in his right hand, the one walking in the midst of the seven golden **lampstands**,

            a) ²ᵃ 'I know your works and labor and your *endurance* and that you are not able to *bear* the evil ones,

                b) ²ᵇ and you tested those who say that ***they themselves*** are apostles

                c) ²ᶜ yet they are not

                b') ²ᵈ and you found that ***they*** are lying,

            a') ³ and you **have endurance** and have **borne** up on account of my name but have not tired.

                C ⁴ But I have against you that your **first** love you have let go.

> **D** ⁵ᵃ Remember then whence you have fallen
>
> **C′** ⁵ᵇ and repent and do the **first** works.
>
> **B′** ⁵ᶜ Otherwise, I am coming to you and I will move your **lampstand** from its place, if you do not repent. ⁶ But this you **have**, that you hate the works of the Nicolaitans, which I also hate.
>
> **A′** ⁷ Let the one having an ear hear what the Spirit **is saying** to the **churches**. To the one who conquers I will give him to eat from the tree of the life, which is in the paradise of God (Gen 2:9).'"

The prophetic servant John to whom the revelation of Jesus Christ that God gave to him was sent through an "angel" (1:1) now addresses the "angel," the heavenly representative counterpart and revelatory intermediary, of the church in Ephesus (2:1a). This is one of the "angels" that are the seven stars the exalted Jesus has under his divine authoritative control in his right hand (1:20). That he addresses the church through its angel suggests that what he is to write has implications for the church's heavenly status and participation in heavenly worship.

The exalted Jesus had authorized John to "write" what he observes in a scroll and send it to the seven churches (1:11), and to "write" the things he saw, "the things that are and the things that are about to happen after these things" (1:19). Now he authorizes him to "write" to the first on the list of seven churches, the church in Ephesus (2:1a).¹ What he is to write is a prophetic oracle introduced and spoken by the exalted Jesus as the one not merely having (1:16) but firmly "holding" the seven stars (angels of the churches) in his right hand. He is the one not merely residing passively (1:13) but actively "walking" in the midst of the seven golden lampstands (churches; 1:20) (2:1b).²

The exalted Jesus acknowledges the church's works and labor and "endurance" (2:2a), reminding the audience that they are brothers and fellow sharers with John in the tribulation and kingdom and "endurance" in Jesus (1:9). The church is not able to bear the evil ones,

---

1. On the historical background of Ephesus, see Hemer, *Letters*, 35–56; Oster, *Seven Congregations*, 94–115.

2. "The imagery of 'walking' combines the ideas of concern for and authority over the church" (Osborne, *Revelation*, 112).

and tested those who claim they are apostles—that they were sent to them with authority—yet they were found to be lying (2:2). He again acknowledges that the church has "endurance" and that, as a church not able to "bear" the evil ones (2:2a), "you have borne" up on account of "my name" (2:3)—the essential significance of Jesus Christ as "the witness, the faithful one, the firstborn of the dead, and the ruler of the kings of the earth" (1:5a). That the church has borne up "on account of my name" likens it to John as a prophetic witness on Patmos "on account of" the word of God and the witness of Jesus (1:9). Jesus affirms that "you have not tired" in doing the works and "labor" needed for prophetic endurance (2:3).

But the exalted Jesus, the one who said "I have" the keys of Death and of Hades (1:18), and who "has" in his right hand seven stars (1:16), now says "I have" against the church that it has let go (2:4) of its first "love" of the Jesus Christ who "loves" us (1:5b).[3] As a church praised because "you have not tired" (2:3), it is to remember then whence "you have now fallen" (2:5a) and repent and return to doing the "first works" (2:5b), the "works" for which its endurance has been acknowledged (2:2a) as part of its "first" love (2:4). If it does not repent, the exalted Jesus, the one like a Son of Man who is "coming" with the clouds for judgment (1:7), warns that "I am coming" to it (1:5c).[4] As the one walking in the midst of the seven golden "lampstands" in heaven (2:1b), he will move the church's "lampstand" from its place in heaven as part of the heavenly worship of the exalted Jesus, if it does not repent (2:5c).

In contrast to the exalted Jesus' accusation, "but I have against you" (2:4), he acknowledges, "but this you have," that the church, "you who have endurance" (2:3), hates the works of the Nicolaitans, which Jesus also hates (2:6). The "works" of the Nicolaitans, *hated* by both the church and the exalted Jesus, thus stand in sharp contrast to the first

---

3. "'But I have this against you' (2:4) is a complaint that echoes a judicial charge in a court of law" (Thompson, *Revelation*, 65). On the seven oracles in Revelation 2–3 as covenant lawsuit speeches, see Bandy, *Prophetic Lawsuit*, 168–75; Bandy, "Patterns," 178–205.

4. "In the eucharist believers experience in the present repeated anticipations of the judicial and salvific effects of Christ's final coming. This same background in the letters suggests that Christ is likewise present and 'coming' among the churches, so that his parousia is not merely a definitively future event" (Beale, *Revelation*, 233).

"works" of the church (2:2a, 5b), as part of its first *love* (2:4) of the Jesus Christ who *loves* us (1:5b) and who is the object of our worship (1:6). This implies that the works of the Nicolaitans are not in accord with the church's worship of the exalted Jesus Christ.

The exalted Jesus "having" in the power of his right hand seven stars (angels) (1:16) exhorts each individual within the audience of the seven churches, "Let the one having an ear hear what the Spirit is saying to the churches" (2:7a). This exhortation for the one having in his power an ear to "hear" reinforces the introductory beatitude that blessed are those in the audience who "hear" the words of the prophecy in Revelation and keep the things written in it (1:3). The divine "Spirit" is the "Spirit" in which John experienced his vision of the exalted Jesus (1:10), earlier referred to as the full seven "Spirits" before God's throne (1:4). What it is "saying" is synonymous with the things the exalted Jesus is "saying," not only to the "church" in Ephesus (2:1) but to all of the "churches."

As part of the revelation which God "gave" to him (1:1), the exalted Jesus promises that to the one who conquers, which includes hating the works of the Nicolaitans (2:6) as one who hears and does what the Spirit is saying (2:7a), "I will give to eat from the tree of the life, which is in the paradise of God" (2:7b).[5] With its allusion to the "tree of the life in the paradise" of Eden as an image of heaven (LXX Gen 2:9), to eat from the "tree of the life, which is in the paradise of God," is a promise to share in the eternal life of the exalted Jesus, the one who is "living" for the ages of the ages (1:18).[6] The fulfillment of this promise for everyone in the audience who is to conquer is anticipated by the eucharistic eating of the supper of the Lord Jesus whom God raised to eternal life after his

---

5. "Their [Nicolaitans'] name is derived from a combination of Greek words that means 'conqueror of people,' which suggests that they conquer God's people by advocating accommodation to the norms and values of the dominant culture" (Resseguie, *Revelation*, 86). "To conquer is to witness resistantly" (Blount, *Revelation*, 52).

6. "The phrase ['tree of the life'] is a reference to Gen 3:22, where God forbids the fallen Adam to eat from the tree of life to prevent him from living forever. What was forbidden to Adam is here promised to the victor; this reversal of human destiny is the result of the salvific death of Jesus Christ on the wood of the cross" (Lupieri, *Apocalypse*, 117). See also Wong, "Tree of Life," 211–26.

PART ONE—*Shown What Must Happen Soon (1:1—3:22)*

death on an earthly "tree" (Acts 5:30-31; 10:39-40; 13:29-30; Gal 3:13; 1 Pet 2:24), which now has as its heavenly counterpart the "tree of the life" in the paradise of God.[7]

2b) Oracle to the Angel of the Church in Smyrna (2:8-11)

A [8a] And to the angel of the **church** in Smyrna write: "These things **is saying**

B [8b] the first and the last, who **became** dead but **lived**.

C [9] 'I know your **tribulation** and poverty, but you are rich, and the blasphemy of those who say that they themselves are Jews yet they are not but are a synagogue of Satan.

D [10a] Do not fear the things you **are about** to suffer.

D' [10b] Behold the Devil **is about** to throw some of you into prison so that you may be tested

C' [10c] and you will have **tribulation** for ten days.

B' [10d] **Become** faithful unto death, and I will give you the crown of the **life**.

A' [11] Let the one having an ear hear what the Spirit **is saying** to the **churches**. The one who conquers shall never be harmed by the second death.'"

In his prophetic oracle to the angel of the church in Smyrna the exalted Jesus directs John to write: "These things is saying the first and the last, who became dead but lived" (2:8).[8] This recalls the exalted Jesus' identification of himself to John as "the first and the last" (1:17), thus reinforcing his divine sovereignty and eternality. That he "became dead but lived" recalls his telling John that once "I was dead but behold I am living" for the ages of the ages (1:18). This emphasis upon the eternality

---

7. On the promise to the one who conquers in 2:7b, see Wilson, *Victor Sayings*, 106–12. On the rational argumentation involved in the oracle to Ephesus, see deSilva, "Appeals to Reason," 130–34.

8. On the historical background of Smyrna, see Hemer, *Letters*, 57–77; Graves, "Local References," 88–96; Oster, *Seven Congregations*, 116–32.

of the exalted Jesus further establishes for the audience that he is the source of their eternal life and thus worthy of their doxological worship for the ages of the ages (1:6).

That the exalted Jesus knows "your tribulation" (2:9) likens the situation of the church to that of John as their fellow sharer "in the tribulation and kingdom and endurance in Jesus" (1:9). The exalted Jesus knows their material poverty but assures them that they are spiritually rich (2:9). His acknowledgment of the blasphemy of those who "say that they themselves are Jews yet they are not" (2:9) recognizes that they are threatened similarly as is the church in Ephesus by those who "say they themselves are apostles yet they are not" (2:2).[9] Their "blasphemy" is a reviling or slandering that ultimately amounts to a false worship of God, which is confirmed by the charge that they are a "synagogue," a gathering for worship, of Satan rather than of God (2:9).

The exalted Jesus who encouraged John, "Do not fear. I am the first and the last" (1:17), now encourages the church, "Do not fear the things you are about to suffer" (2:10a). The things "you are about" to suffer will come from the Devil who "is about" to throw some of them into prison.[10] Consequently, they are told that "you will be tested" (2:10b), ultimately by God (divine passive), in contrast to the Ephesian church—"you" who "tested" those who say they are apostles (2:2). This tribulation they will have from imprisonment will be for a significant but limited period of ten days (2:10c).[11]

The exalted Jesus who "became" dead but lived (2:8b) now exhorts the church to "become" faithful unto death (2:10d). They are to become

---

9. "Some of the Jews of Smyrna and Philadelphia are labeled a 'synagogue of Satan' because they oppose God's people and have allied themselves by default with God's arch-nemesis. This is not to imply that all Jews are of Satan in John's eyes or that John is intending here to be anti-Semitic or even anti-Jewish." (Mayo, *Jews*, 61). For discussions of "those who call themselves Jews," see Lambrecht, "Jewish Slander," 421–29; Frankfurter, "Jews," 403–25; McKelvey, "Jews," 175–94; Duff, "Synagogue of Satan," 147–68; Mayo, *Jews*, 51–76.

10. "By using both 'Satan' and 'devil,' John emphasizes the fact that he is the 'adversary' of God's people" (Osborne, *Revelation*, 133).

11. "A relatively short, manageable time span is meant by ten days, an allusion to the ten-day test of faith of the young Israelites in the Babylonian court (Dan. 1:12, 14)" (Roloff, *Revelation*, 48–49).

"faithful" unto "death" like Jesus—"the witness, the faithful one, the firstborn of the dead, and the ruler of the kings of the earth" (1:5), the one who has the "keys of death" (1:18). Reinforcing his promise to give the one who conquers to eat from the tree of eternal "life" (2:7b), the exalted Jesus now promises to give the church that is to become faithful unto death the triumphal crown or wreath of eternal "life" (2:10d). After again exhorting the audience to hear what the Spirit is saying to all of the churches (2:7a,11a), the exalted Jesus emphatically underlines his promise of eternal life to the one who "conquers" (2:7b). He now promises that the one who "conquers" by becoming faithful unto "death" shall never be harmed by the "second death" (2:11b), the final death that deprives one of eternal life.[12]

3c) Oracle to the Angel of the Church in Pergamum (2:12–17)

> A ¹²ᵃ And to the angel of the **church** in Pergamum write: "These things **is saying**
>
> > B ¹²ᵇ the one having the sharp two-edged **sword**,
> >
> > > a) ¹³ᵃ 'I know where you *inhabit*, where the throne of *Satan* is,
> > >
> > > > b) ¹³ᵇ yet you are holding to *my* name and have not denied *my faith*,
> > > >
> > > > > c) ¹³ᶜ even in the days of Antipas,
> > > >
> > > > b') ¹³ᵈ *my* witness, *my faithful one*, who was killed among you,
> > >
> > > a') ¹³ᵉ where *Satan inhabits*.
> >
> > C ¹⁴ᵃ But I have against you a few things, that **you have** there **those holding to the teaching** of Balaam, who **taught** Balak to throw a stumbling block before the sons of Israel:

---

12. "On the promise to the one who conquers in 2:11b, see Wilson, *Victor Sayings*, 113–21. On the rational argumentation involved in the oracle to Smyrna, see deSilva, "Appeals to Reason," 134–36.

D **¹⁴ᵇ** to eat food sacrificed to idols and to engage in prostitution.

C′ ¹⁵ Thus **you have**, even you, **those holding to the teaching** of the Nicolaitans likewise.

B′ ¹⁶ Repent then. Otherwise, I am coming to you soon and I will battle against them with the **sword** of **my** mouth.

A′ ¹⁷ Let the one having an ear hear what the Spirit **is saying** to the **churches**. To the one who conquers I will give him some of the hidden manna and I will give to him a white stone, and upon the stone a new name written that no one knows except the one receiving it.'"

In the prophetic oracle to the angel of the church in Pergamum the exalted Jesus directs John to write: "These things is saying the one having the sharp two-edged sword" (2:12).[13] This recalls that in John's vision of the exalted Jesus a "sharp two-edged sword" was coming out from his mouth (1:16), thus reinforcing the divine authority of Jesus to execute judgment by uttering the word of God.[14] Jesus knows that the church inhabits where the "throne" of Satan is (2:13a), the focus of the false worship of the Roman emperor and of pagan gods in contrast to the focus of true worship before the "throne" of God in heaven (1:4).[15] Whereas the church in Smyrna is threatened by the slanderous blasphemy of Jews, which amounts to their false worship as a "synagogue of Satan" (2:9), the church in Pergamum is threatened by the false worship associated with the "throne of Satan" which is in its midst.

The exalted Jesus who is firmly "holding" the seven stars in his right hand (2:1), which are the angels of the seven churches (1:20), acknowledges to the church in Pergamum that "you are holding" to my

---

13. On the historical background of Pergamum, see Hemer, *Letters*, 78-105; Oster, *Seven Congregations*, 133-45.

14. "In the context of life in a provincial capital where the proconsul was granted the 'right of the sword' (*ius gladii*), the power to execute at will, the sovereign Christ with the two-edged sword would remind the threatened congregation that ultimate power over life and death belongs to God" (Mounce, *Revelation*, 79).

15. On the "throne of Satan" as a reference to the great altar of Pergamum, which probably served as an altar of burnt offerings for idolatrous worship, see Yarbro Collins, "Satan's Throne," 26-39.

name (2:13b). Just as the church in Ephesus has borne up on account of "my name" and has not tired (2:3), so the church in Pergamum is firmly and tenaciously holding to "my name," that is, to the notable characteristic of Jesus Christ as "the witness, the faithful one, the firstborn of the dead, and the ruler of the kings of the earth" (1:5a). And the church has not denied "my faith" (2:13b), that is, the faith that Jesus Christ has demonstrated as the "faithful one" (1:5a), as well as the faith that not only the church in Smyrna but the audience of all of the churches are to demonstrate by becoming "faithful," like Jesus, until death (2:10), in accord with what the Spirit is saying to all of the churches (2:11).

Whereas the church in Smyrna will have tribulation for ten "days" in the future (2:10), the church in Pergamum has already had tribulation in the "days" of Antipas (2:13c), one of its distinguished members. That he is described as "my witness, my faithful one, who was killed among you" (2:13d) likens him to Jesus Christ, "the witness, the faithful one, the firstborn of the dead" (1:5a), and thus as a model for the witness and faithfulness of the audience. And that Antipas was killed where "Satan inhabits" (2:13e) emphatically underlines the threat of false worship facing the church, as "you inhabit," where the throne of "Satan" is (2:13a).

The exalted Jesus reproached the church in Ephesus, "But I have against you that your first love you have let go" (2:4). And now he similarly reproaches the church in Pergamum, "But I have against you a few things, that you have there those holding to the teaching of Balaam, who taught Balak to throw a stumbling block before the sons of Israel" (2:14a). In contradiction to the fact that "you are holding to my name" (2:13), the church has those "holding to the teaching of Balaam," the false Israelite prophet who deceptively taught the Moabite king Balak to throw a stumbling block before the sons of Israel by leading them into idolatrous worship (Num 25:1–3; 31:16).[16] This misleading teaching to "throw" a stumbling block of idolatrous worship before the people of Israel associates it with the Devil who is about to "throw" some from the church in Smyrna into prison (2:10).

---

16. "Like Balaam, this was a group of false prophets who were encouraging participation in idol feasts by teaching that such permission was permissible for Christians" (Beale, *Revelation*, 249).

In a stark contrast to the promise of the exalted Jesus to give the one who conquers by not engaging in false worship to "eat" from the tree of eternal life (2:7), those holding to the teaching of Balaam teach their followers to "eat" food sacrificed to idols, and thus to partake of the fellowship of idolatrous worship (2:14).[17] They also teach their followers to "engage in prostitution" (2:14b), a biblical metaphor for idolatrous worship (Hos 9:1; Jer 3:6; Ezek 23:19; 1 Chr 5:25), based on the portrayal of the covenant between God and his people as a nuptial union.[18] Not only does the church in Pergamum have "those holding to the teaching" of Balaam (2:14a) but "those holding to the teaching" of the Nicolaitans (2:15), whose works associated with false worship both the exalted Jesus and the church in Ephesus hate (2:6).[19]

To the church in Ephesus the exalted Jesus exhorted, "Repent and do the first works. Otherwise, I am coming to you and I will move your lampstand from its place, if you do not repent" (2:5). And now to the church in Pergamum he similarly exhorts, "Repent then. Otherwise, I am coming to you soon and I will battle against them with the sword of my mouth" (2:16). The church in Pergamum is to repent from any association with those teaching idolatrous practices. If they do not repent, so that the false teachers and their followers in turn will also repent, then the Jesus having the "sharp two-edged sword" (2:12) promises that he is coming to battle against these false teachers and their followers with the "sword of my mouth." This recalls that "from his mouth a two-edged sword is coming" (1:16), which underscores his authority to execute judgment with the word of God that is like a two-edged sword.

After his exhortatory refrain, "Let the one having an ear hear what the Spirit is saying to the churches" (2:7a, 11a, 17a), the exalted Jesus promises, "To the one who conquers I will give him some of the hidden manna and I will give him a white stone, and upon the stone a new name is written that no one knows except the one receiving it" (2:17b).

---

17. On eating food sacrificed to idols, see Aune, *Revelation 1–5*, 191–94.

18. BDAG, 854. "In the OT, the idolatry of Israel is frequently condemned through the use of the metaphor of prostitution and sexual immorality (Jer 3:2; 13:27; Ezek 16:15–58; 23:1–49; 43:7; Hos 5:4; 6:10)" (Aune, *Revelation 1–5*, 188).

19. On the idolatrous worship referred to in 2:14–15, see Coutsoumpos, "Social Implications," 23–27.

PART ONE—Shown What Must Happen Soon (1:1—3:22)

The exalted Jesus already promised that "to the one who conquers I will give him to eat from the tree of the life" (2:7b), the tree of the eternal life in heaven. Now he similarly promises that "to the one who conquers I will give him some of the hidden manna," the metaphorical manna to eat as the bread hidden by God (divine passive) in heaven (LXX Ps 77:24), and thus another promise of eternal life. In a pointed contrast to the eating of food sacrificed to idols (2:14), the eating from both the tree of life and from the hidden manna are anticipated by the audience's eating of the Eucharist.[20]

The additional promise by the exalted Jesus that "I will give him a white stone" (2:17b) suggests that the one who conquers by overcoming the threat of false worship will have an association in heaven with the exalted Jesus whose "head and hair were white as white as wool" (1:14).[21] That upon the stone a new "name" is written (2:17b) by God (divine passive) further suggests an association with the "name" of the Jesus exalted to heaven by God (2:3, 13) as "the firstborn of the dead" (1:5a), and thus indicates a share in his risen, eternal life. As the exalted Jesus is the one who declared, "I know" the situation of the churches (2:2, 9, 13), so no one "knows" the new name written on the white stone, a symbol of resurrection to eternal life, except the one receiving and thus experiencing it (2:17b)—Jesus and anyone who conquers with him.[22]

---

20. "According to the tradition that surrounded the destruction of Jerusalem by the Babylonians, the prophet Jeremiah hid the ark of the covenant, which contained some of the Exodus manna, so that it would not be captured. The ark's location was lost and was promised to remain a secret until the final age" (Blount, *Revelation*, 60). "If one also considers that in primitive Christianity the interpretation of the manna as a type of Lord's Supper was well known (1 Cor. 10:3ff.), one is justified in concluding that this promise describes participation in the messianic meal at the time of salvation, a meal toward which the church looks each time it celebrates the Eucharist (1 Cor. 11:26)" (Roloff, *Revelation*, 52).

21. "The 'white stone' also enforces the idea of the 'manna' as a heavenly reward, since the OT describes the heavenly manna as resembling white bdellium stones (cf. Exod. 16:31 and Num. 11:7)" (Beale, *Revelation*, 253).

22. "The 'new name' symbolizes new life, here the new life given by Christ to the victor, who alone can receive it" (Harrington, *Revelation*, 62). On the promise to the one who conquers in 2:17b, see Wilson, *Victor Sayings*, 121–33; Wong, "Hidden Manna," 346–54. On the rational argumentation involved in the oracle to Pergamum, see deSilva, "Appeals to Reason," 137–39.

4d) Oracle to the Angel of the Church in Thyatira (2:18–29)

A ¹⁸ And to the angel of the **church** in **Thyatira** write: "These things **is saying** the Son of God, the one having his eyes as a flame of fire and his feet like burnished bronze, ¹⁹ 'I know **your works** and love and faith and service and your endurance, and that **your** last **works** are greater than the first.

B ²⁰ But I have against you that you are letting continue the woman Jezebel, who says that she herself is a prophetess and teaches and misleads my servants to **engage in prostitution** and to eat food sacrificed to idols. ²¹ª And I gave **her** time so that she may **repent**,

B′ ²¹ᵇ but she does not wish to **repent** from **her prostitution**. ²² Behold I am throwing **her** to a bed and those committing adultery with **her** to a great tribulation, if they do not **repent** from **her** works, ²³ª and **her** children I will kill with death

A′ a) ²³ᵇ and all the *churches* will know that I am the one searching minds and hearts, and *I will give* to you, to each one, according to **your works**. ²⁴ But to you I say, to the rest who are in **Thyatira**, as many as do not have this teaching, who do not know the deep things of Satan, as they say, I am not throwing upon you another burden,

    b) ²⁵ however, what you have hold *until* I come.

        c) ²⁶ª And the one who conquers

    b′) ²⁶ᵇ and the one who keeps *until* the end my **works**,

a′) ²⁶ᶜ *I will give* him authority over the nations ²⁷ and he will shepherd them with an iron staff, as clay vessels are crushed (Ps 2:8–9), ²⁸ as I myself received from my Father, and *I will give* him the morning star. ²⁹ Let the one having an ear hear what the Spirit **is saying** to the *churches*.'"

In the prophetic oracle to the angel of the church in Thyatira the exalted Jesus directs John to write: "These things is saying the Son of God, the one having his eyes as a flame of fire and his feet like burnished bronze"

(2:18).²³ The exalted Jesus is not only one like the heavenly "Son" of Man (1:13) but also the divine "Son" of God. That he is "the one having his eyes as a flame of fire and his feet like burnished bronze" recalls that in his vision John saw "his eyes as a flame of fire and his feet like burnished bronze" (1:14–15). This reminds the audience of the penetrating divine knowledge and heavenly sovereignty of the exalted Jesus as the focus of true worship.²⁴

The exalted Jesus tells the church in Thyatira that "I know your works and love and faith and service and your endurance, and that your last works are greater than the first" (2:19). As he praised the church in Ephesus that "I know your works and labor and your endurance" (2:2) and "that you have endurance" (2:3), so he now praises the church in Thyatira that "I know your works and faith and service and your endurance."²⁵ And as he praised the church in Pergamum that "you have not denied my faith" (2:13), so he now praises the church in Thyatira that he knows "your faith." Jesus blamed the church in Ephesus "that your first love you have let go" (2:4), so that this church must "repent and do the first works" (2:5). In contrast, Jesus, who identified himself as "the first and the last" (1:17; 2:8), now praises the church in Thyatira for its "love" and "that your last works are greater than the first."

Just as he did for the churches in Ephesus (2:4) and in Pergamum (2:14), so the exalted Jesus admonishes the church in Thyatira, "But I have against you" (2:20). Whereas he had against the church in Ephesus "that your first love you have let go" (2:4), he has against the church in Thyatira "that you are letting continue the woman Jezebel" (2:20), a reference to someone in Thyatira who is like King Ahab's queen, who advocated idolatrous worship in Israel (2 Kgs 9:22).²⁶

Recalling that in Ephesus are "those who say that they themselves are apostles yet they are not" (2:2), and that in Smyrna is "the blasphemy

---

23. On the historical background of Thyatira, see Hemer, *Letters*, 106–28; Oster, *Seven Congregations*, 146–60.

24. "Thus the living Christ has eyes that will penetrate to the heart of the false worship that is being promoted in Thyatira" (Fee, *Revelation*, 38–39).

25. "The 'works' for which this church is first recognized are not mere general deeds of Christian 'service' but are works of persevering witness to the outside world" (Beale, *Revelation*, 260).

26. BDAG, 469.

of those who say that they themselves are Jews yet they are not" (2:9), this Jezebel deceptively "says that she herself is a prophetess" (2:20). Just as Balaam "taught" Balak to mislead the people of God into idolatrous worship—"to eat food sacrificed to idols and to engage in prostitution" (2:14)—so Jezebel "teaches and misleads my servants to engage in prostitution and to eat food sacrificed to idols" (2:20). That Jezebel misleads "my servants" emphatically underlines the threat of her idolatrous teaching for the audience of Revelation, who have been designated as "his servants"—the servants of God and/or Jesus Christ (1:1).[27]

The exalted Jesus Christ, the one to whom God "gave him" the revelation as a divine gift (1:1), now declares that "I gave her" time as a divine gift so that she may repent. But this Jezebel, who teaches the servants of Jesus "to engage in prostitution" (2:20), does not wish to repent from her "prostitution" (2:21), her idolatrous worship. The churches in Ephesus and in Pergamum were both exhorted to "repent" (2:5, 16). And the exalted Jesus warned the church in Ephesus that there will be consequences "if you do not repent" (2:5). The implication, then, is that for this false prophetess Jezebel to whom the exalted Jesus graciously gave time that she may "repent," but who is unwilling to "repent," there will be consequences.

The exalted Jesus warned the church in Smyrna, "Behold the Devil is about to throw some of you into prison so that you may be tested and you will have tribulation for ten days" (2:10). Now, in ironic contrast, he pronounces the consequences of Jezebel's unwillingness to repent: "Behold I am throwing her to a bed and those committing adultery with her to a great tribulation, if they do not repent from her works" (2:22). The reference to those "committing adultery" with Jezebel extends the imagery of sexual misconduct to dramatically describe those servants of Jesus who allow themselves to be seduced into the idolatrous worship of "prostitution" taught by this false prophetess. Ironically, the "bed" suggestive of the place of her seductive adultery/idolatry will become the place of the pain of her great tribulation.[28]

---

27. "All we can speculate is that she [Jezebel] was a woman whose prophetic utterances made her the leader of the movement (most likely Nicolaitan, as at Ephesus and Pergamum) at Thyatira" (Osborne, *Revelation*, 156).

28. "With drastic vividness the announcement is made that the bed—a symbolic

PART ONE—*Shown What Must Happen Soon (1:1—3:22)*

Those committing idolatrous "adultery" with Jezebel, who was given time to "repent," but does not wish to "repent" from her idolatrous "prostitution" (2:21) are thus exhorted so that they may "repent" from her works of idolatry (2:22). The church in Ephesus was warned by the exalted Jesus that "I will move your lampstand from its place, if you do not repent" (2:5). And now those committing adultery with Jezebel are warned of a great tribulation, "if they do not repent from her works" (2:22). Like the church in Ephesus that hates the idolatrous "works" of the Nicolaitans (2:6), so those committing adultery with the false prophetess Jezebel are to repent of her idolatrous "works."

The reference to the followers of the teaching of the false prophetess Jezebel as "her children" (2:23a) further develops the imagery of immoral sexual conduct for idolatrous worship, as it suggests that they are the metaphorical offspring of her "adultery/idolatry" (2:22). In ironic contrast to the faithful witness Antipas, who was "killed" in Pergamum (2:13), the exalted Jesus warns that the idolatrous "children" of Jezebel "I will kill with death" (2:23a). The rhetorically emphatic redundancy that he will "kill with death" reinforces the exhortation for the audience to become faithful until "death" in order to receive the crown of eternal life (2:10), and never be harmed by the second (eternal) "death" (2:11). It underscores the exalted Jesus' sovereignty over eternal life and death as the one who is living forever and has the "keys of Death and of Hades" (1:18).

As the one who declared that "I am the first and the last" (1:17), in continuity with the Lord God who says that "I am the Alpha and the Omega" (1:8), the exalted Jesus promises that "all the churches will know that I am the one searching minds and hearts, and I will give to you, to each one, according to your works" (2:23b; cf. Jer 17:10).[29] That "I will give to you, to each one" reinforces the previous promises of the reward of eternal life that "I will give" to each one who conquers (2:7, 10, 17) by remaining faithful and prevailing over the threat of idolatrous worship. And that "I will give to you, to each one, according to your

---

image for lewdness and debauchery—would become a sickbed for her" (Roloff, *Revelation*, 55).

29. "'He who searches the minds and hearts' explains the literal meaning of the prior picture of Christ's 'eyes like a flame of fire' (v. 18)" (Beale, *Revelation*, 264).

Prophetic Oracles to the Seven Churches

works" reinforces the exhortation for the audience to repent from "her works," the idolatrous works of the false prophetess Jezebel (2:22).[30]

After the exalted Jesus encouraged all the churches with the promise that "I will give to you, to each one, according to your works" (2:23), he encourages the church in Thyatira: "But to you I say, to the rest who are in Thyatira, as many as do not have this teaching, who do not know the deep things of Satan, as they say, I am not throwing upon you another burden" (2:24).[31] As many as do not have this "teaching" refers to not having the teaching of Jezebel, who "teaches" idolatrous worship (2:20), as well as not having the idolatrous "teaching" of Balaam (2:14) and of the Nicolaitans (2:15). As among those who will "know" that the exalted Jesus is the one searching minds and hearts (2:23), the rest who are in Thyatira do not "know" the so-called "deep things of Satan"—the idolatrous worship connected with the Satan whose synagogue is in Smyrna (2:9) and whose throne is in Pergamum (2:13).

In contrast to Jezebel whom "I am throwing" to a bed of pain (2:22), to Balak whom Balaam taught to "throw" a stumbling block before Israel (2:14), and to the Devil who is about to "throw" some of those in Smyrna into prison (2:10), the exalted Jesus promises the rest in Thyatira that "I am not throwing upon you another burden" (2:24). Although they "do not have this teaching" (2:24), they are exhorted by Jesus to hold "what you do have" until he comes (2:25) for final judgment (1:7). The exalted Jesus is sovereignly and protectively "holding" the seven stars (angels of the seven churches) in his authoritative right hand (2:1). He praised the church in Pergamum that "you are holding to my name" (2:13) in contrast to those "holding" to the idolatrous teaching of Balaam (2:14) and of the Nicolaitans (2:15). And now he exhorts the rest who are in Thyatira and who are not engaged in idolatrous worship that "you hold what you have until I come."

The exalted Jesus promised that "I will give to you," to each one among all the churches, according to "your works" (2:23). And now he

---

30. For a possible relation of 2:18–23 to magic and witchcraft, see Duff, "Witchcraft Accusations," 116–33.

31. "[W]hat may have appeared to the false teachers as 'depths' of esoteric knowledge revealed by God about Satan was truly nothing more than 'the depths of Satan,' which only the ungodly fathom" (Beale, *Revelation*, 265–66).

promises that the one who conquers and the one who keeps "until" the end, "until" he comes (2:25), "my works," in contrast to "her works"—the idolatry of Jezebel (2:22), "I will give him authority over the nations and he will shepherd them with an iron staff, as clay vessels are crushed" (2:26–27; cf. Ps 2:8–9). This continues the refrain of promises for the one who conquers by prevailing over the threat of idolatrous worship (2:7, 11, 17). The promise for the one "who keeps until the end my works" reinforces the exhortation for the audience to hear the words of the prophecy of Revelation and "keep the things written in it, for the time is near" (1:3).

The exalted Jesus promised to give the one who conquers over idolatrous worship authority over the nations (2:26), further suggesting that he will shepherd them away from idolatry to the true worship of God with the powerful authority symbolized by the "iron staff" that can crush clay vessels (2:27).[32] He will give this authority that he himself, as the "Son of God" (2:18), received from his "Father" (2:28), reminding the audience that Jesus Christ "made us into a kingdom, priests for his God and Father" (1:6). The exalted Jesus who promised that "I will give him," the one who conquers, authority over the nations also promises that "I will give him" the "morning star" (2:28), suggestive of a share in the risen and eternal life of the exalted Jesus himself. With this prophetic oracle to Thyatira, the central and pivotal oracle within the chiastic subsection of seven oracles (2:1–3:22), the refraining appeal, "Let the one having an ear hear what the Spirit is saying to the churches" (2:7, 11, 17, 29), now occurs after rather than before the promise to the one who conquers.[33]

---

32. Contrary to many translations, "as clay vessels are crushed" does not mean that the nations will be crushed like clay vessels. Rather, it further describes the powerful and protective authority involved in shepherding the nations with an iron staff. "The verb means 'to shepherd' and should be taken in the sense of wielding the shepherd's staff or club to ward off the attacks of marauding beasts" (Mounce, *Revelation*, 90). "Revelation can also depict a positive destiny for the nations and even their rulers, converted to the fear and worship of God" (Bauckham, *Climax*, 314).

33. On the promise to the one who conquers in 2:26–29, see Wilson, *Victor Sayings*, 133–41. On the rational argumentation involved in the oracle to Thyatira, see deSilva, "Appeals to Reason," 139–42.

5c′) Oracle to the Angel of the Church in Sardis (3:1–6)

A ³:¹ᵃ And to the **angel** of the **church** in **Sardis** write:

    a) ¹ᵇ "These things **is saying** the one **having** the seven **Spirits** of **God** and the seven stars,

        b) ¹ᶜ 'I know *your works*

            c) ¹ᵈ *that* **you have** a **name**

            c′) ¹ᵉ *that* you are **living**, but you are dead. ²ᵃ Become watching and strengthen the rest who are about to die,

        b′) ²ᵇ for I have not found *your works* fulfilled

    a′) ²ᶜ **before** my **God**.

B ³ᵃ Remember then how you received and heard and keep and repent. If then you do **not** watch, **I will come** as a thief

B′ ³ᵇ and you will **never** know at what hour **I will come** upon you.

A′   **a)** ⁴ᵃ But **you have** a few *names* in **Sardis**

        b) ⁴ᵇ who have not defiled their *garments*, and they will walk with me in *white*,

            c) ⁴ᶜ for worthy are they.

        b′) ⁵ᵃ The one who conquers thus will be clothed in *white garments*

    a′) ⁵ᵇ and never will I wipe away his *name* from the scroll of the **life** and I will confess his *name* **before** my Father and **before** his **angels**. ⁶ Let the one *having* an ear hear what the **Spirit is saying** to the **churches**.'"

In the prophetic oracle to the angel of the church in Sardis (3:1a) the exalted Jesus directs John to write: "These things is saying the one having the seven Spirits of God and the seven stars" (3:1b).[34] That the exalted Jesus has the "seven Spirits" of God means that he possesses the fullness

---

34. On the historical background of Sardis, see Hemer, *Letters*, 129–52; Oster, *Seven Congregations*, 161–72.

PART ONE—*Shown What Must Happen Soon (1:1—3:22)*

of the divine Spirit, a source of John's opening greeting of grace and peace to the audience from the "seven Spirits" before God's throne (1:4). This reinforces his exhortations to hear what this sevenfold "Spirit" is saying to each of the seven churches (2:7, 11, 17, 29; 3:6, 13, 22). And that he is the one "having" the "seven stars" recalls John's vision of him as the one "having" in his authoritative right hand "seven stars" (1:16), the "seven stars" that are the angels of the seven churches (1:20). This reinforces his divine authority to address the angel representative of the heavenly status of each church (2:1, 8, 12, 18, 3:1).

As he told the church in Ephesus (2:2) and in Thyatira (2:19), so the exalted Jesus now tells the church in Sardis, "I know your works" (3:1c). In contrast to the new "name," suggestive of the new, risen and eternal life, written upon the white stone promised to the one who conquers (2:17), and to the "name" of the risen and exalted Jesus (2:3, 13), the church in Sardis has a different "name" (3:1d), one associated with death rather than life. The exalted Jesus previously informed John that "once I was dead but behold I am living for the ages of the ages" (1:18). In an ironic twist, the exalted Jesus who is living eternally knows the works of the church in Sardis that indicate its spiritual death rather than a living for eternal life—that this church has a name "that you are living, but you are dead" (3:1e).

Since the church in Sardis is spiritually "dead," the exalted Jesus exhorts it to "become watching" (3:2a)—to become watchful for the attainment of eternal life, as this exhortation resonates with the exhortation for the church in Smyrna to "become faithful until death, and I will give you the crown of the [eternal] life" (2:10). The church in Sardis will thereby be able to "strengthen the rest who are about to die" (3:2a) spiritually, resonating with the exhortation to the "rest who are in Thyatira" (2:24) to hold what they have until the exalted Jesus comes (2:25) to give them eternal life.

The exalted Jesus who has the seven Spirits of God, which are "before his throne" (1:4), the focus of royal worship, further admonishes the church, "for I have not found your works fulfilled before my God" (3:2bc). That he has not found "your works fulfilled before my God" indicates that the church has not fulfilled the role he gave to all believers to be "a kingdom, priests for his God and Father" (1:6). In other words, its works do not fulfill the royal and priestly service of rendering worship pleasing before God and his throne. This is why the church is spiritually "dead" and not living for the attainment of eternal life (3:1). This church is not performing a proper worship for eternal life in the Spirit of prophecy.

To the church in Ephesus the exalted Jesus exhorted, "Remember then whence you have fallen and repent and do the first works" (2:5). And now to the church in Sardis he exhorts, "Remember then how you received and heard and keep and repent" (3:3a). "As I myself received from my Father" divine authority (2:28), so the exalted Jesus tells the church to remember "how you received" from him the authority to perform proper worship as "priests for God his Father" (1:6). That the church is to remember what "you heard and keep and repent" reinforces the exhortations that everyone "hear what the Spirit is saying to the churches" (2:7, 11, 17, 29). And this further reinforces the promise that blessed are "those who hear the words of the prophecy and keep the things written in it" (1:3), which includes being "one who keeps until the end my works" (2:26).

In the central and pivotal unit (2:18–29), the oracle to the angel of the church in Thyatira, of this seven unit subsection (2:1–3:22) the audience heard three calls for repentance with verbs in the third person directed to those threatening the church. The exalted Jesus gave the idolatrous false prophetess Jezebel time so that she may "repent," but she does not wish to "repent" of her idolatrous "prostitution" (2:21). And he warned that a great tribulation is coming to those who do not "repent" of her works of idolatrous worship (2:22). With this next unit (3:1–6), the oracle to the angel of the church in Sardis, the audience begin to hear a return to calls for repentance with verbs in the second person addressed directly to the churches themselves.

The exalted Jesus warned the church in Pergamum, "Repent then. Otherwise, I am coming to you soon" (2:16). He warned the church in Ephesus, "Repent and do the first works. Otherwise, I am coming to you and I will move your lampstand from its place, if you do not repent" (2:5). And now he warns the church in Sardis, which is to "repent" by watching, "If then you do not watch, I will come as a thief and you will never know at what hour I will come upon you" (3:3).

PART ONE—*Shown What Must Happen Soon (1:1—3:22)*

The church is told that "you will never know" when Jesus will come to be its judge (3:3). Jesus is the one whom all the churches will "know," including those who do not "know" the deep things of Satan (2:24), as the judge who searches minds and hearts (2:23). That as judge Jesus will give to all, to each one, according to "your works" (2:23) reinforces the exhortation for the church in Sardis to repent of the works rendering it spiritually dead rather than living "for I have not found your works fulfilled before my God" (3:2).

The church in Pergamum the exalted Jesus admonished, "But I have against you a few things, that you have there those holding to the teaching of Balaam" (2:14), which leads to idolatrous worship. But now he praises the church in Sardis, "But you have a few names in Sardis who have not defiled their garments" (3:4), that is, a few individuals who have not "defiled" or "stained" their "garments," a metaphorical representation of themselves and their conduct, by engaging in idolatrous worship. He promises that those who do not defile themselves with idolatrous worship will "walk" with him, who "walks" in the midst of the seven golden lampstands that represent the heavenly status of the seven churches (2:1), in white, for worthy are they (3:4). They will walk in heaven with Jesus in the "white" indicative of their share in the new risen and eternal life suggested by the "white" stone (2:17) promised by the exalted Jesus whose head and hair are "white" as "white" wool (1:14).

And the exalted Jesus now promises that the one who conquers, including anyone with "garments" undefiled by idolatrous worship (3:4), will thus be worthy of being clothed in the "white garments" (3:5a) indicative of their possession of heavenly eternal life. In contrast to the fact that "you have a name that you are living, but you are dead" (3:1), Jesus acknowledged that "you have a few names" who have not engaged in idolatrous worship (3:4), and promises that he will never wipe away or erase the "name" of the one who conquers the threat of idolatry from the scroll or book of "*the* life"—eternal life (3:5). This reinforces the promises of the exalted Jesus to give the one who becomes faithful until death the triumphal crown of "*the* life" (2:10), and to give the one who conquers the threat of idolatry to eat from the tree of "*the* life" (2:7).[35]

---

35. "The possibility of having one's name erased from the Book of Life suggests

54

Although he has not found the works of the church fulfilled "before my God" (3:2), Jesus promises through its "angel" (3:1) that he will confess the name of the one who conquers "before my Father" and "before his angels" in heaven (3:5). In contrast to the "name" of the Sardian church that "you are living, but you are dead" (3:1), Jesus promises that he will not wipe away the "name" of the one who conquers but rather that he will confess his "name" in the heavenly realm. The Jesus who received authority from "my Father" to shepherd the nations (2:28) promises the one who conquers by being a priest for "his God and Father" (1:6) that he will confess his name before "my Father" (3:5) in heaven at the final judgment.

Through what the exalted Jesus, the one "having" the seven "Spirits" of God, "is saying" to the angel of the "church" in Sardis (3:1), anyone in the audience "having" an ear is exhorted to "hear" what the "Spirit is saying" to all of the "churches" (3:6). This reinforces not only the exhortations to "hear" in the previous prophetic oracles (2:7, 11, 17, 29) but the exhortation for the audience to be those who "hear" the words of the prophecy and keep the things written in it (1:3) by avoiding idolatry and engaging in the true worship of God. In other words, the audience of Revelation are to be those who worship for eternal life in the Spirit of prophecy.[36]

6b') Oracle to the Angel of the Church in Philadelphia (3:7–13)

> **A** [7a] And to the angel of the **church** in Philadelphia write: "These things **is saying** the holy one, the true one, the one **having** the key of David,
>
> **B** a) [7b] who opens and no one will close and closes and no one opens (Isa 22:22), [8a] 'I know your works, **behold I**

---

that fidelity to God rather than any type of predestinarian system is the reason for having one's name inscribed in the Book of Life in the first place" (Aune, *Revelation 1–5*, 223).

36. On the promise to the one who conquers in 3:5, see Wilson, *Victor Sayings*, 141–51. On the rational argumentation involved in the oracle to Sardis, see deSilva, "Appeals to Reason," 142–45.

PART ONE—Shown What Must Happen Soon (1:1—3:22)

> ***have given*** before you a door opened, which no one is able to close it,
>
> b) ⁸ᵇ that you have little power but **you have kept** *my* **word**
>
> b') ⁸ᶜ and you have not denied *my* **name**.
>
> a') ⁹ᵃ ***Behold I will give*** from the synagogue of Satan, of those who say that they themselves are Jews yet they are not but are lying. ***Behold*** **I will make** them
>
> C⁹ᵇ come and worship before your feet and they will know that I have loved you.
>
> B' a) ¹⁰ᵃ Because **you have kept** the **word** of *my* endurance,
>
> b) ¹⁰ᵇ I will also **keep** you from the hour of the testing that is about to ***come*** upon the whole world to test those inhabiting upon the earth.
>
> b') ¹¹ I am ***coming*** soon. Hold what you have, so that no one may receive your crown.
>
> a') ¹² The one who conquers, **I will make** him a pillar in the temple of *my* God and from it he will never come out and I will write upon him the **name** of *my* God and the **name** of the city of *my* God, of the new Jerusalem that is descending out of heaven from *my* God, and *my* **name**, the new one.
>
> A' ¹³ Let the one **having** an ear hear what the Spirit **is saying** to the **churches**.'"

In the prophetic oracle to the angel of the church in Philadelphia the exalted Jesus directs John to write: "These things is saying the holy one, the true one, the one having the key of David, who opens and no one will close and closes and no one opens" (3:7).[37] That the exalted Jesus, as the divine holy one and the true one, has the "key" of David, with its

---

37. On the historical background of Philadelphia, see Hemer, *Letters*, 153–77; Oster, *Seven Congregations*, 173–83. "God as 'the holy one' is frequent in the OT, and the title refers to God/Christ as 'set apart' from this world, as Wholly Other and alone worthy of worship" (Osborne, *Revelation*, 187).

Prophetic Oracles to the Seven Churches

allusion to David's authoritative power (Isa 22:22), resonates with his having the "keys" of Death and Hades (Rev 1:18), and indicates his authoritative power to grant entrance into his heavenly eternal life. Jesus promised to give to the one who conquers a white stone, and upon the stone a new name, indicative of his new, risen and eternal life, is written that "no one" knows except the one receiving it (2:17). Similarly, that Jesus opens and "no one" will close and closes and "no one" opens emphasizes the definitive sovereignty of his power and authority to grant an entrance into his new heavenly and eternal life with its heavenly worship.

As he told the church in Ephesus (2:2), in Thyatira (2:19), and in Pergamum (3:1), so the exalted Jesus tells the church in Philadelphia that "I know your works" (3:8a). Jesus declared that "I gave" her—the false prophetess Jezebel—time to repent, but she does not wish to repent from her "prostitution," her idolatrous worship (2:21). In contrast, he now declares that "I have given" before the church a door "opened" (3:8a), with the use of the perfect tenses of these verbs emphasizing that the door has been and still is definitively "given" and "opened" for the church. That the door is opened, which "on one" is able to "close" (3:8a), further underscores the definitive sovereignty of the exalted Jesus' power and authority, as the one who "opens and no one will close and closes and no one opens" (3:7), to grant an entrance into his new heavenly and eternal life.

As the one "having" the sovereign power of the key of David (3:7), the exalted Jesus knows of this church that "you have little power but you have kept my word and you have not denied my name" (3:8bc). Like the one who "keeps" until the end "my" works (2:26), "you have kept my word." This makes the church a model for the audience, who are to be those who hear the "words" of the prophecy, which is the book of Revelation, and "keep" the things written in it (1:3). And it likens the church to John as a prophetic servant who witnessed to the "word" of God and the witness of Jesus (1:2, 9). The Jesus who told the church in Pergamum that "you are holding to my name and have not denied my faith" (2:13) now tells the church in Philadelphia that "you have not denied my name," similar to the church in Ephesus who has borne up on

57

account of "my name" (2:3). His "name" includes especially his identity and status as the one once dead who is now living eternally (1:18).

The exalted Jesus who declared, "Behold I have given before you a door opened" (3:8), now declares, "Behold I will give from the synagogue of Satan, of those who say that they themselves are Jews yet they are not but are lying. Behold I will make them come and worship before your feet and they will know that I have loved you" (3:9).[38] This recalls what Jesus said to the church in Smyrna about the "blasphemy," the idolatrous worship, "of those who say that they themselves are Jews yet they are not but are a synagogue of Satan" (2:9). The Jesus who promised that "I will come" for final judgment (2:25; 3:3) assures that these Jewish false worshipers ultimately "will come" and worship the true God before the feet of those in the church. As they join in the true worship of the church, which includes the acknowledgement of Jesus as the one who "loves us" (1:5), they will know that "I have loved you."

Not only "have you kept my word" (3:8), but the exalted Jesus adds, "Because you have kept the word of my endurance, I will also keep you from the hour of the testing that is about to come upon the whole world to test those inhabiting upon the earth" (3:10). As he acknowledged the "endurance" of the churches in Ephesus and Thyatira (2:2–3, 19), so Jesus acknowledges that the church in Philadelphia has kept the word of my "endurance." This further likens the church to John as their "brother and fellow sharer in the tribulation and kingdom and endurance in Jesus" (1:9). In other words, they have endured in resisting the idolatrous worship that only leads to the "second," eternal death (2:11, 23) and in maintaining the true worship that leads to heavenly eternal life in accord with the prophetic witness given by and to the risen and exalted Jesus.

Although the church in Sardis will never know at what "hour" Jesus will come for final judgment (3:3), he promises to keep the church in Philadelphia from the "hour" of the testing (3:10). The exalted Jesus warned the church in Smyrna that the Devil "is about" to throw some of them into prison so that "you may be tested" and have tribulation for ten days (2:10). He now assures the church in Philadelphia that he will keep them from the hour of the "testing" that "is about" to come

38. On "those who call themselves Jews" in Philadelphia, see Mayo, *Jews*, 67–76.

upon the whole world to "test" those inhabiting upon the earth (3:10). Jesus told the church in Pergamum that he knows where "you inhabit," where the throne of Satan is (2:13) with its threat of idolatrous worship. But he will keep the church in Philadelphia from being tested like those "inhabiting upon" the earth—those involved in the idolatrous worship that takes place on earth rather than in the true worship that takes place in heaven.

The exalted Jesus exhorted the church in Pergamum to repent, otherwise, "I am coming to you soon" (2:16) and the church in Thyatira, "what you have hold until I come" (2:25). Now he exhorts the church in Philadelphia, "I am coming soon. Hold what you have, so that no one may receive your crown" (3:11). The church is to hold what it has, particularly its true worship, so that no one may receive and thus take away its "crown," that is, the "crown" of eternal life Jesus promised to those becoming faithful until death (2:10)—faithful to true worship even if it results in death.[39]

To the church in Philadelphia the exalted Jesus promised that "I will make" the false Jews come and worship the true God before the feet of the church (3:9). And now he adds to his previous promises to "the one who conquers" over the threat of idolatrous worship (2:7, 11, 17, 26; 3:5). He promises, "The one who conquers, I will make him a pillar in the temple of my God and from it he will never come out and I will write upon him the name of my God and the name of the city of my God, of the new Jerusalem that is descending out of heaven from my God, and my name, the new one" (3:12).[40]

In contrast to his not finding the works of the Sardian church fulfilled before "my God" (3:2), and in fulfillment of his having "made us into a kingdom, priests for his God and Father" (1:6), Jesus promises to make the one who conquers a "pillar," a permanent fixture, in the heavenly temple of "my God" (3:12) and thus a priestly participant in

---

39. "[T]he probable eucharistic context in which the Apocalypse was originally read may be important here, for in such a context Christ comes to his expectant people, anticipating his final coming" (Boxall, *Revelation* 73).

40. "The idea of the heavenly Jerusalem stems from Ezekiel's vision of the eschatological temple in Ezek. 40–48, specifically chapter 48" (Osborne, *Revelation*, 198).

heavenly worship.⁴¹ Jesus promised to give the one who conquers a white stone, and upon the stone a "new name" is "written" signifying the new, risen, and eternal life offered by Jesus (2:17). He now promises that "I will write" upon the one who conquers the "name of my God and the name of the city of my God, of the new Jerusalem that is descending out of heaven from my God" (3:12), emphatically underlining a heavenly status with "my God." As the church has not denied "my name" (3:8), so Jesus promises to write "my name, the new one" (3:12), the one that indicates the new, risen, and eternal life, upon the one who conquers.⁴²

The exalted Jesus, the one "having" the authoritative "key of David" (3:7), exhorts anyone in the audience "having" an ear to hear what the Spirit is saying not just to the church in Philadelphia but to all of the churches (3:13). This repeats and so reinforces the exhortation given in each of the previous prophetic oracles to the churches (2:7, 11, 17, 29; 3:6). The worshiping audience are thus to listen to the Spirit speaking in each of these prophetic oracles through the Jesus who has been exalted to risen, eternal life, in order for them to worship for eternal life in the Spirit of prophecy.

7a′) Oracle to the Angel of the Church in Laodicea (3:14–22)

> A ¹⁴ And to the angel of the **church** in Laodicea write: "These things **is saying** the Amen, the witness, the faithful and true one, the beginning of the creation of God,
>
> B a) ¹⁵ᵃ 'I *know* your works,
>
> b) ¹⁵ᵇ that you are ***neither cold nor hot***. Would that you were ***cold*** or ***hot***!
>
> c) ¹⁶ᵃ So because you are lukewarm,
>
> b′) ¹⁶ᵇ and ***neither cold nor hot***, I am about to vomit you from my mouth,

---

41. Wong, "Pillar," 297–307.

42. On the promise to the one who conquers in 3:12, see Wilson, *Victor Sayings*, 151–62. On the rational argumentation involved in the oracle to Philadelphia, see deSilva, "Appeals to Reason," 145–49.

> **a′)** ¹⁷ for you are saying that "I am **rich** and have **become rich** and I have need of nothing," but you do not ***know*** that you are wretched and pitiable and poor and blind and **naked**.
>
> **C** ¹⁸ᵃ I advise you to buy from me gold refined from fire
>
> **B′** ¹⁸ᵇ so that you may **become rich**, and white garments so that you may be clothed and the shame of your **nakedness** not be manifested, and eye salve to anoint your eyes, so that you may observe. ¹⁹ I, as many as I may love, reprove and discipline. Be zealous then and repent.
>
> **A′ a)** ²⁰ᵃ Behold I stand at the door and I am knocking, if anyone ***hears*** my sound and opens the door,
>
>> **b)** ²⁰ᵇ I will come in to him and I will dine ***with*** him and he ***with*** me. ²¹ᵃ The one who ***conquers***, I will give him to ***sit with*** me on my ***throne***,
>>
>> **b′)** ²¹ᵇ as I also ***conquered*** and ***sat with*** my Father on his ***throne***.
>
> **a′)** ²² Let the one having an ear ***hear*** what the Spirit **is saying** to the **churches**.'"

In the prophetic oracle to the angel of the church in Laodicea the exalted Jesus directs John to write: "These things is saying the Amen, the witness, the faithful and true one, the beginning of the creation of God" (3:14).[43] Having twice voiced their own "Amen" as an emphatic affirmation in the initial liturgical dialogue (1:6-7), the audience now hear the exalted Jesus identify himself as "the Amen," the personified ultimate divine affirmation in worshipful response to God.[44] His self-identification as "the witness, the faithful one" not only reinforces John's description of him as "the witness, the faithful one" (1:5), but recalls the model that the martyred Antipas provides for the audience as "my witness, my faithful one" (2:13). Again described as the "true one" (3:7,

---

43. On the historical background of Laodicea, see Hemer, *Letters*, 178–209; Oster, *Seven Congregations*, 184–97.

44. BDAG, 53–54.

14), Jesus is also the "beginning," the preeminent first creature, of God's creation.

Just as for previous churches (2:2; 3:1, 8), the exalted Jesus "knows the works" of the church in Laodicea (3:15a). That metaphorically "you are neither cold nor hot," but rather "lukewarm" (3:15–16), indicates that the works of the church do not provide anything to attract Jesus to share with them a meal that includes appropriately hot or cold drinking water. Because they are unappealingly "lukewarm," Jesus is "about to vomit you from my mouth" (3:16), metaphorical imagery for rejecting them as dining partners.[45] By way of an ironic contrast, this means that the works of the church do not accord with the word of God, symbolized by the sharp two-edged sword that is coming "from his mouth" (1:16), by the sword "of my mouth" (2:16)—the mouth of the exalted Jesus.

The exalted Jesus told the church in Smyrna that he knows its tribulation and poverty, but it is "rich" metaphorically or spiritually (2:9). In ironic deviance from this positive sense of being rich, the church in Laodicea boasts that it is "rich" materially and has become rich and has need of nothing (3:17).[46] The arrogant boast of this church that "I have need of nothing" betrays its need to heed the call for repentance indicated by the exalted Jesus who told other churches, "But I have against you" (2:4, 14, 20), and its need to overcome the power of death through the Jesus who announced, "I have the keys of Death and of Hades" (1:18). The Jesus who declared that "I know your works" (3:15a) now chastises this church that "you do not know that you are wretched and pitiable and poor and blind and naked" (3:17).[47] As spiritually "blind" and "naked," this church lacks a share in the heavenly qualities displayed by the

---

45. For the evidence that the references to hot, cold, and lukewarm draw on common dining practices rather than on any particular peculiarities of the Laodicean water supply, see Koester, "Message to Laodicea," 407–24, esp. 411–16.

46. On the function of the imputed speech in 3:17 as a marker of deviance, see Mathews, "Imputed Speech," 319–38.

47. "The final three adjectives almost certainly contain allusions to the city's local scene. Despite its financial wealth, it is 'poor'; despite its medical school and famous eye-salve, it is 'blind'; and, in the face of its flourishing textile industry, it is 'naked'" (Smalley, *Revelation*, 99).

exalted Jesus "dressed in a robe reaching to the feet and girded at the breasts with a golden belt" (1:13) and with "eyes as a flame of fire" (1:14).

The church that thinks it is so rich in earthly things that it has need of nothing (3:17) the exalted Jesus advises metaphorically or spiritually "to buy" emphatically *from me* "gold refined from fire" (3:18a).[48] It may then have a share in his heavenly splendor as one "with a golden belt" (1:13). He also walks in the midst of the "seven golden lampstands" (2:1), the "seven golden lampstands" that indicate a corresponding heavenly status for the churches (1:12, 20). And he has "feet like burnished bronze, as in a furnace of refining" (1:15). This church that falsely boasts that "I have become rich" (3:17) is told that with the "gold" that transcends earthly gold and that they are to "buy" from the exalted Jesus truly "you may become rich" (3:18) as those who possess a share in the eternal life of the exalted Jesus.

The exalted Jesus further advises this church to "buy" from him "white garments" so that "you may be clothed" and the "shame of your nakedness"—being "naked" despite the claim to be rich (3:17)—not be manifested (3:18). They will thereby be likened to those in Sardis who have not defiled their "garments" through false worship, so that they will walk in heaven with the exalted Jesus in "white" (3:4), as a conqueror "clothed" in "white garments" (3:5), apparel appropriate for heavenly worship. The church is also to "buy" from the exalted Jesus whose "eyes" are as a flame of fire (1:14; 2:28) "eye salve to anoint your eyes, so that you may observe" (3:18). This will liken them to John who turned to "observe" the exalted Jesus (1:12) when he was told to write in a scroll what "you observe" (1:11), and prepare them for their role in the fulfillment of the prophetic promise that every "eye" will see the exalted Jesus at his final coming (1:7).

The exalted Jesus then declares that he reproves and disciplines "as many as I may love" (3:19; cf. Prov 3:11–12), with the implication that they are to be among the "as many as" do not follow the idolatrous teaching of the false prophetess Jezebel (2:24). Consequently, this church, whom he wishes were cold or "hot" (3:15), is to "be zealous" and "repent" (3:19), just as the churches of Ephesus, Pergamum, and Sardis

---

48. "They think they are rich but are actually poor; the only way they can be truly wealthy is to 'purchase' gold from Jesus. Yet this cannot be bought; it must be accepted as a gift on the basis of faith" (Osborne, *Revelation*, 209).

are to "repent" (2:5, 16; 3:3). They are thus to be unlike Jezebel, whom Jesus gave time that she may "repent," but she did not wish to "repent" of her idolatrous "prostitution" (2:21). They will thereby avoid the great tribulation coming upon those who do not "repent" from her works of false worship (2:22).

The exalted Jesus introduced the metaphorical "open door" to the church in Philadelphia, "Behold I have given before you a door opened" (3:8). He now invites those in the Laodicean church to complement this by metaphorically "opening the door" for his entrance into their liturgical assembly. He may then appropriately join and be in meal fellowship with each of them, especially for the celebration of the Eucharist: "Behold I stand at the door and I am knocking, if anyone hears my sound and opens the door, I will come in to him and I will dine with him and he with me" (3:20).[49]

John was in Spirit on the Lord's day when "I heard behind me a great sound" (1:10), the sound of the voice of the exalted Jesus (1:12–16). Now the exalted Jesus invites anyone who "hears my sound" (3:20), that is, hears and heeds the sound of his voice calling for repentance (3:19), to "open the door" by repenting of any association with false worship. In contrast to those committing "adultery"—idolatrous worship—"with her," the false prophetess Jezebel (2:22), Jesus will dine "with him"—the one who repents of such worship (3:20). Those who have not defiled their garments through idolatrous worship will walk "with me" in white (3:4). Similarly, anyone who becomes "zealous" (3:19), rather than "lukewarm," so that Jesus will not reject him as a dining partner (3:16), and repents of false worship, will dine "with me" in a heavenly meal fellowship anticipated by the audience's celebration of the Eucharist.[50]

Adding to his previous six promises, which indicate a share in eternal life for the one who "conquers" (2:7, 11, 17, 26; 3:5, 12) by overcoming the deadly threat of false worship, the exalted Jesus announces a seventh: "The one who conquers, I will give [cf. 2:7, 10, 17, 23, 26, 28] to him to sit with me on my throne" (3:21a). Not only will the one who

---

49. "The meal to be shared by Jesus and the worshiper may be construed as the Lord's Supper" (Aune, *Revelation 1–5*, 254). See also Streett, *Subversive Meals*, 280.

50. According to Beale, *Revelation*, 309, a eucharistic setting could be discernible from the verb "dine" and "the cognate noun of the Last Supper in Luke 22:20; John 13:2, 4; 21:20; and the Eucharist in 1 Cor. 11:20, 21, 25."

"opens the door" by repenting of false worship dine in meal fellowship "with me" (3:20)—the exalted and risen Jesus who now lives eternally—but the one who conquers will sit in a ruling fellowship "with me on my throne." The one who conquers is "to sit" in a position of eternal fellowship and ruling authority not only with the conquering Jesus on "my throne" but with God on his throne—"as I also conquered and sat with my Father on his throne" (3:21b).[51]

God's "throne" before which are the divine seven Spirits (1:4) is the focus of heavenly rule and worship in contrast to the "throne" of Satan (2:13). The Jesus who received divine authority from "my Father" (2:28) and who will confess the name of the one who conquers before "my Father" (3:5) sits with "my Father" on his throne, and the one who conquers will sit with him (3:21). This promise to the one who conquers over the false worship that contradicts the worship for eternal life thus reinforces the audience's doxological worship of Jesus as the one "who has made us into a kingdom, priests for his God and Father, to him be glory and might for the ages of the ages. Amen!" (1:6). The final exhortation for the one having an ear to "hear" what the Spirit is saying to all of the churches (3:22) reinforces this refrain in the previous six prophetic oracles (2:7, 11, 17, 29; 3:6, 13), especially appealing for anyone to "hear" the sound of the exalted Jesus' invitation to dine and sit in heavenly fellowship with him (3:20-21).

Summary on 2:1—3:22

The audience hear the seven units in this subsection (2:1—3:22) in a chiastic pattern with the theme of both encouraging the churches who encounter the deadly threat of idolatrous worship to withstand it and exhorting them to repent of any associations with it, so that they may participate in the worship and eternal life of heaven. In the first (a) unit (2:1-7) the church in Ephesus is to repent and return to its first works associated with proper worship (2:5). In the second (b) unit (2:8-11) the church in Smyrna is encouraged to withstand the threat of idolatry from "those who say that they themselves are Jews yet they are not but are a

---

51. For a suggestion that the promises to the conquerors in Revelation 2-3 follow the biblical salvation-historical order, see den Dulk, "Promises," 516-22.

synagogue of Satan" (2:9). In the third (c) unit (2:12–17) the church in Pergamum is to repent from idolatrous teachings (2:16).

In the central fourth (d) unit (2:18–29) the exalted Jesus tells the church in Thyatira that he gave the idolatrous false prophetess Jezebel time "that she may repent, but she does not wish to repent" (2:21), and he warns those following her of tribulation "if they do not repent" (2:22). With this pivotal fourth unit the refrain that recurs in each unit, "Let the one having an ear hear what the Spirit is saying to the churches" (2:7, 11, 17, 29; 3:6, 13, 22), begins to be heard as the final exhortation climactically concluding the remaining units. In the fifth (c') unit (3:1–6) the church in Sardis is to repent of its death-bringing idolatry (3:3). In the sixth (b') unit (3:7–13) the church in Philadelphia is encouraged to withstand the idolatrous "synagogue of Satan, of those who say that they themselves are Jews yet they are not" (3:9). And in the seventh (a') unit (3:14–22) the church in Laodicea is to be zealous and repent (3:19) of idolatry in order to be in a true worshipful fellowship with the exalted Jesus.

The risen and exalted Jesus issues a promise suggestive of sharing in his eternal life to each of the seven churches in return for their repenting and overcoming the deadly threat of idolatrous worship. They are promised: to eat from the tree of the eternal life, which is in the paradise of God (2:7); to be given the crown of the eternal life, and thus never be harmed by the second—eternal—death (2:10–11); to be given a white stone upon which is written a "new" name indicating a share in the new risen and eternal life of Jesus (2:17); to be given the "morning star" suggestive of rising to eternal life with Jesus (2:28); to be permanently inscribed in the scroll of the eternal life (3:5); to possess a permanent place in the heavenly temple and the "new" name of Jesus for a share in his eternal life (3:12); to sit in eternal fellowship with Jesus on his heavenly throne as the one who conquered death and sat with his Father on his throne (3:21). These seven prophetic oracles thus exhort the audience to continue to engage in true worship for eternal life in the Spirit of the prophecy that is presented to them in the book of Revelation (1:3).

PART TWO

John in Spirit Shown What Must Happen after These Things (4:1—16:21)

4

John's Visions of Lamb Opening the Seals and Worship around the Throne in Heaven

Revelation 4:1—7:17

1a) Vision of the One Sitting on the Throne in Heaven (4:1–5a)

    A [4:1] After these things I saw, and behold a door opened in heaven, and the **sound**, the first one, which I heard as a trumpet speaking with me, saying, "Ascend here, and I will show you the things it is necessary to happen after these things."

    B [2] Immediately I was in Spirit, and behold a throne was lying in heaven and upon the throne one **sitting**,

    B′ a) [3a] and the one ***sitting***

        b) [3b] was in vision like a stone, jasper and carnelian, and a rainbow was ***around the throne*** in vision like emerald.

        b′) [4a] And ***around the throne*** were twenty-four thrones, and upon the thrones twenty-four elders,

PART TWO—*Shown What Must Happen after These Things (4:1—16:21)*

>   **a′)** ⁴ᵇ ***sitting*** clothed in white garments and upon their heads golden crowns.
>
> **A′** ⁵ᵃ And from the throne were going out lightnings and **sounds** and thunders.

The heavenly visions of John continue as he declares that "after these things I saw" (cf. 1:12, 17), and "behold" there was a "door opened" by God (divine passive) in heaven (4:1). This door already opened in heaven differs from but resonates with the door on earth that believers are to open for Jesus to come in and share meal fellowship with them: "Behold I stand at the door and I am knocking, if anyone hears my sound and opens the door, I will come in to him and I will dine with him and he with me" (3:20). The door opened in heaven for John also resonates with what the exalted Jesus announced to the church in Philadelphia: "Behold I have given before you a door opened, which no one is able to close it" (3:8).

John then refers to "the sound, the first one, which I heard as a trumpet speaking with me" (4:1). This recalls what John reported when his vision of the exalted Jesus began: "I heard behind me a great sound as a trumpet" (1:10) and "I turned to observe the sound that was speaking with me" (1:12). That same sound of the exalted Jesus that John now hears again is saying, "Ascend here, and I will show you what must happen after these things" (4:1). Thus, before the fulfillment of his promise to the audience regarding the new Jerusalem that is to be "descending" to earth "out of heaven" (3:12), the exalted Jesus has invited John to "ascend" here and enter the door opened "in heaven" (4:1).

The exalted Jesus' offer to John that "I will show you the things it is necessary to happen after these things" (4:1) promises to provide additional content for John to fulfill the mandate given him by Jesus to write "the things that are about to happen after these things" (1:19). And it will further develop for the audience the content of the "revelation of Jesus Christ which God gave to him to show his servants the things it is necessary to happen soon" (1:1). The Jesus who has been raised from the dead and exalted to heaven thus invites John to ascend to heaven for the continuation of his initial revelatory vision into heaven while on earth (1:1–20) after the interlude of the prophetic oracles to the seven churches (2:1—3:22) representative of the audience of the book of Revelation.

John previously reported that "I was in Spirit" on the Lord's day of worship when his initial vision of the exalted Jesus in heaven began (1:10). And now he relates again that "immediately I was in Spirit" (4:2). The initial focus of his present vision—"behold a door opened in heaven" (4:1)—now progresses to "behold a throne was lying in heaven" (4:2). This heavenly "throne" thus stands in contrast to the "throne" of Satan on earth (2:13), even as it recalls the reference to the heavenly "throne" of God before which are the seven divine Spirits (1:4). That upon this "throne" in heaven was one "sitting" (4:2) recalls the promise of the exalted Jesus that he will give the one who conquers "to sit with me on my throne, as I also conquered and sat with my Father on his throne" (3:21).

Whereas in his vision while on earth John saw the exalted Jesus as "one like a Son of Man" (1:13), now in his vision while in heaven he sees that the "one sitting was in vision like a stone, jasper and carnelian, and a rainbow was around the throne in vision like emerald" (4:3). The audience are thus to identify the one "sitting" upon the "throne" in heaven (4:2) with God, the Father with whom the exalted Jesus, as the one who conquered, sat on his "throne" (3:21). Not only was an emerald-like rainbow "around the throne" (4:3) but "around the throne were twenty-four thrones, and upon the thrones twenty-four elders" (4:4).[1] That the twenty-four elders were "sitting" (4:4) "upon the thrones" closely associates them with the heavenly rule of God as the one "upon the throne sitting" (4:2).[2]

The twenty-four elders in heaven were "clothed in white garments" (4:4). This establishes them as role models not only for the church in Laodicea, which is to "buy" from the exalted Jesus "white garments so that you may be clothed" (3:18), but also for the entire audience, each of whom is to be one who conquers and thus "will be clothed in white

---

1. The elders "are identified with the twelve tribes and the twelve apostles, thus representing the entire community of the redeemed of both testaments" (Beale, *Revelation*, 322).

2. For various suggestions regarding the identity of the twenty-four elders, see Aune, *Revelation 1–5*, 288–92; Beale, *Revelation*, 323–26.

garments" (3:5). That upon the heads of the elders were golden "crowns" (4:4) suggests that they have received the "crown" of the eternal heavenly life promised to the audience who are to become faithful until death (2:10) and allow no one to take away their "crown" (3:11). That upon their heads were "golden" crowns associates the elders not only with the exalted Jesus girded with a "golden" belt (1:13), but also with the seven "golden" lampstands representative of the seven churches (1:12, 20), the "golden" lampstands in the midst of which walks the risen and exalted Jesus (2:1).[3]

And from the throne in heaven were "going out" lightnings and sounds and thunders indicative of the divine power emanating from God (4:5a). This resonates with what John saw "going out" from the mouth of the exalted Jesus—a sharp two-edged sword, symbolic of the powerful word of God (1:16). The great "sound" of the voice of the exalted Jesus that John heard as a trumpet speaking with him (1:10, 12; 4:1) the audience can now identify as one of the divinely powerful "sounds" coming out from the throne in heaven.[4]

2b) Worship of the One Sitting on the Throne in Heaven (4:5b–11)

> **A** [5b] And seven torches of fire are burning **before the throne,** which are the seven Spirits of **God,** [6a] and **before the throne** something as a glassy sea like crystal,
>
> > **B** [6b] and in the midst of the throne and **around** the throne **four living creatures full of eyes** in front and in back,
> >
> > > **C** [7a] and the first living creature is **like** a lion and the second living creature is **like** an ox

---

3. On the background of the golden crowns, see Stevenson, "Golden Crown Imagery," 257–72. "The number twenty-four may be suggested by the twenty-four classes of priests in 1 Chr 24:1–19; significantly, the elders of Revelation have a cultic role (4:9–10; 5:8–11; 11:16–18; 19:4). And they are kings, seated on thrones and wearing crowns. They fittingly represent the people of God, that 'royal house of priests' (1:6)" (Harrington, *Revelation*, 79).

4. On the significant role of 4:5–6a within Revelation, see Giblin, "From and before the Throne," 500–513.

> > **D** ⁷ᵇ and the third living creature has the face as of a human being
>
> > **C′** ⁷ᶜ and the fourth living creature is **like** an eagle flying,
>
> > **B′** ⁸ᵃ and the **four living creatures**, each one of them having six wings apiece, **around** and within are **filled with eyes** (Ezek 1:5–21),
>
> **A′ a)** ⁸ᵇ and they do not have rest day and night *saying*, "Holy, holy, holy is the **Lord God**, the Almighty, who was and who is and who is coming."
>
> > **b)** ⁹ And whenever the living creatures will give glory and honor and thanksgiving to *the one sitting on the throne, the one living for the ages of the ages*,
>
> > **b′)** ¹⁰ᵃ the twenty-four elders will fall **before** *the one sitting on the throne* and they will worship *the one living for the ages of the ages*
>
> **a′)** ¹⁰ᵇ and they will throw their crowns **before the throne saying**, ¹¹ "Worthy are you, our **Lord** and **God**, to receive the glory and the honor and the power, for you yourself have created all things and on account of your will they existed and were created."

"And seven torches of fire are burning before the throne, which are the seven Spirits of God" (4:5b). That the seven Spirits are seven torches of "fire" closely associates them with the exalted Jesus, who has eyes as a flame of "fire" (1:14; 2:18), and who advised the church in Laodicea to buy from him gold refined from "fire" (3:18). "The seven Spirits that are before his throne" (1:4), the "seven Spirits of God" the exalted Jesus has (3:1), are thus more specifically identified for the audience. They are "the seven Spirits of God" that are seven torches of fire burning "before the throne" of God in heaven.

In contrast to the often chaotic, dark, and rough seas on earth, before the throne of God in heaven is "something as a glassy sea like crystal" (4:6a).⁵ And in the midst of the throne and around the throne

---

5. "Here the crystal-clear sea of glass symbolizes God's transcendent holiness and his awesome sovereignty that is a source of worship (4:6) and then becomes

of God in heaven are "four living creatures full of eyes in front and in back" (4:6b). In contrast to those in the church of Laodicea whose "eyes" need to be anointed so that they may properly observe (3:18), these four living creatures are full of "eyes," having them in front as well as in back, underlining their capacity to observe. This associates them with the exalted Jesus, who has penetrating "eyes" as a flame of fire (2:18; cf. 1:14).

The first living creature is like a lion, and thus represents a heavenly counterpart to all of the wild animals living on earth. The second living creature is like an ox, and thus represents a heavenly counterpart to all of the domestic animals living on earth. The third living creature has the face as of a human being, and thus represents a heavenly counterpart to all human beings living on earth. Whereas the first living creature is "like" a lion and the second "like" an ox (4:7a), the third has the face as of a "human being" (4:7b) in contrast to the exalted Jesus who is "like a Son of Man" (1:13). The fourth living creature is "like" an eagle flying (4:7c), and thus represents a heavenly counterpart to all of the animals living on earth who do not walk on it—those who fly in the sky or swim in the sea. In sum, the four living creatures together represent a heavenly counterpart to all creatures living on earth.

Not only are the "four living creatures" who are around the throne of God in heaven "full of eyes" in front and in back (4:6b), but the "four living creatures," each one of them having six wings apiece (cf. Isa 6:2), around and within are "filled with eyes" (4:8a; cf. Ezek 1:5–21). This further accentuates for the audience the comprehensive powers of observation and vigilance on the part of the four living creatures in heaven.

And the four living creatures do not have rest day and night as they take part in heavenly worship saying, "Holy, holy, holy is the Lord God, the Almighty, who was and who is and who is coming" (4:8b; cf. Isa 6:3). That they worship God as "holy, holy, holy" reaffirms the worthiness of the exalted Jesus, who identified himself as "the holy one" (3:7), as also an object of worship. Their heavenly worship of "the Lord God, the Almighty, who was and who is and who is coming" serves as a model inviting the audience to join them. The audience may thereby respond with their own act of worship to the epistolary/liturgical greeting of

---

the basis of judgment (15:2) when God will eradicate evil from his creation (21:1)" (Osborne, *Revelation*, 232).

grace and peace from "the one who is and who was and who is coming" (1:4). The audience are thus being led to worship the "Lord God" who says, "I am the Alpha and the Omega," "the one who is and who was and who is coming, the Almighty" (1:8).[6]

"And whenever the living creatures will give glory and honor and thanksgiving to the one sitting upon the throne, the one living for the ages of the ages" (4:9), "the twenty-four elders will fall before the one sitting upon the throne" (4:10a). This is the one "upon the throne sitting" (4:2), "who was in vision like a stone, jasper and carnelian" (4:3). "And they will worship the one living for the ages of the ages" (4:10a).

The worship of the living creatures who will give "glory" to, and of the twenty-four elders who will worship, "the one living for the ages of the ages" (4:9, 10a) resonates with worship of the exalted Jesus. The audience were led to join in a communal worship of Jesus Christ as the one to whom be "glory and might for the ages of the ages" (1:6). That the twenty-four elders "will fall," as a gesture of worship, before the Lord God sitting upon the throne (4:10a) recalls John's report that "I fell," as a gesture of worship, toward the feet of the exalted Jesus (1:17) who declared, "I am living for the ages of the ages" (1:18). That both the Lord God and Jesus are identified as living forever indicates their dynamic oneness as objects of true worship. And that the elders "will worship" the One living forever (4:10a) anticipates the fulfillment of the promise of Jesus that those of the synagogue of Satan "will worship" the God who lives forever (3:9).[7]

Seven torches of fire, which are the seven Spirits of God, are burning "before the throne" (4:5b) and "before the throne" is something as a glassy sea like crystal (4:6a). In addition, "before the throne" of God in heaven, the twenty-four elders will throw their "crowns," the golden "crowns" upon their heads (4:4b), as a gesture of worshipful homage (4:10b). Their gesture is accompanied by the words of their worship:

---

6. "It is as if the whole of creation (whether knowingly or not) is caught up in the worship and praise of God, through their heavenly representatives around the divine throne" (Boxall, *Revelation*, 87).

7. "With John, we enter heaven to see and hear what we now understand to be a ceaseless round of immediate, liturgical adoration; and this embraces the worship of the saints on earth" (Smalley, *Revelation*, 123).

PART TWO—*Shown What Must Happen after These Things (4:1—16:21)*

"Worthy are you, our Lord and God, to receive the glory and the honor and the power, for you have created all things and on account of your will they existed and were created" (4:11).

The four living creatures worship by declaring, "Holy, holy, holy is the Lord God" (4:8b), when they give "glory" and "honor" and thanksgiving (4:9a). The twenty-four elders complement and extend this worship with a direct address, "Worthy are you, our Lord and God, to receive the glory and the honor and the power" (4:11a). In correspondence to those in Sardis who are "worthy" to participate in heavenly worship, as those who will walk with the exalted Jesus in white (3:4), the elders acknowledge our Lord and God as "worthy" of worship. In contrast to the church in Philadelphia which has little "power" (3:8), our Lord and God is worshiped as worthy to receive the "power," which further associates the Lord God with the exalted Jesus whose face appeared as the sun in its "power" (1:16). And that "you yourself have created" all things that were "created" (4:11b) closely unites the Lord God to the exalted Jesus as "the beginning of the creation of God" (3:14).[8]

3c) Vision of the Scroll and the Mighty Angel (5:1–5)

    A   a) [5:1a] ***Then I saw*** upon the right of the one sitting upon the throne a scroll

            b) [1b] ***written*** within and in back,

            b′) [1c] ***sealed*** with **seven seals**.

       a′) [2a] ***Then I saw*** a mighty angel proclaiming in a great sound,

    B   a) [2b] "Who is ***worthy*** to open the scroll and release its seals?"

            b) [3a] But no one was able in heaven or upon ***the earth***

---

8. For a discussion of the title "our Lord and God" as indicative of the date of Revelation, see Parker, "Our Lord and God," 207–31. On worship in 4:1–11, see MacLeod, "Adoration of God," 198–218. For a discussion of the relationship between the praise utterances in 4:8, 11 and first-century acclamations, see Seal, "Shouting in the Apocalypse," 339–52.

John's Visions of Lamb Opening the Seals and Worship

> **b')** ³ᵇ or under ***the earth*** to open the scroll or to observe it.
>
> **a')** ⁴ And I was **weeping** much, for no one ***worthy*** was found to open the scroll or to observe it.
>
> **B'** ⁵ᵃ Then one from the elders says to me, "Do not **weep**,
>
> **A'** ⁵ᵇ behold the lion, the one from the tribe of Judah, the root of David, has conquered to open the scroll and its **seven seals**."

John saw a scroll (5:1a) on the right—the position of divine authority—of "the one sitting upon the throne," as the object of heavenly worship from both the four living creatures and the twenty-four elders (4:2–3, 9–10).[9] That the scroll is upon the "right" relates it to the divinely authoritative activity of the exalted Jesus. In his "right" hand he holds the seven stars (1:16; 2:1), the seven stars John saw upon his "right" hand, which are the angels of the seven churches (1:20). And he placed his "right" hand upon John (1:17) when he identified himself as the one once dead but now living eternally (1:18). The "scroll" that John now sees will thus become part of the content of the "scroll" in which the exalted Jesus directed him to write what he observes and send it to the seven churches (1:11), the "scroll" which comprises the book of Revelation.

The scroll was "written" by God (divine passive) within and in back (5:1b) like the new name "written" upon the white stone and promised to the one who conquers (2:17). The contents of the scroll are thus included among the things "written" in the prophecy of the book of Revelation, which the audience are to hear and keep (1:3). Whereas the four living creatures are totally filled with eyes—in front and "in back" (4:6) and around and "within" (4:8)—the scroll is filled with writing "within and in back." Not only is the scroll "written" in a thoroughly complete manner—within and in back—but, as an alliterative chiastic parallel, it is "sealed" in a thoroughly complete manner: with seven seals (5:1c).

The report that "then I saw" a comprehensively written and sealed scroll (5:1) continues with the report that "then I saw a mighty angel

---

9. Stefanovic, "Meaning," 42–54.

PART TWO—*Shown What Must Happen after These Things (4:1—16:21)*

proclaiming with a great sound" (5:2a). That the mighty "angel" is proclaiming, and thus revealing something, reminds the audience that it was through an "angel" that the revelation of Jesus Christ that God gave him was sent (1:1). John heard behind him a "great sound" as a trumpet (1:10) before his vision of the exalted Jesus. That he now sees a mighty angel proclaiming in a "great sound" suggests a further revelation regarding the exalted Jesus.

Proclaiming with a great sound, the mighty angel (5:2a) asks, "Who is worthy to open the scroll and release its seals" (5:2b)? The question of who is "worthy" suggests that a divinely granted qualification is needed, as it recalls that God himself is "worthy" to receive the worship of the elders (4:11). And there are a few in Sardis who have been deemed "worthy" to walk with the exalted Jesus in the white garments that qualify them to share in his eternal life and participate in heavenly worship (3:4). The audience already have a good idea regarding who might be worthy to "open" the scroll. They have heard that the exalted Jesus has a unique and absolute power as the one who "opens and no one will close and closes and no one opens" (3:7). The Jesus who "released us from our sins by his blood" (1:5) would thus seem to be uniquely worthy to "release" the scroll's seals.

John's report that apparently "no one was able" in heaven or upon the earth or under the earth to "open" the scroll or to observe it (5:3) reaffirms for the audience that it is only the exalted Jesus who has this power. The door "opened" by him "no one is able" to close (3:8), and "no one opens" what only he "opens" (3:7). That the "scroll," which is "written" within and in back (5:1), is something to "observe" accentuates its relevance for the fulfillment of the command the exalted Jesus issued to John: "What you observe write in a scroll and send it to the seven churches" (1:11).

John was weeping much, for initially no one worthy was found to open the scroll or to observe it (5:4). But then one from the elders told him, "Do not weep, behold the lion, the one from the tribe of Judah, the root of David, has conquered to open the scroll and its seven seals" (5:5). Whereas the first living creature is like a "lion" (4:7), John is told about *the* "lion," the one "from the tribe of Judah." He thus fulfills the scriptural prophecy for the arrival of a metaphorical "lion," one who "lies down

78

to sleep as a lion" (LXX Gen 49:9), "a ruler from Judah" (49:10), with the implication that he has the power to conquer. That he is the "root of David," and thus the one who "arises to rule over nations" as "the root of Jesse" (LXX Isa 11:10; cf. 11:1)," the father of David, identifies him as the exalted Jesus, "the one having the key of David" with the absolute divine power to open and close (3:7). Everyone in the audience can be one who "conquers" (2:7, 11, 17, 26; 3:5, 12, 21), because he "conquered" to open the scroll and its seven seals.

4d) Vision of and New Song to the Lamb (5:6–10)

> **A a)** ⁶ᵃ Then I saw in the midst of the **throne** and of the four living creatures and in the midst of the elders a Lamb standing, as one having been **slaughtered**,
>
>> **b)** ⁶ᵇ having ***seven*** horns
>>
>> **b′)** ⁶ᶜ and ***seven*** eyes, which are the ***seven*** Spirits of God sent into **all** the **earth**.
>
> **a′)** ⁷ Then he came and received from the right of the one sitting upon the ***throne***.
>
>> **B** ⁸ᵃ And when he **received the scroll**, the four living creatures and the twenty-four elders fell before the Lamb having, each one, a harp and golden bowls filled with incense,
>>
>>> **C** ⁸ᵇ which are the prayers of the holy ones,
>>
>> **B′** ⁹ᵃ and they are singing a new song saying, "Worthy are you to **receive the scroll** and open its seals,
>
> **A′** ⁹ᵇ for you were **slaughtered** and bought for God with your blood those from **every** tribe and tongue and people and nation ¹⁰ and you made them for our God a kingdom and priests, and they will reign upon the **earth**."

John has already reported that around the throne of God in heaven were twenty-four thrones upon which were the twenty-four elders (4:4). And "in the midst of the throne" and around the throne were the four living creatures (4:6), who were joined by the elders in an act of heavenly worship (4:8–11). And now, as John's heavenly vision continues, he reports that he saw "in the midst of the throne and of the four living creatures and in the midst of the elders a Lamb standing, as one having been slaughtered, having seven horns and seven eyes, which are the seven Spirits of God sent into all the earth" (5:6).[10]

The audience are to realize that Jesus became "the lion" who conquered to open the scroll and its seven seals (5:5) by first becoming the Lamb slaughtered, with its connotations of sacrificial worship, but now standing as the risen and exalted Jesus (5:6a).[11] The Jesus who declared that "behold I stand at the door" as the risen and exalted one ready to dine with anyone who opens for him (3:20) is the Lamb now "standing" as one risen to eternal life after having been slaughtered. The Jesus who identified himself as "the one who is living, once I was dead but behold I am living for the ages of the ages and I have the keys of Death and of Hades" (1:18) is the Lamb "having seven horns" (5:6b) symbolic of the full and complete power needed to open the scroll's "seven seals" (5:5).

Whereas the four living creatures are filled with "eyes" (4:6, 8), the Lamb has the complete number of "seven eyes, which are the seven Spirits of God sent into all the earth" (5:6c; cf. Zech 4:10). The "seven Spirits of God" signify the fullness of the divine Spirit, which is the Spirit of prophecy. It is the Spirit through which John received the prophecy (1:10; 4:2) he communicates in Revelation (1:3), and the Spirit that speaks prophetically to each of the churches (2:7, 11, 17, 29; 3:6, 13, 22). The seven torches of fire burning before the throne in heaven (4:5; cf.

---

10. For suggestions regarding the background of the divine throne here, see Hannah, "Rev 5:6 in Context," 528–42.

11. The depiction of the "Lamb" as one having been "slaughtered" alludes to the description of the violent yet sacrificial death foreseen for the prophet Jeremiah, who declared, "I was as an innocent lamb led to be sacrificed" (LXX Jer 11:19), and to the suffering servant in Isaiah described as a "sheep led to the slaughter" (LXX Isa 53:7). It also resonates with the ritual slaughtering of the Passover male lamb/goat ("they will slaughter it"), as the sacrifice that saved the people of Israel from death during the Exodus event (LXX Exod 12:6). On Jesus as the "Lion-Lamb" who is simultaneously conqueror and savior, see Charles, "Imperial Pretensions," 85–97. On the shift from the lion to the lamb imagery in 5:5–6, see Strawn, "Why Does the Lion Disappear," 37–74. On Jesus as the Lion/Lamb who conquers through sacrifice or the purpose of witness, providing a role-model for his followers, see Skaggs and Doyle, "Lion/Lamb," 362–75.

1:4) are thus vigilantly and observantly active on earth as the seven eyes of the Lamb, the "seven Spirits of God sent into all the earth." That the seven eyes of the Lamb, who is the risen and exalted Jesus, are the seven Spirits of God "sent" by God (divine passive) into all the earth further develops for the audience the earthly relevance of the revelation of Jesus Christ that God "sent" through his angel to his servant John (1:1).

The exalted Jesus, who referred to the authority over the nations (2:26) that "I myself received from my Father" (2:28), now, as the Lamb, came and "received from the right of the one sitting upon the throne" (5:7). That is, he received from the authoritative right side of God the scroll that John saw "on the right of the one sitting upon the throne" (5:1).[12]

When the Lamb received the scroll, the twenty-four elders, who "will fall" in worship "before" the one sitting upon the throne (4:10), "fell," along with the four living creatures, "before" the Lamb (5:8a). Each one of them had a harp, an instrument for worship. And in correspondence to the seven "golden" lampstands, which represent the heavenly counterpart to the seven churches (1:20; cf. 1:12; 2:1), each also had "golden" cultic bowls filled with incense, which are the prayers of the holy ones (5:8; cf. Ps 141:2), the members of the churches representative of the audience of believers. They were made "holy ones," those set apart and consecrated to God especially for worship of the God who is "holy, holy, holy" (4:8), by Jesus, the "holy one" (3:7), who made "us" believers into "a kingdom, priests for his God and Father" (1:6). The prayers of the "holy ones," of the audience who have been consecrated to worship as "priests" on earth, are thus part of the worship performed by the living creatures and elders in heaven.

In correspondence to the "new" name or status of Jesus as the one exalted to a new, eternal life in heaven (3:12; cf. 2:17), as well as to the "new" heavenly Jerusalem (3:12), the living creatures and the elders are singing a "new" song in their heavenly worship (5:9a). In answer to the question of who is "worthy to open the scroll and release its seals" (5:2), they sing to the Lamb, "[W]orthy are you to receive the scroll and open its seals" (5:9a). The elders worshiped God by declaring, "Worthy are you, our Lord and God, to receive the glory and the honor and the

---

12. For an exposition of 5:1–7, see MacLeod, "The Lion Who Is a Lamb," 323–40.

PART TWO—*Shown What Must Happen after These Things (4:1—16:21)*

power" (4:11). And now, similarly, the living creatures and the elders worship the Lamb by declaring, "Worthy are you to receive the scroll and open its seals." This reinforces for the audience the dynamic oneness of God and the exalted Jesus, the Lamb, as objects of worship.

Continuing their worship of the Lamb, the living creatures and elders acknowledge that the sacrificial death of Jesus as the "slaughtered" Lamb (5:6) effected salvific redemption. They declare to the Lamb that "you were slaughtered and bought for God with your blood those from every tribe and tongue and people and nation" (5:9b). As the slaughtered, sacrificial Lamb, "you bought" and thus redeemed for the salvation of eternal, heavenly life with God those from all peoples. The exalted Jesus thus advises believers to "buy" from him "gold refined from fire," a metaphor suggestive of heavenly existence, and the metaphorical "white garments" needed to participate in the eternal life and liturgy of heaven (3:18).

The audience were previously invited to participate in an act of communal worship of Jesus as the one who effected with his sacrificial blood salvation of us believers for eternal life, the one who "has released us from our sins by his blood" (1:5). And now they are invited to join in the heavenly worship of Jesus as the slaughtered Lamb who effected with his sacrificial blood a salvation for eternal life that embraces those from all peoples. He is the one who "bought for God with your blood those from every tribe and tongue and people and nation" (5:9b).[13]

As they listen to this heavenly worship in their liturgical assembly, the audience become participants in it. They realize that the Jesus who has "made" *us* believers into a "kingdom, priests for *his* God and Father" (1:6), is also the Lamb who, through his sacrificial death, itself an act of priestly worship, did this for those who come from all peoples (5:9b). In their worship they declare to the Lamb that "you made" *them*—those from all peoples—for "*our* God a kingdom and priests." And those from "every" tribe and tongue and people and nation (5:9b)—ultimately will reign, in and through their worship as "priests," upon the "earth" (5:10), "all" the "earth" into which the seven Spirits of God were sent as the seven eyes of the Lamb in heaven (5:6). In this act of heav-

---

13. There was also a salvific role of the "blood" of the Passover lamb for the Exodus event (Exod 12:7).

enly worship the audience share in the hope that those from all peoples will ultimately become believers who perform authentic worship—the worship for eternal life in the Spirit of prophecy—upon earth.[14]

5e) Vision of Universal Worship of the Lamb and One Sitting on the Throne (5:11–14)

> A [11] Then I saw, and **I heard** the sound of many angels around **the throne** and the **living creatures** and **the elders**, and the number of them was ten thousands of ten thousands and thousands of thousands, [12] **saying** with a great sound, "Worthy is **the Lamb**, the one who has been slaughtered, to receive the power and wealth and wisdom and strength and **honor** and **glory** and **blessing**."
>
> B [13a] Then **every** creature in heaven
>
>> C [13b] and **upon the earth**
>>
>> C' [13c] and under **the earth** and **upon** the sea
>
> B' [13d] and **all** the things in them
>
> A' [13e] **I heard saying**, "To the one sitting upon **the throne** and to **the Lamb**, the **blessing** and the **honor** and the **glory** and the might for the ages of the ages." [14] And the four **living creatures** were saying, "Amen!" And **the elders** fell down and worshiped.

John previously reported that "I heard" the "sound" who invited him to ascend to heaven for the vision (4:1), the same great "sound" from the exalted Jesus that "I heard" on Patmos (1:10). Now, as the vision continues, he reports, "I heard a sound of many angels around the throne and the living creatures and the elders, and the number of them was ten thousands of ten thousands and thousands of thousands" (5:11).

---

14. "Already God's people share in the Kingdom, and share with the angels in priestly ministry, able to offer true worship to God, and to mediate on behalf of the world. This would be particularly powerful when Revelation's canticles were heard—and perhaps repeated by the congregation—in a liturgical setting: in the liturgy, the gulf between present reality and future hope is temporarily bridged" (Boxall, *Revelation*, 101).

PART TWO—*Shown What Must Happen after These Things (4:1—16:21)*

Now not only are the four living creatures "around the throne" (4:6), but "around the throne" in heaven are the living creatures, the elders, and an extremely large number of angels.

Previously John saw a mighty angel proclaiming in a "great sound," "Who is worthy to open the scroll and release its seals" (5:2)? The huge crowd of many angels (5:11) answer in an act of worship with a "great sound": "Worthy is the Lamb, the one who has been slaughtered, to receive the power and wealth and wisdom and strength and honor and glory and blessing" (5:12; cf. 1 Chr 29:11). This reinforces the new song of worship being sung by the living creatures and elders, who declared to the Lamb, "Worthy are you to receive the scroll and open its seals, for you were slaughtered" (5:9). And they worship the Lamb in a manner similar to their worship of God himself: "Worthy are you, our Lord and God, to receive the glory and the honor and the power" (4:11a).

The living creatures and elders completed their worship of God by declaring that "you yourself have created all things and on account of your will they existed and were created" (4:11b). In an appropriate response now "every creature" in heaven (5:13a) and upon the earth (5:13b) and under the earth (5:13c) and upon the sea and "all the things" in them (5:13d) worship both God, the creator, and the Lamb, "the beginning of the creation of God" (3:14). John heard them declaring, "To the one sitting upon the throne and to the Lamb, the blessing and the honor and the glory and the might for the ages of the ages" (5:13e).

No one was able "in heaven or upon the earth or under the earth" to open the scroll or to observe it (5:3). But now every creature "in heaven and upon the earth and under the earth" and upon the sea and all the things in them participate in this universal worship of both God and the Lamb (5:13), the one worthy to open the scroll (5:9). Our Lord and God was worshiped in heaven as worthy to receive "glory" and "honor" (4:11). And similarly but separately the Lamb was worshiped in heaven as worthy to receive "honor" and "glory" (5:12). But now all of creation worships God and the Lamb together, acknowledging for both of them "the blessing and the honor and the glory and the might for the ages of the ages" (5:13).

In declaring to both God and to Jesus as the Lamb "the glory and the might for the ages of the ages" (5:13), the worship of all of creation resonates with and complements the audience's worship of Jesus as the one to whom "be the glory and the might for the ages of the ages" (1:6). In proclaiming the liturgical affirmation of "Amen!" the worship of the four living creatures (5:14) resonates with and complements the audience's own "Amen!" in their worship of Jesus (1:6, 7). And the elders, the twenty-four elders who "will fall" before the one sitting upon the throne and "will worship" the one living for the ages of the ages (4:10), "fell" down and "worshiped" (5:14) both the one sitting upon the throne and the Lamb (5:13).

The audience are to appreciate that both the Jesus who said "I am living for the ages of the ages" (1:18) and the God "living for the ages of the ages" (4:9, 10) are worthy of their worship. These scenes of the heavenly worship of both God and the Lamb in Revelation 4–5 are thus part of the prophecy John experienced in the Spirit of prophecy (1:10; 4:2), the prophecy the audience of Revelation are to keep (1:3). In hearing these scenes of heavenly worship in their liturgical assembly the audience are made participants of the worship for eternal life—a share in the life of the ever-living creator and his ever-living "beginning of creation" (3:14).[15]

6e′) First Four Seals: The Four Horsemen (6:1–8)

A a) [6:1a] *Then I saw*

      b) [1b] when the Lamb opened **one of the** seven seals,

         c) [1c] and I heard

      b′) [1d] **one of the** four living creatures saying **as a sound** of thunder, "Come!"

    a′) [2] *Then I saw*, and **behold** a white horse, and the one sitting upon it has a bow and a crown **was given** to him and he came out conquering even so that he might conquer.

---

15. Stuckenbruck, "Revelation 4–5," 235–48; MacLeod, "Adoration of God the Redeemer," 454–71; Charles, "Apocalyptic Tribute to the Lamb," 461–73.

PART TWO—*Shown What Must Happen after These Things (4:1—16:21)*

> **B** ³ And when he opened the seal, the second one, **I heard the second living creature saying**, "Come!" ⁴ᵃ Then another horse, fiery red, came out,
>
>> **C** ⁴ᵇ and to the one sitting upon it, it **was given to him**
>>
>>> **D** ⁴ᶜ to take the peace from the earth even so that each other they will slaughter
>>
>> **C′** ⁴ᵈ and a great dagger **was given to him**.
>
> **B′** ⁵ᵃ And when he opened the seal, the third one, **I heard the third living creature saying**, "Come!"
>
> **A′** a) ⁵ᵇ *Then I saw*, and *behold* a black *horse*, and *the one sitting upon it* has a scale in his hand,
>
>> b) ⁶ᵃ and I heard something **as** a *sound* in the midst of the four living creatures saying,
>>
>>> c) ⁶ᵇ "A *quart* of wheat for a *denarius*
>>>
>>> c′) ⁶ᶜ and three *quarts* of barley for a *denarius*, and the olive oil and the wine do not harm."
>>
>> b′) ⁷ And when he opened the seal, the fourth one, I heard a *sound* of the fourth living creature saying, "Come!"
>
> a′) ⁸ *Then I saw*, and *behold* a pale green *horse*, as for *the one sitting over it*, a name for him is Death, and Hades was following with him and authority **was given** to them over the fourth of the earth to kill with sword and with famine and with death and by the beasts of the earth.

After the worship of the "Lamb" (5:8) as the one worthy to receive the scroll and "open" its "seals" (5:9), John saw (6:1a) when the "Lamb opened" one of the seven "seals" (6:1b). John had reported that "I heard" all of creation worshiping God and the Lamb (5:13), including the "four living creatures" who were worshiping by "saying," "Amen!" (5:14). And now he reports that "I heard" (6:1c) one of the "four living creatures saying" as a sound of thunder, "Come!" (6:1d). That their command was as a "sound of thunder" associates it with the divine power coming out of the heavenly throne in the form of "lightnings and sounds and thunders" (4:5a). The audience realize that the four living creatures, the heavenly counterparts to all of creation, not only worship God and the Lamb with an affirmative "Amen!," but upon the Lamb's opening of the first seal issue the powerfully authoritative "Come!"

Both God (1:4, 8; 4:8) and Jesus (1:7; 2:5, 16; 3:11; 5:7) have often been the subject of the verb "come." But after one of the four living creatures issued the divinely authoritative command to "Come!" (6:1), John again saw, "and behold a white horse, and the one sitting upon it has a bow and a crown was given to him and he came out conquering even so that he might conquer" (6:2). The audience initially associates the one sitting on this "white" horse with the exalted Jesus, whose head and hair were "white" as "white" wool (1:14), a heavenly color. Jesus promised to give the one who conquers a "white" stone associated with heaven (2:17). Those who do not defile their garments will walk with the exalted Jesus in "white" (3:4), clothed in "white" garments (3:5), as he is the one who issues the "white" garments appropriate for heavenly worship (3:18). Indeed, the twenty-four elders who worshiped in heaven were clothed in "white" garments (4:4).

Since the act of "sitting upon" was heard previously only of God (4:2, 9, 10; 5:1, 7, 13) or the elders (4:4) as those "sitting upon" thrones in heaven, that one is "sitting upon" a white horse (6:2) would seem to give him a further association with heaven. But in contrast to the exalted Jesus as the heavenly Lamb "having" seven horns and seven eyes, which are the seven Spirits of God sent into all the earth (5:6), the one sitting upon the white horse is "having" a "bow" (6:2), a weapon for violent destruction on earth. A "crown" was given to him (6:2) by God (divine passive) as part of the mysterious divine plan symbolized by the sealed scroll, but an earthly crown symbolic of military victory, not the heavenly "crown" of eternal life (2:10; 3:11) or one of the golden "crowns" of those in heaven (4:4, 10).[16]

And in contrast to the one "conquering" who will never "come out" of the heavenly temple (3:12), the one sitting upon the white horse "came out" as one "conquering." But he came out not as one "conquer-

---

16. "The description of the rider closely resembles the Parthians, the only military force in the ancient world feared by the Romans since they had defeated a Roman army twice, in 55 BC and AD 62" (Osborne, *Revelation*, 277).

PART TWO—*Shown What Must Happen after These Things (4:1—16:21)*

ing" so as to participate in the eternal life of heaven (2:7, 11, 17, 26; 3:5, 12, 21), but even so that he might continue to "conquer" destructively on earth (6:2). The audience are to conclude that although the one sitting upon the white horse appears to have characteristics that could closely identify him with the heavenly exalted Jesus, this is quite deceptive. Whereas the one sitting upon the white horse came out "conquering even so that he might conquer" violently and destructively on earth, Jesus was exalted to heaven as the "lion" from the tribe of Judah. He "conquered" (5:5) ironically and paradoxically by becoming a victim of violent destruction—the Lamb slaughtered on earth (5:6).[17]

When the Lamb opened the seal, the one pointedly designated as the second, John heard the second living creature issuing the same divinely authoritative command as the first—"Come!" (6:3; cf. 6:1). The one sitting upon the white horse "came out conquering even so that he might conquer" (6:2) This time another horse, fiery red, "came out and to the one sitting upon it, it was given to him to take the peace from the earth even so that each other they will slaughter and a great dagger was given to him" (6:4).

An earthly crown "was given" by God (divine passive) to the one sitting upon the white horse to go along with the bow that he has as a weapon of destruction (6:2). Similarly, a great dagger, another weapon of destruction, "was given" to the one sitting upon the fiery red horse, and it "was given" to him to "take" the "peace," which is a divine gift (1:4), from the "earth" (6:4). The one on the fiery red horse thus stands in stark contrast to the Lamb who is worthy to "receive" the scroll and open its seals (5:9), and to both the Lamb and God as those worthy to "receive" worship (4:11; 5:12) from every creature on and under the "earth" (5:13). The "slaughtered" Lamb (5:6, 12) was a victim of those who "will slaughter" each other on earth (6:4). But the Lamb is worthy to be worshiped for "you were slaughtered," and those he redeemed from all peoples (5:9) he made "for our God a kingdom and priests, and they will reign on the earth" (5:10), and thus restore its peace.

When the Lamb opened the seal, the one pointedly designated as the third, John heard the third living creature issuing the same divinely authoritative command as the first and second—"Come!" (6:5a; cf. 6:1, 3).

17. Boxall, "White Horse," 76–88; de Villiers, "Role of Composition," 125–53.

John then saw, "and behold a black horse, and the one sitting upon it has a scale in his hand" (6:5b). This closely parallels and follows as a consequence of what John saw when the first seal was opened—"and behold a white horse, and the one sitting upon it has a bow and a crown was given to him and he came out conquering even so that he might conquer" (6:2). Whereas the rider on the white horse "has a bow," a weapon used in conquering people, and the rider on the fiery red horse takes the peace from the earth as people slaughter each other (6:4), the rider on the black horse "has a scale" in his hand. The exalted Jesus "has in his right hand" seven stars (1:16), indicating his authority over the angels of the seven churches (1:20). The rider on the black horse similarly "has a scale in his hand," indicating his authority to regulate economic matters.

That John heard something "as a sound" (6:6a) points to an authoritative sound from heaven, as it resonates with the command of the first living creature "as a sound of thunder" (6:1). And that John heard something as a sound "in the midst" of the four living creatures (6:6a) suggests the authoritative sound of the heavenly Lamb, as it recalls that John saw "in the midst" of the heavenly throne and of the four living creatures and "in the midst" of the elders a Lamb standing, as one having been slaughtered (5:6). The Lamb directs the rider with the scale to regulate the high cost of food staples necessary to preserve life in the famine that accompanies the destruction indicated at the opening of the first two seals. A denarius, an entire day's wage, buys only a quart of wheat (6:6b) and only three quarts of barley (6:6c).[18] He is told that "you do not harm" the olive oil and the wine, as a life-preserving measure, just as the one who conquers is "never to be harmed" by the second death (2:11).

When the Lamb opened the seal, the one pointedly designated as the fourth, John heard the fourth living creature issuing the same divinely authoritative command as the first three—"Come!" (6:7; cf. 6:1, 3, 5a). Whereas each of the first three riders who came out of an opened seal was sitting "upon" his horse (6:2, 4, 5), the rider of the fourth horse, the pale green one, was sitting "over" or "above" it, underlining how the threat of his death-bringing power extends over and above the horse

---

18. "The denarius was a Roman silver coin equivalent to the daily wage of a working man" (Mounce, *Revelation*, 144).

PART TWO—Shown What Must Happen after These Things (4:1—16:21)

itself (6:8).[19] In contrast to the previous occurrences of the term "name" associated with divine life (2:3, 13, 17; 3:1, 5, 8, 12), and to the previous three unnamed riders (6:2, 4, 5), the "name" of this rider is "Death" personified, and "Hades" as the personified realm of death was following with him (6:8). But the audience have already been assured of the exalted Jesus' superior power over death as the one who lives eternally and has the "keys of Death and of Hades" (1:18).

Each of the first two riders "was given" destructive authority on earth (6:2, 4) by God (divine passive) as part of the mysterious divine plan contained in the sealed scroll. Similarly, authority "was given" to Death and Hades, but only "over the fourth of the earth to kill with sword and with famine and with death and by the beasts of the earth" (6:8). This limited "authority" stands in noteworthy contrast to the "authority" over the nations that the exalted Jesus promises to each member of the audience who, by refusing to practice false worship, conquers (2:26) death to live eternally and to shepherd the nations toward true worship for eternal life (2:27).

The audience have already been reminded of the authority of Death and Hades to "kill with death" (6:8), as the faithful witness Antipas was "killed" among them (2:13). But the exalted Jesus promised that "I will kill with death" the "children"—those who practice the idolatrous worship, of the false prophetess Jezebel (2:23). Whereas Death and Hades have authority to kill with "sword," with physical death (6:8), the exalted Jesus promised to come and battle those who practice idolatrous worship with a different sword—"with the sword of my mouth" (2:16). This is the sharp two-edged "sword" (2:12), the "sword" coming from his mouth (1:16), symbolic of the prophetic word of God to execute judgment regarding eternal life and death.

Death and Hades have been given authority to kill by means of the beasts of the "earth," but only over the fourth of the "earth" (6:8). The slaughtered Lamb, however, is worshiped in heaven, as well as on and under the "earth" (5:13), as the one who bought for God with his blood those from every tribe and tongue and people and nation (5:9).

---

19. On the visionary nature of the distinctive colors of the four horses, see Peachey, "Horse of a Different Colour," 214–16.

He made them for our God a kingdom and priests to offer the true worship by which they will reign on the "earth" (5:10).

This scene of the Lamb's opening of the first four seals (6:1–8) has thus assured the audience that God and the Lamb—the heavenly exalted Jesus, hold the ultimate divine power over eternal life and death. Their authoritative power greatly transcends the limited power of physical death and destruction that the audience have known, presently know, and will continue to know and experience on earth, as the opening of the first four seals indicate. This dramatic scene thus reinforces the exhortation for the audience to worship for eternal life in the Spirit of the prophecy that this book of the revelation of Jesus Christ signifies for them (1:1–3).

7d′) Fifth Seal: Prayer of the Slaughtered Souls under the Altar (6:9–11)

A a) [9a] And **when** he opened the fifth seal, I saw under the altar the souls of those slaughtered

    b) [9b] **on account of** the word of God

    b′) [9c] and **on account of** the witness that they had.

  a′) [10] And they cried out with a great sound saying, "**Until when**, Master, holy and true, do you not judge and vindicate our blood from those inhabiting upon the earth?"

B [11a] And it was given **to them**, to each one,

  C [11b] a white robe

B′ [11c] and it was said **to them** that they will rest yet a little time,

A′ [11d] **until** would be fulfilled both their fellow servants and their brothers who are about to be killed even as they.

When the Lamb opened the first four seals, the ordinal adjective designating each seal followed the term "seal" (6:1, 3, 5, 7). In contrast, the ordinal adjective "fifth" precedes the term "seal" when the Lamb "opened the fifth seal" (6:9a). This break in the pattern alerts the audience to expect the scene of the opening of the fifth seal (6:9–11) to be

PART TWO—*Shown What Must Happen after These Things (4:1—16:21)*

set off from and to differ significantly from that of the opening of the first four seals (6:1–8).

When the Lamb opened the fifth seal, John reports that "I saw under the altar the souls of those slaughtered on account of the word of God and on account of the witness they had" (6:9). In contrast to those "under" the earth (5:3, 13) the slaughtered souls are "under" the altar located in heaven. The audience are to realize that these "slaughtered" souls are among the victims of those who "will slaughter" as they take the peace from the earth, as indicated in the opening of the second seal (6:4). But the association of the "slaughtered" souls with the "slaughtered" Lamb (5:6, 12) reminds the audience why the Lamb is worshiped in heaven as worthy to receive the scroll and open its seals: "for you were slaughtered" (5:9). The slaughtered souls under the altar in heaven are thus among those whom the slaughtered Lamb "bought for God with your blood from every tribe and tongue and people and nation and you made them for our God a kingdom and priests, and they will reign on the earth" (5:9–10).

The souls under the altar were slaughtered "on account of the word of God and on account of the witness they had" (6:9). The audience recall that this is the same reason John was on the island of Patmos, namely, "on account of the word of God and the witness of Jesus" (1:9). Indeed, the book of Revelation contains the "words of the prophecy" (1:3) God gave to his prophetic servant John, who witnessed to "the word of God and the witness of Jesus Christ" (1:2). The souls were thus slaughtered on account of the prophetic word from and about God and on account of the witness "they had"—the exemplary witness they had in Jesus as the Lamb who was slaughtered, as well as the consequent witness they possessed and provided as those slaughtered like Jesus. The audience are thus to realize that their own witness may lead to some of their members being slaughtered like Jesus and the souls or to being exiled like John.

Many angels, the living creatures, and the elders (5:11) performed an act of doxological worship, "saying with a great sound": "Worthy is the Lamb, the one who has been slaughtered, to receive the power and wealth and wisdom and strength and honor and glory and blessing" (5:12). And now the slaughtered souls perform an act of supplicatory worship, as they cried out "with a great sound saying": "Until when, Master, holy and true, do you not judge and vindicate our blood from those inhabiting upon the earth?" (6:10). The time "when" the Lamb opened the fifth seal (6:9a) provokes the souls to pray for the time "when" at last the Lamb will vindicate them. Their prayer is addressed to Jesus the Lamb as "the Master, holy and true," resonating with the self-identification of the exalted Jesus as "the holy one, the true one" (3:7).

The souls' act of supplicatory worship in praying for the time when the Lamb will judge and vindicate their "blood" (6:10) indicates that their position under the altar as slaughtered souls who have shed their blood for God is itself an act of sacrificial worship.[20] Their sacrificial blood further associates them with the slaughtered Lamb whom the living creatures and elders worship as the one who "bought" or "redeemed" people for God with his sacrificial "blood" (5:9). It aligns them with the Jesus whom the audience worshiped as the one who has released us from our sins by his sacrificial "blood" (1:5). The slaughtered souls pray for the time when the divine Lamb will judge and vindicate their blood from their enemies, from "those inhabiting upon the earth" (6:10). They thus associate themselves with those who have kept the word of Jesus' endurance in distinction from "those inhabiting upon the earth," those who will be tested in the testing that is about to come upon the whole world (3:10).

Authority "was given to them"—to personified Death and Hades—by God (divine passive) "over the fourth of the earth to kill with sword and with famine and with death and by the beasts of the earth" (6:8). In contrast, and as a preliminary answer to their prayer for vindication, it "was given to them"—to the slaughtered souls in heaven—"to each one, a white robe" (6:11ab). A white robe was "given" to them, to "each one," for their role in heavenly worship, just as "each one" of the living creatures and elders has a harp for their role in heavenly worship (5:8). As part of their divine judgment and vindication, the giving of a white robe to each one of the souls reinforces the exalted Jesus' promise to the churches that "I will give to you, to each one, according to your works" (2:23). The "white robe" thus resonates with the "white garments" in

---

20. "The mention of the 'altar' here in association with those slain evokes the sacrificial nature of their suffering" (Beale, *Revelation*, 391).

PART TWO—Shown What Must Happen after These Things (4:1—16:21)

which those who conquer will be clothed to participate in heavenly worship (3:4–5, 18) and in which the worshiping elders in heaven are clothed (4:4).[21]

Paralleling what was divinely "given to them" (6:11a) is what was divinely "said to them"—to the slaughtered souls in answer to their prayer of supplication (6:11c). They are told that they will rest in heaven yet a little "time" (6:11c), which suggests a correspondence to the time given for people to repent on earth, as it resonates with Jesus' declaration that he gave the false prophetess Jezebel "time" so that she may repent (2:21). In answer to their prayer of "until" (ἕως) when will their blood be judged and vindicated (6:10), the souls were told that they will rest "until [ἕως] would be fulfilled both their fellow servants and their brothers who are going to be killed even as they" (6:11d). In contrast to the works of the Sardian church not being "fulfilled" before God (3:2), there is still to be "fulfilled" by God those who are going to be killed like the slaughtered souls.[22]

That "fellow servants" and "brothers" of the slaughtered souls are yet to be killed (6:11d) warns the audience that not only John himself but other members of the churches could be killed for their prophetic witness. John identified himself as both a "brother" and "fellow sharer" with his audience in the tribulation and kingdom and endurance in Jesus (1:9). He is a "servant" along with them as his fellow prophetic "servants" (1:1), Jesus' "servants" who are being misled to engage in idolatrous worship (2:20). That some in the audience are about to be "killed" like the slaughtered souls means they will be victims of personified Death and Hades, who were given authority over the fourth of the earth "to kill" (6:8). Indeed, one member of the churches, Antipas, has already been "killed" (2:13). Yet that each of the slaughtered souls was given a heavenly white robe encourages the audience to continue to

---

21. "But the juxtaposition of the altar with the specific word John uses for robe may suggest an additional priestly role: they fulfil the priestly role of intercession on behalf of the world, their prayers being especially effective because of their proximity to God's throne" (Boxall, *Revelation*, 116).

22. "John uses the term 'fulfilled,' and at no point says that the fulfillment of the martyrs consists in their reaching a certain number" (Lupieri, *Apocalypse*, 146).

worship for eternal life in the Spirit of prophecy, even if it means some of them may be killed.[23]

8c') Sixth Seal: The Anger of God and the Lamb (6:12–17)

A   a) [12a] Then I saw when he opened the seal, the sixth one, and a ***great earthquake*** came to be

      b) [12b] and the sun ***became*** black ***as*** sackcloth made of hair

      b') [12c] and the whole moon ***became as*** blood

  a') [13] and the stars of heaven fell to the earth, as a fig tree throws its unripe figs ***shaken*** by a ***great*** wind,

B   a) [14a] and heaven was displaced as a scroll being rolled up and every ***mountain***

      b) [14b] and island were moved from ***their*** places.

          c) [15a] And the kings of the earth and the great ones and the commanders and the rich and the mighty and everyone, slave and free,

      b') [15b] hid ***themselves*** in the caves

  a') [15c] and in the ***rocks*** of the ***mountains***

B' [16] and they are saying to the ***mountains*** and to the ***rocks***, "Fall upon us [Hos 10:8] and ***hide*** us from the face of the one sitting upon the throne and from the anger of the Lamb,

A' [17] for the ***great*** day of their anger has come, and who is able to stand?"

When the Lamb opened the first four seals, the ordinal adjective designating each seal followed the term "seal" (6:1, 3, 5, 7). In contrast, the ordinal adjective "fifth" preceded the term "seal" when the Lamb opened the fifth seal (6:9a). Now the pattern of the first four seals resumes, as John saw when the Lamb opened the seal, the one pointedly designated as the sixth (6:12a). This confirms how the scene of the opening of the

---

23. Heil, "Fifth Seal," 220–43.

PART TWO—*Shown What Must Happen after These Things (4:1—16:21)*

fifth seal, with its focus on the heavenly response to the sacrificial worship and prayer of the slaughtered souls (6:9-11), is set off and highlighted for the audience as distinctive from, though interrelated to, the scenes of the opening of the first four seals (6:1-8) and of the sixth seal (6:12-17).

Upon the opening of the fifth seal (6:9) the slaughtered souls under the heavenly altar cried out their prayer of supplication to the Lamb with a "great" sound (6:10). And then a "great" earthquake came to be as a divine cosmic response, when the Lamb opened the sixth seal (6:12a). And the sun, comparable to the powerful countenance of the exalted Jesus (1:16), "became black as" sackcloth made of hair (6:12b), an appropriate cosmic response to the destructive plague associated with the "black" horse of the third seal (6:5). And the "whole" moon, resonating with the "whole" world that is about to undergo the testing (3:10), "became as" blood (6:12c), paralleling the sun becoming black as sackcloth.[24] That the whole moon became as "blood" serves as a further cosmic response to the prayer of the slaughtered souls for the divine judgment and vindication of their "blood" from those inhabiting upon the earth (6:10).

That the "stars" of heaven fell to the earth (6:13) further indicates to the audience that the divine authority of God and the Lamb stands behind this cosmic response to the prayer of the slaughtered souls (6:10). The seven "stars" that are the angels of the seven churches are in the authoritative right hand of the exalted Jesus (1:20) as part of his control over the stars of heaven. As part of their heavenly worship the living creatures and elders had golden bowls filled with incense, which are the prayers of the holy ones and thus would include the prayer of the slaughtered souls. They "fell" down as they offered these prayers in their worship of God and the Lamb (5:8, 14). As an ironic response to these prayers the stars of the heaven "fell" to the earth.

That the stars of heaven fell to the "earth" (6:13) begins to answer the souls' prayer for vindication from those inhabiting upon the "earth" (6:10). And the stars fell "to the earth" as a result of the divine authority

---

24. "Joel 2:31 stands behind the picture in 6:12b of the sun being darkened and the moon becoming like blood. And likening the darkening of the sky to 'sackcloth' was suggested by Isa. 50:3" (Beale, *Revelation*, 397).

John's Visions of Lamb Opening the Seals and Worship

of the Lamb whose seven eyes are the seven Spirits of God sent "into all the earth" (5:6). In their heavenly worship the elders "will fall" before and "throw" their crowns before the heavenly throne (4:10). In ironic contrast, the stars of heaven "fell" to the earth, as a fig tree "throws" its unripe figs "shaken" by a "great" wind (6:13) in correspondence to the "great earthquake" that came to be (6:12).

As a further divine cosmic response to the prayer of the slaughtered souls for vindication of their blood from those inhabiting upon the earth (6:10), "the heaven was displaced as a scroll being rolled up and every mountain and island were moved from their places" (6:14).[25] In ironic contrast to the sealed "scroll" being opened by the Lamb (5:1–5, 8–9), the heaven was displaced as a "scroll" being rolled up. Every mountain and "island" were moved from their places, thus eliminating them as locations of either refuge or exile, recalling that John was in refuge and/or exile on the "island" called Patmos (1:9). That every mountain and island were "moved" from "their places" confirms this as a divine response to the prayer of the slaughtered souls. It recalls the divine authority of the heavenly exalted Jesus, who warned the church in Ephesus that "I will move your lampstand from its place" (2:5).

The divinely authoritative response to the slaughtered souls' prayer for divine judgment and vindication of their blood from those inhabiting upon the "earth" (6:10) continues as "the kings of the earth and the great ones and the commanders and the rich and the mighty and everyone, slave and free, hid themselves in the caves and in the rocks of the mountains" (6:15). That divine authority stands behind this event is evident as the reference to the "kings of the earth" reminds the audience that Jesus Christ is the "ruler of the kings of the earth" (1:5). In ironic contrast to the "mighty" angel in heaven (5:2) the "mighty" on earth are frantically trying to hide themselves from a superior divine authority. Despite every "mountain" being moved from its place (6:14), all of these earth-dwellers desperately hid themselves in the rocks of the "mountains."

As all of those inhabiting upon the earth "hid" themselves in the caves and in the "rocks of the mountains" (6:15), they are saying to the "mountains and to the rocks"—"Fall upon us [cf. Hos 10:8] and hide

---

25. See Isa 34:4 for OT background to Rev 6:13–14a.

PART TWO—*Shown What Must Happen after These Things (4:1—16:21)*

us from the face of the one sitting upon the throne and from the anger of the Lamb" (6:16).[26] Not only did the stars of the heaven "fall" to the earth (6:13), but those inhabiting upon the earth plead to the mountains and to the rocks, "Fall upon us." They beg to be hidden not from the "face" of a human being (4:7) but from the "face" of God himself as the "one sitting upon the throne" in heaven, recalling that the sealed scroll was in the authoritative right hand of the "one sitting upon the throne" (5:1, 7). And they beg to be hidden from the anger of the slaughtered Lamb worthy to open the sealed scroll and reveal the plan of God for all peoples (5:6, 12; 6:1), including the judgment of those inhabiting upon the earth (6:10).

All of those inhabiting upon the earth conclude their desperate plea with the declaration and query, "for the great day of their anger has come, and who is able to stand?" (6:17).[27] Now that the Lamb "came" and received the sealed scroll from the right of the one sitting upon the throne (5:7), the great day of the anger of the Lamb and the one sitting upon the throne "has come." With the "great" earthquake that came to be (6:12) as well as the "great" wind (6:13), the "great" day of their anger has come. The audience are thus prompted to answer the question of "who is able to stand?" This question recalls the similar question of "Who is worthy to open the scroll and release its seals?" (5:2). But no one was "able" (5:3), except the Lamb "standing," as one having been slaughtered (5:6). The implication is that the souls slaughtered (6:9) like the Lamb, whose prophetic witness the audience are to imitate, and not the evil earth-dwellers, are those able to stand on the great day of anger, the day of divine judgment.

The slaughtered souls under the altar in heaven directed their prayer of supplication to the divine Lamb, "Until when, Master, holy and true, do you not judge and vindicate our blood from those inhabiting upon the earth?" (6:10). Ironically, all those inhabiting upon the earth direct their pseudo-prayer of supplication to the mountains and rocks on the earth. The prayer of their pseudo-worship, "Fall on us and

---

26. "The petition alludes to Hos. 10:8, which, like Isaiah 2, speaks of judgment on idolaters and portrays them seeking refuge from divine wrath in mountains and rocks" (Beale, *Revelation*, 400).

27. See Joel 2:10–11 and Nah 1:5–6 for OT background to Rev 6:17.

hide us from the face of the one sitting upon the throne and from the anger of the Lamb" (6:16), stands in stark contrast to the authentic worship that comes from the whole universe: "To the one sitting upon the throne and to the Lamb, the blessing and the honor and the glory and the might for the ages of the ages" (5:13). Consequently, this scene of the opening of the sixth seal (6:12–17) further exhorts the audience to practice authentic worship for eternal life in the Spirit of prophecy, the prophetic witness, presented to them in the book of Revelation.[28]

9b′) Vision and Audition of 144,000 Who Had Been Sealed (7:1–8)

A   a) [7:1a] After this *I saw* four **angels** standing upon the four corners of the earth,

> b) [1b] holding the four **winds** of the earth
>
> b′) [1c] so that **wind** may not blow upon the earth nor upon the sea nor upon any tree.
>
> a′) [2a] Then *I saw* another **angel** ascending from east of the sun having a **seal** of the living **God**,

B [2b] and he cried out with a great sound to the four angels to whom it was given to them to **harm** the earth and the sea,

C [3a] saying,

B′ [3b] "Do not **harm** the earth nor the sea nor the trees,

A′   a) [3c] until we have *sealed* the servants of our **God** upon their foreheads." [4] Then I heard the number of those who had been *sealed*, one hundred forty-four thousand, having been *sealed* from every tribe of the sons of Israel. [5a] From the tribe of Judah twelve thousand had been *sealed*,

> b) [5b] from the tribe of Reuben twelve thousand, from the tribe of Gad twelve thousand,
>
> [6] from the tribe of Asher twelve thousand, from the tribe of Napthtali twelve thousand, from the tribe

---

28. On 6:12–17, see de Villiers, "Sixth Seal," 1–30.

PART TWO—*Shown What Must Happen after These Things (4:1—16:21)*

> of Manasseh twelve thousand, ⁷ from the tribe of Simeon twelve thousand, from the tribe of Levi twelve thousand, from the tribe of Issachar twelve thousand, ⁸ᵃ from the tribe of Zebulun twelve thousand, from the tribe of Joseph twelve thousand,
>
> **a′)** ⁸ᵇ from the tribe of Benjamin twelve thousand had been ***sealed***.

At the conclusion of the scene of the opening of the sixth seal (6:12–17) the audience were presented with the question of who is able to "stand" before the anger of God and the Lamb on the great day of judgment (6:17). Through the recurrence of the verb "stand" the audience experience the transition to the next scene (7:1–8), as John reports that after this he saw "four angels standing upon the four corners of the earth, holding the four winds of the earth so that wind may not blow upon the earth nor upon the sea nor upon any tree" (7:1). Whereas the exalted Jesus in heaven is "holding the seven stars" that represent the angels of the seven churches (1:20) in his authoritative right hand (2:1), the four angels are "holding the four winds" under their control upon earth.

In contrast to the fig tree shaken by a great "wind" in the description of how the stars of the heaven fell to the earth (6:13), the four angels are holding the four "winds" of the earth so that "wind" may not blow upon the earth (7:1). The universal worship of God and the Lamb comes from every creature in the heaven and "upon the earth" and under the earth and "upon the sea" and all the things in them (5:13). That the four angels do not allow the wind to blow "upon the earth nor upon the sea" thus protects the people who offer authentic worship to God and the Lamb from those locations.

John was invited to "ascend" from earth to heaven for his revelatory visions (4:1). Now he reports that he saw another angel "ascending" from east of the sun (7:2a), that is, from the heavenly region of paradise thought to be from the "rising" or "east" (cf. Gen 2:8) of the sun that became black at the opening of the sixth seal (6:12). This angel has a "seal" of the living God (7:2a), a sign of divine authority and protective control, resonating with the seven "seals" that sealed the scroll John saw upon the authoritative right of God (5:1). The Lamb is worthy to open each "seal" and reveal divinely guarded aspects of the scroll that contains God's plan for the salvation of all peoples (5:2, 5, 9; 6:1, 3, 6, 7, 9, 12). That it is a seal of the eternally "living" God indicates to the audience that it comes from the God worshiped in heaven as the one "living" for the ages of the ages (4:9, 10), just as John on earth worshiped the exalted Jesus who is likewise eternally "living" for the ages of the ages (1:18).

The slaughtered souls "cried out with a great sound" their prayer to the Lamb for the vindication of their blood (6:10). Resonating and in close continuity with their prayer, the other angel John saw "cried out with a great sound to the four angels to whom it was given to them to harm the earth and the sea" (7:2b). In contrast to the slaughtered souls to whom it "was given to them," to each one, a heavenly white robe in answer to their prayer for vindication (6:11), to the four angels it "was given to them" to harm the earth and the sea. This is similar to the divine authority that "was given to them," to Death and Hades, over a fourth of the earth to kill (6:8). That it was divinely given to the four angels to harm the "earth" and the sea continues to answer the prayer of the slaughtered souls for vindication of their blood from those inhabiting upon the "earth" (6:10).

The other angel John saw said to the four angels who were given authority to "harm" the earth and the sea (7:2), but who were holding the four winds of the earth so that the wind may not blow upon the earth nor upon the sea nor upon any tree (7:1): "Do not harm the earth nor the sea nor the trees, until we have sealed the servants of our God upon their foreheads" (7:3). Whereas the Lamb directed the rider of the black horse, "Do not harm" the olive oil and the wine (6:6), the other angel directs the four angels not to harm the earth nor the sea nor the trees. The angels are to do no harm until "we have sealed," with the "seal" of the living God (7:2), the foreheads of the servants of our God, thus designating them for eternal life with the living God in heaven. These "servants" of our God include the members of the audience, who are being shown the revelation of Jesus Christ as "servants" of God (1:1). They are also the "servants" of Jesus (2:20) and "fellow servants" of the slaughtered souls (6:11).

PART TWO—*Shown What Must Happen after These Things (4:1—16:21)*

Whereas the "number" of worshipers John saw and heard in heaven was ten thousands of ten thousands and "thousands of thousands" (5:11), he heard that the "number" of those who had been sealed was "one hundred forty-four thousand" from every tribe of the sons of Israel (7:4). That amounts to a vastly complete number composed of the traditional total of the twelve tribes of Israel, the chosen people of God, squared and multiplied by one thousand.[29] In contrast to the stumbling block of idolatrous worship Balak threw before the "sons of Israel" (2:14), one hundred forty-four thousand from every tribe of the "sons of Israel" had been sealed and thus authorized to participate in true heavenly worship. Indeed, the full number from "every tribe" of the sons of Israel are included among those from "every tribe" whom the slaughtered Lamb, worshiped in heaven, bought for God with his blood (5:9).

The list of the traditional twelve tribes (7:5–8) begins with the tribe of Judah from which twelve thousand had been "sealed" (7:5) and concludes with the tribe of Benjamin from which twelve thousand likewise had been "sealed" (7:8).[30] The "tribe of Judah" appropriately heads the list, since the Lamb is also the lion from the "tribe of Judah" who conquered to open the scroll and its seven seals (5:5). Indeed, the Lamb is worshiped in heaven as the one worthy to receive the scroll and open its seals (5:9). Included among the divinely sealed servants of God (7:3), some members of the audience may be killed in their prophetic witness as fellow servants of the slaughtered souls (6:11). Nevertheless, the audience are to appreciate that they have been divinely sealed as prophetic and priestly servants of God, who are included among the chosen people of God, and thus designated to participate in the heavenly worship of the Lamb for eternal life in the Spirit of prophecy.

---

29. "That there are 144,000 (12,000 from each tribe of Israel) is a symbolic way of stressing that the church is the eschatological people of God who have taken up Israel's inheritance. Their being sealed does not protect them from physical death but insures entrance into the heavenly kingdom" (Mounce, *Revelation*, 158).

30. Smith, "Portrayal of the Church," 111–18; Smith, "Tribes of Revelation 7," 213–18; Bauckham, "List of the Tribes," 99–115.

10a′) Vision of a Great Crowd Standing before the Throne and Worshiping God (7:9–17)

A a) ⁹ᵃ After these things I saw, and behold a large crowd, which no one was able to number it, from every nation and tribes and peoples and tongues standing before the **throne** and before the **Lamb**,

>b) ⁹ᵇ clothed with white robes and palm branches in their hands,

a′) ¹⁰ and they are crying out with a great sound saying, "The salvation to our God, **the one sitting upon the throne**, and to the **Lamb**."

B ¹¹ And all the angels stood around the throne and **the elders** and the four living creatures and fell before the throne upon their faces and worshiped God

>C ¹²ᵃ saying, "**Amen!**

>>D ¹²ᵇ The blessing and the glory and the wisdom and the thanksgiving and the honor and the power and the strength to our God for the ages of the ages.

>C′ ¹²ᶜ **Amen!**"

B′ a) ¹³ Then replied one of **the elders** saying **to me**, "**These** who are clothed with the white robes, who are they and whence have they **come**?"

>b) ¹⁴ᵃ Then I said to him, "My lord, you know."

a′) ¹⁴ᵇ And he said **to me**, "**These** are those **coming** from the great tribulation

A′ a) ¹⁴ᶜ and they have washed their robes and whitened them in the blood of the **Lamb**, ¹⁵ᵃ on account of this they are before the throne of **God** and they offer worship to him day and night in his temple,

>b) ¹⁵ᵇ and **the one sitting upon the throne** will dwell **over them**.

       c) ¹⁶ᵃ They will not hunger *again*

       c′) ¹⁶ᵇ nor will they thirst *again*

    b′) ¹⁶ᶜ nor may the sun ever fall *over them* nor any burning,

a′) ¹⁷ for the **Lamb** who is in the middle of the throne will shepherd them and lead them to life's springs of waters [Isa 49:10], and **God** will wipe away every tear from their eyes [25:8]."

John introduced the first unit (4:1–5a) in this ten unit subsection (4:1–7:17) with the words "after these things I saw, and behold" (4:1a). Now, at the beginning of this tenth unit (7:9–17), the audience hear a literary inclusion with the first unit, as John with exactly the same words reports that "after these things I saw, and behold" (7:9a).[31] In the first unit John saw a door opened in heaven through which he ascended from earth to be shown the revelatory visions recounted in the book (4:1). In this tenth unit John in heaven saw a large crowd standing before the heavenly throne and before the Lamb (7:9).

The "number" John heard of those who had been sealed by the angels on earth was one hundred forty-four thousand (7:4), and the "number" of angelic worshipers around the heavenly throne was ten thousands of ten thousands and thousands of thousands (5:11). But the large crowd that John saw no one was able to "number" (7:9). That "no one was able" to number it means that it was of a virtually unlimited, divinely determined size. It recalls that "no one was able" to open the scroll except the divine Lamb (5:3), and that "no one is able" to close the door opened by the divinely exalted Jesus (3:8).

That the large crowd John saw standing before the throne and before the Lamb was from "every" nation and "tribes" and peoples and tongues (7:9) means that it includes the one hundred forty-four thousand that he heard were sealed from "every tribe" of the sons of Israel (7:4). In contrast to the four angels "standing" upon the four corners of the earth (7:1), the large crowd is "standing" in heaven before the throne and before the Lamb, whom John saw likewise "standing" as one having

---

31. These are the only occurrences of this formula in Revelation.

been slaughtered (5:6). This large crowd thus includes those who are able to "stand" (6:17) before the face of the one sitting upon the throne and before the anger of the Lamb (6:16).

The large crowd John saw was "from every nation and tribes and peoples and tongues" (7:9), identifying them with those whom the slaughtered Lamb bought for God with his blood "from every tribe and tongue and people and nation" (5:9). That the large crowd were standing "before the throne" and "before the Lamb" (7:9) places them in an honored position of participating in heavenly worship. It resonates with the heavenly worship performed by the living creatures and elders "before the throne" (4:10) and "before the Lamb" (5:8).

Like the elders who were "clothed" in "white" garments (4:4) for their participation in heavenly worship, the large crowd were "clothed" similarly with "white" robes (7:9). That the large crowd were clothed with "white robes" assimilates them to the slaughtered souls under the heavenly altar, each of whom was given a "white robe" (6:11). Whereas the rider of the black horse has a scale "in his hand" for his authoritative regulation of the dreadful time of famine (6:5), the exalted Jesus has "in his right hand" seven stars (1:16), symbolizing his authority over the angels of the seven churches (1:20). That the large crowd have celebratory palm branches "in their hands" thus underlines their authority to participate in heavenly worship (7:9).[32]

The slaughtered souls under the heavenly altar "cried out with a great sound saying," as they introduced their prayer to the divine Lamb (6:10). And now, the large crowd likewise "are crying out with a great sound saying," as they introduce their heavenly worship of God and the Lamb. Standing before the "throne" and before the "Lamb" (7:9a), they worship them declaring, "The salvation to our God, the one sitting upon the throne, and to the Lamb" (7:10).

The large crowd include the sealed servants of "our God" (7:3) and those whom the slaughtered Lamb made for "our God" a kingdom and priests (5:10). In their heavenly worship they appropriately acknowledge that salvation belongs to "our God" and the Lamb. Their worship

---

32. "Since Jews carried palm fronds around and into the temple in Jerusalem in connection with the celebrations of the Feast of Tabernacles, it is possible to understand the palms in Rev 7:9 in that connection" (Aune, *Revelation 6–16*, 469).

directed to "the one sitting upon the throne and to the Lamb" echoes, as it participates in, the universal worship of every creature likewise directed to "the one sitting upon the throne and to the Lamb" (5:13).

John had heard "a sound of many angels around the throne and the living creatures and the elders" (5:11), as they worshiped the divine Lamb in heaven (5:12). And now he reports that "all the angels stood around the throne and the elders and the four living creatures and fell before the throne upon their faces and worshiped God" (7:11). That they "fell before" the heavenly throne and "worshiped" God recalls that the living creatures and elders "fell before" the divine Lamb (5:8) as they worshiped him (5:9–10). John reported that the elders "will fall" before God as they "will worship" him (4:10). And the elders "fell down" and "worshiped" (5:14), as they participated in the universal worship of both God and the divine Lamb (5:13).

All the angels, elders, and living creatures worshiped God (7:11) saying, "Amen! The blessing and the glory and the wisdom and the thanksgiving and the honor and the power and the strength to our God for the ages of the ages. Amen!" (7:12). This list of seven attributes directed to "our God" echoes the worship of the large white-robed crowd (7:9), likewise directed to "our God" but also to the Lamb (7:10). This further confirms the participation of the large crowd in heavenly worship. Indeed, the worship by the large crowd complements that by all the angels, elders, and living creatures as it explicitly includes the worship of the Lamb. But the worship by all the angels, elders, and living creatures of our God implicitly includes the worship of the divine Lamb, as it resonates with worship of God and/or the Lamb heard previously by the audience: "blessing" (5:12, 13), "glory" (1:6; 4:9, 11; 5:12, 13), "wisdom" (5:12), "thanksgiving" (4:9), "honor" (4:9, 11; 5:12, 13), "power" (4:11; 5:12), and "strength" (5:12).

The worship performed by all the angels, elders, and living creatures draws in the audience to join them and the large white-robed crowd in their heavenly worship. The audience have already been led to participate in the worship of Jesus Christ, who identified himself as the "Amen" (3:14), by employing the liturgical acclamation of "Amen" at the beginning (1:6) and conclusion of their doxological worship (1:7). The doxological heavenly worship offered by all the angels, elders, and liv-

John's Visions of Lamb Opening the Seals and Worship

ing creatures similarly begins and ends with "Amen" (7:12). Their worship of God, which concludes with the words "for the ages of the ages. Amen!" (7:12), resonates with the universal worship by every creature, which attributes to both God and the divine Lamb "might for the ages of the ages" (5:13), to which the four living creatures add, "Amen!" (5:14). This echoes and embraces the audience's worship, which attributes to Jesus "might for the ages of the ages. Amen!" (1:6).

When John wept because no one was able to open the sealed scroll (5:4), "one from the elders" told him not to weep since the lion from the tribe of Judah has conquered to open the scroll (5:5). And now the audience hear that again "one from the elders," the "elders" engaged in heavenly worship (7:11), replied to John. He asked him who are these "clothed with the white robes," that is, the large crowd, "clothed with white robes" (7:9), who were also participating in heavenly worship (7:10), and whence have they come (7:13). With an address of "my Lord," until now reserved for the "Lord" God (1:8; 4:8, 11), and in contrast to "you," the church in Laodicea, who does not "know" its true identity (3:17), John said to the elder that "you," that is, emphatically "you are the one," who "knows" the identity of the large crowd (7:14a).

The elder then said to John that these who are clothed with the white robes (7:13) "are those coming from the great tribulation" (7:14b). That the large crowd are those coming from the "great tribulation" further associates them with John and his audience. John is a fellow sharer with his audience in the "tribulation" involving the prophetic witness of Jesus (1:9), which includes the refusal to engage in idolatrous worship. The exalted Jesus acknowledged the "tribulation" that those in Smyrna experience as a result of the false worshipers among them (2:9, 10). And the exalted Jesus is throwing the false prophetess Jezebel and those engaged in idolatrous worship with her to a "great tribulation," if they do not repent from her idolatry (2:22). The large crowd coming from the great tribulation are thus those who have refused to engage in or who have repented from their engagement with false worship. They are now clothed with white robes for their participation in true heavenly worship.[33]

---

33. "Some assume that the people are a select group who have been martyred for their faith because they have died during the tribulation. But it is not clear that martyrdom is in mind. Nevertheless, even if these people are martyrs, it would be best

PART TWO—Shown What Must Happen after These Things (4:1—16:21)

The elder goes on to explain to John that the large crowd "have washed their robes and whitened them in the blood of the Lamb" (7:14c). That they have metaphorically washed their robes and paradoxically whitened them in the red "blood" of the Lamb reaffirms that they are included within the kingdom and priests (5:10) that the slaughtered Lamb made for God with his "blood" (5:9). They are among those released from their sins by the sacrificial "blood" of Jesus Christ (1:5).[34] They include the slaughtered souls who prayed to the slaughtered Lamb for the vindication of their "blood " (6:10), which resulted in the moon becoming as "blood" (6:12).

"On account of this they are before the throne of God and they offer worship to him day and night in his temple" (7:15a). This suggests that the large crowd washed their robes and whitened them in the blood of the Lamb (7:14c) by becoming like the souls slaughtered "on account of" the word of God and "on account of" the witness that they had (6:9). That the large crowd are "before the throne" of God reaffirms that they are standing "before the throne" and before the Lamb (7:9), together with all the angels, elders, and living creatures who fell "before the throne" in their heavenly worship (7:11). The large crowd offer worship "day and night" in heaven just like the four living creatures who do not have rest "day and night" as they worshiped in heaven (4:8). That they "offer worship" in his "temple" reinforces for the audience the promise that the exalted Jesus will make the one who conquers the threat of idolatrous worship a pillar in the heavenly "temple" (3:12).

The elder then assures John that the one "sitting upon the throne," that is, the God whom the large crowd worshiped as the one "sitting upon the throne" together with the Lamb (7:10), will dwell over them (7:15b). When the "sun" became black (6:12), those on earth pleaded to the mountains and to the rocks, "Fall upon us and hide us from the face of the one sitting upon the throne and from the anger of the Lamb"

---

to view them as representative of all believers who must suffer" (Beale, *Revelation*, 432–33).

34. "The metaphorical character of the white robes is evident in this passage, where they are washed white by the blood of the Lamb; i.e., the sin of those who wear them has been atoned for by the sacrificial death of Christ" (Aune, *Revelation 6-16*, 475).

(6:16). But the large crowd in heaven "will not hunger again nor will they thirst again nor may the sun ever fall over them nor any burning" (7:16; cf. Isa 49:10). In other words, they will enjoy a heavenly, eternal life.

John saw the Lamb standing, as one having been slaughtered, in the "midst" of the heavenly throne and of the four living creatures and in the "midst" of the elders (5:6). One from the elders now reassures John and his audience that the Lamb who is in the "middle" of the throne "will shepherd them and lead them to life's springs of waters, and God will wipe away every tear from their eyes" (7:17; cf. Isa 49:10; 25:8). That the Lamb "will shepherd" the large crowd to springs of waters of eternal life reinforces the promise that the one who conquers false worship "will shepherd" the nations (2:27) to eternal life. And that the Lamb will shepherd them to springs of waters of eternal "life," and God "will wipe away" every tear from their eyes reinforces the promise of the exalted Jesus that never "will I wipe away" the name of the one who conquers from the scroll of the eternal "life" (3:5). Indeed, he will give to the one who conquers the crown of the eternal "life" (2:10) and to eat from the tree of the eternal "life" (2:7).

John's vision (7:9–17) encourages his audience to become part of the very large crowd engaged in the true heavenly worship of God and the Lamb. They are exhorted to join those who have "washed their robes and whitened them in the blood of the Lamb" (7:14) through the prophetic witness of their resistance to and repentance from false, idolatrous worship. In other words, in and through their liturgical celebrations on earth they are to practice a true, heavenly worship for eternal life in the Spirit of prophecy.[35]

---

35. "[T]here may be eucharistic as well as baptismal echoes here. If so, this would underline the degree to which participation in these eschatological blessings can be experienced by the churches now through their liturgical celebrations" (Boxall, *Revelation*, 128). See also Perry, *Rhetoric of Digressions*, 208–24; Morton, "Revelation 7:9–17," 1–11; Yates, "Function," 215–33; Yates, "Rewards," 322–34; Tavo, *Woman*, 135–72.

PART TWO—*Shown What Must Happen after These Things (4:1—16:21)*

Summary on 4:1—7:17

The audience hear the ten units of this subsection (4:1—7:17) in a chiastic pattern centering around the theme of encouraging believers on earth to participate in heavenly worship. At the center of this subsection the audience experience a pivot of chiastic parallels from the fifth (e) unit (5:11-14) to the sixth (e′) unit (6:1-8), based on the transition from references to the four "living creatures" as a whole (5:11, 14) to references of each individual "living creature" (6:1, 3, 5, 7). In the (e) unit John saw the participation of the four living creatures in the universal worship of the Lamb by every earthly and heavenly creature. Then, in the (e′) unit, when the Lamb began to open the seven-sealed scroll (5:1) containing the divine plan, each of the four living creatures commanded a different colored horse and its rider to come forth and reveal its destructive role on earth. But the audience are assured that this destruction is part of God's plan that will ultimately culminate in the heavenly worship of the Lamb by all of creation.

When the audience hear the (d′) unit (6:9-11), they experience a progression of chiastic parallels from the (d) unit (5:6-10), based on references to "blood" and "each one." In the (d) unit the slaughtered Lamb is worshiped in heaven as the one who bought for God those from every tribe and tongue and people and nation with his "blood" (5:9). In the (d′) unit this progresses to the prayer of supplication from under the heavenly altar by the souls slaughtered for their prophetic witness (6:9). They pray for the Lamb to vindicate their "blood" (6:10). That "each one" of the living creatures and elders had a harp and golden bowls filled with incense for their role in heavenly worship (5:8) progresses to "each one" of the slaughtered souls being given a white robe (6:11) for their participation in heavenly worship.

Based on references to "mighty" and "being able," the audience experience a progression of chiastic parallels from the (c) unit (5:1-5) to the (c′) unit (6:12-17). When a "mighty" angel in heaven asked who was worthy to open the scroll and release its seals (5:2), no one was "able" (5:3) to open it (except the divine Lamb). This progresses to the "mighty" of the earth who tried to hide themselves (6:15) from God and the anger of the divine Lamb (6:16) after the opening of the sixth seal, raising the question of who (except those redeemed by the Lamb) is "able" to stand (6:17) in the final judgment and/or heavenly worship.

Based on references to the eternally "living" God, the audience experience a progression of chiastic parallels from the (b) unit (4:5b-11) to the (b') unit (7:1–8). The living creatures and the elders worship God in heaven as the one "living" for the ages of the ages in the (b) unit (4:9, 10). This progresses to the seal of the eternally "living" God (7:2) with which the servants of God were divinely sealed to protect them from harm on earth and designate them for participation in heavenly worship in the (b') unit.

Based on the introductory formula, "after these things I saw, and behold," and references to being "clothed in white" garments or robes, the audience experience a progression of chiastic parallels from the (a) unit (4:1–5a) to the (a') unit (7:9–17). The same formula (4:1; 7:9) introduces both units, forming a literary inclusion embracing the first and last units of this ten-unit subsection. In the (a) unit the twenty-four elders were sitting "clothed in white" garments (4:4) for their participation in heavenly worship. In the (a') unit this progresses to the universal large crowd of believers "clothed in white" robes (7:9, 13) for their participation in heavenly worship because in and through their prophetic witness "they washed their robes and whitened them in the blood of the Lamb" (7:14). The audience are exhorted to do the same, so that they may likewise participate in the heavenly worship for eternal life in and through their witness in the Spirit of prophecy.

5

John's Visions of the Seven Angels Trumpeting Their Seven Trumpets

Revelation 8:1—11:19

1a) Seventh Seal and Seven Angels Given Seven Trumpets (8:1–5)

    A [8:1] And when he opened the seal, the seventh one, there **came to be** silence in heaven for about half an hour.

        B   a) [2a] Then I saw the seven *angels* who before God *stand*,

            b) [2b] and seven trumpets were given to them.

            a') [3a] And another *angel* came and *stood* over the altar, having a golden **censer**,

        C [3b] and much **incense** was given to him, so that he will give it with **the prayers** of all **the holy ones** upon the golden altar that is **before** the throne.

        C' [4] And the smoke of the **incense** ascended with **the prayers** of **the holy ones** from the hand of the angel **before** God.

B′ ⁵ᵃ Then the angel received the **censer** and filled it from the fire of the altar and threw it to the earth,

A′ ⁵ᵇ and there **came to be** thunders and sounds and lightnings and an earthquake.

"When he opened the seal, the seventh one" (8:1a), the series of the Lamb's opening of each of the seven seals of the scroll (6:1) containing the divine plan resumes from when the Lamb "opened the seal, the sixth one" (6:12a). At the opening of this final and climactic seventh seal, "there came to be silence in heaven for about half an hour" (8:1b). In sharp contrast to the moon that "became" as blood, to the sun that "became" black, and to the great earthquake that "came to be" on earth at the opening of the sixth seal (6:12), at the opening of the seventh seal there "came to be" silence in heaven. This stark silence "in heaven" of a limited duration of about half an hour creates a dramatic pause in the worship of God and the Lamb by every creature "in heaven" (5:13). John has thus provocatively prepared his audience for something significant to take place in view of such a suspenseful silence in heaven.[1]

John then "saw the seven angels who before God stand" (8:2a), recalling that the "seven" stars that John saw upon the authoritative right hand of the exalted Jesus are the "angels" of the "seven" churches that include the audience (1:20). Whereas John saw four "angels standing" upon the four corners of the earth holding back the wind (7:1), he now saw the seven "angels" who "stand" before God in heaven. Like the large crowd "standing before" the heavenly throne and "before" the Lamb (7:9), the seven angels stand "before" God in a position of worship. They are included among all the "angels" who "stood" around the throne and the elders and the four living creatures. They fell "before" the throne upon their faces and worshiped God (7:11). The seven angels stand before God, the God who will wipe away every tear from the eyes (7:17) of the large crowd who offer worship "before" the throne of God in heaven (7:15).

---

1. "In short, there are two primary reasons for this dramatic pause: the hushed expectancy of God's judgment about to unfold, and the liturgical silence of heaven in light of the incense and the prayers of the saints in 5:8; 6:9–11; and 7:3–4" (Osborne, *Revelation*, 338).

PART TWO—*Shown What Must Happen after These Things (4:1—16:21)*

The slaughtered souls under the altar in heaven prayed for the divine vindication of their blood from those inhabiting upon the earth (6:10). In response, a white robe "was given to them" by God (divine passive) appropriate for their participation in heavenly worship (6:11). As a further response to their prayer for vindication on earth, "it was given to them," to the four angels standing upon the four corners of the earth (7:1), to harm the earth and the sea (7:2). And now, seven trumpets "were given to them," to the seven angels who before God stand ready to perform an act of worship (8:2). The sound of the divinely exalted Jesus, which John heard twice, was "as a trumpet" (1:10; 4:1). This suggests that the sounds to be made by the seven "trumpets" given to the seven angels will likewise involve a divine communication in response to the prayer of the slaughtered souls.

John saw "another angel" ascending from east of the sun "having" a seal of the living God (7:2) for the protection of the servants of God on earth (7:3). And now, similarly, "another angel" that John saw came and stood over the altar in heaven, "having" a golden censer (8:3a). The "golden" censer resonates with the "golden" bowls filled with incense that each of the living creatures and elders were "having," when they fell before the Lamb in worship (5:8). The angel stood over the "altar," the same "altar" in heaven under which the slaughtered souls offered their prayer of supplication (6:9).

Whereas seven trumpets "were given to them," the seven angels who stand before God (8:2), much "incense was given to him," the other angel, "so that he will give it with the prayers of all the holy ones upon the golden altar that is before the throne" (8:3b). The "much" incense appropriately accords with the "large" crowd of heavenly worshipers (7:9). This complements the worship by the living creatures and elders having golden bowls filled with "incense," which are the "prayers" of the "holy ones" (5:8).[2]

In correspondence to the "golden" censer (8:3a), the angel gives the incense upon the "golden altar" over which he stands (8:3a) and

---

2. "Given that these prayers . . . are, in effect, acts of worship, and worship operates by ritual prescriptions that allow the presentations to God to be acceptable in God's sight. The incense performs that ritual, liturgical function here" (Blount, *Revelation*, 165).

under which the slaughtered souls offer their prayer (6:9). This further confirms that their prayer is included among the prayers of all the holy ones with whom the audience are to identify. The golden altar is "before the throne," that is, "before the throne" where heavenly worship takes place (7:9, 11, 15).

The smoke of the incense given to the other angel to give with the "prayers" of all the "holy ones" (8:3b), "ascended with the prayers of the holy ones from the hand of the angel before God" (8:4). Palm branches were in the "hands" of the large crowd as part of their heavenly worship (7:9). And now, the smoke of the incense ascends with the prayers of the holy ones, which include the prayer of the slaughtered souls (6:10) and of the audience, as an act of heavenly worship from the "hand" of the angel. The smoke of the incense upon the golden altar that is "before" the throne (8:3b) ascends "before God" himself, further associating this act of prayerful worship with the seven angels who stand "before God" and to whom were given seven trumpets (8:2).

The Lamb "received" the scroll from the right of the one sitting upon the throne, that is, from God himself (5:7). Similarly, the angel "received" from God himself in answer to the prayers of the holy ones (8:4) the golden censer he had (8:3), and "filled it from the fire of the altar and threw it to the earth" (8:5a). As a divine response to the prayers, the "fire" of the golden altar that is before the throne in heaven (8:3b), is closely associated with the seven torches of "fire" burning before the throne in heaven, which are the seven Spirits of God (4:5b).

The slaughtered souls prayed for judgment and vindication from those inhabiting "upon the earth" (6:10). In response, at the opening of the sixth seal, the stars of the heaven fell "to the earth," as a fig tree "throws" its unripe figs shaken by a great wind (6:13). And now, in further response to the prayer, the angel "threw" the flaming censer "to the earth" (8:5a).

After the angel threw the censer filled with fire to the earth (8:5a), "there came to be thunders and sounds and lightnings and an earthquake" (8:5b). This confirms and underlines the divine response from heaven to the prayers of the holy ones, including the prayer of the slaughtered souls (6:10), as it recalls that from the throne in heaven were coming out "lightnings and sounds and thunders" (4:5a). That there "came to be" not only thunders and sounds and lightnings but an "earthquake" resonates with the great "earthquake" that "came to be" at the opening of the sixth seal (6:12) in answer to the prayer of the slaughtered souls. This divine answer from heaven to the prayers of the holy ones, who include the slaughtered souls as well as the audience, thus resolves the suspense of why there "came to be" a silence in heaven for about half an hour (8:1).[3]

2b) First Four Trumpets and Announcement of Three Woes (8:6–13)

   A [6] Then the seven angels having the seven **trumpets** prepared themselves so that they might trumpet.

      B a) [7a] Then the first trumpeted, and there *came to be* hail

           b) [7b] and fire mixed with blood and it *was thrown* to the earth,

              c) [7c] and a third of the earth was **burned up** and a third of the trees was **burned up** and all the green grass was **burned up**.

              d) [8a] Then the second angel trumpeted,

           c') [8b] and something as a great mountain with fire *burning*

         b') [8c] *was thrown* into the sea,

      a') [8d] and a third of the sea *became* blood. [9] Then **died** a third of the creatures who are in the sea—those having souls and a third of the ships were destroyed.

   C [10a] Then the third angel trumpeted, and a great star burning as a torch **fell** out of heaven

   C' [10b] and it **fell** upon a third of the rivers and upon the springs of the waters,

---

3. On 8:1–5, see Stefanovic, "Angel," 79–94; de Villiers, "Eschatological Celebration," 67–96.

B' **a)** [11] and the name of the *star* is said to be "The Wormwood," and a ***third*** of the waters **became** wormwood and many of the human beings **died** from the waters for they were embittered.

    b) [12a] Then the fourth angel trumpeted,

a') [12b] and a ***third*** of the sun was struck and a ***third*** of the moon and a ***third*** of the ***stars***, so that a ***third*** of them was darkened, and the day did not appear—a ***third*** of it, and the night likewise.

A' [13] Then I saw, and I heard one eagle flying in midheaven saying with a great sound, "Woe, woe, woe to those inhabiting upon the earth from the rest of the sounds of the **trumpet** of the three angels who are about to trumpet."

In answer to the prayers of the holy ones (8:4) the "angel" received from God the censer and filled it from the fire of the altar in heaven and threw it to the earth (8:5a). Now, in further answer to the prayers, "the seven angels having the seven trumpets prepared themselves so that they might trumpet" (8:6). These are the seven "angels" John saw. They stand before God, and seven "trumpets" were given to them by God (8:2). The living creatures and elders fell before the Lamb in worship "having" a harp and golden bowls filled with incense for their act of heavenly worship involving the prayers of the holy ones (5:8). And now, similarly, the seven angels "having" the seven trumpets prepared themselves for their act of worship in further answer to the prayers of the holy ones.

    In continuity with the theophanic storm phenomena—thunders, sounds, lightnings, earthquake—that "came to be" in answer to the prayers of the holy ones (8:5b), there "came to be" hail when the first angel trumpeted (8:7a). When the other angel received the censer, he filled it from the "fire" of the altar in heaven and "threw" it to the earth (8:5a). Similarly, when the first angel trumpeted, there came to be "fire" mixed with blood and it was "thrown" by God (divine passive) to the earth (8:7b). The prayer of the slaughtered souls in heaven, a prayer of the holy ones, was for the divine judgment and vindication of their "blood" from those inhabiting upon the "earth" (6:10). Now, in further

PART TWO—*Shown What Must Happen after These Things (4:1—16:21)*

answer to the prayer, fire mixed with "blood" was thrown to the "earth," and a third of the "earth" was burned up (8:7c).[4]

Whereas the four angels standing upon the four corners of the earth protected every "tree" (7:1), so that the "trees" were not harmed (7:3), now a third of the "trees" was burned up (8:7c). That all the "green" grass was also burned up (8:7c) resonates ironically with the destruction resulting from Death (and Hades), the rider of the "green" horse that John saw at the opening of the fourth seal (6:8a). But the deadly destruction on earth in response to the prayer for judgment and vindication from those inhabiting upon the earth (6:10) now progresses from a "fourth of the earth" (6:8b) to a "third of the earth" (8:7c).

When the first angel trumpeted, there "came to be" hail and "fire" mixed with "blood" and it "was thrown" to the earth, and a third of the earth was "burned up" and a third of the trees was "burned up" and all the green grass was "burned up" (8:7). Similarly, when the second angel trumpeted, something as a great mountain with "fire burning was thrown" into the sea, and a third of the sea "became blood" (8:8). Whereas a third of the "earth" and a third of the "trees" were burned up at the first trumpeting, at the second trumpeting a third of the "sea" became blood, so that then a third of the creatures who are in the "sea" died (8:9a). But the audience have already been assured that they are among the servants of God who have been sealed for God before the angels were to harm the "earth," "sea," and "trees" (7:3).

That a third of the earth was burned up (8:7) and a third of the "creatures" who are in the sea died (8:9) means the destruction of a third of the participants involved in the universal worship John heard. It recalls that every "creature in the heaven and upon the earth and under the earth and upon the sea and all the things in them" were worshiping God and the Lamb (5:13). That a third of the sea became "blood" (8:8), so that then a third of the sea creatures who have "souls" (8:9) died, serves as an ironic response to the prayer of the slaughtered "souls" John saw under the heavenly altar (6:9) for the divine judgment and vindication of their "blood" (6:10). With the second trumpeting the destruc-

---

4. "The first five trumpets, beginning with 8.7, are broadly patterned according to five of the plagues inflicted upon the Egyptians before the Exodus" (Smalley, *Revelation*, 219).

tion progresses from a third of the earth and a third of its vegetation of trees and of all the green grass (8:7) to a third of the sea (8:8) and a third of the animal life within it as well as a third of the ships, which imply human life (8:9).[5]

At the opening of the sixth seal (6:12) the "stars" of the "heaven fell" to the earth (6:13). Now, similarly, when the third angel trumpeted, a great "star" burning as a torch "fell" out of "heaven" (8:10a). Whereas something as a "great" mountain with fire "burning" was thrown into the sea at the second trumpeting (8:8), at the third trumpeting a "great" star "burning" as a torch fell out of heaven. The divine origin of the great star burning as a "torch" is confirmed and underlined, as it recalls the seven "torches" of fire "burning" before the throne in heaven that are the seven Spirits of God (4:5b). This reinforces the promise that God will dwell over the large crowd of worshipers in heaven, so that the sun may never "fall" over them nor any "burning" (7:16).

The great star burning as a torch that "fell" out of heaven (8:10a), "fell upon a third of the rivers and upon the springs of the waters" (8:10b). Whereas a third of the sea, which contains non-drinkable salt water, became blood at the second trumpeting (8:8), at the third trumpeting a great burning star fell upon a third of the sources of drinkable sweet water—the rivers and springs of the waters. And whereas the Lamb will shepherd and lead the large crowd of heavenly worshipers to the metaphorical "springs of waters" of eternal life in heaven (7:17), the great burning star fell upon the physical "springs of the waters" crucial for life on earth.

That the "name" of the deadly destructive star is said to be "The Wormwood" (8:11a) resonates with the "name" of Death for the one sitting over the pale green horse at the opening of the fourth seal (6:8). At the first trumpeting there "came to be" hail (8:7), at the second trumpeting a third of the sea "became" blood (8:8). And now, at the third trumpeting, a third of the "waters," that is, of the drinkable "waters" from the springs (8:10), "became" wormwood and many of the human beings died from the "waters" for they were embittered (8:11b). Whereas a third of the sea creatures, that is, animal life, "died" at the second trum-

---

5. Perry, "Things Having Lives," 105–13.

PART TWO—*Shown What Must Happen after These Things (4:1—16:21)*

peting, at the third trumpeting many of the human beings "died" from the waters for they were embittered by God (divine passive).[6]

At the opening of the sixth seal the "sun" became black, the whole "moon" became as blood (6:12), and the "stars" of the heaven fell to the earth (6:13). But when the fourth angel trumpeted (8:12a), the destructive, darkening effects were more limited. Only a third of the "sun" was struck and a third of the "moon" and a third of the "stars," so that a third of them was darkened, "and the day did not appear—a third of it, and the night likewise" (8:12b). This emphatically and climactically completes the significant but limited destruction of thirds as the four angels trumpeted—a third of the earth, trees (8:7), sea (8:8), sea creatures, ships (8:9), rivers (8:10), waters (8:11), sun, moon, stars, day, and night (8:12).[7]

When the Lamb opened the first of the seven seals, John reported that "I saw" and "I heard one" of the four living creatures "saying" as a "sound" of thunder, "Come!" (6:1). Now he reports that "I saw" and "I heard one eagle flying," recalling that the fourth living creature is like an "eagle flying" (4:7), in midheaven "saying" something with a great "sound" (8:13a). The audience have thus been attuned to hear a noteworthy divine declaration.

Indeed, the flying eagle dramatically announces, "Woe, woe, woe to those inhabiting upon the earth from the rest of the sounds of the trumpet of the three angels who are about to trumpet" (8:13b). The threefold "woe" here is the obverse of the threefold "holy" addressed to God in heavenly worship (4:8). It indicates to the audience that the various destructions affecting a third of the earth at the sounding of the first four of the seven "trumpets" of the seven angels (8:6) serve as a divine response to the slaughtered souls' prayer for judgment and vindication from "those inhabiting upon the earth" (6:10). But it also prepares the audience for further responses to the prayer from the rest of the sounds of the "trumpet" of the three angels who are about to trumpet.

---

6. "According to Jer 9:15 and 23:15, wormwood was also an appropriate punishment for the crime of idolatry" (Blount, *Revelation*, 169).

7. "John uses the expression 'one-third' insistently in this passage (12 times between verses 7 and 12; cf. also 9.15, 18; 12.4). The fraction cannot be taken literally. It rather indicates that God's judgement is not yet final" (Smalley, *Revelation*, 220).

3c) Vision of Fifth Trumpet: A Fallen Star Given the Key to the Abyss (9:1–12)

A a) ⁹:¹ᵃ Then the fifth **angel** trumpeted, and I saw a star that had fallen out of heaven **to the earth**,

    b) ¹ᵇ and the key of the shaft of the ***abyss*** was given to it.

    b′) ²ᵃ and it opened the shaft of the ***abyss***,

  a′) ²ᵇ and smoke ascended from the shaft as smoke of a great furnace, and the sun was darkened, and the air, from the smoke of the shaft, ³ᵃ and from the smoke locusts **came out to the earth**,

B a) ³ᵇ and **authority *was given*** to them as the ***scorpions*** of the earth have **authority**, ⁴ᵃ and it was said to them ***that*** they will ***not*** harm the grass of the earth nor anything green nor any tree, but only the human beings,

    b) ⁴ᵇ those who do not have the seal of God upon the foreheads,

  a′) ⁵ and it ***was given*** to them ***that*** they may ***not*** kill them, but only that they will be tormented for **five months**, and their torment is as the torment of a ***scorpion*** when it stings a human being,

C ⁶ᵃ and in those days human beings will seek **death** and they will not find it,

  D ⁶ᵇ and they will desire to die

C′ ⁶ᶜ but **death** will flee from them.

B′ a) ⁷ And the likenesses of the locusts were like **horses** prepared ***for battle***, and upon their heads as crowns like gold, and their faces as faces of **human beings**,

    b) ⁸ᵃ ***they had*** hair as hair of women,

        c) ⁸ᵇ and their teeth were as of lions,

    b′) ⁹ᵃ and ***they had*** breastplates as breastplates of iron,

PART TWO—*Shown What Must Happen after These Things (4:1—16:21)*

a') ⁹ᵇ and the sound of their wings as a sound of chariots of many **horses** running *for battle*, ¹⁰ and they have tails like **scorpions**, and stingers, and in their tails is their **authority** to harm *human beings* for **five months**.

A' ¹¹ They have over them as king the **angel** of the **abyss**, a name for him in Hebrew is Abaddon, and in Greek he has the name Apollyon. ¹² One woe **has gone away**. Behold, coming still are two woes after these.

At the opening of the sixth seal (6:12) the "stars" of the "heaven fell" to the "earth" (6:13) in divine response to the slaughtered souls' prayer for judgment and vindication from those inhabiting upon the "earth" (6:10). And at the third trumpeting a great "star" burning as a torch "fell" out of "heaven" upon the sources of drinking water on earth (8:10). John now saw a "star" that had "fallen" out of "heaven" to the "earth" as a further response to the prayer. This happened when the fifth angel "trumpeted" (9:1a), thus signaling the inauguration of the woes to those inhabiting upon the "earth" from the rest of the sounds of the trumpet of the three angels who are about to "trumpet" (8:13).

Much incense "was given to him," the other angel who stood over the heavenly altar, to offer with the prayers that include the prayer of the slaughtered souls under the altar (8:3). Now, in further divine response to that prayer, the key of the shaft of the abyss "was given to it," the angelic star (9:1b), by God (divine passive).[8] The angelic star "opened" the shaft of the abyss (9:2a) with the "key" that was given to it, further indicating that this is a divinely authoritative action in answer to the prayer. It recalls that the divinely exalted Jesus is the one having not only the "key" of David, who "opens" and no one will close (3:7), but also the "keys" of Death and Hades (1:18), a virtual synonym of the abyss as the realm of the dead.[9]

As an ironic response to the prayer of the slaughtered souls included in the prayers of the holy ones with which the "smoke" of the incense "ascended" (8:4), "smoke ascended" from the shaft of the abyss

---

8. See 1:20 for the close connection between stars and angels.
9. BDAG, 2.

John's Visions of the Seven Angels Trumpeting Their Seven Trumpets

(9:2b). It ascended from the realm of the dead as smoke of a great "furnace" (9:2b), recalling that the feet of Jesus, who was exalted from the dead, are like burnished bronze, as in a "furnace" of refining (1:15). At the opening of the sixth seal the "sun" became black as sackcloth made of hair (6:12) as part of the divine response to the prayer of the slaughtered souls. At the fourth trumpeting a third of the "sun" was struck, so that it was "darkened" by God (8:12). And now the audience hear that at the fifth trumpeting the "sun" was "darkened," as well as the air, from the smoke of the shaft (9:2b) opened with the key God gave to the angelic star fallen out of heaven (9:1–2). This continues the progression of divine responses to the prayer of the slaughtered souls.

From the smoke locusts "came out" to the "earth" (9:3a), resonating with the fiery red horse that "came out" to take peace from the "earth" (6:4). "Authority was given to them," the locusts, as the deadly scorpions of the "earth" have authority (9:3b). This recalls that similarly "authority was given to them," Death and Hades, over the fourth of the "earth" to kill (6:8). The divine authority given to the locusts on earth in response to the prayer of the slaughtered souls thus corresponds to the divine authority given to Death and Hades responsible for the slaughter of the souls.

"It was said to them," the locusts who came out to the earth with authority as the scorpions of the earth (9:3), "that they will not harm the grass of the earth nor anything green nor any tree, but only the human beings, those who do not have the seal of God upon the foreheads" (9:4). This corresponds to the divine response to the prayer of the slaughtered souls, recalling that "it was said to them" that they will need to rest yet a little time (6:11) until their blood is vindicated from those inhabiting upon the earth (6:10), those among the human beings not having the seal of God. At the first trumpeting a third of the "earth," of the "trees," and all the "green grass" were burned up (8:7). But at the fifth trumpeting the locusts are not to harm the "grass" of the "earth" nor anything "green" nor any "tree." At the third trumpeting many of the "human beings" died from the embittered waters (8:11). But now the locusts are only to harm those "human beings" not having the seal of God.

The locusts "will not harm" the grass of "earth" nor any "tree," but only those human beings who do not have the "seal of God upon the foreheads" (9:4). This recalls the angel having a "seal of the living God" (7:2), who directed the four angels, "Do not harm the earth nor the sea nor the trees, until we have sealed the servants of our God upon their foreheads" (7:3). As among the divinely sealed servants (1:1; 2:20) designated for participation in eternal heavenly life and worship (7:4–17), the audience are thus reassured that they are not to be harmed by the locusts of the fifth trumpeting.

Authority "was given" by God to the locusts as the deadly scorpions of the earth have authority (9:3b). But it "was given" to them that they may not "kill" those human beings not having the seal of God, but only that they will be tormented for a limited period of five months, and their torment is as the torment of a scorpion when it stings a human being (9:5). This further indicates to the audience that they are not to be tormented by the locusts, since among the audience are the slaughtered souls' fellow servants and brothers who are going to be "killed" even as they (6:11). That the torment is that of a "scorpion" when it stings a "human being" underscores that the authority the "scorpions" of the earth have and that was given to the locusts (9:3b) is to be exercised only against those "human beings" not having the seal of God (9:4).

In ironic contrast to "in the days" of Antipas who was killed (2:13) by human beings not having the seal of God, "in those days human beings will seek death and they will not find it, and they will desire to die but death will flee from them" (9:6). At the third trumpeting many of the "human beings died" from the embittered waters (8:11). But at the fifth trumpeting those "human beings" not having the seal of God will desire to "die" but death will flee from them. Despite the fact that "Death" and Hades were given the authority to kill a fourth of the earth (6:8), human beings will seek "death" but "death" will flee from them. This underlines for the audience the ultimate divine authority the exalted Jesus has over death as the one who has the keys of "Death" and of Hades (1:18).

The likenesses of the locusts that came out to the earth (9:3) from the smoke of the shaft of the abyss (9:2) were like horses prepared for battle (9:7a). The seven angels "prepared" themselves to trumpet the seven trumpets (8:6) that bring woe to those inhabiting upon the earth

(8:13). Similarly, the locusts of the fifth trumpeting that initiates the final three woes (8:13) were like horses "prepared" for battle on earth.[10]

The dramatic description of the strikingly supernatural appearance of the locusts suggests their heavenly authority and source (9:7–10). That they had "upon their heads as crowns like gold" (9:7b) associates them with the twenty-four elders in heaven, recalling that they had "upon their heads golden crowns" (4:4). That the locusts have faces "as faces of human beings" (9:7c) likens them to the third of the four living creatures in heaven, the one who has the "face as of a human being" (4:7). It is also appropriate for the divine authority given to them to harm only those "human beings" not having the seal of God (9:4).

In contrast to the divinely exalted Jesus whose "hair" is a heavenly white (1:14), the locusts, with faces as faces of human beings, had "hair" as "hair" of "women" (9:8a) and thus of female human beings on earth. This associates them with the "woman" Jezebel, the false prophetess who teaches and misleads members of the audience to engage in idolatrous worship (2:20). That teeth of the locusts were "as of lions" (9:8b) gives them heavenly associations. The first of the four living creatures is the one "like a lion" (4:7) in heaven. And Jesus conquered death and was exalted to heaven as the "lion" of the tribe of Judah (5:5).

Whereas the one who conquers will shepherd the nations to eternal life in heaven with an "iron" staff (2:27), the locusts had breastplates as breastplates of "iron" (9:9:a) for their battle on earth. The reference to the "wings" of the locusts (9:9b) likens them to the four living creatures in heaven, each one of whom has six "wings" (4:8). The sound of the wings of the locusts was "as a sound of chariots of many horses running for battle" (9:9b). This dramatically underscores and intensifies for the audience that the locusts, with their heavenly associations, were "like horses prepared for battle" on earth (9:7).

The locusts "have tails like scorpions, and stingers, and in their tails is their authority to harm human beings for five months" (9:10). This emphatically reinforces that "authority" was given to the locusts as

---

10. "That idolatry is one of the major sins for which these people are being punished is evident from 8:13, which labels the victims of the last three trumpets as 'earth-dwellers,' a technical term in the Apocalypse for idolaters" (Beale, *Revelation*, 498).

the "scorpions" of the earth have "authority" (9:3). But the locusts, with faces as those of "human beings" (9:7), "will harm" only those "human beings" not having the seal of God (9:4). They will torment them for a significant but limited period of "five months" with the torment of a "scorpion" when it stings a "human being" (9:5).

The locusts have over them not an earthly king, like the "kings" of the earth who hid themselves from the anger of the divine Lamb (6:15), the ruler of the "kings" of the earth (1:5). But they have over them as "king" the angel of the abyss (9:11a). The star that had fallen out of heaven to the earth when the fifth "angel" trumpeted, the star to which was given by God the key of the shaft of the "abyss" (9:1), so that it opened the shaft of the "abyss" (9:2a), is thus now explicitly identified as "the angel of the abyss." A "name for him in Hebrew is Abaddon ['Destruction'] and in Greek he has the name Apollyon ['Destroyer']" (9:11b).[11] This associates the angel of the abyss with the rider over the pale green horse, recalling that a "name for him" is Death (6:8). But his deadly destruction is authoritatively controlled by the divinely exalted Jesus, who has the keys of Death and of Hades (1:18). The audience are thus assured that the locusts are also ultimately under divine, heavenly, angelic control.

After the vision of the locusts which "came out" to the earth from the smoke of the shaft of the abyss opened by the angelic star at the fifth trumpeting (9:3), the vision of the first woe correspondingly "has gone away" (9:12a). That "coming still are two woes after these" (9:12b) recalls the eagle's announcement of the visions of the three "woes" yet to come "from the rest of the sounds of the trumpet of the three angels who are about to trumpet" (8:13). The audience have thus been attuned to listen for the report of two more woes to those inhabiting upon the earth (8:13) in divine response to the prayer of the slaughtered souls for judgment and vindication from those inhabiting upon the earth (6:10).

---

11. "John translates the Hebrew for the sake of the mixed, Jewish-Hellenistic audience in his community" (Smalley, *Revelation*, 234).

4d) Vision of Sixth Trumpet: Release of the Four Angels/ Horses with Riders (9:13–21)

A   a) [13] Then the sixth *angel* trumpeted, and I heard one sound from the *four* horns of the **golden** altar before God, [14a] saying to the sixth *angel*,

      b) [14b] the one having the trumpet,

   a′) [14c] "Release the *four angels* who are bound at the great river Euphrates." [15a] Then were released the *four angels* who had been prepared for this hour and day and month and year,

B   a) [15b] so that they may **kill** a **third of the human beings**, [16] and the number of the armies of *horsemen* was twenty thousand of ten thousands, I heard their number. [17a] And thus I saw the *horses* in the vision

      b) [17b] and those sitting upon them,

   a′) [17c] having breastplates fiery red and dark blue and sulfurous yellow, and the heads of the *horses* as heads of lions, and **from their mouths was going out fire** and **smoke** and **sulfur**.

B′   a) [18a] From these three *plagues* were *killed* a **third of** *the human beings*,

      b) [18b] from the **fire** and the **smoke** and the **sulfur going out from their** *mouths*.

      c) [19a] For the authority of the **horses**

      b′) [19b] is in their *mouth* and in their tails, for their tails are like serpents, having heads and they harm with them.

   a′) [20a] Then the rest of *the human beings*, those who were not *killed* by these *plagues*,

A′   a) [20b] *did not repent* from the works of their hands,

PART TWO—*Shown What Must Happen after These Things (4:1—16:21)*

> b) [20c] so that they will not worship *the* demons and *the* idols—
>
> b′) [20d] *the* **golden** and *the* silver and *the* bronze and *the* stone and *the* wooden, which are able neither to observe nor hear nor walk—
>
> a′) [21] and they **did not repent** of their murders nor of their sorceries nor of their prostitution nor of their robberies.

The audience experience a transition from the summary notice that "one" woe has gone away but two more are on the way (9:12) to the "one" sound when the sixth angel trumpeted (9:13), indicating the introduction of the next woe. Indeed, the three woes were introduced when John reported that "I heard one eagle flying in midheaven saying with a great sound, 'Woe, woe, woe to those inhabiting upon the earth from the rest of the sounds of the trumpet of the three angels who are about to trumpet'" (8:13). And now, when the sixth angel trumpeted, the second of the three angels still to trumpet, John reports that "I heard one sound from the four horns of the golden altar before God" (9:13).

That one unified sound comes from the four "horns" of the golden altar before God (9:13) suggests a divine power and authority akin to that of the Lamb, who has seven "horns" (5:6).[12] The one sound comes from the four horns of the "golden altar before God." This is the "golden altar" upon which were the prayers of all the holy ones which include the prayer of the slaughtered souls (8:3). The prayers that ascended from the hand of the angel "before God" (8:4) were answered by God when the angel threw the censer filled from the fire of the "altar" in heaven down to the earth (8:5). This is in response to the prayer of the slaughtered souls under the "altar" (6:9) for judgment and vindication from those inhabiting upon the earth (6:10). Thus, the one sound from the four horns of the golden altar before God introduces the next woe as a further response to the prayer of the slaughtered souls.

The sixth angel to whom the one sound speaks (9:14a), the sixth angel who trumpeted (9:13), is redundantly referred to as the one having the "trumpet" (9:14b) to underline the identity of the sixth trum-

---

12. "'Four' connotes completeness and 'horns' represent power" (Beale, *Revelation*, 506).

peting with the rest of the sounds of the "trumpet" of the three angels about to trumpet (8:13). The divine Lamb was the one worthy to open the scroll and "release" its seals (5:2), and the audience have worshiped Jesus Christ as the one who "released" us from our sins by his blood (1:5). Communicating a divine power akin to that of the Lamb, the one sound from the four horns commands the sixth angel, "Release the four angels who are bound at the great river Euphrates" (9:14c).[13] In contrast to the "four angels" standing upon the four corners of the earth, holding back the destructive force of the four winds of the earth so that wind may not blow upon the earth (7:1), these "four angels" are to be released so that they can unleash their destructive force upon the earth in further answer to the prayer of the slaughtered souls.

In precise response to the divine command to the sixth angel to "release" the "four angels" bound at the great river Euphrates (9:14), then were "released" the "four angels who had been prepared for this hour and day and month and year, so that they may kill a third of the human beings" (9:15). At the fifth trumpeting the destructive locusts were like horses "prepared" for battle (9:7) to harm "human beings" for five months (9:10). And now, by way of progression to this destruction, the four angels had been "prepared" to kill a third of the "human beings." Whereas the locusts were not allowed to "kill" human beings (9:5), now the angels are to "kill" a "third" of the human beings, complementing the previous destructions of a "third" of non-human created things (8:7–12).

That the four angels had been prepared to kill a third of the human beings at "this hour and day and month and year" (9:15) underscores the divinely appointed time for the woe from the sixth trumpeting. The reference to this "hour" resonates with the "hour" of the testing that is about to come upon the whole world to test those inhabiting upon the earth (3:10), as well as with the anticipated divinely appointed "hour" of Jesus' final coming (3:3). The reference to this "day" resonates with the divinely appointed great "day" of the anger of God and the Lamb (6:17), the day of final judgment. And the reference to this "month" recalls the

---

13. "The Euphrates River represented the eastern edge of the Roman Empire, beyond which are presumed to be sinister and threatening nations" (Roloff, *Revelation*, 118).

divinely appointed period of five "months" for the torment and harm of human beings (9:5, 10).

In a further progression to the locusts who were like "horses" prepared for battle (9:7), whose wings had the sound of many "horses" running for battle (9:9), the number of the angelic armies of "horsemen" that resulted when the sixth angel released the four angels "was twenty thousand of ten thousands" (9:16). The large "number" of the armies of horsemen, twenty thousand of "ten thousands," is emphasized as John adds, "I heard their number" (9:16). Such a large number underlines the divine heavenly source and authority of the armies, as it resonates with John's report that "I heard" the sound of the heavenly worshipers, and "their number" was "ten thousands of ten thousands" and thousands of thousands (5:11). It also recalls his report that "I heard" the large "number" of one hundred forty-four thousand of those sealed for heavenly life and worship (7:4).

At the fifth trumpeting the locusts were compared to "horses" (9:7) and had the sound of many "horses" (9:9). But now, in further progression, at the sixth trumpeting John saw actual "horses" in the vision (9:17a) and those sitting upon them (9:17b), that is, the angelic "horsemen" (9:16). That he saw the horses in the "vision" and those "sitting" upon them further connotes their heavenly association, as it recalls that John saw God himself in "vision" as one "sitting" upon the heavenly throne (4:3). Whereas the locusts had "breastplates" as "breastplates" of iron (9:9), the horses and their riders have "breastplates" that are "fiery red and dark blue and sulfurous yellow, and the heads of the horses as heads of lions, and from their mouths was going out fire and smoke and sulfur" (9:17c).

Whereas at the fifth trumpeting there were on the "heads" of the locusts crowns like gold (9:7) and their teeth were "as of lions" (9:8), at the sixth trumpeting the "heads" of the horses were "as heads of lions" (9:17). John previously saw that "from the mouth" of the exalted Jesus a sharp two-edged sword is "going out" to execute divine judgment (1:16). Similarly and in close continuity, fire and smoke and sulfur was "going out" "from the mouths" of the horses to execute divine judgment (9:17) on a third of the human beings (9:15). This further responds to

John's Visions of the Seven Angels Trumpeting Their Seven Trumpets

the prayer of the slaughtered souls for judgment and vindication of their blood from those inhabiting upon the earth (6:10).

The "fire" from the mouths of the horses (9:17) is in continuity with the "fire" of the altar (8:5), the "fire" mixed with blood (8:7), and the mountain with "fire" burning (8:8) as responses to the prayer of the slaughtered souls. The "smoke" from the mouths of the horses (9:17) is in continuity with the "smoke" that ascended from the shaft of the abyss as "smoke" of a great furnace (9:2), the "smoke" from which locusts came out to the earth (9:3). It corresponds to the "smoke" of the incense that ascended with the prayers of the holy ones (8:4). In accord with the "fiery red," "dark blue," and "sulfurous yellow" colors of the breastplates of the angelic horsemen, the "fire" and "smoke" and "sulfur" was going out of the mouths of the horses (9:17). This continues the divine response to the prayer of the slaughtered souls for judgment and vindication of their blood from those inhabiting upon the earth (6:10).

From these "three" plagues, which are part of the second of the three woes to come from the rest of the sounds of the trumpet of the "three" angels about to trumpet (8:13), "were killed a third of the human beings" (9:18a). This fulfills the purpose for the release of the four angels, namely, "so that they may kill a third of the human beings" (9:15). It is emphasized that the divine authority of the "horses" to kill (9:19a) is in their "mouth" (9:19b). Indeed, from the "mouths" of the "horses was going out fire and smoke and sulfur" (9:17). And it is precisely and pointedly "from the fire and the smoke and the sulfur going out from their mouths" that a third of the human beings were killed (9:18).

At the fifth trumpeting the destructive locusts had "tails" like scorpions and in their "tails" is their divine "authority" to "harm" human beings for five months (9:10). And now, similarly, at the sixth trumpeting the divine "authority" of the horses is in their "tails," for their "tails" are like serpents, having heads and they "harm" with them (9:19). The rest of the "human beings," the two-thirds who were not "killed" by these "plagues" (9:20a), that is, precisely and pointedly from the three "plagues" from which were "killed" a third of the "human beings" (9:18), remarkably "did not repent from the works of their hands" (9:20b).

That the human beings who were still living did not "repent" from the "works" of their hands (9:20) recalls that the exalted Jesus gave the false prophetess Jezebel time so that she may "repent," but she does not wish to "repent" from her "prostitution," her idolatrous worship (2:21). He promises a great tribulation for those committing the "adultery" of idolatry with her, if they do not "repent" from her "works" of idolatry (2:22). In poignant contrast to those who "will worship" the true God (3:9; 4:10), and those who "worshiped" the true God (5:14; 7:11), they did not repent, so that they "will not worship" the demons and the idols, which are merely works made with their own hands (9:20).

The idols the unrepentant worship are "the golden and the silver and the bronze and the stone and the wooden, which are able neither to observe nor hear nor walk" (9:20).[14] Ironically, they worship "golden" idols rather than the true God before whom is the "golden" altar in heaven (9:13). And, ironically, they worship idols which are "able neither to observe" nor hear nor "walk" rather than the divine Lamb who is worthy to open the scroll which no one was "able" neither to open "nor observe" it (5:3), and who is "walking" in the midst of the seven golden lampstands in heaven (2:1).

The human beings still living after the sixth trumpeting did not "repent" from the works of their hands, which are the "idols" they worship (9:20) and their murders, sorceries, idolatrous "prostiution," and robberies (9:21). This includes the immoral behavior that results from and is closely identified with their false worship.[15] Their emphatic failure to repent reinforces the repeated exhortations for the audience to "repent" (2:5, 16; 3:3, 19) from any association with idolatrous worship. They are thus not to eat the "food sacrificed to idols" or "engage in prostitution" (2:14, 20), but to "repent" of the false prophetess Jezebel's "prostitution" (2:21), her idolatrous worship. They are to repent and thus worship the true God and the divine Lamb Jesus Christ for eternal life in the Spirit of authentic prophecy.

---

14. "Jewish and Christian denunciations of idolatry frequently include a list of the materials out of which pagan deities were constructed, with the implication that this is incompatible with the belief that they are living beings" (Aune, *Revelation 6–16*, 542).

15. "Such sins are either part of the activities involved in idolatry or they actually become acts of idolatry themselves" (Beale, *Revelation*, 519–20).

5c′) Vision of the Mighty Angel with the Small Scroll (10:1–11)

A   a) ¹⁰:¹ᵃ Then I saw another mighty angel descending **out of heaven** clothed with a cloud,

    b) ¹ᵇ and a rainbow ***upon*** his head

      c) ¹ᶜ and his face **as** the sun and his ***feet as*** pillars of fire,

        d) ²ᵃ and having in his hand a **small scroll** that **had been opened**,

      c′) ²ᵇ and he placed his right ***foot***

    b′) ²ᶜ ***upon*** the sea, and his left ***upon*** the earth,

  a′) ³ and cried out with a great **sound** just as a lion roaring, and when he cried out, the seven thunders **spoke their own sounds**, ⁴ and when the seven thunders **spoke, I was about** to write, but **I heard** a **sound *out of heaven*** saying, "Seal the things the seven thunders **spoke**, and do not write them."

B ⁵ Then the angel, whom I saw standing upon the **sea** and upon the **earth**, raised his right hand to **heaven**

  C ⁶ᵃ and swore by the one living for the ages of the ages,

B′ ⁶ᵇ who created **heaven** and the things in it and the **earth** and the things in it and the **sea** and the things in it,

A′   a) ⁶ᶜ "There will be no more time, ⁷ but in the days of the **sound** of the seventh angel, whenever **he may be about** to trumpet, then is completed the mystery of God, **as** he brought good news to **his own** servants the ***prophets***." ⁸ᵃ Then the **sound** which **I heard out of heaven** is *again* speaking with me and **saying**,

    b) ⁸ᵇ "Go, *receive* the scroll that **had been opened** in **the hand of the angel** standing upon the sea and upon the earth." ⁹ Then I went to the angel, **saying** for him to give me the ***small scroll***, and he **says** to me, "*Receive* and ***devour it***, and it will ***embitter*** your ***stomach***, but in your ***mouth*** it will be ***sweet as honey.***"

b′) ¹⁰ Then I ***received*** the ***small scroll*** from ***the hand of the angel*** and ***I devoured it***, and in my ***mouth*** it was ***sweet as honey*** but when I had eaten it, my ***stomach*** was ***embittered*** (Ezek 2:8—3:3).

a′) ¹¹ Then they are **saying** to me, "It is necessary that you ***again prophesy*** about many peoples and nations and tongues and kings."

When John saw the scroll sealed with seven seals upon the right of the one sitting upon the throne in heaven (5:1), he reported, "I saw a mighty angel proclaiming in a great sound, 'Who is worthy to open the scroll and release its seals?'" (5:2). And now he reports, "I saw another mighty angel descending out of heaven" (10:1a). Whereas the first mighty angel was in heaven, this second mighty angel is "descending out of heaven," recalling the promise of the exalted Jesus that the new Jerusalem is "descending out of heaven" from my God (3:12). The slaughtered souls in heaven prayed for judgment and vindication from those inhabiting upon the "earth" (6:10). In response, at the fifth trumpeting an angelic star fell "out of heaven" to the "earth" (9:1), and then destructive locusts came out to the "earth" (9:3). But now, the mighty angel with a small scroll descended "out of heaven" (10:1) and placed his left foot upon the "earth" (10:2).

Similarities with the exalted Jesus highlight the divine authority of this mighty angel. The exalted Jesus is coming with the "clouds" from heaven (1:7), and the mighty angel is descending out of heaven clothed with a "cloud" (10:1a). The "head" and hair of the exalted Jesus are a heavenly white, his eyes "as a flame of fire" (1:14; 2:18), "his feet" like burnished bronze, as in a furnace of refining (1:15; 2:18), and his countenance appears "as the sun" (1:16). On the "head" of the mighty angel is a "rainbow" with divine associations (10:1b), recalling that a "rainbow" was around the throne of God in heaven (4:3). And his face is "as the sun" and "his feet as pillars of fire" (10:1c). In contrast to the destructive locusts with faces "as faces of human beings" (9:7), the divinely authori-

John's Visions of the Seven Angels Trumpeting Their Seven Trumpets

tative mighty angel has a "face as the sun," suggesting a brighter, more favorable task for him.[16]

The rider of the black horse "has a scale in his hand" (6:5), indicating his authority over the price of food (6:6). The exalted Jesus "has in his right hand" seven stars (1:16), indicating his authority over the angels of the seven churches (1:20). Similarly, the mighty angel "has in his hand" a small scroll (10:2a), indicating his authority over it. In contrast to the human beings who did not repent of the works coming from their merely human "hands" (9:20), the mighty angel has a small scroll in his divinely authoritative "hand." That the "small scroll had been opened" (10:2a) by God (divine passive) closely associates it with the sealed "scroll" (5:1–9), each of whose seven seals the divine Lamb "opened" (6:1, 3, 5, 7, 9, 12; 8:1).[17] In contrast to the angelic star who "opened" the shaft of the abyss so that the "sun" was darkened (9:2), the mighty angel with the "opened" small scroll has a face as bright as the "sun" (10:1c).

The exalted Jesus performed a divinely authoritative gesture when he "placed" his "right" hand "upon" John (1:17), and identified himself as eternally living with power over death (1:18). Similarly, the mighty angel with the heavenly rainbow "upon" his head (10:1b) performed a divinely authoritative gesture when he "placed" his "right" foot (10:2b) "upon" the sea, and his left "upon" the earth (10:2c). That the mighty angel placed his right foot "upon the sea" and his left "upon the earth" indicates a universal dimension for the opened small scroll in his hand. It resonates with the universal dimension of the protection provided by the four angels holding back the four winds of the earth so that wind may not blow "upon the earth" nor "upon the sea" (7:1). And it resonates with the universal dimension of the worship of God and the Lamb from every creature "upon the earth" and "upon the sea" (5:13).

The angel John saw having a seal of the living God "cried out with a great sound" to the four angels given the authority to harm the "earth" and the "sea" (7:2). He told them not to harm the "earth" nor the "sea" nor the trees, until they have sealed the servants of God (7:3). Similarly,

---

16. "[T]his angel is not Christ but is the special herald of Christ and shares in his glory and his mission" (Osborne, *Revelation*, 394).

17. "[T]he scroll might become 'small' because it has to be swallowed by John" (Lupieri, *Apocaplypse*, 168).

PART TWO—*Shown What Must Happen after These Things (4:1—16:21)*

the mighty angel with his feet upon the "sea" and upon the "earth" (10:2) that John saw "cried out with a great sound" just as a lion roaring (10:3a). This resonates with the worship not only of the large crowd who "are crying out with a great sound" as they worship God and the Lamb (7:10), but of the slaughtered souls who "cried out with a great sound" as they prayed for divine judgment and vindication from those inhabiting upon the "earth" (6:10). The locusts and horsemen had features of "lions" (9:8, 17), but the mighty angel cried out just as a "lion" roaring, further associating him with Jesus, the "lion" who conquered to open the sealed scroll (5:5).

When the Lamb opened the first seal, one of the four living creatures issued the command to come as a "sound of thunder" (6:1), underlining its divine authority. Lightnings and "sounds" and "thunders" come from the throne of God in heaven (4:5a). When the angel threw the fiery censer from the altar in heaven to the earth, there came to be "thunders" and "sounds" and lightnings and an earthquake (8:5) in divine response to the prayers of the holy ones (8:3–4), which include the prayer of the slaughtered souls under the altar (6:9). And now, when the mighty angel cried out, the seven "thunders" in heaven spoke their own "sounds" (10:3b) suggestive of divine revelation authoritatively proclaimed.[18]

When John was in Spirit on the Lord's day, he heard a great "sound" as a trumpet (1:10). It told him to "write" what he was to observe in a scroll and send it to the seven churches (1:11). He then observed the "sound" that was "speaking" with him (1:12) the divine revelation he was to include in the scroll that is the book of Revelation. That same "sound," which John heard "speaking" with him, called him to ascend to heaven and "I will show you the things it is necessary to happen after these things" (4:1), that is, more of the "revelation of Jesus Christ that God gave him to show his servants the things it is necessary to happen soon" (1:1), the content of Revelation. When the seven thunders "spoke" their own "sounds" (10:3), John was about to "write." But he heard a "sound out of heaven," closely associated with the mighty angel

---

18. "Nearly all agree that this echoes Ps. 29 (indicated by the article pointing to the OT allusion), where God speaks like thunder seven times" (Osborne, *Revelation*, 396).

descending "out of heaven" (10:1). It said, "Seal the things the seven thunders spoke, and do not write them" (10:4).

John is thus not to write the things the seven thunders in heaven authoritatively spoke as divine revelation in the scroll which is the book of Revelation. That there are things divinely spoken that John heard but did not write down for his audience enhances his prophetic authority and underlines the sovereignty of God. He has heard revealed even more of the prophetic word of God than he has written in the book.[19] This is confirmed as he was given the divine authority to "seal" the things the seven thunders spoke (10:4), a divine authority analogous to that of "we" angels who have "sealed" the servants of God (7:3, 4, 5, 8). That the things the seven thunders spoke are to be "sealed" accentuates the audience's focus on the small scroll in the hand of the mighty angel that has been "opened" (10:2).

The angel whom John saw "standing upon the sea" and "upon the earth" (10:5a) was the mighty angel who performed a gesture of divine authority when he placed his right foot "upon the sea" and his left "upon the earth" (10:2). This repeated reference to the authoritative action by the mighty angel serves to emphasize the universal relevance of the small scroll in his hand. It recalls the universal protection provided by the four angels "standing" upon the four corners of the earth, so that wind may not blow "upon the earth" nor "upon the sea" nor upon any tree (7:1). This mighty angel, who had a small scroll in his "hand" and authoritatively placed his "right" foot upon the sea (10:2), raised his "right hand" to heaven (10:5b), the source of his universal divine authority.

The mighty angel then swore by the one living for the ages of the ages (10:6a). This is the one who created the heaven to which the angel raised his right hand as the source of his authority (10:5), the things in it, the earth and the sea upon which the angel stands with divine authority (10:5), and the things in them (10:6b). The mighty angel swore by the "one living for the ages of the ages," who "created" everything in heaven, earth, and sea. This means that he swore by the divine authority of both

---

19. "The major message is one of sovereignty. God is in control, and the saints do not need to know all the details" (Osborne, *Revelation*, 398). See also Ruiz, "Hearing," 91–111.

PART TWO—*Shown What Must Happen after These Things (4:1—16:21)*

God and the Lamb. The living creatures and the elders in heaven worship God as the "one living for the ages of the ages" (4:9, 10), who "created" all things (4:11). And John worshiped the exalted Jesus, the divine Lamb, as the one who declared that "I am living for the ages of the ages" (1:18), the one who is the beginning of the "creation" of God (3:14).

The souls under the altar in heaven were divinely informed that they will rest "yet" a little "time," until would be fulfilled both their prophetic "fellow servants" and their brothers who are about to be killed even as they (6:11). But now the mighty angel swore that there will be "no more time" (10:6c), "but in the days of the sound of the seventh angel, whenever he may be about to trumpet, then is completed the mystery of God, as he brought good news to his own servants the prophets" (10:7). At the fifth trumpeting, "in the days" when human beings seek death, they will not find it (9:6) in accord with God's plan. But "in the days" of the seventh trumpeting the mystery of God, which includes the death of his prophetic servants, is completed. That the seventh angel, the last of the three angels "about to trumpet" the final three woes (8:13), is "about to trumpet" suggests ramifications for the prophetic servants "about to be" killed like the slaughtered souls (6:11).

At the seventh trumpeting the "mystery" of God will be completed (10:7), which involves the heavenly status and destiny of the audience represented by the seven churches. According to the "mystery" of the seven stars and seven golden lampstands, the seven churches have angels and lampstands, indicating their heavenly status and destiny (1:20).[20] The audience were initially addressed as "servants" of God (1:1), exhorted to hear the words of the "prophecy" and keep the things written in the book of Revelation (1:3). Included in the audience are prophetic "servants" of Jesus being misled by the false "prophetess" Jezebel (2:20). The audience are to identify themselves with the prophetic "servants" of God, who have been divinely sealed (7:3) for participation in the eternal life and worship of heaven. At the seventh trumpeting God will bring

---

20. "Mystery" is a term that "occurs four times in Revelation (with 1:20, 17:5, 7), and its background is in its apocalyptic function to designate those divine secrets that have been hidden from past generations and only revealed to the people of God in these last days" (Osborne, *Revelation*, 400).

good news to his own "servants" the "prophets" (10:7), among whom are the audience called to worship for eternal life in the Spirit of prophecy.

The "sound" John reported that "I heard out of heaven," recalling the "sound" that "I heard out of heaven," which told John to seal the things the seven thunders "spoke" as divine revelation (10:4), is again "speaking" to John with divine authority (10:8a). When the Lamb "received the scroll" (5:8) from God (5:7), he was worshiped as worthy to "receive the scroll" and "open" its seals (5:9). Since the Lamb has already opened the sealed scroll, the sound out of heaven directed John to go, "receive the scroll" that "had been opened," that is, the "small scroll" that "had been opened" (10:2), in the hand of the angel standing upon the sea and upon the earth (10:8b). The sealed scroll that the Lamb received from God and opened is the same as the small scroll that had been opened in the hand of the mighty angel. This accords with the revelation God gave to Jesus Christ and sent through his angel to John (1:1).

When John went to tell the angel to give him the small scroll, the mighty angel said to him, "Receive and devour it, and it will embitter your stomach, but in your mouth it will be sweet as honey" (10:9).[21] What John then did corresponds precisely to what the angel told him and alludes to the divine commissioning of the prophet Ezekiel (Ezek 2:8–3:3). John reports, "Then I received the small scroll from the hand of the angel and I devoured it, and in my mouth it was sweet as honey but when I had eaten it, my stomach was embittered" (10:10).

That the small scroll was in John's "mouth" sweet as honey (10:9, 10) indicates the prophetic authority it gives John as the word of God with a pleasant taste. It accords with the divine authority in the "mouth" of the horses at the sixth trumpeting (9:19). And it recalls that a two-edged sword is coming out from the "mouth" of the exalted Jesus (1:16; 2:16), symbolic of the word of God with its power to execute judgment. That the stomach of John was "embittered" by the small scroll (10:10) containing the prophetic word of God connotes its death-bringing

---

21. "Revelation's first audiences, probably hearing this read out during a eucharistic celebration, might detect echoes of Jesus' command at the Last Supper. The Lord's words, no less than his body and blood, are to be taken and devoured" (Boxall, *Revelation*, 157).

dimension. It recalls that at the third trumpeting many of the human beings died from the waters for they were "embittered" (8:11).

The mighty angel who was "saying" to John (10:9), and the sound out of heaven that was "saying" to him (10:4, 8), are now "saying" to him (10:11a), "It is necessary that you again prophesy about many peoples and nations and tongues and kings" (10:11). In accord with the divine necessity that forms the purpose of the book of Revelation—to show the things "it is necessary" to happen (1:1; 4:1)—"it is necessary" that John again prophesy. And in accord with the sound he heard out of heaven "again" speaking divine revelation with him (10:8a) after the seven thunders spoke (10:3–4), John is "again" to prophesy. Because of his prophetic witness, John, as a brother and fellow sharer with his audience, was on the island called Patmos on account of the word of God and witness of Jesus (1:9). That he is again to "prophesy" will thus provide a further example to be imitated by his audience, who are to hear the words of the "prophecy" and keep the prophetic things written in the book of Revelation (1:3).

John is to prophesy about the participation of many "peoples" and "nations" and "tongues" and kings (10:11) in the universal heavenly worship of God and the divine Lamb.[22] The numberless large crowd John saw in heaven worshiping God and the Lamb (7:10) were from every "nation" and tribes and "peoples" and "tongues" (7:9). These groups, representative of all humankind, are to participate in heavenly worship and eternal life, because the Lamb bought for God with his blood those from every tribe and "tongue" and "people" and "nation" (5:9).

John, a brother and fellow sharer with his audience in the "kingdom" (1:9), is to prophesy about many "kings" (10:11), because they are to be included among those the Lamb made into a "kingdom" and priests for the worship of God, and they "will reign" upon the earth (5:10; 1:6). Rather than be subject to the destructive locusts whose "king" is the angel of the abyss (9:11), they are to be subject to Jesus, the ruler of the "kings" of the earth (1:5). He has made it possible for the "kings" of the earth not to hide from, but to worship God and the Lamb (6:15). Thus, John is to prophesy about all humankind, who are

22. It seems that "about" rather than "against" is the better translation for the preposition in 10:11; see Osborne, *Revelation*, 405.

to participate in the heavenly worship of God and the divine Lamb for eternal life in the Spirit of prophesy.

6b′) Martyrdom and Vindication of the Two Prophetic Witnesses (11:1–14)

A a) ¹¹:¹ Then was *given* to *me* a rod like a staff, **saying**, "Rise and measure the temple of God and the altar and those worshiping in it,

    b) ²ᵃ but the *outer* courtyard of the temple

    b′) ²ᵇ leave *out* and do not measure it,

  a′) ²ᶜ for it was *given* to the nations, and they will trample the holy city for forty-two months. ³ Then I will *give* to *my* two witnesses and they will prophesy one thousand two hundred sixty days clothed with sackcloth." ⁴ These are the two olive trees and the two lampstands that before the Lord of the earth are **standing** (Zech 4:1–3, 11–14),

B a) ⁵ and if anyone *wishes* to harm them, fire goes out from their mouth and devours their enemies. And if anyone may *wish* to harm them, it is thus necessary that he be **killed**.

    b) ⁶ᵃ These **have** the *authority* to close heaven,

      c) ⁶ᵇ so that rain may not fall during the days of their **prophecy**,

    b′) ⁶ᶜ and they **have authority** over the waters to turn them into blood

  a′) ⁶ᵈ and to strike the earth with every plague as often as they may *wish*. ⁷ And when they have completed their witness, the beast ascending from the abyss will make with them a battle and will conquer them and will *kill* them.

C ⁸ᵃ And their **corpse** is on the main street of the great city,

PART TWO—*Shown What Must Happen after These Things (4:1—16:21)*

> **D** ⁸ᵇ which is called spiritually Sodom and Egypt, where also their Lord was crucified,
>
> **C'** ⁹ then those from the peoples and tribes and tongues and nations observe their **corpse** three and a half days and their **corpses** they would not let be placed in a tomb.
>
> **B'** a) ¹⁰ᵃ Then *those inhabiting upon the earth*
>
> > b) ¹⁰ᵇ rejoice *over them*
> >
> > c) ¹⁰ᶜ and celebrate
> >
> > b') ¹⁰ᵈ and they will send gifts *to one another*,
>
> a') ¹⁰ᵉ for these two **prophets** tormented *those inhabiting upon the earth*.
>
> **A'** a) ¹¹ᵃ But after *three* and a half days a Spirit of life from *God came in* among them and they **stood** on their feet,
>
> > b) ¹¹ᵇ and *great fear fell*
> >
> > c) ¹¹ᶜ upon those *watching* them.
> >
> > > d) ¹²ᵃ Then they heard a great sound out of heaven **saying** to them, "*Ascend* here!"
> > >
> > > d') ¹²ᵇ so they *ascended* to heaven in a cloud,
> >
> > c') ¹²ᶜ and their enemies *watched* them.
> >
> > b') ¹³ᵃ Then at that hour there came to be a *great* earthquake and a tenth of the city *fell* and seven thousand names of human beings were killed and the rest became *fearful*
>
> a') ¹³ᵇ and they **gave** glory to the *God* of heaven. ¹⁴ The second woe **has gone away**. Behold, the *third* woe is coming soon.

In continuity with what the divinely authoritative voices are saying to "me," John (10:11), then was given to "me" by God (divine passive) a rod like a "staff" (11:1a). The comparison associates this rod with the iron "staff" (2:27) by which the audience, as those who are to conquer

142

the threat of idolatrous worship, will shepherd the nations into heavenly worship and eternal life with the divine authority given them by Jesus (2:26–28; 7:17). The divinely authoritative voices are "saying" to John, "It is necessary that you again prophesy about many peoples and nations and tongues and kings" (10:11). Then the voice of the divine being who gave John the rod is "saying" (11:1), "Rise and measure the temple of God and the altar and those worshiping in it, but the outer courtyard of the temple leave out and do not measure it, for it was given to the nations, and they will trample the holy city for forty-two months" (11:1–2). Thus, John's measuring is a prophetic gesture that is part of his prophesying about the nations.

The divinely authoritative voice directs John to rise and metaphorically to "measure," that is, to take account of, "the temple of God and the altar and those worshiping in it" (11:1) as key elements in the holiness of true heavenly worship.[23] The "temple of God" John is to "measure" is the heavenly "temple of my God" in which the exalted Jesus promises to make the one who conquers false worship a permanent "pillar" (3:12). It is the heavenly "temple" in which the numberless large crowd offer worship to God day and night (7:15). The "altar" is the heavenly "altar" under which the slaughtered souls offer their prayer (6:9), the "altar" upon which are the prayers of all the holy ones (8:3b), and the "altar" from which comes a heavenly response to the prayers (8:3a, 5; 9:13). Those "worshiping" in the temple are those who "will worship" (3:9; 4:10; 9:20) and "have worshiped" not idols but the true God (5:14; 7:11).[24]

But John is emphatically to "leave out" the "outer" courtyard, the earthly dimension, of the heavenly temple (11:2a) and not to "measure" it as part of true heavenly worship (11:2b).[25] Just as the measuring rod was divinely "given" to John (11:1), so the outer courtyard of the temple was divinely "given" to the "nations" (11:2c), the "nations" over which

---

23. "The background to this passage is Ezek. 40–42 itself, where the measuring of the eschatological temple provides a detailed description of the future temple" (Smalley, *Revelation*, 271). "Measuring the sanctuary seems to function to mark it out as belonging to God" (Boxall, *Revelation*, 160).

24. Dalrymple, "Revelation 11,1," 387–94.

25. The outer court "is the earthly expression of the temple" (Beale, *Revelation*, 568).

PART TWO—*Shown What Must Happen after These Things (4:1—16:21)*

Jesus promised that "I will give" to the one who conquers idolatry the divine authority (2:26) to shepherd them to heavenly worship and eternal life (2:27-28; 7:17). But before the nations are led to heavenly worship, God has allowed them metaphorically to "trample" with their idolatrous worship the holy "city," the "city of my God," the heavenly Jerusalem (3:12), for forty-two months (11:2c). Just as human beings will be tormented by the locusts at the fifth trumpeting for a limited period of five "months" (9:5, 10), so the nations will "trample" the holy city for a divinely limited period of forty-two "months."[26]

A measuring rod was divinely "given" to John (11:1) as part of his task to "prophesy" (10:11). Similarly, a divine voice promises that "I will give" to my two witnesses and "they will prophesy" one thousand two hundred sixty days (11:3), the equivalent of the forty-two months the nations will trample the holy city (11:2). The reference to "my witnesses" associates them with Antipas, who was killed as "my witness" (2:13), as well as with Jesus, the faithful "witness" (1:5; 3:14). It also associates them with John, who in his prophetic ministry "witnessed" to the word of God and the "witness" of Jesus Christ, as did the slaughtered souls (1:2, 9; 6:9). The two witnesses, then, are representative examples for the audience, who, like John, have been given a prophetic task of hearing the words of the "prophecy" and keeping the things written in it (1:3).[27]

The two witnesses will be clothed with sackcloth when they prophesy (11:3) during the same divinely limited period of time that the nations will "trample" the holy city (11:2) through their involvement with idolatrous worship. They will be "clothed" with sackcloth in ironic contrast to their destiny of being "clothed" with white robes for their participation in heavenly worship and eternal life (7:13; cf. 3:5, 18; 4:4; 7:9). By being clothed with "sackcloth" indicative of mourning death, the two witnesses prophetically witness to and warn of the destructive

---

26. Jauhiainen, "Measuring," 507-26; Tavo, "Outer Court," 56-72; Hitchcock, "Temple," 219-36; den Dulk, "Measuring," 436-49. "The temporal designation of 42 months (11:2; 13:5) is also given in Revelation as 1,260 days (11:3; 12:6) and 'a time, times and half a time' (12:14) . . . It became a standard symbol for that limited period of time during which evil would be allowed free rein" (Mounce, *Revelation*, 215).

27. Dalrymple, *Two Witnesses*. The two witnesses "represent the whole community of faith, whose primary function is to be a prophetic witness" (Beale, *Revelation*, 573).

destiny of eternal death in store for those who do not repent from any engagement in or association with idolatrous worship. Their prophetic clothing recalls and resonates with the deadly destruction connoted by the sun becoming black as "sackcloth" made of hair at the opening of the sixth seal (6:12).[28]

That "these are the two olive trees and the two lampstands that before the Lord of earth are standing" (11:4; cf. Zech 4:1–3, 11–14) indicates the destiny of the two witnesses to be part of the large crowd of heavenly worshipers. They were similarly referred to as "these are" those coming from the great tribulation and they have washed their robes and whitened them in the blood of the Lamb (7:14).[29] That the two witnesses are the two "lampstands" further associates them with heavenly life and worship. It recalls that the seven "lampstands" indicate the heavenly dimension of the seven churches (1:20). As part of their prophetic task the two witnesses stand before the divine "Lord" of the earth in a prophetic gesture indicating that the "Lord" God is the object of true heavenly worship (1:8; 4:8, 11). And that the two witnesses are "standing" "before" the Lord of the earth further associates them with the large crowd "standing before" the throne and "before" the Lamb in heavenly worship (7:9).

The false prophetess Jezebel does not "wish" to repent from her "prostitution," her idolatrous worship (2:21). But if anyone "wishes" to harm the two prophetic witnesses against idolatrous worship, "fire goes out from their mouth and devours their enemies. And if anyone may wish to harm them, it is thus necessary that he be killed" (11:5). Anyone who wishes to "harm" the prophetic witnesses would be usurping the divine authority to "harm" human beings, as indicated at the fifth trumpeting (9:10). But ironically the prophetic witnesses make those who would harm them victims of the divine authority to kill, as "fire goes out from their mouth and devours them." This resonates with the divine authority of the angelic horsemen at the sixth trumpeting. "From their mouths was going out fire" (9:17), so that a third of the human beings were killed from the "fire going out from their mouths" (9:18).

---

28. "Their clothing indicates that the two are preachers of repentance: the sackcloth is a robe symbolizing sorrow and repentance" (Roloff, *Revelation*, 132).

29. Dalrymple, "These Are the Ones," 396–406.

PART TWO—*Shown What Must Happen after These Things (4:1—16:21)*

In ironic continuity with the prophetic task given to John after he reported that "I devoured" the small scroll and it became sweet as honey in "my mouth" (10:10; cf. 10:9), out of the "mouth" of the two prophetic witnesses fire comes out and "devours" their enemies (11:5). It is divinely "necessary" that John prophesy about many nations (10:11). Accordingly, it is thus divinely "necessary" for anyone who may wish to harm the witnesses closely associated with John, who will prophesy while the nations trample the holy city (11:2), to be killed (11:5) by God (divine passive).

At the sixth trumpeting a third of the human beings were "killed" by God (divine passive) from the plagues coming from the angelic horsemen under divine authority (9:18). But the rest of the human beings who were not "killed" by these plagues did not repent of their idolatrous worship (9:20). Thus it is divinely necessary that anyone who wishes to harm the two prophetic witnesses, rather than repent of the idolatrous worship against which the two witnesses prophesy, be "killed" (11:5). This accords with the warning of the exalted Jesus that "I will kill with death" (2:23) those who do not repent of the idolatrous worship practiced and taught by the false prophetess Jezebel (2:20–22).

The two prophetic witnesses "have" the "authority" to close heaven and they "have authority" over the waters to turn them into blood (11:6). They thus have divine destructive authority like that of the destructive locusts to whom were given authority as the scorpions of the earth "have authority" (9:3). The authority the two witnesses have to "close" heaven is a divine authority, resonating with that of the exalted Jesus, who has the authority to "close" that no other human being has (3:8; cf. 3:7). The witnesses have the destructive authority to close heaven so that rain may not fall during the "days" of their "prophecy" (11:6), that is, during the one thousand two hundred sixty "days" that they "will prophesy" against idolatrous worship (11:3). This reinforces the exhortation for the audience to hear the words of the "prophecy" written in the book of Revelation (1:3) by likewise witnessing against idolatrous worship.[30]

---

30. "Like Elijah, they are able to ward off their adversaries with fire (2 Kgs. 1:10; Sir. 48:3) and obstruct the sky so that no rain falls (1 Kgs. 17:1; Sir. 48:3); like Moses, they have the authority to change water into blood and thus intimidate their opponents with plagues (Exod. 7:17, 19–20)" (Roloff, *Revelation*, 130).

The two prophetic witnesses have divine destructive authority over the "waters" to turn them into "blood" (11:6). This recalls that at the second trumpeting the sea became "blood" (8:8) so that a third of its creatures died (8:9), and at the third trumpeting a third of the "waters" became wormwood and many of the human beings died (8:11). The two prophetic witnesses also have the divine destructive authority to strike the earth with every "plague" (11:6). This recalls that at the sixth trumpeting a third of the human beings were killed from three destructive "plagues" (9:18), but those who were not killed by these "plagues" did not repent of their idolatrous worship (9:20). In ironic contrast to anyone who "may wish" to harm them (11:5) rather than repent of idolatrous worship, the two prophetic witnesses have divine destructive authority to strike the earth with every plague as often as they "may wish" to encourage repentance from idolatrous worship (11:6).

When the two prophetic witnesses have "completed" their witness (11:7), they will have played a role in the mystery of God that is "completed" at the seventh trumpeting (10:7). The reference to the completion of their "witness" against idolatrous worship further associates them with the souls slaughtered on account of the "witness" they had (6:9). It also furthers their close association with John, who witnessed to the "witness" of Jesus Christ (1:2, 9).

When the two prophetic witnesses have completed their witness against idolatry, "the beast ascending from the abyss will make with them a battle and will conquer them and will kill them" (11:7). In contrast to the heavenly origin of the destructive angel of the "abyss" (9:11), the destructive "beast" from the "abyss" has an earthly association. It is like the destructive "beasts" of the earth by which the fourth horseman, personified Death, killed a fourth of the earth (6:8). Whereas the other angel John saw, the one having a seal of the living God, was "ascending" from a heavenly realm east of the sun (7:2), the destructive beast is "ascending" from the abyss under the earth. Whereas the destructive locusts were like horses prepared for "battle" (9:7, 9), the destructive beast will make a "battle" with the two prophetic witnesses.

That the destructive beast will "conquer" and will kill the two prophetic witnesses (11:7) associates him with the destructive first horseman, who came out "conquering" even so that he might "conquer" (6:2).

PART TWO—*Shown What Must Happen after These Things (4:1—16:21)*

But, ironically, the Lamb, as one having been slaughtered and thus a victim of such deadly destruction, has paradoxically "conquered," despite being killed, in and through his prophetic witness (5:5). The audience have been repeatedly exhorted to participate in such paradoxical "conquering" (2:7, 11, 17, 26; 3:5, 12, 21) in and through their prophetic witness against idolatrous worship. Indeed, as the exalted Jesus promised, "The one who conquers, I will give him to sit with me on my throne, as I also conquered and sat with my Father on his throne" (3:21).

It is necessary for anyone who would harm the two prophetic witnesses to be "killed" in accord with divine heavenly authority (11:5). But the beast will "kill" the two prophetic witnesses in accord with earthly authority (11:7). This further associates the two prophetic witnesses with Antipas, who, as a prophetic witness, was "killed" by earthly authorities (2:13). And it further indicates how the two prophetic witnesses serve as examples for the prophetic witness against idolatrous worship to be rendered by the audience, even if it means that some of them will be slaughtered like the souls and the Lamb. Indeed, among the audience are the fellow servants and brothers of the slaughtered souls who are about to be "killed," even as they, by earthly authorities (6:11).

The corpse of the two prophetic witnesses is on the main street of the great earthly "city" (11:8a) in contrast to the heavenly holy "city" that the nations will "trample" for forty-two months (11:2). The city is "called" spiritually "Sodom," notorious for its immorality, and "Egypt", notorious for its deadly oppression, where also the Lord of the two prophetic witnesses was crucified (11:8b).[31] This recalls that John was on the island "called" Patmos, the location of his prophetic witness to the word of God and witness of Jesus (1:9), which the crucifixion of Jesus epitomizes. Thus, the two prophetic witnesses, as those standing before the divine "Lord" of the earth, the object of true heavenly wor-

---

31. "[T]he peculiar indirect description indicates that at stake here is not a real city but a typical one. What it characterizes is its spiritual name—that is, the disclosure, made possible by the Spirit, of that which determines its reality before God: it is both Sodom, the prototype of the city that rejects God's commandment and will (Isa. 1:10; Jer. 23:24), and Egypt, the typical place of alienation and slavery of the people of God (Matt. 2:13–23; Acts 13:17) . . . here Jerusalem is expanded, as it were, beyond its purely geographic area into the picture of the world hostile to God; indeed, the picture of Jerusalem blends with that of Rome" (Roloff, *Revelation* 133).

ship (11:4), were killed in the same "city," the earthly domain of death and destruction, in which their "Lord" Jesus was crucified.

Those from the peoples and tribes and tongues and nations observe the "corpse" of the two witnesses on the main street of the great city (11:8a) for three and a half days and would not let their "corpses" be placed in a tomb (11:9). In ironic contrast to those who did not repent from worshiping idols unable to "observe" (9:20), those from the peoples and tribes and tongues and nations "observe" their corpse. That those from the "peoples and tribes and tongues and nations" observe their corpse recalls that John and the two witnesses were to prophesy about many "peoples and nations and tongues and kings" (10:11). This reminds the audience that the Lamb bought for God those from every "tribe and tongue and people and nation" (5:9), and that the large crowd of worshipers of God and the Lamb are from every "nation and tribes and peoples and tongues" (7:9).

In contrast to the one thousand two hundred sixty "days" that the two prophetic witnesses prophesied (11:3, 6), their corpse was observed for only three and a half "days" (11:9). The exalted Jesus has against the church in Thyatira that "you are letting" continue the false prophetess Jezebel, who teaches and misleads his servants to engage in idolatrous worship (2:20). In ironic contrast, those who observe the corpses of the two witnesses, who prophesied against such idolatrous worship, would not "let" them be placed in a tomb (11:9), thus depriving them of a proper burial to further disgrace them.

The exalted Jesus gave John a divine commission to write in a scroll what "you observe," which will include scenes of true heavenly worship, and "send" it, as a heavenly gift, to the seven churches (1:11). In ironic contrast, those from the peoples and tribes and tongues and nations "observe" the corpse of the two witnesses who prophesied against false earthly worship (11:9). Then those inhabiting upon the earth, in an ironic parody of true heavenly worship, rejoice "over them," the two prophetic witnesses, and celebrate and they will "send" earthly gifts "to one another" (11:10). These two "prophets," who during the days of their "prophecy" against idolatrous worship exercised divine destructive authority to strike the "earth" (11:6), tormented those inhabiting upon the "earth" (11:10), those promoting and engaged in idolatrous worship.

At the fifth trumpeting the locusts were given divine authority so that the human beings will be "tormented" for five months. Their "torment" is as the "torment" of a scorpion when it "stings" a human being (9:5). Similarly, these two prophets, who have the divine authority to "strike" the earth with every plague as often as they may wish (11:6), "tormented" those inhabiting upon the earth (11:10) to encourage their repentance from false worship.

These two prophets tormented "those inhabiting upon the earth," who engage in a parody of true worship by celebrating and rejoicing over the two dead prophets (11:10). Their tormenting resonates with the testing that is about to come upon the whole world to test "those inhabiting upon the earth" (3:10). As an anticipation of the woes to "those inhabiting upon the earth" from the final three trumpets (8:13), their tormenting continues to respond to the slaughtered souls' prayer for vindication from "those inhabiting upon the earth" (6:10).

But after the three and a half days that their corpse was observed (11:9), "a Spirit of life from God came in among them and they stood on their feet, and great fear fell upon those watching them" (11:11). That the divine Spirit of "life" from God, that is, eternal life, came in among them reinforces the previous promises the audience have heard regarding eternal, heavenly life. The Lamb will shepherd the large crowd of heavenly worshipers and lead them to "life's" springs of waters (7:17). The exalted Jesus will never wipe away the name of the one who conquers from the scroll of the "life" (3:5). He will give those who become faithful until death like the two witnesses the crown of the "life" (2:10), and to the one who conquers he will give to eat from the tree of the "life" (2:7). And that the Spirit of life from God "came in" among them reinforces the promise of Jesus that "I will come in" to the one who hears his sound and opens the door (3:20).

A "Spirit" of life from God came in among the two prophetic witnesses whom the beast killed (11:7), so that they "stood" on their "feet" (11:11), thus raised to life, as a result of the sacrificial death and resurrection of the Lamb (5:9–10). As one having been slaughtered, the Lamb, with "feet" like burnished bronze (1:15; 2:18), "stood," as raised to life, having seven horns and seven eyes, which are the seven "Spirits" of God sent into all the earth (5:6). Jesus, who became dead but lived (2:8), exhorted the church in Smyrna not to "fear" the things they are about to suffer (2:10). He exhorted John, who reported that "I fell" toward his feet as if dead, not to "fear" death (1:17), because he is the one living eternally with the keys of Death and Hades (1:18). In ironic contrast, great "fear" emphatically "fell upon" those watching the two prophetic witnesses, who became dead but lived (11:11).

John saw a door opened in "heaven," and the "sound," the "great sound I heard" earlier (1:10), told him to "ascend here" and "I will show you the things it is necessary to happen after these things" (4:1). John was then shown scenes of heavenly worship (4:2—5:14). And now, the two prophetic witnesses "heard" a "great sound" out of "heaven" telling them to "ascend here" to participate in heavenly life and worship (11:12a). So they "ascended" to heaven in a "cloud" (11:12b), a means of heavenly travel, recalling the mighty angel descending out of heaven clothed with a "cloud" (10:1), and that Jesus is coming from heaven with the "clouds" (1:7). And their remaining enemies not devoured by fire from the mouth of the two witnesses (11:5) "watched" them (11:12c), as among those "watching" upon whom great fear fell (11:11).[32]

Then at that "hour," resonating with the "hour" of the testing that is about to come upon the whole world to test those inhabiting upon the earth (3:10; cf. 11:10), "there came to be a great earthquake" (11:13a). This recalls and resonates with "a great earthquake came to be" at the opening of the sixth seal (6:12) in response to the slaughtered souls' prayer for judgment and vindication from those inhabiting upon the earth (6:10). A tenth of the "city," the great earthly "city" where the two prophetic witnesses were killed (11:8), "fell" (11:13a) in accord with the great fear that "fell" upon those watching the two witnesses (11:11).

In accord with the divine necessity that anyone who wished to harm the two witnesses be "killed" (11:5), there were "killed" seven thousand names of human beings (11:13a). In ironic contrast to the "names" of those who will walk with Jesus in heaven (3:4), seven thousand "names" of human beings were killed. The "rest" of the "human

---

32. "God has them—again like Elijah (2 Kgs. 2:11; Sir. 48:9) and Moses (Jos. *Ant.* 4.8.48)—rise and bodily ascend into heaven" (Roloff, *Revelation*, 130).

PART TWO—*Shown What Must Happen after These Things (4:1—16:21)*

beings," those who were not "killed" by the three plagues, did not repent from their idolatrous worship (9:20). In contrast, seven thousand names of "human beings" were "killed" and the "rest" became "fearful" (11:13a), in accord with the great "fear" that fell upon those watching the two witnesses (11:11). Indeed, that they "gave glory" to the "God" of heaven (11:13b), in response to the Spirit of life from "God" that raised the two witnesses from death (11:11), associates them with the heavenly worshipers who "will give glory" to the eternally living God (4:9).[33]

After a Spirit of life from God "came in" among the two dead prophetic witnesses (11:11), the second woe "has gone away" (11:14a). After the destruction by the locusts at the fifth trumpeting John announced that one woe "has gone away," and "behold, coming" still are two woes after these (9:12). And now, similarly, after the destruction by the great earthquake and the repentance of those who gave glory to the God of heaven (11:13) he announces that the second woe "has gone away," and "behold," the third woe is "coming" soon (11:14). That the third woe is "coming soon" reinforces the exhortation for the audience to repent from any association with idolatrous worship, since Jesus promised that "I am coming soon" for judgment (2:16; 3:11; cf. 1:7; 2:5). John has thus placed the audience in suspenseful expectation of a third woe of divinely authoritative destruction, calling for repentance from false worship. This woe is still to come.[34]

7a') Seventh Trumpet: Sounds of Worship and Appearance of the Ark in Heaven (11:15-19)

A a) ¹⁵ Then the seventh angel trumpeted and **there came to be** great **sounds in heaven** saying, "There has come to be the **kingdom** of the world of our Lord and of his Christ, and it **will reign** for the ages of the ages."

---

33. "Here in 11:13, giving glory to God is clearly the consequence of repentance" (Aune, *Revelation 6–16*, 628).

34. Dean, "Chronological Issues," 217–26; McLean, "Chronology," 460–71; Tavo, *Woman*, 173–223.

      b) ¹⁶ Then the twenty-four elders who are sitting before **God** on their thrones fell upon their faces and worshiped **God**,

         c) ¹⁷ᵃ saying, "We give thanks to you,

     b′) ¹⁷ᵇ Lord **God**, the Almighty, who is and who was,

  a′) ¹⁷ᶜ for you have received your great power and **have reigned**,

B ¹⁸ᵃ and the nations **were made angry**,

B′ ¹⁸ᵇ and your **anger** has come and the time for the dead to be judged and to give the reward to your servants the prophets and to the holy ones and to those who fear your name, the small and the great, and to destroy those destroying the earth."

A′ ¹⁹ Then there was opened the temple of **God in heaven** and the ark of his covenant appeared in his temple, and **there came to be** lightnings and **sounds** and thunders and an earthquake and great hail.

Then the "seventh angel trumpeted" (11:15a), recalling the mighty angel's announcement that in the days of the sound of the "seventh angel," whenever he may be about to "trumpet," "then is completed the mystery of God, as he brought good news to his own servants the prophets" (10:7). In contrast to the "great" earthquake that "there came to be" so that those who were not killed by it "became" fearful and performed an act of true worship, as they gave glory to the God of "heaven" (11:13), when the seventh angel trumpeted, "there came to be great" sounds in "heaven" (11:15b). In contrast to the silence for about half an hour that came to be "in heaven" when the seventh seal was opened (8:1), at the seventh trumpeting great sounds came to be "in heaven." These great heavenly sounds were saying, "There has come to be the kingdom of the world of our Lord and of his Christ, and it will reign for the ages of the ages" (11:15c).

    That the "kingdom" of the world and of "our" Lord "will reign" (11:15) resonates with the worship of the Lamb as the one who made for "our" God those from every tribe and tongue and people and nation a "kingdom" and priests, and they "will reign" upon the earth (5:10). That it is the kingdom of our "Lord" recalls that the two prophetic witnesses are standing before the "Lord" of the earth (11:4) as the object of true worship. That it is also the kingdom of his "Christ" recalls the worship of Jesus "Christ" (1:5) as the one who has made us into a "kingdom," priests for his God and Father (1:6). And that this kingdom will reign "for the ages of the ages" (11:15) resonates with the divine authority and the worship of God and/or Jesus, which is "for the ages of the ages" (1:6, 18; 4:9, 10; 5:13; 7:12; 10:6).

John saw that there were twenty-four "thrones" in heaven, and upon the "thrones" twenty-four elders, "sitting" clothed in white garments for their role in heavenly worship (4:4). The twenty-four elders "will fall" before God sitting upon the throne and they "will worship" the God living eternally (4:10). The twenty-four elders "fell" before the Lamb in worship, each one offering the prayers of the holy ones (5:8). The twenty-four elders participated in the scene of the universal worship of God and the Lamb (5:13), as they "fell" down and "worshiped" (5:14). And now the audience hear that, in continuity with their role in heavenly worship, the twenty-four elders, who are "sitting" before God on their "thrones," "fell" upon their "faces" and "worshiped God" (11:16). This likens them to all the angels who "fell" before the throne upon their "faces" and "worshiped God" (7:11).

The "great" heavenly sounds were "saying" that the "kingdom" of the world of our "Lord" and of his Christ has come to be, and it "will reign" for the ages of the ages (11:15). Resonating with this, the twenty-four elders sitting before "God" as they worshiped "God" (11:16) are "saying," "We give thanks to you, Lord God, the Almighty, who is and who was, for you have received your great power and have reigned" (11:17). God has already identified himself and been worshiped as the "Almighty," who "is" and who "was" and who "is coming" (1:8; 4:8). But now, with his third woe "coming" soon (11:14), God is worshiped simply as the "Almighty," who "is" and who "was," emphasizing that his reign has already begun. The Lamb was worshiped as worthy to "receive" the "power" (5:12), so also God is now worshiped because "you have received" your great "power."

It was given to the "nations" by God (divine passive) to "trample" the heavenly holy city through their idolatrous worship on earth (11:2). And those from the "nations" observed the corpses of the two prophets killed because of their witness against idolatry (11:9). But now, in their act of worship, the twenty-four elders acknowledge that the "nations were made angry" by God (11:18a) because of his vindication of the prophetic witness against idolatrous worship. Indeed, the elders go on to acknowledge that "your anger has come and the time for the dead to be judged and to give the reward to your servants the prophets and to the holy ones and to those who fear your name, the small and the great, and to destroy those destroying the earth" (11:18b). This recalls that the great day of the "anger" of God and of the Lamb now "has come" (6:17) to judge those who have killed the prophetic witnesses against idolatrous worship.

Recalling the initial notice that the "time" is near (1:3), the "time" now has come for the "dead" to be "judged" (11:18b) by the risen Jesus as the firstborn of the "dead" (1:5). This is in response to the prayer of the slaughtered souls who cried out to the divinely exalted Jesus, "Until when, Master, holy and true, do you not judge and vindicate our blood from those inhabiting upon the earth?" (6:10). That the time has come to give your "servants" the "prophets" the reward (11:18b) of vindication for their prophetic witness against idolatry accords with the notice that God brought good news to his own "servants" the "prophets" at the seventh trumpeting (10:7). And the time has come for God to give the reward to the "holy ones" (11:18b) in response to the prayers of the "holy ones" for vindication (5:8; 8:3, 4).

That the time has come for God to give the reward to all those who "fear" his name, the small and the great (11:18b), recalls that all those not killed by the great earthquake became "fearful;" they repented of their false worship and performed an act of true worship as "they gave glory to the God of heaven" (11:13). The audience are to identify themselves with those who fear God's "name" by turning away from idolatrous worship in order to engage in the true worship of God. Indeed, they have been exhorted to conquer false worship in accord with the promise of the exalted Jesus to write upon them the "name of my God" for their participation in heavenly worship (3:12). And that the time has come for God to "destroy" those "destroying" the earth (11:18b) accords with the fact that those having souls and a third of the ships were "destroyed" by God at the second trumpeting (8:9) in an effort to bring about the repentance of the idolatrous worshipers destroying the earth.

Then there was opened by God (divine passive) "the temple of God in heaven and the ark of the covenant appeared in the temple, and there came to be lightnings and sounds and thunders and an earthquake and great hail" (11:19). The "temple of God" that was "opened in heaven," recalling the door "opened in heaven" for John's visions of heavenly worship (4:1), refers to the "temple of God" John was to "measure" as an integral part of true heavenly worship (11:1). That the ark of God's covenant indicating his faithfulness and abiding presence with his people appeared in the opened temple in heaven reinforces the elders' worshipful acknowledgment that God has indeed answered (11:18) the prayer of the slaughtered souls (6:10).[35] In accord with the great "sounds" that "there came to be in heaven" at the seventh trumpeting (11:15), now "in heaven there came to be" lightnings and "sounds" and thunders and an earthquake and great hail.

At the beginning of John's visions of heavenly worship he saw that from the throne of God were coming out "lightnings and sounds and thunders" (4:5a). When, in response to the prayers of the holy ones (8:4), the angel filled the censer from the fire of the altar in heaven and threw it to the earth, "there came to be" not only "thunders and sounds and lightnings" but an "earthquake" (8:5). And now, as a further progression and intensification of the divine response to the prayers of the holy ones that include the prayer of the slaughtered souls for judgment and vindication (6:10), "there came to be" not only "lightnings and sounds and thunders and an earthquake" but "great hail" (11:19). This emphatically impressive divine response to the prayers of those who have prophetically witnessed against idolatrous worship encourages the audience likewise to witness against false worship and to engage in a true heavenly worship for eternal life in the Spirit of prophecy.

---

35. "In the OT the ark of the covenant was a symbol of the abiding presence of God" (Mounce, *Revelation*, 228).

John's Visions of the Seven Angels Trumpeting Their Seven Trumpets

Summary on 8:1—11:19

The audience hear the seven units of this subsection (8:1—11:19) in a chiastic pattern centering around the theme of the ongoing divine response to the prayer of the souls slaughtered because of their prophetic witness against idolatrous worship (6:9-11). In the unparalleled central (d) unit (9:13-21) of this subsection the audience hear that the rest of the human beings not killed by the plagues of the second of the final threes woes (8:13; 9:12), as a divine response to the prayer of the slaughtered souls, emphatically did not repent of their idolatrous worship (9:20-21). This reinforces the repeated exhortations for the audience to repent from any association with idolatrous worship (2:5, 14, 16, 20, 21; 3:3, 19) and engage in true, heavenly worship.

When the audience hear the (c') unit (10:1-11), they hear a chiastic progression of the (c) unit (9:1-12). At the fifth trumpeting the angelic star that had fallen "out of heaven" (9:1) "opened" the shaft of the abyss (9:2), so that destructive locusts could harm those engaged in idolatrous worship (9:10) as the first of the three final woes (9:12) in divine response to the prayer of the slaughtered souls. This progresses to a mighty angel descending "out of heaven" (10:1) with an "opened" small scroll (10:2, 8) for John to devour as the basis for prophetic witness against idolatrous worship. John and his audience are to prophesy about many "kings" (10:11), because they are to be included among those the Lamb made into a "kingdom" and priests for the worship of God, and they "will reign" upon the earth (5:10; 1:6). Rather than be subject to the destructive locusts whose "king" is the angel of the abyss (9:11), they are to be subject to Jesus, the ruler of the "kings" of the earth (1:5). He has made it possible for the "kings" of the earth not to hide from, but to worship God and the Lamb (6:15).

When the audience hear the (b') unit (11:1-14), they hear a chiastic progression of the (b) unit (8:6-13). The two prophetic witnesses, as models for the audience, tormented "those inhabiting upon the earth" who engage in a parody of true worship by celebrating and rejoicing over the two dead prophets (11:10). As an anticipation of the woes to "those inhabiting upon the earth" from the final three trumpets (8:13), their tormenting continues to respond to the slaughtered souls' prayer

PART TWO—*Shown What Must Happen after These Things (4:1—16:21)*

for judgment and vindication from "those inhabiting upon the earth" (6:10). Following upon the prophetic tormenting, the rest of the human beings not killed by the great earthquake, as the second of the final three woes to "those inhabiting upon the earth" (8:13), became fearful, repented from their idolatrous worship, and performed an act of true worship, as they gave glory to the God of heaven (11:13).

When the audience hear the final (a') unit (11:15–19), they hear a chiastic progression of and inclusion with the initial (a) unit (8:1–5). When, in response to the prayers of the holy ones (8:4), the angel filled the censer from the fire of the altar in heaven and threw it to the earth, "there came to be" not only "thunders and sounds and lightnings" but an "earthquake" (8:5). As a further progression and intensification of the divine response to the prayers of the holy ones that include the prayer of the slaughtered souls for judgment and vindication (6:10), "there came to be" not only "lightnings and sounds and thunders and an earthquake" but "great hail" (11:19). This emphatically impressive divine response to the prayers of those who have prophetically witnessed against idolatrous worship encourages the audience likewise to witness prophetically against idolatrous worship on earth and to engage in a true heavenly worship of God and the Lamb for eternal life in the Spirit of prophecy.

6

Worship of Dragon and Beasts on Earth and Worship of Lamb in Heaven

Revelation 12:1—14:20

1a) Appearances in Heaven of Signs of Woman with Child and of Dragon (12:1–6)

    A a) [12:1a] Then a great *sign appeared in heaven*,

          b) [1b] a **woman** clothed with the sun and the moon under *her* feet

          b') [1c] and upon *her* head a crown of twelve **stars**, [2] and she is pregnant, and crying out, laboring and being tormented, **to give birth**.

      a') [3a] Then there *appeared* another *sign in heaven*,

    B [3b] and behold a great fiery red dragon having **seven heads**

        C [3c] and ten horns

    B' [3d] and upon his **heads seven** diadems,

PART TWO—*Shown What Must Happen after These Things (4:1—16:21)*

> **A′** ⁴ᵃ and his tail swept a third of the **stars** of **heaven** and threw them to the earth.
>> **a)** ⁴ᵇ Then the dragon stood before the ***woman*** about **to give birth**,
>>> **b)** ⁴ᶜ so that when she **gave birth** he might devour ***her child***.
>>>> **c)** ⁵ᵃ So she **gave birth** to a son, a male, who is about to shepherd all the nations with an iron staff.
>>> **b′)** ⁵ᵇ Then ***her child*** was caught up to God and to his throne
>> **a′)** ⁶ and the ***woman*** fled into the wilderness, where she has there a place prepared by God, so that there they are nourishing her for one thousand two hundred and sixty days.

When the temple of God was opened "in heaven," the ark of his covenant "appeared" in his temple, and there came to be lightnings and sounds and thunders and an earthquake and "great" hail (11:19). This focus on appearances in heaven continues, as a "great" sign then "appeared in heaven" (12:1a). The "woman" Jezebel, rather than being legitimately commissioned by God for true prophecy, calls herself a prophetess and teaches and misleads the servants of Jesus to engage in idolatrous, rather than true heavenly worship (2:20). In contrast, the "woman" of the great sign that appeared in heaven has a genuine heavenly status bestowed by God, as indicated by her being "clothed with the sun and the moon under her feet and upon her head a crown of twelve stars" (12:1).

As their creator, God has authority over and control of the sun, moon, and stars as heavenly bodies. At the opening of the sixth seal, in divine response to the prayer of the slaughtered souls for judgment and vindication from those inhabiting upon the earth (6:10), the "sun" became black, the "moon" became as blood (6:12), and the "stars" of heaven fell to the earth (6:13). At the fourth trumpeting, in divine response to the prayers of all the holy ones (8:1–5), a third of the "sun" was struck by God (divine passive), a third of the "moon," and a third of the "stars," so that a third of them was darkened (8:12). God has given the woman of the great sign that appeared in heaven a share in his authority over cosmic creatures and a heavenly status. She is clothed by God with the "sun," the "moon" was placed by God under her feet, and a crown of twelve "stars" was placed upon her head (12:1).

That the woman was "clothed" by God with the sun indicates her destiny to participate in the eternal life and worship of heaven (12:1). It recalls and resonates with the promise that the one who conquers false worship will be "clothed" in heavenly white garments (3:5), available from the exalted Jesus so that one may be properly "clothed" (3:18). John saw the twenty-four elders and the large crowd of worshipers in heaven "clothed" in white (4:4; 7:9; cf. 7:13), and the mighty angel descending from heaven "clothed" with a cloud (10:1). But being "clothed" by God also associates the woman with the divine authority and commission given to the two witnesses to prophesy against idolatrous worship "clothed" with sackcloth (11:3).

That the moon is placed by God in a position of submission "under" the feet of the woman (12:1) points to her role in bringing about the universal worship of God and the Lamb from both earthly and heavenly realms. Although no one was able in heaven or upon the earth or "under" the earth to open the scroll (5:3), every creature in heaven and upon the earth and "under" the earth is a participant in the universal worship of God and the Lamb (5:13). The slaughtered souls' act of prayerful worship comes from "under" the altar in heaven (6:9). The exalted Jesus promised the church in Philadelphia that he will make those from the synagogue of Satan who falsely claim to be Jews come and worship God from a position of submission before their "feet" (3:9). Similarly, the moon has been placed under the "feet" of the woman in a position to participate in the universal worship of God and the Lamb by all of creation.

That "upon the head" of the woman is a crown of twelve stars (12:1) further indicates her heavenly status and destiny to triumph over false worship and participate in true heavenly worship. She has a heavenly status similar to the mighty angel with a heavenly rainbow "upon the head" (10:1). And she has a heavenly triumphant "crown" similar to the true golden "crowns upon the heads" of the twenty-four elders positioned for heavenly worship (4:4), in contrast to the "crowns" merely like gold "upon the heads" of the destructive locusts on earth (9:7).

But that her crown is of "twelve stars" (12:1) indicates that the woman is a corporate figure representative of the people of God, traditionally numbered as "twelve" tribes (7:5-8) that have been symbolized as "stars" in conjunction with the sun and moon (LXX Gen 37:9). According to the mystery of the seven "stars," they represent the angels of the seven churches as part of the heavenly status of the churches, which includes their participation in heavenly worship (1:20). Similarly, the woman's crown of twelve stars underlines the role the audience, as part of the people of God, are to have in triumphantly overcoming idolatrous earthly worship through their prophetic witness in order to participate in true heavenly worship.[1]

In the past the people of God compared themselves to a woman who "cried out," "laboring to give birth" (LXX Isa 26:17). Similarly, the woman of the great heavenly sign representative of the people of God is pregnant, and "crying out," "laboring" and being tormented, "to give birth" (12:2). She is "being tormented" by God (divine passive), indicating that she is now located not in heaven but on earth. At the fifth trumpeting the destructive locusts were given authority by God so that only the human beings on earth "will be tormented" for five months (9:5). And under divine authority the two prophets "tormented" those inhabiting upon the earth (11:10). That she is "crying out" in response to being tormented within the realm of divine authority on earth anticipates not only the anguished prayer by the souls who "cried out" in heaven after being slaughtered on earth (6:10), but the triumphant worship of the large crowd now "crying out" in heaven (7:10).

Closely following upon the "great sign" that "appeared in heaven" (12:1), then there "appeared" another "sign in heaven," "and behold a great fiery red dragon having seven heads and ten horns and upon his heads seven diadems" (12:3). "His tail swept a third of the stars of

---

1. The heavenly woman "is an image of the end-time salvation community, a symbol of the church. She is the heir of the promises of the Old Testament people of God; pointing to this is the reference to the twelve stars (cf. Gen 37:9), which symbolize the holy twelve tribes in their end-time fullness and perfection" (Roloff, *Revelation*, 145).

heaven and threw them to the earth" (12:4a). That the great dragon is "fiery red" associates him with the destructive power connoted by the "fiery red" horse whose rider was given authority to take peace from the "earth" by people slaughtering each other (6:4). And the depiction of the dragon as "having" seven "heads" and a "tail" with which he threw stars from heaven to earth associates him with the destructive power of the angelic horsemen, the "tails" of whose horses are like serpents, "having heads" and they harm with them (9:19).[2]

That the Lamb is depicted as "having seven horns" and "seven" eyes, which are the "seven" Spirits of God sent into all the "earth" (5:6), indicates his divine authority over the earth. In pointed contrast, the great fiery red dragon is similarly depicted as "having seven" heads and ten "horns" and upon his heads "seven" diadems (12:3). And his tail threw a third of the stars of heaven to the "earth" (12:4a), indicating his demonic authority over the earth.

The woman of the "great" sign has "upon her head" a heavenly "crown" of twelve heavenly "stars" (12:1), underlining her heavenly status. In noteworthy contrast, the "great" dragon has "upon his heads" seven "diadems" (12:3). And his tail threw a third of the "stars" of heaven to the earth (12:4a), underlining his destructive earthly authority, especially toward the people of God symbolized by the twelve stars.

In contrast to the mighty angel who has "upon his head" a heavenly rainbow (10:1), and to the twenty-four elders who have "upon their heads" heavenly golden crowns (4:4), the dragon has "upon his heads" seven diadems (12:3) in accord with his authority to rule on earth. In accord with divine authority, a "third of the stars" was struck by God at the fourth trumpeting (8:12). But in accord with his demonic destructive authority, the dragon threw a "third of the stars" of heaven to the earth (12:4a). In divine response to the prayers of all the holy ones, an angel "threw" a censer filled from the "fire" of the heavenly altar "to the earth" (8:5). In ironic contrast, the "fiery red" dragon "threw" a third of

---

2. "As in ancient Oriental myths, the chaotic power on which God has declared war appears in the Old Testament embodied in the form of a sea monster, Leviathan, whose name is rendered in the LXX as 'dragon' (Ps. 74:14; Job 7:12; Amos 9:3)" (Roloff, *Revelation*, 146).

the stars of heaven "to the earth," a dramatic gesture of cosmic violence ominous for the woman laboring to give birth on earth (12:2).

John saw the large, numberless crowd from every nation "standing before" the throne in heaven and "before" the Lamb (7:9), poised for their participation in heavenly worship (7:10–17). He also saw the seven angels who "before" God "stand" ready for their role in heavenly worship (8:2). The two prophetic witnesses have as their heavenly correspondence the two olive trees and the two lampstands that are "standing before" the Lord of the earth as the object of true heavenly worship (11:4). In a tense contrast, the dragon "stood before" the woman divinely authorized "to give birth" (12:4b), the heavenly woman now on earth crying out, laboring and being tormented, "to give birth" (12:2). The dragon stands before the woman not in a position to perform an act of heavenly worship, but so that when the woman gave birth he might devour her child (12:4).

The woman "is about to," that is, in accord with an imminent necessity determined by God, give birth (12:4), resonating with the divine imminent necessity of the testing that "is about to" come upon the whole world (3:10). The exalted Jesus promised that "her children," that is, the metaphorical offspring who engage in the idolatrous worship taught and promoted by the "woman" Jezebel (2:10), "I will kill with death" (2:23). In ironic contrast, the great fiery red dragon stood before the "woman" of the great sign in heaven, destined by God to participate in true heavenly worship, so that when she gave birth he might devour "her child" (12:4).

That the dragon might "devour" the child the woman destined for heavenly worship was divinely authorized to bring to birth on earth indicates that he is an enemy who would thwart God's plan for universal heavenly worship. But, as John reported, "I devoured" it (10:10), the scroll containing the word of God's plan, after being directed by the mighty angel to "devour" it (10:9), as the basis for John and his audience to prophesy against false worship in order to bring about true heavenly worship (10:11). And God promised that if anyone wishes to harm his prophetic witnesses, who are closely aligned with the heavenly woman, fire comes out of their mouth and "devours" their enemies (11:5). The audience thus expect God to prevent the great fiery red dragon, an enemy of God and the woman, from devouring the woman's child.

The tension mounts as the woman "gave birth to a son, a male" (12:5a; cf. LXX Isa 66:7), the child the dragon, who stood before the woman about to "give birth," wants to devour when she "gave birth" (12:4). That she gave birth to a "son" identifies him as Jesus, the one like a "Son of Man" (1:13) as well as the "Son of God" (2:18). The redundant addition that her son is a "male" (ἄρσεν), a neuter adjectival noun, links him to Jesus as the "Lamb [ἀρνίον]" (5:6, 12; 6:1; 7:17), a similar sounding neuter noun.³ This identity is confirmed with the notice that the woman's son "is about to," in accord with the imminent necessity of God's plan, "shepherd all the nations" with an "iron staff" (12:5a). It recalls that the Lamb "will shepherd" (7:17) the large crowd from "every nation" (7:9). Furthermore, the exalted Jesus promised that he will give to the one who conquers false worship authority over the "nations" (2:26) so that he "will shepherd" them with an "iron staff" (2:27).

But then the tension is relieved as "her child," whom the dragon wanted to devour (12:4), "was caught up to God and to his throne" (12:5b). This underscores the identity of the woman's son with the divinely exalted Jesus as the Lamb. It recalls that the Lamb, who will shepherd the large crowd from every nation, is in the middle of the "throne" of God in heaven (7:17; cf. 5:6).⁴

In ironic contrast to the human beings who sought death—though death "will flee" from them (9:6)—the woman "fled" from death into the wilderness, where she has there a "place" prepared by God (12:6) on earth, complementing the church's "place" in heaven (2:5). As horses "prepared" by God for battle on earth (9:7), and the four angels "prepared" by God for their task on earth (9:15), so the woman has a place "prepared" by God for her prophetic witness on earth. There "they," implicitly God and "her child caught up to God" (12:5), are nourishing

---

3. That the neuter form for "male" is used intentionally here to promote identification with the neuter form of "lamb" is further indicated in 12:13, which employs the masculine form: "who had given birth to the male." See also Tavo, *Woman*, 271.

4. On the significance of the death of Jesus not being explicitly mentioned here, see Pataki, "Non-Combat Myth," 258–72.

her for "one thousand two hundred and sixty days" (12:6), identical to the "one thousand two hundred and sixty days" God's two witnesses will prophesy against idolatrous worship (11:3).[5] The divine nourishment provided for the woman during the time of her prophesying thus encourages the audience, who are to identify with her, to witness to true heavenly worship for eternal life in the Spirit of prophecy.[6]

2b) Dragon Thrown Down to Earth and Sound in Heaven (12:7–12a)

A a) [7a] Then **there came to be** a battle *in heaven*:

    b) [7b] **Michael** and *his angels* to **battle** against *the dragon*,

    b') [7c] and *the dragon* **battled** and also *his angels*,

  a') [8] but they were not strong nor was a place found for them still *in heaven*.

B [9a] Then **was thrown** the great dragon,

    C [9b] the ancient serpent, the one called Devil and the Satan, who misleads the whole world,

B' [9c] he **was thrown** to the earth, and his angels **were thrown** with him.

A' a) [10a] Then I heard a great sound *in heaven* saying, "Now **there has come to be** the salvation and the power

    b) [10b] and the kingdom of *our God* and the authority of his Christ,

        c) [10c] for was thrown the *accuser* of our brothers,

        c') [10d] who *accuses* them

    b') [10e] before *our God* day and night,

---

5. "This is the same period as in 11:2–3, where for that length of time God protects the church as his invisible, inviolable temple and gives it power to witness despite ongoing persecution" (Beale, *Revelation*, 642).

6. On 12:1–6, see Tavo, *Woman*, 256–73.

a′) ⁱⁱ but they conquered him on account of the blood of the Lamb and on account of the word of their witness and they did not love their soul unto death. ¹²ᵃ Therefore celebrate, you **heavens** and those dwelling in them.

Whereas the locusts were like horses prepared for "battle" on earth (9:7, 9), and the beast ascending from the abyss will make with the two prophetic witnesses a "battle" on earth (11:7), John now reports that there came to be a "battle" in heaven (12:7a). After the focus on the encounter between the dragon and the woman on earth (12:4-6), the notice that a battle took place "in heaven" returns the focus to where the great sign of the woman and the other sign of the great fiery dragon appeared—"in heaven" (12:1, 3). The exalted Jesus warned that "I will battle against" those engaged in idolatrous worship on earth (2:16). But in heaven, Michael, the traditional angelic guardian of the people of God (Dan 10:13, 21; 12:1), and his fellow angels were to "battle against" the dragon (12:7b), and the dragon and his angels also "battled" (12:7c). Thus, as a prelude to when the dragon stood before the woman to devour her child on earth (12:4), the dragon battled against Michael in heaven.[7]

In contrast to the "strength" that the divine Lamb was worthy to receive as an object of heavenly worship (5:12) and the "strength" attributed to God (7:12) as an object of heavenly worship, the dragon and his angels were not "strong" nor was a place found for them still in heaven (12:8). Whereas a "place" was prepared by God for the woman who fled into the wilderness on earth (12:6), no "place" was "found" for the dragon and his angels in heaven. This accords with the fact that no one except the Lamb in heaven was "found" worthy to open the scroll (5:4). Thus, as a result of the battle that came to be "in heaven" (12:7), no place was found for the great fiery dragon and his angels "in heaven."

Out of heaven, in which no place was still found for him (12:8), was thrown the great dragon (12:9a) by God (divine passive). The great dragon is further identified as "the ancient serpent, the one called Devil and the Satan, who misleads the whole world" (12:9b). As the ancient "serpent," the great dragon is the primordial ancestor in inflicting the

---

7. "Michael was seen as the angel of Israel who superintends the angels of the nations. As general of the divine armies he is responsible for combatting Satan" (Roloff, *Revelation*, 148).

harm on human beings on earth that is associated with the tails of the angelic horses which are like "serpents" (9:19). Being "called" in the book of Revelation signals a significant role to play in the divine plan. John was on the island "called" Patmos because it was the place God destined him to be on account of the word of God and the witness of Jesus (1:9). Because the "great city" is the place where both the two prophetic witnesses and their Lord were killed, it is "called" spiritually Sodom and Egypt (11:8). That, as the ancient serpent, the great dragon is "called" Devil and the Satan similarly points to his key role within the divine plan.

Indeed, that the great dragon, the ancient serpent, is called "Devil" (12:9b) means that he is the "Devil" who is "about to," in accord with imminent divine necessity, throw some members of the audience into prison so that they may be tested with regard to their witness against idolatrous worship (2:10). And that he is called the "Satan" (12:9b) recalls the threat of idolatrous worship associated with the "synagogue of Satan" (2:9; 3:9), "the place where Satan inhabits" (2:13), and "the deep things of Satan" (2:24). And that he "misleads" the "whole world" (12:9b) indicates that he is the diabolic cause behind the false prophetess Jezebel, who "misleads" members of the audience to engage in idolatrous worship (2:20), as well as the testing that is about to come upon the "whole world" (3:10).

The great dragon who "was thrown" by God out of heaven "was thrown to the earth," and his angels "were thrown" with him (12:9c). This recalls that at the first trumpeting fire mixed with blood similarly "was thrown to the earth" so that a third of it was destroyed (8:7). Previously, angels were symbolized as stars (1:20). That his angels were thrown to the earth with the great dragon thus resonates with how his tail swept a third of the stars of heaven and "threw" them "to the earth" (12:4). But now the great dragon himself was also thrown to the earth, intensifying the ominous nature of this event for all those on earth.

John reported that "I was in Spirit on the Lord's day and I heard behind me a great sound" (1:10) before his vision of the heavenly character and status of the exalted Jesus (1:11–16). Now he reports that, as a result of the outcome of the battle that there came to be "in heaven" (12:7), so that no place was found for the great dragon and his angels "in heaven" (12:8), "I heard a great sound in heaven" (12:10a). As a result of the outcome of the battle that "there came to be" in heaven, the great sound was that of those worshiping in heaven, saying, "Now there has come to be the salvation and the power and the kingdom of our God and the authority of his Christ, for was thrown the accuser of our brothers, who accuses them before our God day and night" (12:10).

What John heard the "great sound in heaven" saying provides the basis for the heavenly worship he has experienced. Now that there has come to be the "salvation" (12:10), the large crowd are crying out with a "great sound" saying, "The salvation to our God" (7:10). Now that there has come to be the "power" (12:10), worshipers acknowledge the "power" that belongs to God (7:12) and the "power" attributed to God and the Lamb (4:11; 5:12; 11:17). Now that "there has come to be" the "kingdom" of our God and the authority of "his Christ" (12:10), there came to be "great sounds in heaven" saying that "there has come to be" the "kingdom" of the world of our Lord and of "his Christ" (11:15; cf. 5:10). And the "authority" of his Christ includes the "authority" the exalted Jesus promised to give over the nations to enable them to participate in universal heavenly worship (2:26).

That emphatically the accuser of our brothers "was thrown" (12:10) refers to the great dragon who "was thrown" by Michael and his angels out of heaven to the earth (12:9). Included among our "brothers" are members of the audience, the "brothers" who are about to be killed for their prophetic witness against idolatrous worship even as the slaughtered souls (6:11). In ironic contrast to the worship that takes place "before God" (8:2, 4; 9:13; 11:16), the accuser accuses our brothers "before our God" (12:10). And rather than participating in the true worship of God that takes place "day and night" (4:8; 7:15), the accuser accuses our brothers "day and night" (12:10) because of their true worship of God.

The great sound in heaven continues its declaration, adding that our brothers conquered their diabolic accuser "on account of the blood of the Lamb and on account of the word of their witness and they did not love their soul unto death" (12:11). In contrast to the beast from the abyss who "will conquer" the two prophetic witnesses (11:7), our brothers "conquered" their accuser, the great dragon. They conquered him on account of the "blood of the Lamb," the Lamb who "conquered" (5:5), so that he is worshiped as the one who was slaughtered and who bought for God with "your blood" those from every nation (5:9) to participate in heavenly worship. Indeed, the large crowd of heavenly worshipers are those who washed and whitened their robes in the "blood of the Lamb" (7:14). That our brothers conquered the diabolic accuser thus reinforces the repeated exhortations for everyone in the audience to be one who "conquers" false worship (2:7, 11, 17, 26; 3:5, 12, 21).

That "they," our brothers, conquered the diabolic accuser "on account of the word of their witness" (12:11) likens them to "they" (6:11), the souls slaughtered "on account of the word of God and on account of the witness" they had (6:9). It also likens them to John, who witnessed to the "word of God and the witness" of Jesus Christ (1:2), so that he was on the island called Patmos "on account of the word of God and the witness" of Jesus (1:9). That our brothers did not love their "soul" unto death (12:11) underlines their likeness to the "souls" slaughtered for their witness against false worship (6:9). And that they did not love their soul "unto death" makes them a paradigm for the fulfillment of the exalted Jesus' exhortation for the audience to become faithful "unto death" (2:10) in their prophetic witness against idolatrous worship.[8]

That the expulsion of the great dragon and his angels out of heaven to the earth is a basis for true heavenly worship is confirmed as the great sound in "heaven" declares, "Therefore celebrate you heavens and those dwelling in them" (12:12a). In ironic contrast to the parody of true worship that takes place when those inhabiting upon the earth "celebrate" the death of the two prophetic witnesses (11:10), the heavens and those dwelling in them are exhorted to "celebrate" with true heavenly worship (cf. LXX Isa 49:13; Deut 32:43). Those "dwelling" in the heavens include the large numberless crowd in heaven of those who worship the Lamb and the one sitting upon the throne, the one who "will dwell" over them (7:15). The audience are to join those dwelling in heaven by their witness to and practice of the worship for eternal life in the Spirit of prophecy.

---

8. "Many have said that all believers in the Apocalypse were to become martyrs. On the basis of 2:10 and 12:11, that is not so. All will be persecuted, but not all will die" (Osborne, *Revelation*, 477).

Worship of Dragon and Beasts on Earth and Worship of Lamb in Heaven

3c) The Devil/Dragon/Serpent and the Woman (12:12b–18)

A ^{12b} Woe to the earth and the **sea**,

> B a) ^{12c} for the Devil has descended to you, having great fury, knowing that he has little *time*."
>
>> b) ^{13a} Then when the **dragon** saw that he had been thrown to the earth, he pursued the *woman*,
>>
>>> c) ^{13b} who gave birth to the male,
>>
>> b') ^{14a} but the two wings of the great eagle were given to the *woman*,
>
> a') ^{14b} so that she could fly into the wilderness to her place, where she is nourished there, a *time* and *times* and half a *time*, from the face of the **serpent**.
>
> B' a) ¹⁵ Then the **serpent** *threw from his mouth* water behind the **woman** as a *river*, so that he might *make* her be swept away by a river.
>
>> b) ^{16a} But *the earth* helped the **woman**
>>
>> b') ^{16b} and *the earth* opened its mouth
>
> a') ^{16c} and swallowed the *river* that the **dragon** *threw from his mouth*. ¹⁷ Then the **dragon** was made angry at the **woman** and went forth to *make* a battle against the rest of her offspring who keep the commandments of God and have the witness of Jesus.

A' ¹⁸ And it stood upon the sand of the **sea**.

The great sound that John heard in heaven (12:10–12a) concludes with the threatening announcement, "Woe to the earth and the sea, for the Devil has descended to you, having great fury, knowing that he has little time" (12:12bc). Having heard that the second "woe" has gone away and the third "woe" is coming soon (11:14; cf. 8:13; 9:12), the audience now hear the pronouncement of "woe" to the earth and the sea, in contrast to the exhortation to the heavens and those dwelling in them to celebrate (12:12a). John saw the mighty angel "descending" out of heaven (10:1) and "having" the small scroll of divine revelation (10:2). He placed his right foot upon the "sea," and his left upon the "earth" (10:2). But the Devil, who is the great dragon, the ancient serpent, and the Satan (12:9), "descended" to the "earth" and the "sea," ominously "having" great fury. Since the "time" is near (1:3), and the "time" for judgment has come (11:18), the devil knows he has little "time" for his great fury.

The dragon saw that he had been "thrown to the earth" (12:13a). This emphatically underscores that, as the ancient serpent, the one called Devil and the Satan, the great dragon was "thrown to the earth" (12:9) by God. Consequently, the dragon pursued the woman (12:13a) on earth, who "gave birth" to the "male" (12:13b). This is the heavenly woman, representative of the people of God, who "gave birth" to a son, a "male"—Jesus, the Lamb, who was caught up to God and to his throne (12:5) in heaven.

But the two wings of the great eagle were given by God to the "woman" (12:14a), the "woman" the dragon pursued (12:13a). The two "wings" have heavenly, angelic connotations, recalling the sound of the "wings" of the destructive locusts (9:9) under the authority of the angel of the abyss (9:11) and the "wings" of each of the four living creatures in heaven (4:8). Similar to the fourth living creature like an "eagle flying" (4:7) and to the "eagle flying" in midheaven (8:13), the woman could "fly" with the two wings of the great "eagle" (12:14b).

John previously reported that the woman fled "into the wilderness," where she has "there" a "place" prepared by God, so that "there they are nourishing" her for one thousand two hundred and sixty days (12:6), the period of the church's prophetic witness against idolatrous worship (11:3). This is now reiterated as she was able to fly "into the wilderness" to her "place," where she "is nourished there" by God (divine passive) for an equivalent period—"a time and times and half a time" (12:14b). In ironic contrast to those false worshipers who pleaded to be hidden "from the face" of God at the opening of the sixth seal (6:16), the woman witnessing to the true worship of God is able to fly into the wilderness "from the face" of the "serpent" (12:14b), the ancient "serpent," who is the great dragon (12:9).[9]

---

9. "As Israel has been miraculously fed then by manna, so also will the church be nourished and kept alive by God" (Roloff, *Revelation*, 151).

Worship of Dragon and Beasts on Earth and Worship of Lamb in Heaven

If anyone may wish to harm the two prophetic witnesses, fire comes "out of their mouth" and devours their enemies (11:5). In contrast, although the woman was able to fly from the face of the "serpent" (12:14), the "serpent" threw "from his mouth" water behind the woman as a river, "so that he might make her be swept away by a river" (12:15). But, just as the two wings of the great eagle were given by God to the "woman" (12:14), so the earth under divine authority helped the "woman" (12:16a) "as it opened its mouth" (12:16b) and "swallowed the river that the dragon threw from his mouth" (12:16c).[10] The "dragon" who pursued the woman (12:13) reappears as the "dragon" who "threw from his mouth" the "river," that is, the water the serpent "threw from his mouth" as a "river" (12:15). Thus, the woman has twice been rescued from the dragon/serpent.

Just as the nations "were made angry" by God (11:18), so the dragon who pursued the "woman" (12:13), "was made angry" at the "woman" and "went away to make a battle against the rest of her offspring who keep the commandments of God and have the witness of Jesus" (12:17). The first and second woe "went away," but the third is ominously coming soon (9:12; 11:14). Similarly, the dragon "went forth" to make a battle, as part of the woe to the earth and the sea (12:12b), ominous for the woman's offspring with whom the audience are to identify. Indeed, since the beast from the abyss "will make" a "battle" against the two prophetic witnesses and kill them (11:7), that the dragon went forth "to make" a "battle" against the offspring of the woman could mean death for some of them.

The audience have been exhorted to be those who hear the words of the prophecy, the words or commandments of God, and "keep" the things written in it, as they are recorded in the book of Revelation (1:3). Thus the audience are to see themselves as part of the rest of the offspring of the woman who "keep" the commandments of God and have the prophetic witness of Jesus (12:17). As part of those who "have" the "witness of Jesus," the audience are further likened to the souls slaughtered on account of the "witness" that they "had" (6:9), and to John,

---

10. "The image of the earth as having a 'mouth' that can 'swallow' is a fairly common one; the earth usually swallows enemies or adversaries for the purpose of protecting the holy ones (Num 16:30–34)" (Lupieri, *Apocalypse*, 199–200).

who witnessed to the "witness of Jesus" Christ (1:2), so that he was on Patmos on account of the "witness of Jesus" (1:9).

The devil/dragon/serpent then ominously "stood upon the sand of the sea" (12:18). As John previously reported, another angel "stood" over the altar in heaven to offer the prayers of all the holy ones as an act of worship before God (8:3). In contrast, the devil/dragon/serpent "stood" upon the sand of the "sea," poised to be part of the woe to the earth and the "sea" (12:12b). The earth and the sea define the location of those in the audience who are to keep the commandments of God and have the witness of Jesus (12:17), those who are to witness to true heavenly worship for eternal life in the Spirit of prophecy.[11]

4d) Vision of the Beast from the Sea (13:1–10)

A a) [a] ^{13:1a} Then I saw from the sea a ***beast*** ascending,

    [b] ^{1b} having ten horns and seven ***heads***

      [c] ^{1c} and upon its horns ten diadems

    [b′] ^{1d} and upon its ***heads* names** of **blasphemy**.

  [a′] ^{2a} And the ***beast*** that I saw was like a leopard and its feet as of a bear and its **mouth** as a **mouth** of a lion

    b) ^{2b} and the dragon gave it ***his*** power

    b′) ^{2c} and ***his*** throne and **great** authority.

  a′) ³ And one of its ***heads*** as one having been **slaughtered** to death, but the plague of its death was healed. And the whole **earth** marveled after the ***beast***

B ^{4a} and **they worshiped** the dragon, for he gave the authority to the beast,

B′ ^{4b} and **they worshiped** the beast saying, "Who is like the beast and who is able to battle against it?"

A′ a) [a] ⁵ And a **mouth** *was given to it* to speak **great** things and **blasphemies**, and *authority was given to it to do* this for forty-

---

11. Paul, "Old Testament in Revelation 12," 256–76.

two months, ⁶ᵃ and it opened its **mouth** for **blasphemies** to God to **blaspheme** *his name*

[b] ⁶ᵇ and his *dwelling*,

[b'] ⁶ᶜ those in heaven *dwelling*,

[a'] ⁷ and it *was given to it to do* battle against the **holy ones** and to conquer them, and *authority was given to it* over every tribe and people and tongue and nation. ⁸ Then all those inhabiting upon the **earth** will worship it, for each of whom *his* **name** has not been written in the scroll of the life of the Lamb who has been **slaughtered** from the foundation of the world.

b) ⁹ *If anyone* has an ear, let him hear!

b') ¹⁰ᵃ *If anyone* is to go into captivity, into captivity he goes. *If anyone* is to be killed by the dagger, he is by the dagger to be killed.

a') ¹⁰ᵇ Here is the endurance and the faith of the **holy ones**.

As the dragon stood ominously upon the sand of the "sea" (12:18), John saw from the "sea a beast ascending, having ten horns and seven heads and upon its horns ten diadems and upon its heads names of blasphemy" (13:1). That a "beast" is "ascending" from the sea adds to the ominousness, as it resonates with the "beast ascending" from the abyss that will make against the two prophetic witnesses a battle and will conquer them and will kill them (11:7). Like the great fiery red dragon having "seven heads" and "ten horns" (12:3), the beast has "ten horns" and "seven heads." But whereas the dragon has upon his "heads seven diadems" (12:3), the beast has upon its horns "ten diadems" and upon its "heads" names of blasphemy. The names of "blasphemy" connote an association with false worship, recalling the "blasphemy" of those who are a synagogue of Satan (2:9).

Whereas in heaven the first living creature is "like" a lion, the second "like" an ox, and the fourth "like" an eagle flying (4:7), on earth the beast was "like" a leopard (13:2a), in contrast to the exalted Jesus in heaven "like" a Son of Man (1:13). Regarding the heavenly Jesus, "his feet" were like burnished bronze (1:15; 2:18). Regarding the heavenly mighty angel, "his feet" were as pillars of fire (10:1). But regarding the earthly beast, "its feet" were as of a bear (13:2a). The teeth of the destructive locusts were "as" of "lions" (9:8) and the heads of the destructive horses were "as" heads of "lions" (9:17). Similarly, the mouth of the beast was "as" a mouth of a "lion" (13:2a), suggesting its destructiveness as a fiercely wild beast.[12]

In contrast to the revelation of Jesus Christ that God "gave him" (1:1), the diabolical dragon "gave" the earthly beast his power (13:2b). In contrast to God, worshiped in heaven as the one who has received "great power" and reigned (11:17), the dragon gave to the beast his "power" and his throne and "great" authority on earth (13:2c). In contrast to the child Jesus Christ being caught up to God and to "his throne" in heaven (12:5), the dragon gave the beast "his throne" on earth, that is, the "throne" of Satan (2:13), the dragon (12:9), associated with idolatrous worship. The heavenly "authority" of the Christ of God (12:10) includes the "authority" that the exalted Jesus Christ promised that "I will give" to those who conquer false worship over the nations to lead them to heavenly worship and eternal life (2:26). But the dragon "gave" to the beast great "authority" on earth, implicitly to prevent true heavenly worship.

John saw in the midst of the throne in heaven a Lamb standing, "as one having been slaughtered," having seven horns and seven eyes, which are the seven Spirits of God sent into all the "earth" (5:6). As a parody to this, John saw one of the "heads," one of the seven "heads" of the beast, upon whose "heads" are names of blasphemy (13:1), "as one having been slaughtered" to death, but the plague of its death was healed. And the whole "earth" marveled after the "beast" (13:3), the earthly "beast" John saw ascending from the sea (13:1). In contrast to the Lamb who was slaughtered but caught up to God and his throne in heaven (12:5), the beast was slaughtered but healed so that it remained operative on

---

12. "There is little doubt that for John the beast was the Roman Empire as persecutor of the church . . . Yet the beast is more than the Roman Empire . . . The beast has always been, and will be in a final intensified manifestation, the deification of secular authority" (Mounce, *Revelation*, 244, 246).

Worship of Dragon and Beasts on Earth and Worship of Lamb in Heaven

earth. That the "whole" earth marveled after the beast resonates with the dragon misleading the "whole" world with idolatrous worship (12:9).[13]

In contrast to those in heaven who "worshiped God" (7:11; 11:16), the whole earth "worshiped the dragon," for he gave the authority to the beast (13:4a), and so "they worshiped the beast" also saying, "Who is like the beast and who is able to battle against it?" (13:4b). This implicitly unanswerable rhetorical question the audience can answer. Michael and his angels are able "to battle" against the dragon (12:7), who gave his authority to the beast. Furthermore, the audience can appreciate the arrogantly boastful question of their idolatrous worship ("Who is like the beast?"), as an ironic mimicry of the meaning of the name "Michael" ("Who is like God?"), which indicates the object of true worship.

A "mouth" was given to the beast, whose "mouth" is as the "mouth" of a lion (13:2), "to speak great things and blasphemies, and authority was given to it to do this for forty-two months" (13:5). In accord with the "great" authority the dragon gave it (13:2, 4), as well as the names of "blasphemy" upon its heads (13:1), the beast spoke "great" things and the "blasphemies" associated with idolatrous worship. That it "was given authority," the great "authority" the dragon gave it (13:2, 4), to do this for "forty-two months" coincides with the limited period of "forty-two months" that "was given" by God to the nations to "trample" the holy city on earth with idolatrous worship (11:2).

Under divine authority the earth helped the woman, as it "opened" its "mouth" and swallowed the river that the dragon threw from his mouth (12:16). In ironic contrast, the beast "opened" its "mouth for blasphemies to God to blaspheme his name and his dwelling, those in heaven dwelling" (13:6). In accord with the "names" of "blasphemy" upon its heads (13:1), the beast opened its mouth for idolatrous "blasphemies" to God to "blaspheme" his "name." In ironic contrast to the child being caught up "to God" in heaven (12:5), the beast on earth issued idolatrous blasphemies "to God." Rather than fearing the "name" of God in heavenly worship (11:18), the beast blasphemed his "name." In contradiction to the exhortation for the "heavens" and those "dwell-

---

13. "The wound represents a Satanic attempt to imitate the death and resurrection of Jesus Christ, for the purpose of tricking 'the entire earth' and claiming the worship that properly belongs to Christ" (Lupieri, *Apocalypse*, 203).

ing" in them to celebrate with heavenly worship (12:12a), the beast on earth blasphemed those in "heaven dwelling."

A mouth "was given to it," the beast, by God (divine passive) to speak great things and blasphemies, and "authority was given to it to do" this for forty-two months (13:5). In parallel progression to this, it "was given to it to do" battle against the holy ones and to conquer them, and "authority was given to it" over every tribe and people and tongue and nation (13:7). That it was given to the beast "to do battle" against the holy ones and "to conquer" them accords with the dragon going away "to make a battle" against the rest of the woman's offspring who keep the commandments of God and have the witness of Jesus (12:17), that is, the holy ones with whom the audience are to identify. It likewise accords with the beast ascending from the abyss who "will make" against the two prophetic witnesses, with whom the audience are to identify, a "battle" and it "will conquer" them and will kill them (11:7).

The slaughtered Lamb bought for the true heavenly worship of God those from "every tribe and tongue and people and nation" (5:9). The large numberless crowd engaged in heavenly worship were from "every nation and tribes and peoples and tongues" (7:9). It was divinely necessary for John to prophesy about many "peoples and nations and tongues and kings" (10:11). And those from the "peoples and tribes and tongues and nations" observe the corpse of the two witnesses who prophesied against idolatrous worship (11:9). But now the audience hear that authority was given to the beast over "every tribe and people and tongue and nation" (13:7), implicitly to prevent them from engaging in true heavenly worship.

The whole "earth" (13:3) "worshiped" the beast (13:4). Reiterating and further developing this, then all those inhabiting upon the "earth will worship" it, "for each of whom his name has not been written in the scroll of the life of the Lamb who has been slaughtered from the foundation of the world" (13:8). "Those inhabiting upon the earth" celebrated and rejoiced over the two witnesses killed for prophesying against idolatrous worship (11:10). Accordingly, all "those inhabiting upon the earth" will engage in idolatrous worship of the beast.

The exalted Jesus promised that he will never wipe away "his name," the name of the one who conquers false worship, from the "scroll of the

Worship of Dragon and Beasts on Earth and Worship of Lamb in Heaven

life" and he will confess "his name" before his Father (3:5). In ironic contrast, for each of those who will worship the beast who blasphemed "his name," the name of God (13:6), "his name" has not been written by God (divine passive) in the "scroll of the life" of the Lamb (13:8). In contrast to one of the heads of the beast having been "slaughtered" but healed (13:3), so that the whole earth engaged in idolatrous worship of the beast (13:4), the Lamb has been "slaughtered" from the foundation of the world (13:8), and thus became an object of true heavenly worship. Indeed, the Lamb has been slaughtered from the foundation of the world whose heavenly kingdom has come to be, as acknowledged in the heavenly worship of the Lord God and his Christ, the Lamb (11:15).

The exhortation, "If anyone has an ear, let him hear!" (13:9), recalls and reinforces the exhortations in each of the prophetic oracles to the seven churches: "Let the one having an ear hear what the Spirit is saying to the churches" (2:7, 11, 17, 29; 3:6, 13, 22). What "anyone" in the audience is to hear is that if "anyone" is destined to go into captivity for prophetic witness against idolatrous worship, then into captivity he goes, and if "anyone" is destined to be killed by the dagger for prophetic witness against idolatrous worship, then he is by the dagger to be killed (13:10a). That he is by the "dagger" to be killed accords with the opening of the second seal in which the rider of the fiery red horse was given a great "dagger" to take the peace from the earth so that they will slaughter each other (6:4).

It is divinely necessary that "anyone" who may wish to harm the two prophetic witnesses be "killed" (11:5). Similarly, if "anyone" is to be "killed" for his prophetic witness, then he is to be "killed" in accord with divine necessity (13:10a). This recalls and resonates with the fact that some members of the audience, the fellow servants and brothers of the slaughtered souls, are about to be, in accord with the imminence of divine necessity, "killed" even as the slaughtered souls (6:11)—for their prophetic witness against idolatrous worship.

Informed that they may go into captivity or be killed for their prophetic witness against idolatrous worship (13:10a), the audience are exhorted: "Here is the endurance and the faith of the holy ones" (13:10b). This recalls the praise of the exalted Jesus for the members of the church at Thyatira because he knows their "faith" and "endur-

PART TWO—*Shown What Must Happen after These Things (4:1—16:21)*

ance" (2:19), before he challenges them to prophetic witness against the idolatrous worship of the false prophetess Jezebel (2:20-23). Since it was given to the beast to do battle against the "holy ones" (13:7), with whom the audience are to identify, they are exhorted to have the endurance and faith of the "holy ones" in their prophetic witness against idolatrous worship. This resonates with the heavenly worship that declares God's reward to the "holy ones" (11:18), to those in the audience who are willing to go into captivity or be killed for their witness to the true heavenly worship for eternal life in the Spirit of prophecy.

5e) Vision of the Beast from the Earth (13:11–18)

A a) ¹¹ Then I saw another beast ascending from the earth, and it **had** two horns like a lamb but it was speaking as a dragon,

    b) ¹²ᵃ and **all** the authority of the first beast it ***activates before*** it, and it ***activates*** the earth and those ***inhabiting*** on it so that they will worship the first beast,

      c) ¹²ᵇ whose plague, the one of its death, was healed,

    b′) ¹³ and it ***activates great*** signs, so that it may even ***make*** fire descend out of heaven to the earth ***before*** the **human beings**, ¹⁴ᵃ and it misleads those ***inhabiting*** upon the earth on account of the signs that are given to it to ***make before*** the beast, telling those who ***inhabit*** upon the earth to ***make*** an image for the beast,

  a′) ¹⁴ᵇ who ***has*** the plague of the dagger but lived.

B ¹⁵ᵃ Then it was given to it to give a spirit to **the image of the beast**,

  C ¹⁵ᵇ so that the image of the beast could even speak

B′ ¹⁵ᶜ and could make it so that as many as do not worship **the image of the beast** would be killed,

A′ a) ¹⁶ and it ***activates all***, the small and the **great**, and the rich and the poor, and the free and the slaves, so that they give to them a mark upon their right hand or upon their forehead,

180

ⁱ⁷ even so that no one may be able to buy or sell unless he is **one having** the mark—the name of the beast or the **number** of its name.

    b) ¹⁸ᵃ Here is the wisdom.

a′) ¹⁸ᵇ Let **one having** a mind calculate the **number** of the beast, for it is a **number** of a **human being**, and its **number**: six hundred sixty-six.

Having seen a beast "ascending" from the sea (13:1), John then saw another beast "ascending" from the "earth" (13:11), the "earth" upon which those inhabiting will worship the beast from the sea (13:8). The beast from the earth had two "horns" like a lamb (13:11), making it deceptively but imperfectly resemble the Lamb having the perfect number of seven "horns" (5:6). Furthermore, it was "speaking" as a dragon (13:11). This links it to the dragon that gave "great authority" to the beast from the sea (13:2) to "speak great things" together with the blasphemies of idolatrous worship (13:5).

All the great authority that the dragon gave to the beast from the sea (13:2, 4, 5, 7), the beast from the earth activates before it (13:12a). That it activates the "earth" and those "inhabiting" on it so that they "will worship" the first beast (13:12a) reinforces the assertion that all those "inhabiting" upon the "earth will worship" the first beast (13:8). And that this first beast is the one whose "plague," the one of "its death," was "healed" (13:12b) recalls that the first beast was slaughtered to death, but the "plague" of "its death" was "healed," so that the whole earth marveled after the beast (13:3), and worshiped both the dragon and the first beast (13:4).

Similar to the first beast who speaks "great" things (13:5), this second beast activates "great" signs (13:13), but signs that indicate that it is a false prophet. In contrast to the two true prophets, out of whose mouth "fire" comes and devours their enemies (11:5), the second beast makes "fire descend out of heaven to the earth before the human beings" (13:13). In contrast to the mighty angel "descending out of heaven" with a scroll containing true prophecy (10:1), and to the true prophecy of a new Jerusalem "descending out of heaven" (3:12), the second beast, as one of the signs of its false prophecy, makes fire "descend out of heaven."

That it makes fire descend before "the human beings" resonates with the fact that the rest of "the human beings" not killed by the plagues did not repent of their idolatrous worship (9:20).

The false prophetess Jezebel "misleads" the prophetic servants of Jesus to engage in idolatrous worship (2:20). The great dragon is the ancient serpent, the one called Devil and the Satan, who "misleads" the whole world (12:9). Similarly, the second beast, as a false prophet, "misleads" those "inhabiting" upon the "earth" (13:14a), so that those "inhabiting" on the "earth" will worship the first beast (13:12a). It misleads on account of the signs which are given to it to "make before" the first beast (13:14a), since all the authority of the first beast it "activates before" it (13:12a). As part of the signs misleading to false worship, it tells those inhabiting upon the earth, those who will worship the first beast, to make an image for the beast (13:14a), implicitly to promote and facilitate the idolatrous worship of it.

That the second beast "had" two horns like a lamb (13:11), in contrast to the Lamb (5:6), indicates that it is a deceptive false Christ like the first beast who "has" the "plague" of the dagger but lived (13:14b), recalling that its "plague" of death was healed (13:12b). Indeed, unlike one who witnesses to the true Christ and is thus killed by the "dagger" (13:10), the first beast has the plague of the "dagger" but lived. The first beast has the plague of the dagger "but lived" because it was healed (13:3, 12b) to continue its life on earth. In contrast, the true Christ became dead "but lived" (2:8) as one who is living forever in heaven (1:18).

The divine "Spirit" of life from God came in among the two prophetic witnesses who were killed (11:11) but then exalted to life in heaven (11:12). In ironic contrast, it was given to the second beast to give a human "spirit" to the humanly made image of the first beast (13:15a), so that the image of the beast could even "speak" (13:15b), like the beast who was "speaking" as a diabolical dragon (13:11). This accords with the fact that a mouth was given to the first beast to "speak" the "great things" that include the blasphemies of idolatrous worship (13:5).

The second beast could make it so that as many as do not "worship the image of the beast" would be killed (13:15c). This adds to the emphatic focus upon "the image of the beast" that is made by those inhabiting upon the earth (13:14a), and to which the second beast gave a human spirit (13:15a), since it activates those inhabiting on the earth so that they "will worship" the first beast (13:12a). That those who refuse to engage in idolatrous worship would be "killed" reinforces the exhortation for the audience to faithfully endure in their prophetic witness against false worship, even if some of them must be "killed" (13:10). Indeed, some of the brothers of the slaughtered souls are about to be "killed" even as they (6:11)—for their refusal to engage in idolatrous worship.

The second beast, who "activates all" the authority of the first beast and the earth and those inhabiting on it so that they will worship the first beast (13:12a), "activates all," "the small and the great, and the rich and the poor, and the free and the slaves, so that they give to them a mark upon their right hand or upon their forehead" (13:16). In ironic contrast to "the small and the great" who fear the name of God by their true worship (11:18), the second beast activates "the small and the great" so that they are given a mark associating them with idolatrous worship. That they will give the mark to the "rich" and the "poor" recalls the irony that one who thinks he is "rich" is actually "poor" (3:17) and vice versa (2:9). And that they will give the mark to the "free" and the "slaves" associates them with the "slave" and "free" included among the false worshipers seeking to avoid (6:15) the judgment of God and the Lamb (6:16).

The servants of God are sealed upon "their foreheads" in accord with their participation in true heavenly worship (7:3; 9:4). The large crowd of worshipers in heaven have palm branches in "their hands" (7:9). The mighty angel raised his "right hand" to heaven in reverential acknowledgment of the true and eternally living God (10:5). But the second beast activates all so that they will be given a mark upon their "right hand" or upon "their forehead" (13:16), a mark that makes them part of the economic system associated with idolatrous worship. This is confirmed as "no one may be able to buy or sell unless he is one having the mark—the name of the beast or the number of its name" (13:17).[14]

---

14. For the "mark" as a reference to Roman coinage and its significance for the provenance of Revelation, see Taylor, "Monetary Crisis," 580–96. "The 'mark' of the beast symbolizes a person's allegiance to and participation in the religious, social, economic, and political rites associated with the imperial cult" (Blount, *Revelation*, 259).

PART TWO—*Shown What Must Happen after These Things (4:1—16:21)*

The exalted Jesus, who is worshiped as the Lamb—"you who bought" for the true heavenly worship of God those from every nation (5:9)—advised the church in Laodicea to "buy" from him the things necessary to participate in true heavenly worship (3:18). But, ironically, no one may be able to "buy" or sell on earth unless he is one having the mark that associates him with idolatrous worship of the beast (13:17). No one is able to do business unless he has the "name" of the beast or the number of "its name" (13:17), the beast who opened its mouth for idolatrous blasphemies to God, ironically, to blaspheme "his name" (13:6). But for each of all those inhabiting upon the earth who worship the beast, "his name" has not been written in the scroll of the eternal, heavenly life of the Lamb (13:8).

The audience were exhorted that "here" they are to have the endurance and the faith of the holy ones, calling them to persevere in their witness against idolatrous worship (13:10). Now they are similarly exhorted that "here" they are to have the "wisdom" (13:18a), calling them to recognize and share in the divine "wisdom" for which both God and the Lamb are worshiped (5:12; 7:12). In contrast to one "having" the mark of idolatrous worship (13:17), anyone in the audience "having" a mind oriented to true worship is exhorted to "calculate the number of the beast, for it is a number of a human being, and its number: six hundred sixty-six" (13:18b). The number of the beast is a number of a mere "human being," like one of the "human beings" before whom the second beast, as part of its false prophecy, makes fire descend out of heaven to the earth (13:13).

The "number" of the angels worshiping the Lamb in heaven is a divinely unlimited "ten thousands of ten thousands and thousands of thousands" (5:11). The "number" that John heard of those sealed for heavenly worship is a divinely determined "one hundred forty-four thousand" (7:4). And the "number" of the angelic armies of horsemen of the sixth trumpeting was a divinely unlimited "twenty thousand of ten thousands" (9:16). But the "number" of the beast, the object of false worship, is a humanly limited "six hundred sixty-six" (13:18). Since the number seven is a divinely perfect number, the human number of 666 indicates triple imperfection, underlining the unworthiness of the

Worship of Dragon and Beasts on Earth and Worship of Lamb in Heaven

beast as an object of true heavenly worship.[15] Consequently, rather than engaging and associating with the idolatrous worship of the beast on earth, the audience are to participate in the true heavenly worship for eternal life in the Spirit of prophecy.

6e') Vision of the Lamb with 144,000 (14:1–5)

    A a) ^{14:1} Then I saw, and behold the **Lamb** was standing upon Mount Zion, and with him were one hundred forty-four thousand having his name and the name of his Father written upon *their* foreheads,

        b) ^{2a} and *I heard* a *sound* out of heaven as a *sound* of many waters and as a *sound* of great thunder,

        b') ^{2b} and the *sound* that *I heard*

    a') ^{2c} was as harpists harp-playing with *their* harps,

    B ^{3a} and they are singing a new **song** before the throne and before the four living creatures and the elders,

    B' ^{3b} and no one was able to learn the **song** except the one hundred forty-four thousand, those who have been bought from the earth.

    A' a) ^{4a} These *are* those who have not been defiled with women, for they *are* virgins,

        b) ^{4b} those who are following the **Lamb** wherever he may go.

        b') ^{4c} Those were bought from human beings as first fruits for God and the **Lamb**,

    a') ⁵ and in *their* mouth is not found falsehood, unblemished *are* they.

John saw the "Lamb" in the midst of the throne in heaven "standing" as one having been slaughtered (5:6). Now, in contrast to the dragon

---

15. "Some writers take the number more as a symbol than a cryptogram. 666 is the number that falls short of perfection in each of its digits . . . It is the trinity of imperfection" (Mounce, *Revelation*, 262).

PART TWO—*Shown What Must Happen after These Things (4:1—16:21)*

who "stood upon" the sand of the sea on earth (12:18), the "Lamb" was "standing upon" the heavenly, spiritual Mount Zion, "and with him were one hundred forty-four thousand having his name and the name of his Father written upon their foreheads" (14:1). The "one hundred forty-four thousand" with him refers to the "one hundred forty-four thousand" who were divinely sealed from every tribe of Israel for participation in heavenly worship (7:4).

No one was able to buy or sell anything on earth unless he was among those having the mark, the "name" of the beast or the number of "its name" (13:17), upon "their forehead" (13:16). In contrast, the one hundred forty-four thousand with the Lamb on the heavenly Mount Zion have "his name" and the "name" of his Father written upon "their foreheads" (14:1). This recalls and resonates with the fact that the one hundred forty-four thousand, as the servants of God, were sealed upon "their foreheads," divinely designated to participate in heavenly worship (7:3). The name of "his Father" relates them to the audience as among those whom Jesus made into a kingdom, priests to be engaged in true heavenly worship for "his Father" (1:6).

When John heard the seven "thunders" speak, he reported that "I heard a sound out of heaven" saying, "Seal the things the seven thunders spoke" (10:4). Now he reports that "I heard a sound out of heaven as a sound of many waters" and as a sound of great "thunder" (14:2a). This recalls that the sound of the exalted Jesus in heaven was "as a sound of many waters" (1:15). And the "sound" that "I heard" (14:2b) was as "harpists harp-playing with their harps" (14:2c). This emphatically resonates with the "harp" that each of the twenty-four elders had for their role in heavenly worship (5:8). And the reference to harpists harp-playing with "their" harps further associates with heavenly worship those with the name of the Lamb and of his Father written upon "their" foreheads (14:1), those with whom the audience are to identify.

When the Lamb received the scroll, the "four living creatures" and the twenty-four "elders" fell before the Lamb (5:8), and "they are singing a new song" as they worship the Lamb (5:9). The one hundred forty-four thousand are participants in this heavenly worship as "they are singing a new song" before the throne and before the "four living creatures" and the "elders" (14:3a). "No one was able" to open the scroll (5:3) except the

Lamb in heaven (5:5–6). "No one was able" to number the large crowd participating in heavenly worship (7:9). Similarly, "no one was able" to learn the "song," the new "song" of heavenly worship (14:3a), except the one hundred forty-four thousand (14:3b).

No one "may be able" to "buy" or sell anything on earth without the mark—the name of the beast or the number of its name (13:17). In contrast, no one "was able" to learn the new song of worship in heaven except the one hundred forty-four thousand, those who have been "bought" from the earth (14:3b). They are among those whom the Lamb "bought" for the heavenly worship of God (5:9). In contrast to those inhabiting upon the "earth" (13:14), who engage in the idolatrous worship of the image of the beast (13:14–15), the one hundred forty-four thousand have been bought from the "earth" so that they may live and worship in heaven.

Regarding the participants in heavenly worship who are clothed with white robes (7:13), one of the elders told John that "these are" those who have metaphorically "washed their robes and whitened them in the blood of the Lamb" (7:14) through their prophetic witness against idolatrous worship. Regarding the heavenly dimension of the two prophetic witnesses against idolatrous worship on earth (11:3), "these are" the two olive trees and the two lampstands that are standing (11:4) before the Lord of the earth, as the object of true heavenly worship. Similarly, regarding the one hundred forty-four thousand bought from the earth to participate in heavenly worship (14:3), "these are" those who have not been metaphorically "defiled with women," for they are "virgins" (14:4a), those who have not engaged in the "prostitution" of idolatrous worship.

They have not been defiled with "women" (14:4a) like the "woman" Jezebel, the false prophetess who misleads the servants of Jesus to engage in the "prostitution" of idolatrous worship (2:20). They have not been "defiled," and thus not disqualified for heavenly worship, like those who have not "defiled" their garments through idolatrous worship on earth, so that they will walk with the exalted Jesus in white (3:4), prepared to participate in heavenly worship.[16] They are metaphorical "vir-

---

16. "The verb [defile] is not sexual for John; it applies rather to idolatry and the lack of resistance to that idolatry. John could craft such a connection (see 2:14, 20)

gins" (14:4a) who have not engaged in the "prostitution" or "adultery" of idolatrous worship (2:20–22).[17] As those who follow the Lamb wherever he may "go" (14:4b), any one of them may need to "go" into captivity or be killed like the Lamb for their prophetic witness (13:10). But as those who are following the "Lamb" wherever he may go, they are with the "Lamb" standing on Mount Zion to worship in heaven (14:1).

The one hundred forty-four thousand who have been "bought" from the earth (14:3) are those who were "bought" by God (divine passive) from "the human beings" on earth (14:4c). These are "the human beings" the second beast misleads into idolatrous worship by making fire descend from heaven to earth before them (13:13), and the rest of "the human beings" who did not repent of their idolatrous worship (9:20). They were bought from the human beings as metaphorical "first fruits" for the heavenly worship of "God" and the Lamb with whom they are standing on Mount Zion in heaven (14:1). They are thus among those the Lamb "bought" for the heavenly worship of "God" (5:9).[18]

The first beast opened "its mouth" for idolatrous blasphemies to God (13:6). But as for the one hundred forty-four thousand, who have the name of the Lamb and of his Father written upon "their" foreheads (14:1), in "their mouth is not found falsehood, unblemished are they" (14:5). In contrast to the dragon and his angels for whom a place was not "found" by God (divine passive) in heaven (12:8), in the mouth of the one hundred forty-four thousand is not "found" the falsehood associated with idolatrous worship, thus qualifying them for a place among the worshipers in heaven.[19] The one hundred forty-four thousand "are" those who have not been "defiled with women" through idolatrous wor-

---

because idolatry had long been imaged as improper sexuality" (Blount, *Revelation*, 268).

17. "That the group described in 14:1–5 is in contrast with the beast-worshipers in 13:11–18 also suggests that the idea of virgins is figurative, since the followers of the beast are guilty primarily not of immorality but of idolatry. Consequently, the followers of the Lamb are primarily characterized by loyalty to him and not idolatry of the beast, and virginity is one way of portraying that loyalty" (Beale, *Revelation*, 741).

18. "The first fruit is the part of the harvest to which God has claim, which is therefore presented to him as a sacrifice" (Roloff, *Revelation*, 172).

19. Olson, "Those Who Have Not Defiled," 492–510.

ship, for they "are" metaphorical "virgins" (14:4a), and thus morally unblemished or blameless "are" they to participate in heavenly worship. They thus provide an encouraging model for the audience to join them in the true heavenly worship for eternal life in the Spirit of prophecy.

7d') Announcement of God's Judgment and Fall of Babylon (14:6–8)

> **A** ⁶ Then I saw another angel flying in midheaven, having everlasting good news to bring good news upon those sitting upon the earth and upon **every nation** and tribe and tongue and people,
>
> > **B** ⁷ᵃ **saying** with a great sound,
> >
> > > **C** ⁷ᵇ "Fear God and give **him** glory,
> > >
> > > **C'** ⁷ᶜ for has come the hour of **his** judgment, and worship the one who made the heaven and the earth and sea and springs of waters."
> >
> > **B'** ⁸ᵃ Then another angel, a second, followed **saying**,
>
> **A'** ⁸ᵇ "Fallen, fallen has Babylon the great, who from the wine of the fury of her prostitution made drink **all the nations**."

John saw and heard one eagle "flying in midheaven" with a bad news message of woe to those inhabiting upon the earth (8:13). In contrast, he now saw another angel "flying in midheaven," "having everlasting good news to bring good news upon those sitting upon the earth and upon every nation and tribe and tongue and people" (14:6). The bad news of woe is for those "inhabiting upon the earth," those engaged in idolatrous worship (13:8, 12, 14). But the good news is for those "sitting upon the earth," those in a position of being included among the one hundred forty-four thousand who have been bought from the "earth" to engage in heavenly worship (14:3). With the completion of the mystery of God at the seventh trumpeting, God "brought good news" to his own servants the prophets (10:7). But now the angel is to "bring good news" upon a universal group from every nation and tribe and tongue and people.

PART TWO—*Shown What Must Happen after These Things (4:1—16:21)*

Authority was given to the first beast over "every tribe and people and tongue and nation" (13:7), to cause all those inhabiting upon the earth to engage in the idolatrous worship of the beast (13:8, 12, 14). But now the angel is to bring good news upon those sitting upon the earth, upon "every nation and tribe and tongue and people" (14:6). This recalls that the slaughtered Lamb bought for God those from "every tribe and tongue and people and nation"—for the true and universal heavenly worship of God (5:9). Indeed, the large numberless crowd of those worshiping God and the Lamb in heaven were from "every nation and tribes and peoples and tongues" (7:9).

"Saying with a great sound," the eagle flying in midheaven announced bad news of woe from the sounds of the final three trumpets for those inhabiting upon the earth, those engaged in idolatrous worship (8:13). But now, "saying with a great sound," the angel flying in midheaven having everlasting good news issues an invitation for all those on earth to participate in true and universal heavenly worship: "Fear God and give him the glory, for the hour of his judgment has come, and worship the one who made the heaven and the earth and sea and springs of waters" (14:7). The rest of the human beings not killed by the great earthquake following the ascension to heaven of the two prophetic witnesses against idolatrous worship became "fearful" and performed an act of true worship, as they "gave glory" to the "God" of heaven (11:13). And now the angel with good news invites all on earth to join in this true worship, to "fear God" and "give" him "glory."

The souls slaughtered on account of their prophetic witness against idolatrous worship (6:9) cried out in prayerful worship, "Until when, Master, holy and true, do you not judge and vindicate our blood from those inhabiting upon the earth?" (6:10). In answer to their prayer the heavenly worship at the seventh trumpeting announced that the time for the dead to be "judged" has come and to give the reward to God's servants the prophets and to the holy ones and to those who "fear" God's name through proper worship (11:18). And now, with a further answer to the prayer of the slaughtered souls, the angel issues a universal call to proper worship, to "fear" God and give "him" glory (14:7b), for the hour of "his judgment" (14:7c) has come.

Worship of Dragon and Beasts on Earth and Worship of Lamb in Heaven

There are those who may falsely "worship" the humanly made image of the beast (13:15), which those inhabiting upon the earth are to "make" (13:14). But in ironic contrast to this, the angel invites all those sitting upon the earth, those from everywhere, to truly "worship" the God who "made the heaven and the earth and sea and springs of waters" (14:7). This call to the universal worship of God as the one who made the "heaven" and the "earth" and "sea" appropriately complements the universal heavenly worship of God and the Lamb from every creature in "heaven" and upon the "earth" and under the "earth" and upon the "sea" and all the things in them (5:13). That God made "springs of waters" recalls that he made not only the "springs of the waters" on earth (8:10), but also eternal life's "springs of waters" in heaven to which the Lamb will lead those who truly worship God (7:17).

Whereas the first angel was "saying" with a great sound (14:7a), yet another angel, a second, followed the first (14:6) "saying," "Fallen, fallen has Babylon the great, who from the wine of the fury of her prostitution made drink all the nations" (14:8; cf. Isa 21:9; Jer 51:7-8). That "fallen, fallen" has Babylon the "great" recalls that a tenth of the city, the "great" city, which is called spiritually Sodom and Egypt, where both the two prophetic witnesses and their Lord were killed (11:8), "fell" after the divine vindication of the two prophets for their witness against idolatrous worship (11:13). The wine of the "fury" of Babylon resonates ominously with the great "fury" of the devil (12:12). And the wine of the fury of "her prostitution," her idolatrous worship, associates Babylon with the false prophetess Jezebel, who does not wish to repent from "her prostitution" (2:21), and with the rest of the human beings who did not repent of "their prostitution" (9:21).[20]

The great Babylon who made all the nations "drink" from the metaphorical "wine" of her fury and thus promoted a universal participation in her "prostitution," her false worship that contradicts the eucharistic dining with Jesus (3:20), has emphatically and conclusively fallen (14:8). This dramatic announcement reinforces the exhortation

---

20. "Here Babylon is naturally used as a pseudonym for Rome, not so much to disguise what is truly meant but to reveal its true meaning. The capital city of the new Babylonian empire, Babylon, was understood, since the time of the exile, as the epitome of the satanic world power" (Roloff, *Revelation*, 175).

PART TWO—*Shown What Must Happen after These Things (4:1—16:21)*

resulting from the everlasting good news upon "every nation" (14:6), the exhortation for everyone to participate in the true and universal heavenly worship of the God who made everything (14:7). Indeed, although Babylon made "all the nations" drink of the wine of the fury of her idolatrous worship, the heavenly woman gave birth to a son, a male, who is about to shepherd "all the nations" into the eternal life and worship in heaven (12:5). Rather than being deceived and seduced into participating in the false worship promoted by the great Babylon, the audience are to participate in the true and universal heavenly worship of God and the Lamb for eternal life in the Spirit of prophecy.

8c′) Blessed Are Those Who Die for Not Worshiping the Beast (14:9–13)

A ⁹ᵃ Then another angel, a third, **followed** them **saying** with a great **sound**,

> B ⁹ᵇ **"If anyone worships the beast and its image** and **receives** a **mark** upon his forehead or upon his hand, ¹⁰ then he will drink from the wine of the fury **of God** that has been mixed undiluted in the cup of his anger and will be **tormented** with fire and sulfur before **holy** angels and before the Lamb,
>
> B′ ¹¹ and the smoke of their **torment** ascends for ages of ages, and they do not have rest day and night, those **worshiping the beast and its image,** and **if anyone receives** the **mark** of its name." ¹² Here is the endurance of the **holy** ones, those keeping the commandments **of God** and the faith of Jesus.

A′ a) ¹³ᵃ Then I heard a **sound** out of heaven *saying,*

> b) ¹³ᵇ "Write: Blessed are **the** dead,
>
> b′) ¹³ᶜ **the** ones who die in the Lord from now on!"
>
> a′) ¹³ᵈ "Yes," *says* the Spirit, "they will rest from their labors, for their works **follow** with them."

Then another angel, a third, followed "them" (14:9a)," that is, the first (14:6) and the second (14:8) angels. "Saying with a great sound," the first angel brought the good news of calling everyone to participate in the true worship of God (14:7). But now, "saying with a great sound," the third angel issues bad news for anyone who participates in false worship (14:9a).

The second beast, the one from the earth, could make it so that as many as do not "worship" the "image of the beast," the first beast, the one from the sea, would be killed (13:15). And it causes everyone to be given a metaphorical "mark" upon their right "hand" or upon their "forehead" (13:16), corresponding to their full participation in an economic system dominated by idolatrous worship (13:17). But now the third angel issues a stern warning for anyone who "worships" the "beast" and its "image" and receives a "mark" upon his "forehead" or upon his "hand" (14:9b).

Babylon the great made all the nations (14:8) "drink" from the "wine of the fury" of her "prostitution," her idolatrous worship," so that they were seduced into participating in idolatrous worship. In ironic contrast, anyone who engages in idolatrous worship of the beast "will drink" from the "wine of the fury" of God "that has been mixed undiluted in the cup of his anger" (14:10), contradicting the eucharistic dining with Jesus (3:20). Thus, anyone who engages in idolatrous worship will experience the "anger" of the judgment of God against idolatrous worshipers. This recalls the true worship of God which acknowledged that "your anger" has come and the time for the dead to be judged and to give the reward to God's servants the prophets and to the holy ones and to those who fear God's name through proper worship (11:18). At the opening of the sixth seal everyone on earth wanted to hide from being judged by the "anger" of God and the Lamb (6:16), for the great day of their "anger" has come (6:17).

At the fifth trumpeting those human beings without the seal of God designating them as participants in true heavenly worship "will be tormented" by God (divine passive) for five months (9:5). At the sixth trumpeting "fire" and smoke and "sulfur" was coming out from the mouths of the destructive horses (9:17), so that a third of the human beings engaged in idolatrous worship were killed from the "fire" and the smoke and the "sulfur" (9:18). And now anyone who worships the beast and its image "will be tormented" with "fire" and "sulfur before holy angels and before the Lamb" (14:10). Jesus promised that he will confess the name of the one who conquers false worship "before" his Father and "before" his "angels" (3:5). Ironically, anyone who worships the beast and its image rather than worshiping "before the Lamb" (5:8; 7:9) will be tormented "before" holy "angels" and "before the Lamb."

The smoke of their "torment," that is, of those who "will be tormented" with fire and sulfur for worshiping the beast and its image (14:10), "ascends for ages of ages" (14:11). Just as "smoke" complemented the fire and sulfur coming out from the mouths of the destructive horses (9:17), so the "smoke" of their torment complements the fire and sulfur with which the idolatrous worshipers will be tormented. That the smoke of their torment "ascends" resonates with the destructive "smoke" that "ascended" from the shaft of the abyss as "smoke" of a great furnace (9:2). This smoke of torment for false worshipers ironically contrasts the "smoke" of the incense that "ascended" with the prayers of the holy ones as an act of true worship before God (8:4).

The torment experienced by idolatrous worshipers "for ages of ages" (14:11) ironically contrasts the true worship "for the ages of the ages" (1:6; 7:12) of God and the Lamb, who live and reign "for the ages of the ages" (1:18; 4:9, 10; 5:13; 10:6; 11:15). The four living creatures "do not have rest day and night" as they unceasingly perform their liturgy of true heavenly worship (4:8). In ironic contrast, the idolatrous worshipers "do not have rest day and night" from their unremitting torment (14:11).

The third angel warned of torment "if anyone worships the beast and its image" and "receives" a "mark" upon his forehead or upon his hand (14:9b). The repeated reference to those "worshiping the beast and its image" and "if anyone receives" the "mark" of its name (14:11) emphatically reinforces the warning of this torment. Furthermore, the concluding reference to the mark of "its name" recalls the intensely imperfect number of "its name" (13:17), underlining the unworthiness of the beast and its image to be an object of true worship. In contrast, the one hundred forty-four thousand true worshipers of the Lamb have "his name" and the "name" of his Father written upon their foreheads (14:1).

The audience were previously exhorted to have endurance in their prophetic witness against idolatrous worship, whether it leads to their captivity or death: "Here is the endurance and the faith of the holy ones" (13:10). And now this exhortation is reinforced and elaborated: "Here is the endurance of the holy ones, those keeping the commandments of God and the faith of Jesus" (14:12). The idolatrous worshiper will drink from the wine of the fury "of God" (14:10). In contrast, the audience are to be the "holy ones" associated with the "holy" angels (14:10), by keeping the commandments "of God."

The reference to the audience as those who are "keeping the commandments of God and the faith of Jesus" (14:12) resonates with their being among the offspring of the heavenly woman who are "keeping the commandments of God and have the witness of Jesus" (12:17). The exhortation for the audience to be those who "keep" the commandments of God reinforces the exhortation for them to be those who hear the words of the prophecy of God and "keep" the things written in the book of Revelation (1:3).[21] That they are both to have the "witness" of Jesus and to keep the "faith" of Jesus means they are not to deny the "faith" of Jesus like Antipas, "my witness, my faithful one," who was killed for his prophetic witness against idolatrous worship (2:13). In faithfully upholding their prophetic witness to the practice of true heavenly worship the audience are thus to be like Jesus himself, the "witness," the "faithful one" (1:5; 3:14).

Recalling and continuing the previous divine commands for John to "write" for his audience of seven churches (1:11, 19; 2:1, 8, 12, 18; 3:1, 7, 14), John heard a sound out of heaven saying, "Write: Blessed are the dead, the ones who die in the Lord from now on!" (14:13). "The" dead are further clarified; they are not just any dead, but "the" ones who die in the Lord.[22] These "dead" are blessed by God because, in accord with the worship of the Lord God (11:17), the time for the "dead" to be judged and to give the reward to God's servants the prophets and to the

---

21. "'The commandments of God' is a holistic reference to the objective revelation of the old and new covenants, to which the faithful remain loyal" (Beale, *Revelation*, 766).

22. "To 'die in the Lord' means to remain faithful to the very end, to make Christ the sphere of your life" (Osborne, *Revelation*, 544).

holy ones and to those who fear God's name through true worship has come (11:18). "Blessed" by God is each member of the audience who hears the words of the prophecy and keeps the things written in it (1:3). And now "blessed" by God are the dead who die in the Lord from "now" on, because they have kept the things written in the prophecy by their witness against idolatrous worship, and "now" the salvation, power, and kingdom of God and his Christ has come to be (12:10).

Recalling the previous exhortations to hear what "the Spirit is saying" to each of the seven churches of the audience (2:7, 11, 17, 29; 3:6, 13, 22), "Yes," "says the Spirit," "they will rest from their labors, for their works follow with them" (14:13). Those who die in the Lord after a life of prophetic witness against idolatrous worship "will rest" like the souls slaughtered for their prophetic witness against idolatrous worship. These are the souls who "will rest yet a little time, until would be fulfilled both their fellow servants and their brothers who are about to be killed even as they" (6:11). Resonating with Jesus' praise for the "works" and "labor" of those who resist evil ones (2:2), those who die in the Lord will rest from their "labors," for their "works" follow with them.[23]

The threat of personified Death was emphasized with the notice that Hades, the realm of the dead, "was following with him" (6:8). But now the divine judgment of blessedness for those who die in the Lord, those who are "following" the Lamb wherever he may go (14:4), is emphasized. Their works, according to which Jesus will give to each one (2:23), "follow with them" (14:13), just as certainly as the third angel "followed" the first two (14:9a). The Spirit emphatically promises that those who faithfully endure in their lifelong witness against false worship will rest from their labors, for their works follow with them, as those who have promoted and practiced the true heavenly worship for eternal life in the Spirit of prophecy.[24]

---

23. "Emphasis has been placed upon work as maintaining faithful witness" (Boxall, *Revelation*, 211).

24. DeSilva, "Sociorhetorical Interpretation," 65–117; DeSilva, "Seeing Things John's Way," 271–98.

9b′) Vision of Harvesting Earth by One Like a Son of Man for Judgment (14:14–17)

> A ¹⁴ Then I saw, and behold a white cloud, and upon the cloud sitting one like a Son of Man, **having** upon his head a golden crown and in his hand a **sharp sickle**. ¹⁵ᵃ **Then another angel came out from the temple**
>
> > B ¹⁵ᵇ crying out in a great sound to **the one sitting upon the cloud**, "Send **your sickle** and **harvest**, for has come the hour to **harvest**, and dried up is the **harvest** of the **earth**."
> >
> > B′ ¹⁶ Then **the one sitting upon the cloud** threw **his sickle** upon the **earth** and **harvested** was the **earth**.
>
> A′ ¹⁷ **Then another angel came out from the temple** in heaven **having** also, he himself, a **sharp sickle**.

As the first four seals began to be opened, the formula "then I saw, and behold" introduced three of those "sitting" upon a horse and causing havoc for those on earth (6:2, 5, 8). But the same formula "then I saw, and behold" also introduced John's vision of the Lamb "standing" upon Mount Zion in heaven together with one hundred forty-four thousand (14:1). These are those the Lamb bought from the earth, the earth damaged by the destruction depicted at the opening of the seals, to engage in heavenly worship (14:3; cf. 5:9). And now John reports that "then I saw, and behold a white cloud, and upon the cloud sitting one like a Son of Man, having upon his head a golden crown and in his hand a sharp sickle" (14:14). Thus the stage has been set for the execution of divine judgment upon the earth by the exalted Jesus, the one "standing" as the Lamb in heaven but now "sitting" upon a white cloud as one like a Son of Man.

Clouds have been associated with various acts of movement between heaven and earth. Jesus is coming from heaven with the "clouds" (1:7). A mighty angel was descending out of heaven to earth clothed with a "cloud" (10:1). The two prophetic witnesses on earth ascended to heaven in a "cloud" (11:12). And now a white "cloud," the "cloud" upon which is sitting "one like a Son of Man," the heavenly exalted Jesus whom John previously saw as "one like a Son of Man" (1:13), implies an impending movement from heaven to earth (14:14). That the cloud is "white" underlines its heavenly association, resonating with the "white" robe given to each of the slaughtered souls in heaven (6:11). Whereas the one "sitting" upon a "white" horse used it for transportation to conquer those on earth (6:2), the one like a Son of Man "sitting" upon a white cloud used it as an authoritative base or throne in heaven to judge those on earth.[25]

John saw "sitting" upon a heavenly "white" cloud one like a Son of Man, having "upon his head a golden crown" (14:14). This closely associates the one like a Son of Man with the heavenly figures of the twenty-four elders engaged in heavenly worship. John saw them "sitting" clothed in "white" garments and "upon their heads golden crowns" (4:4).

The one sitting upon a black horse "has" a scale "in his hand" (6:5) to regulate economic matters on earth (6:6). The mighty angel descended out of heaven (10:1) "having in his hand" a small scroll containing God's plan for those on earth (10:2). The one like a Son of Man "has in his hand" a sharp sickle (14:14).[26] This "sharp" sickle resonates with the "sharp" two-edged sword coming out of the mouth (1:16) of the one like a Son of Man (1:13), the exalted Jesus who identified himself as the one having the "sharp" two-edged sword (2:12), the metaphorical instrument for executing judgment on earth.[27] The Spirit promised that those who die in the Lord will rest from "their" labors, for "their" works, the works according to which they will be judged (2:23; 11:18), follow with "them" (14:13). Accordingly, the one like a Son of Man has upon "his" head a golden crown and in "his" hand a sharp sickle to execute that judgment (14:14).

Then "another" angel, the fourth "other" angel (14:6, 8, 9), came out from the "temple" (14:15a), the "temple" of God in heaven that was opened so that the ark of God's covenant appeared in his "temple"

---

25. "The white cloud here is not so much a means of transport as it is a kind of throne . . . The 'one like a son of man' is a sovereign about to judge his world" (Osborne, *Revelation*, 550–51).

26. "The symbol of the sickle is taken from Joel 3:13: 'Put in the sickle, for the harvest is ripe. Go in, tread, for the winepress is full. The vats overflow'" (Roloff, *Revelation*, 177).

27. "The emphasis on the 'sharpness' of the sickle brings out the finality and power behind the judgment" (Osborne, *Revelation*, 551).

(11:19a). From this temple "there came to be lightnings and sounds and thunders and an earthquake and great hail" (11:19b), as a further response to the prayers of the holy ones (8:3-5). The angel was "crying out in a great sound" to the one "sitting" upon the "cloud" (14:15b), that is, the one like a Son of Man whom John saw "sitting" upon the white "cloud" (14:14). This recalls and resonates with the slaughtered souls who "cried out with a great sound," as they prayed for divine judgment of those inhabiting upon the earth (6:10). Indeed, the angel was crying out, "Send your sickle and harvest, for has come the hour to harvest, and dried up is the harvest of the earth" (14:15b).

"For has come the hour" to harvest (14:15b) is another way of saying "for has come the hour" of God's "judgment" (14:7). This is in answer to the slaughtered souls' prayer, "Until when, Master, holy and true, do you not judge and vindicate our blood from those inhabiting upon the earth?" (6:10). That the harvest of the "earth" (14:15b) is "dried up" or "ripened" by God (divine passive) emphatically underlines that the hour has come to harvest/judge the earth, including those inhabiting upon the earth, those engaged in idolatrous worship.

Then "the one sitting upon the cloud," that is, the one like a Son of Man (14:14), the one to whom the angel cried out with a great sound as "the one sitting upon the cloud" (14:15b), "threw his sickle upon the earth and harvested was the earth" (14:16). Whereas the dragon "threw" a third of the stars of heaven "to the earth" (12:4), the one sitting upon the white cloud in heaven "threw" his sickle "upon the earth." This further accords with the answer to the prayers of the holy ones, including the prayer of the slaughtered souls for judgment on earth (6:10), as it resonates with the angel who "threw" the censer filled from the fire of the altar in heaven "to the earth" (8:5). Since the hour to "harvest" has come, and the "harvest" of the "earth" (14:15b) is dried up, he threw his sickle upon the "earth" and the "earth" was emphatically "harvested," that is, judged by God (divine passive).

Then yet "another" angel, the fifth "other" angel (14:6, 8, 9, 15b), like the fourth other angel who "came out from the temple" (14:15b), "came out from the temple in heaven having also, he himself, a sharp sickle" (14:17). That the angel came out of the "temple in heaven" further resonates with the "temple" of God "in heaven" from which "there came to be lightnings and sounds and thunders and an earthquake and

PART TWO—*Shown What Must Happen after These Things (4:1—16:21)*

great hail" (11:19). That this angel came out of the temple "in heaven" (cf. 14:15a) further accords with the divine response from the temple "in heaven" in answer to the prayer of the slaughtered souls for divine judgment of those inhabiting "upon the earth" (6:10).

The angel crying out in a "great sound" came out from the temple (14:15a) "in heaven" (14:17), and told the one sitting upon the cloud, the exalted Jesus Christ as the one like a Son of Man, that the time has come for the "harvesting," the divine judgment, of the earth (14:15b). This accords with the "great sound in heaven" that John heard (12:10) after the dragon was thrown to the earth (12:9). The great sound was saying that now that the dragon has been thrown from heaven to earth the authority of God's Christ has come to be (12:10). This includes the divine authority to judge those on earth, including those the dragon misleads to engage in idolatrous worship (12:9).

This fifth "other" angel is referred to with an emphatic and dramatic "he himself" (14:17). Similar to the one like a Son of Man who "has" a "sharp sickle" (14:14), this angel himself also "has" a "sharp sickle," the instrument for executing the "harvesting," the divine judgment, of the earth. This indication of yet a further stage in the divine judgment from the temple in heaven of those engaged in idolatrous worship on earth thus reinforces the ongoing exhortation for the audience to practice and promote the true heavenly worship for eternal life in the Spirit of prophecy.

10a′) Vine of the Earth Thrown into the Winepress of God's Fury (14:18–20)

> A [18a] Then another angel **came out** from the altar having authority over the fire,
>
> > B [18b] and sounded with a **great** sound to the one having the sickle, the sharp one, saying,
> >
> > > C [18c] "Send your sickle, the sharp one, and **gather** the clusters of **the vine of the earth**,
> > >
> > > > D [18d] for its grapes are ripened."

> **C′** ¹⁹ᵃ Then the angel threw his sickle to the **earth** and **gathered the vine of the earth**
>
> **B′** ¹⁹ᵇ and threw it into the winepress of the fury of God, the **great** one,
>
> **A′** ²⁰ and the winepress was trampled outside of the city and blood **came out** from the winepress up to the bridles of the horses for one thousand six hundred stadia.

Then "another" angel, the sixth "other" angel (14:6, 8, 9, 15b, 17), who "came out" of the temple in heaven, "came out" more specifically from the altar of the temple in heaven "having authority over the fire" (14:18a). That this angel came out from the "altar" having authority over the "fire" closely associates, if not identifies, him with the angel who received the censer and filled it from the "fire" of the "altar" in heaven and threw it to the earth (8:5). He did this as a divine response to the prayers of the holy ones offered on the altar (8:4), which include the prayer of the slaughtered souls for divine judgment of those inhabiting upon the earth (6:10).

The fourth other angel was crying out in a "great sound" to the one sitting upon the cloud (14:15), the one like a Son of Man (14:14). Similarly, the sixth angel sounded with a "great sound" to the fifth angel with the sharp sickle (14:18b), similar to Jesus, the one sitting on the cloud (14:14), who also has a "sharp sickle" (14:17). The fourth other angel told Jesus to "send your sickle" and harvest, for has come the hour to harvest, and dried up or ripened is the harvest of the earth (14:15). Similarly, the sixth other angel told the fifth to "send your sickle," the sharp one, and gather the clusters of the vine of the earth (14:18c), for its grapes are ripened (14:18d) like the harvest. Thus, the gathering of "the vine of the earth" intensifies the divine judgment characterized as harvesting "the harvest of the earth."[28]

The sixth other angel, who was told to "gather" the clusters of "the vine of the earth" (14:18c), threw his sickle to the earth and "gathered the vine of the earth" (14:19a). He "threw his sickle to the earth," further intensifying the divine judgment executed by Jesus, who similarly "threw

---

28. "The vintage harvest and the winepress as metaphors for divine judgment are found in Joel 3:13 (MT 4:13)" (Aune, *Revelation 6–16*, 846).

PART TWO—*Shown What Must Happen after These Things (4:1—16:21)*

his sickle upon the earth" (14:16). In addition, this further contrasts with the dragon, who swept a third of the stars of heaven and "threw" them "to the earth" (12:4), contributing to the need for the earth to be harvested/judged. And it further resonates with the angel who "threw to the earth" the censer filled with fire from the altar" (8:5) in answer to the prayer of the slaughtered souls for divine judgment of those inhabiting upon the earth (6:10), those engaged in idolatrous worship.

That the angel threw the vine of the earth into the winepress of the "fury of God," "the great one" (14:19b), reinforces the warning that anyone who worships the beast and its image (14:9) will drink from the wine of the "fury of God" (14:10). This ironically corresponds to the fact that Babylon the great made drink all the nations from the wine of the "fury" of her "prostitution," her idolatrous worship (14:8). In accord with the angel's "great" sound (14:18b), the "great one," with its grammatical ambivalence, serves a richly dual purpose. On the one hand, as a masculine *accusative*, it may appropriately indicate that the "winepress," a feminine *accusative*, is the great winepress of divine judgment. On the other hand, as a *masculine* accusative, the "great one" may underline that this "fury" is of "God," a *masculine* genitive, as *the* one and only divine "great one" in heaven, in contrast to the "great fury" of the devil (12:12), who is a dragon "great" merely on earth (12:3, 9).

The winepress into which the angel threw the vine of the earth (14:19) was trampled by God (divine passive) "outside the city and blood came out from the winepress up to the bridles of the horses for one thousand six hundred stadia" (14:20). The winepress was "trampled" outside of the "city" in ironic contrast to the idolaters who will "trample" the holy "city" for forty-two months (11:2). In accord with the angel who "came out" from the altar in heaven with instructions for a further, intensified act of divine judgment of the earth (14:18), an enormous amount of blood "came out" from the winepress. That this is implicitly the "blood" of those inhabiting upon the earth, those engaged in idolatrous worship, serves as a further response to the prayer of the slaughtered souls for divine judgment and vindication of their "blood" from those inhabiting upon the earth (6:10).

The dramatic portrayal of divine judgment of the earth in terms of a harvest of the earth (14:14–17) as well as a vintage of the earth

Worship of Dragon and Beasts on Earth and Worship of Lamb in Heaven

(14:18-20) both warns and encourages the audience. It warns them not to be involved in the idolatrous worship in their society, so as not to be part of the negative consequences of divine judgment. But it encourages them that they will be rewarded in heaven, like the slaughtered souls, as part of the positive consequences of divine judgment for their faithful witness against false worship, whether it results in their being put to death or not. Consequently, the threat as well as the promise of divine judgment exhorts the audience to foster and maintain true heavenly worship for eternal life in the Spirit of prophecy.

Summary on 12:1—14:20

The audience hear the ten units of this subsection (12:1—14:20) in a chiastic pattern centering around the theme of divine judgment against idolatrous worship on earth in favor of a true and universal worship in heaven. When the audience hear the (e') unit (14:1-5), they hear a chiastic progression of the (e) unit (13:11-18). No one was able to "buy" or sell anything on earth unless he is among those having the mark, the "name" of the beast or the number of "its name" (13:17), upon "their forehead" (13:16) in accord with their participation in idolatrous worship of the beast on earth. But the one hundred forty-four thousand with the Lamb on the heavenly Mount Zion have "his name" and the "name" of his Father written upon "their foreheads" (14:1) in accord with their participation in true worship of God and the Lamb in heaven. And the one hundred forty-four thousand who have been "bought" from the earth (14:3) are those who were "bought" by God from the human beings engaged in idolatrous worship on earth (14:4), so that they may participate in the true worship in heaven.

When the audience hear the (d') unit (14:6-8), they hear a chiastic progression of the (d) unit (13:1-10). Authority was given to the first beast over "every tribe and people and tongue and nation" (13:7), to cause all those inhabiting upon the earth to engage in the idolatrous worship of the beast (13:8, 12, 14). But the angel flying in midheaven is to bring good news upon those sitting upon the earth, upon "every nation and tribe and tongue and people" (14:6), inviting them to participate in the true and universal heavenly worship of God (5:9) by all of creation (5:13).

PART TWO—*Shown What Must Happen after These Things (4:1—16:21)*

When the audience hear the (c′) unit (14:9–13), they hear a chiastic progression of the (c) unit (12:12b-18). The reference to the audience as those who are "keeping the commandments of God and the faith of Jesus" (14:12) resonates with their being among the offspring of the heavenly woman who are "keeping the commandments of God and have the witness of Jesus" (12:17), the faithful witness against idolatrous worship on earth in favor of true worship in heaven. In faithfully upholding their prophetic witness to the practice of true heavenly worship of God and the Lamb the audience are thus to be like Jesus himself, the "witness," the "faithful one" (1:5; 3:14), the Lamb who offered his own blood in sacrificial worship (5:9; 7:14; 12:11).

When the audience hear the (b′) unit (14:14–17), they hear a chiastic progression of the (b) unit (12:7–12a). The angel crying out in a "great sound" came out from the temple (14:15a) "in heaven" (14:17), and told the one sitting upon the cloud, the exalted Jesus Christ as the one like a Son of Man, that the time has come for the "harvesting," the divine judgment, of the earth (14:15b). This accords with the "great sound in heaven" that John heard (12:10) after the dragon was thrown to the earth (12:9). The great sound was saying that now that the dragon has been thrown from heaven to earth the authority of God's Christ has come to be (12:10). This includes the divine authority to judge those on earth, especially those the dragon misleads to engage in idolatrous worship (12:9).

When the audience hear the (a′) unit (14:18–20), they hear a chiastic progression of the (a) unit (12:1–6). The sixth other angel "threw his sickle to the earth" (14:19), further intensifying the divine judgment executed by Jesus, who similarly "threw his sickle upon the earth" (14:16). This serves as an ironic contrast to the dragon, who swept a third of the stars of heaven and "threw" them "to the earth" (12:4), as part of his diabolical deception advocating idolatrous worship, but thus contributing to the need for the earth to be divinely judged. This divine judgment against idolatrous worship on earth in favor of a true and universal worship in heaven thus exhorts the audience to foster and maintain the true and universal heavenly worship of God and the Lamb for eternal life in the Spirit of prophecy.

7

John's Visions of the Seven Angels Pouring out Their Seven Bowls

Revelation 15:1—16:21

1a) Visions of Angels with Seven Last Plagues and of Those Who Conquered (15:1-4)

    A   a) [15:1] Then I saw another sign in heaven, **great and marvelous**, seven angels *having* seven plagues, the last ones, **for** in them is completed the fury *of God*.

           b) [2a] Then I saw something as a *glassy sea* mixed with fire

                c) [2b] and those conquering from the beast and from its image and from the number of its **name**

           b') [2c] standing upon the *glassy sea*,

       a') [2d] *having* harps *of God*,

    B [3a] and they are singing the **song** of Moses (Exod 15:1-18) the servant of God

    B' [3b] and the **song** of the Lamb saying,

  A' a) [3c] "**Great and marvelous** are your works, Lord God, the Almighty! *Righteous* and true are your ways,

PART TWO—*Shown What Must Happen after These Things (4:1—16:21)*

> b) ³ᵈ the king of the **nations**.
>> c) ⁴ᵃ Who will not fear you [Jer 10:7], Lord, and glorify your **name**? **For** you alone are sacred,
>
> b′) ⁴ᵇ **for** all the **nations** will come and worship before you [LXX Ps 85:9],
>
> a′) ⁴ᶜ **for** your **righteous deeds** have been manifested."

As a "great sign" a woman appeared "in heaven" as a representative of the people of God (12:1). Then there appeared "another sign in heaven," a "great" fiery red dragon as the enemy of God's people (12:3). But now John saw "another sign in heaven," "great and marvelous, seven angels having seven plagues, the last ones, for in them is completed the fury of God" (15:1).

The "plague" of the death of the slaughtered head of the beast was healed, so that the whole earth "marveled" after the beast (13:3), and worshiped the dragon and the beast (13:4, 12, 14). In ironic contrast, the seven angels having the seven last "plagues" is a "marvelous" sign, for in these plagues is completed the fury of God (15:1) against such false worship.[1] In them "is completed the fury of God" that is included within the mystery of God's plan, recalling that in the days of the sound of the seventh trumpeting angel, then "is completed the mystery of God" (10:7). In them is completed the "fury of God" involved in the divine judgment against idolatry when the angel threw the vine of the earth into the winepress of the "fury of God" (14:19). Indeed, one who worships the beast and its image (14:9) will drink from the wine of the "fury of God" (14:10) in ironic contrast to drinking the wine of the "fury" of Babylon's idolatry (14:8).

Then John saw something "as a glassy sea" (15:2a), recalling the something "as a glassy sea" before the throne of God in heaven (4:6). As a glassy sea in heaven that was "mixed with fire" (15:2a), it serves as a heavenly correspondent to the "fire mixed" with blood and thrown to the earth at the first trumpeting (8:7). Those on earth worshiped

---

1. "The description of the plagues as the seven *last* plagues connects them with the earlier series of plagues connected with the seven seals (6:1–17; 8:1) and the seven trumpets (8:1—9:21; 11:15–18), though neither of these series is called 'plagues'" (Aune, *Revelation 6–16*, 869; emphasis original).

the "beast" (13:4), to whom authority was given "to conquer" the holy ones (13:7), those who do not worship the "image" of the beast (13:15) or have the "number of its name" (13:17). In ironic contrast, John saw those "conquering" from the "beast" and from its "image" and from the "number of its name standing upon the glassy sea, having the harps of God" (15:2).

John saw the mighty angel authoritatively "standing upon the sea" and upon the earth (10:5, 8). He similarly saw those conquering idolatrous worship (15:2b) authoritatively "standing upon the sea," the "glassy" one (15:2c), that is, the "glassy sea" mixed with fire in heaven (15:2a). The seven angels are those "having" the seven last plagues to complete the fury "of God" that is part of the divine judgment against idolatrous worship on earth (15:1). Aptly, then, those conquering idolatrous worship on earth are "having" harps "of God" in heaven (15:2). They thus possess instruments enabling them to participate in heavenly worship along with the living creatures and elders, each one "having" a "harp" (5:8) to contribute to the sound of worship in heaven, which was like "harpists harp-playing with their harps" (14:2).

The living creatures and elders "are singing" a new "song" as they worship the Lamb in heaven (5:9). The one hundred forty-four thousand standing with the Lamb "are singing" a new "song" as they worship before the throne of God in heaven (14:3). And now those conquering idolatrous worship similarly "are singing" in heaven the "song" of Moses (cf. Exod 15:1–18) the servant of God (15:3a), which is also the "song" of the Lamb (15:3b).[2] "Great and marvelous" is the sign in heaven of the seven angels with the seven last plagues to complete the fury of God (15:1) against idolatrous worship on earth. Accordingly, those conquering idolatrous worship are singing that "great and marvelous are your works, Lord God, the Almighty! Righteous and true are your ways, the king of the nations" (15:3).

In a prophetic word of God at the beginning of the book, God identified himself as the "Lord God" the "Almighty" (1:8). Thus, in heaven the living creatures fittingly worship God as the "Lord God, the Almighty" (4:8). In heaven the elders also worship God as the "Lord

---

2. "The deliverance of which Moses and the people sang in Exod 15:1–18 prefigured the greater deliverance wrought by the Lamb" (Mounce, *Revelation*, 285).

God, the Almighty" (11:17). And now those conquering idolatrous worship on earth are in heaven similarly worshiping God as the "Lord God, the Almighty" (15:3c). Their worshipful acknowledgment that God's ways are righteous and "true" (15:3c) resonates with the slaughtered souls' prayer for judgment with its worshipful acknowledgment of the divine Lamb as holy and "true" (6:10; cf. 3:7, 14). Those "conquering" false worship on earth (15:2) in heaven worship the true God as king of the "nations" (15:3d), by whose authority over the "nations" the one who "conquers" will shepherd them into the eternal life and worship in heaven (2:26).

The angel flying in midheaven invited those from every nation to "fear" God and give him "glory" as they participate in the true and universal worship of the God who created everything (14:7). And now those conquering idolatrous worship on earth worship God in heaven as they ask who will not "fear" the Lord God (cf. Jer 10:7) and "glorify" his "name" (15:4a), rather than engage in the idolatrous worship associated with the number of the "name" of the beast (15:2). The exalted Jesus promised that he will make those engaged in the idolatrous worship of the synagogue of Satan "come and worship" the true God "before" the feet of those in the church of Philadelphia (3:9). In line with this, those conquering idolatrous worship acknowledge in their true worship that God alone is sacred, and "all nations will come and worship before" God (cf. LXX Ps 85:9), "for his righteous deeds have been manifested" (15:4).

In ironic contrast to Babylon the great, who made "all the nations" (14:8) drink from the wine of the fury of her "prostitution," her idolatrous worship, "all the nations" will come and worship before God in heaven (15:4). This accords with the heavenly woman's giving birth to a son, a male, who is about to shepherd "all the nations" into the eternal life and true universal worship in heaven (12:5; cf. 2:26). Corresponding to the ways of God that are "righteous" and true (15:3c), God's "righteous deeds" have been "manifested" (15:4c).[3] Thus, the shame of metaphorical "nakedness" associated with idolatrous worship need not be "manifested" for those participating in true heavenly worship (3:18). John's vision invites the audience to be those who conquer idolatrous worship

---

3. "The result of this revelation should motivate the wayward nations' return to God in fear, glorification, and worship (i.e., repentance)" (Blount, *Revelation*, 289).

John's Visions of the Seven Angels Pouring out Their Seven Bowls

on earth, in order to participate in the true and universal heavenly worship of God and the Lamb for eternal life in the Spirit of prophecy.[4]

2b) Vision of Seven Angels Given Seven Bowls Filled with the Fury of God (15:5–8)

> **A** [5] Then after these things I saw, and there was opened the **temple** of the dwelling of the testimony in heaven, [6a] and the seven angels having the **seven plagues came out** from the **temple**
>> **B** [6b] dressed in pure bright linen and girded around the chests with **golden** belts.
>>> **C** [7a] Then one of the four living creatures gave to the seven angels
>> **B′** [7b] seven **golden** bowls filled with the fury of the God who lives for the ages of the ages.
> **A′** [8] Then the **temple** was filled with smoke from the glory of God and from his power, and no one was able to **come into** the **temple** until were completed the **seven plagues** of the seven angels.

After the heavenly worship that proclaimed the arrival of the time for divine judgment (11:16–18), "there was opened the temple" of God "in heaven" and the ark of the covenant appeared in his "temple" (11:19a). And "there came to be lightnings and sounds and thunders and an earthquake and great hail" (11:19b), as a further divine response to the prayers of the holy ones (8:3–5), implicitly including the slaughtered souls' prayer for divine judgment (6:10). And now John saw that similarly "there was opened the temple" of the dwelling of the testimony "in heaven" (15:5).[5] The reference to the "dwelling" of the testimony in heaven reminds the audience that the first beast, an object of idolatrous

---

4. On the OT background of 15:3–4, see Moyise, "Singing the Song," 347–60.

5. "By 'testimony' is intended the Ten Commandments, or rather the tablets that ratify the covenant and that are preserved in the ark, which in its turn is placed in the tabernacle or dwelling (the 'tent'): the mobile temple that accompanied the Israelites during the exodus" (Lupieri, *Apocalypse*, 234).

PART TWO—*Shown What Must Happen after These Things (4:1—16:21)*

worship along with the dragon (13:4), in accord with this false worship, blasphemed God's name and God's "dwelling" in heaven (13:6).

In continuity with the individual angels who "came out from the temple" to play their role in executing divine judgment (14:15, 17), the seven angels having the seven plagues "came out from the temple" (15:6a). These seven angels "having the seven plagues" are the seven angels "having seven plagues," the last ones, for in them is completed the fury of God (15:1) that is part of the divine judgment against idolaters. They "came out" from the temple to play their role in the divine judgment against idolatrous worship, which reinforces the assertion that all the nations "will come" and truly worship God (15:4). These angels are "dressed" in pure bright linen and "girded" around the chests with "golden belts" (15:6b). This closely associates them with the exalted Jesus whom John saw similarly "dressed" in a robe reaching to the feet and "girded" at the breasts with a "golden belt" (1:13).

When the Lamb received the scroll, the four living creatures and the twenty-four elders fell in worship before the Lamb, each one having a harp and "golden bowls filled" with incense, which are the prayers of the holy ones (5:8). These prayers implicitly include the prayer for divine judgment of those who are inhabiting upon the earth and engaged in idolatrous worship (6:10). And now one of the four living creatures gave to the seven angels (15:7a), girded with "golden" belts (15:6b), seven "golden bowls filled with the fury of the God who lives for the ages of the ages" (15:7b).[6]

The seven golden bowls are filled with the "fury of God" (15:7) since in the seven last plagues is completed the "fury of God" included in the divine judgment against idolatrous worship (15:1). This accords with the angel who played his role in divine judgment by throwing the vine of the earth into the winepress of the "fury of God" (14:19). Indeed, anyone who worships the beast and its image (14:9) will drink from the wine of the "fury of God" (14:10).

The fury of the God who "lives for the ages of the ages" (15:7) recalls that the mighty angel with the scroll containing the prophetic divine plan swore by the God who "lives for the ages of the ages," the

---

6. "The gold bowls are those used in cultic worship, for libations or for holding the ashes from the sacrifices" (Boxall, *Revelation*, 222).

object of true worship as the creator of all things (10:6). Indeed, both the living creatures and the elders worship God as the one "living for the ages of the ages" (4:9, 10). In addition, the exalted Jesus identified himself as one "living for the ages of the ages" (1:18) and thus implicitly an object of true worship along with God. This further reminds the audience that they are to worship the eternally living God and the eternally living divine Lamb and thus share in their eternal life.

The angel who received the censer "filled" it from the fire of the altar in the heavenly temple and threw it to the earth, and "there came to be thunders and sounds and lightnings and an earthquake" (8:5). This is a divine response to the prayers of the holy ones that ascended with the "smoke" of the incense (8:4) and that include the prayer for divine judgment (6:10). Accordingly, the temple in heaven was "filled" with "smoke" from the glory of God and from his power, so that no one was able to enter the temple to worship until the "seven plagues" of the seven angels "were completed" (15:8). These are the "seven plagues" in which "is completed" the fury of God that is part of the divine judgment against idolatrous worship on earth (15:1).[7]

The "smoke" of the torment of those worshiping the beast and its image on earth ascends "for ages of ages," and they do not have rest day and night (14:11). In ironic contrast, the temple in heaven was filled with "smoke" from the "glory" of the God who lives "for the ages of the ages" (15:7b) and from his "power." These are attributes indicating his worthiness as an object of true worship (15:8). Indeed, both God and the divine Lamb are worshiped as those having "glory" and "power" (4:11; 5:12; 7:12).

That "no one was able" to come into the temple to worship until the seven plagues of the seven angels were completed (15:8) expresses human inability regarding divine or heavenly realities. "No one is able" to close the divinely opened door (3:8). "No one was able" to open the scroll in heaven (5:3) except the divine Lamb (5:5). "No one was able" to number the large crowd of heavenly worshipers (7:9). And "no one was

---

7. "In Rev 8:4 the smoke of the incense burned by the angel goes up before God. Here in 15:8, the smoke that fills the heavenly temple would be that produced by the incense burned by the angels on the golden altar of incense" (Aune, *Revelation 6–16*, 880).

able" to learn the new song of heavenly worship except the one hundred forty-four thousand in heaven (14:3). No one was able to "come into" the "temple" to worship until the seven plagues of the seven angels who "came out" from the "temple" were divinely completed (15:6a). The audience are to appreciate that when God completed the plagues of divine judgment against idolatrous worship then one is able to enter the heavenly temple to truly worship God and the Lamb for eternal life in the Spirit of prophecy.

3c) First Four Bowls Poured Out and No Repentance (16:1-9)

A a) ¹⁶:¹ Then I heard a **great** sound out of the temple saying to the seven angels, "Go and ***pour out*** the seven **bowls** of the fury of God ***on the earth***."

b) ²ᵃ Then the first went forth

a') ²ᵇ and ***poured out*** his **bowl on the earth**, and there came to be a sore evil and wicked upon the **human beings** who have the mark of the beast and who worship its image. ³ Then the second ***poured out*** his **bowl** on the sea, and there came to be blood as of a dead man and every living soul died—the things in the sea. ⁴ Then the third ***poured out*** his **bowl** on the rivers and springs of the waters, and there came to be blood.

B ⁵ Then I heard the angel of the waters **saying**, "You are **righteous**, the one who is and the one who was, the sacred one, for these things you have **judged**,

C ⁶ᵃ for the **blood** of holy ones and prophets they poured out

C' ⁶ᵇ but **blood** to them you have given to drink, worthy are they."

B' ⁷ Then I heard the altar **saying**, "Yes Lord God, the Almighty, true and **righteous** are your **judgments**."

A′ ⁸ Then the fourth **poured out** his **bowl** upon the sun, and it was given to it to burn the **human beings** with fire. ⁹ And the **human beings** were burned with a **great** burning and they blasphemed the name of God who has the authority over these plagues and they did not repent to give him glory.

The two prophetic witnesses against idolatry "heard a great sound" out of heaven telling them to ascend from earth to heaven in a cloud, divinely vindicating them in the sight of their enemies, those engaged in idolatrous worship (11:12). Similarly, but involving a movement from heaven to earth, John reports that "I heard a great sound" out of the "temple" in heaven (16:1a), the "temple" no one was able to enter until the seven plagues of the seven angels were completed (15:8).[8] The great sound was saying, "Go and pour out the seven bowls of the fury of God on the earth" (16:1b). These are the "seven golden bowls filled with the fury of the God who lives for the ages of the ages" (15:7), the fury involved in the divine judgment against false worship.[9]

Playing his role in the divine judgment against idolatrous worship on earth, an angel threw his sickle "to the earth" and gathered the vine of the earth and threw it into the winepress of the "fury of God" (14:19). The seven angels are told similarly to pour out the seven bowls of the "fury of God on the earth" (16:1). This implies further divine judgment against those on earth associated with and engaged in idolatrous worship.

The dragon "went forth" to make a battle against the rest of the offspring of the heavenly woman, those who keep the commandments of God and have the witness of Jesus (12:17), including the audience who are to bear prophetic witness against those on earth involved in idolatrous worship. In contrast, the first of the seven angels "went forth" and "poured out his bowl on the earth, and there came to be a sore evil and wicked upon the human beings who have the mark of the beast and

---

8. "Since only God is in the temple (15:8), it must be he who speaks" (Osborne, *Revelation*, 578).

9. Since the "bowls" were used for drink offerings in the temple, divine judgment here is being figuratively portrayed as a drink offering to God, according to Osborne, *Revelation*, 579.

who worship its image" (16:2).[10] The first angel "poured out" his "bowl on the earth," that is, one of the seven "bowls" of the fury of God that the seven angels were to "pour out on the earth" (16:1) in divine judgment against idolatrous worship.

At the fifth trumpeting the destructive locusts were to harm only "the human beings" who do not "have the seal of God upon their foreheads" (9:4), the seal that designates them as participants in true heavenly worship. In accord with this, at the pouring out of the first bowl there came to be a sore evil and wicked upon "the human beings" who "have" the mark of the beast and who worship its image (16:2). If anyone "worships" the "beast" and "its image" and receives a "mark" upon his forehead (14:9), he will drink from the wine of the fury of God (14:10) as part of the divine judgment against idolatrous worship. And those "worshiping" the "beast" and "its image" and receiving the "mark" of its name experience the continual torment (14:11) of this judgment. Similarly, there came to be a sore evil and wicked upon the human beings who have the "mark" of the "beast" and who "worship its image."

At the second trumpeting something as a great mountain with fire burning was thrown "into the sea" and a third of the sea "became blood" (8:8). Then a third of the creatures who are in the sea—those having "souls" (8:9)—"died." But now the second angel poured out his bowl "on the sea," and "there came to be blood" as of a dead man and *every* living "soul died"—"the things in the sea" (16:3). Thus, the destruction of divine judgment against idolatrous worship on earth has progressed from only a third of the sea creatures to *every* living soul in the sea.

At the third trumpeting a great star burning as a torch fell out of heaven upon a third of the "rivers" and upon the "springs of the waters" (8:10). A third of the waters "became" wormwood and many of the human beings died (8:11). But now the third angel poured out his bowl on the "rivers" and "springs of the waters," and "there came to be" blood (16:4), the deadly blood (16:3) implying death for human beings. The destruction of divine judgment against idolatrous worship on earth has progressed again from only a third of the rivers and a third of the waters

---

10. "This plague of festering sores resembles the sixth plague of boils narrated in Exod 9:8–12" (Aune, *Revelation 6–16*, 883).

to all of the rivers and springs of the waters, and the death-bringing wormwood has progressed to the death-bringing blood.

Then John heard the angel of "the waters" (16:5a), that is, the third angel who poured out his bowl on the springs of "the waters" (16:4). Worshiping God, it was saying, "You are righteous, the one who is and the one who was, the sacred one, for these things you have judged, for the blood of holy ones and prophets they poured out but blood to them you have given to drink, worthy are they" (16:5b–6). This angel's true worship, which contradicts the false worship of the image of the beast (16:2), resonates with previous true worship. That God is "righteous" (16:5b) echoes the worshipful acknowledgment that "righteous" are God's ways (15:3), for his "righteous deeds" have been manifested (15:4). God is again identified and worshiped as "the one who is and the one who was" (16:5b; cf. 1:4, 8; 4:8; 11:17). And that God is the "sacred" one (16:5b) echoes the worship of God as the one who alone is "sacred" (15:4).

The angel's worshipful acknowledgment, "for these things you have judged" (16:5b), further answers the prayer of the slaughtered souls asking, "do you not judge and vindicate our blood from those inhabiting upon the earth?" (6:10). Indeed, the "blood" of "holy ones" and prophets that those on earth poured out (16:6a) includes the "blood" of the slaughtered souls, whose prayer is one of the prayers of the "holy ones" (5:8; 8:3, 4). The blood of "prophets" refers to the blood of God's servants the "prophets" to whom God brought good news (10:7). These are the "prophets" God will reward (11:18), as their blood, like that of the slaughtered souls, was poured out because of their witness against idolatrous worship. They include the two "prophets" who were killed for tormenting those inhabiting upon the earth (11:10), those engaged in idolatrous worship.[11]

Since those on earth "poured out" the "blood" of holy ones and prophets (16:6a), the third angel, with appropriate irony, "poured out" his bowl on the rivers and springs of the waters, and there came to be

---

11. "When John refers to the blood of 'saints and prophets,' he is describing one group and not two" (Smalley, *Revelation*, 403). "The Church's prophetic witness has been articulated in Rev. 11:1–13, and so there is a sense in which all God's holy ones are called to be prophets" (Boxall, *Revelation*, 227–28).

"blood" (16:4). Consequently, God has given them "blood," the "blood as of a dead man" (16:3), to drink for their death, since they are worthy of it (16:6b). That God has given them deadly blood to "drink" accords with the warning that anyone who worships the beast and its image (14:9) will "drink" from the wine of the fury of God (14:10), from the "blood" that came out from the winepress (14:20). There are some in Sardis who will walk with the exalted Jesus in white, and thus participate in true heavenly worship, for "worthy are they" (3:4). In ironic contrast, "worthy are they," those God has given deadly blood to drink, because they poured out the blood of those who witnessed against idolatrous worship (16:6), and they failed to acknowledge God and the Lamb as "worthy" of true worship (4:11; 5:9, 12).[12]

But there is an ironic double meaning here based on an ambivalent reference for the pronoun "them" (16:6b). On the one hand, the deadly blood, as of a "dead" man (16:3), was given as drink to "them"—those who poured out the life blood of holy ones and prophets who witnessed against idolatrous worship (16:6a). But on the other hand, the life-giving blood of the Lamb, the one once "dead" but now living eternally (1:18), was given as drink to "them"—holy ones and prophets (16:6a).

As among those who have washed their robes and whitened them in the "blood" of the Lamb (7:14), the holy ones and prophets whose "blood" has been poured out by idolaters on earth will be given the "blood" of the Lamb to drink (16:6) in the form of eternal life's springs of waters to which the Lamb will lead them in heaven (7:17). "Worthy are they" (16:6b) of this, just as some in Sardis will walk with the exalted Jesus in white as heavenly worshipers, for "worthy are they" (3:4). The "springs of the waters" on earth became deadly blood for idolatrous worshipers (16:4), but by his sacrificial blood (1:5; 5:9) the Lamb gives true worshipers to drink the "springs of waters" of eternal life in heaven (7:17; cf. 21:6). The holy ones and prophets among the audience have been given to drink the blood of the Lamb as part of the eucharistic supper that anticipates their drinking the water of eternal life in heaven (3:20; cf. 19:7; 22:2, 17).

12. "In the same way that God (4:11), the Lamb (5:9, 12), and his followers (3:4) are 'worthy' to receive blessing, so also the persecutors are 'worthy' and deserving of their punishment" (Beale, *Revelation*, 819).

The angel of the waters was "saying" in worship to God that "you are righteous," for "these things you have judged" (16:5). Affirming this worshipful acknowledgment, the heavenly altar was "saying," "Yes Lord God, the Almighty, true and righteous are your judgments" (16:7). The angel's address, "Lord God, the Almighty" echoes previous addresses to God as the object of true worship (11:17; 15:3). The words of the personified "altar" in heaven thus further affirm that the prayer of the slaughtered souls under the "altar" in heaven (6:9) for divine judgment is being answered, "Until when, Master, holy and true, do you not judge and vindicate our blood from those inhabiting upon the earth?" (6:10).[13]

Like each of the first three angels who "poured out his bowl" (16:2, 3, 4), the fourth "poured out his bowl upon the sun, and it was given to it to burn the human beings with fire" (16:8). This means to burn "the human beings" who worship the image of the beast (16:2). To burn them redundantly but emphatically "with fire" accords with the warning that anyone who worships the beast and its image (14:9) will be tormented "with fire" (14:10).

In accord with the "great" sound John heard from the temple (16:1), the human beings were burned by the "sun" (16:8) with a "great burning" (16:9) in ironic contrast to the heavenly worshipers over whom neither the "sun" nor any "burning" will fall (7:16). Like the beast who opened its mouth for "blasphemies" to God and to "blaspheme" his "name" (13:6), these idolatrous human beings "blasphemed" the "name" of God (16:9). Similar to the angel "having authority over" the fire (14:18), God "has the authority over" these "plagues" (16:9), the seven last "plagues" in which is completed the fury of God for judgment against the blasphemy of idolatrous worship (15:1, 6, 8).[14]

The rest of the "human beings," those who were not killed by "these plagues" at the sixth trumpeting, "did not repent" of their idolatrous worship (9:20), and they "did not repent" of their idolatrous behavior (9:21). Similarly, the "human beings" who blasphemed the name of the

---

13. "The altar appears personified here—indeed, it becomes a spokesman for the fallen martyrs whose souls lie at its feet (6:9)" (Roloff, *Revelation*, 189).

14. "The blasphemy shows that they have become like the false, beastly god that they worship, since elsewhere outside ch. 16 'blasphemy' is attributed only to the beast (13:1, 5, 6; 17:3)" (Beale, *Revelation*, 823).

PART TWO—*Shown What Must Happen after These Things (4:1—16:21)*

God who has authority over "these plagues" at the pouring out of the first four bowls "did not repent to give him glory" (16:9). Unlike those who became fearful and "gave glory" to the God of heaven (11:13), they refused the invitation to "fear God and give him glory" (14:7). These failures to repent and give God glory thus reinforce the repeated exhortations for the audience to "repent" (2:5, 16; 3:3, 19) of any association with idolatrous worship and give God glory by maintaining the true heavenly worship for eternal life in the Spirit of prophecy.

4c′) Fifth Bowl Followed by No Repentance and Sixth Bowl (16:10–12)

> A ¹⁰ᵃ Then the fifth **poured out his bowl** upon the throne of the beast, and its **kingdom** became darkened,
>
> > B ¹⁰ᵇ and they were biting their tongues **from the pain**,
> >
> > > C ¹¹ᵃ and they blasphemed the God of heaven
> >
> > B′ ¹¹ᵇ **from their pains** and from their sores but did not repent from their works.
>
> A′ ¹² Then the sixth **poured out his bowl** on the great river the Euphrates, and its water was dried up, so that there was prepared the way for the **kings** from east of the sun.

Continuing the series in which each of the first four angels "poured out his bowl" (16:2, 3, 4, 8), the fifth likewise "poured out his bowl" (16:10a). He poured it out upon the "throne" of the "beast" (16:10a), which is the "throne" that the diabolical dragon gave to the beast (13:2), the "beast" whose image the human beings falsely worship (16:2). At the fourth trumpeting a third of the sun was struck and a third of the moon and a third of the stars, so that a third of them was "darkened" (8:12). At the fifth trumpeting the sun was "darkened" by the smoke that ascended from the shaft of the abyss (9:2). And now, at the outpouring of the fifth bowl the kingdom of the beast likewise became "darkened" (16:10a).[15]

---

15. "The resulting darkness is reminiscent of the ninth Egyptian plague (Exod 10:21–29)" (Mounce, *Revelation*, 297).

The worshipers in heaven declared that now there has come to be the "kingdom" of our God and the authority of his Christ (12:10), the "kingdom" of the world of our Lord and of his Christ (11:15). From every tribe and tongue and people and nation the Lamb made this "kingdom" and priests for the true worship of God on earth (1:6; 5:10). It is in this "kingdom," whose rule is true heavenly worship, that John and his audience are brothers and fellow sharers (1:9). Accordingly, the "kingdom" of the beast, whose rule is false worship, became darkened by God (divine passive) at the pouring out of the fifth bowl (16:10a).

The numberless crowd of heavenly worshipers from every nation and tribes and peoples and "tongues" used their tongues for the true worship of God (7:9). And the angel flying in midheaven and bringing good news upon every nation and tribe and "tongue" and people on earth (14:6), invited them to fear God and give him glory by using their tongues to worship the creator God who made everything (14:7). But in ironic contrast, the members of the kingdom of the beast were biting their "tongues" from the pain of the outpouring of the fifth bowl (16:10b).

At the outpouring of the fourth bowl the human beings who were burned "blasphemed" rather than worshiped the name of God (16:9). And now, those biting their tongues from the pain of the fifth bowl (16:10) "blasphemed" rather than worshiped the "God of heaven" (16:11a). This is in ironic contrast to the rest of the human beings not killed by the great earthquake, who performed an act of true worship as they gave glory to the "God of heaven" (11:13). Those biting their tongues "from the pain" of the fifth bowl blasphemed the God of heaven "from their pains" and their "sores" (16:11b), like the evil and wicked "sore" upon the human beings at the outpouring of the first bowl (16:2).

The rest of the human beings, those who were not killed by the plagues at the sixth trumpeting, "did not repent from the works" of their hands, so that they will not worship the idols they made as the works of their hands (9:20). And they "did not repent" of their idolatrous behavior (9:21). And now, similarly, those who blasphemed rather than worshiped the God of heaven "did not repent from their works" (16:11) at the outpouring of the fifth bowl. Indeed, like the human beings who blasphemed the name of God at the outpouring of the fourth bowl, they "did not repent" to give him glory (16:9) by engaging in true heavenly worship rather than the blasphemy of idolatrous worship.

The fifth angel "poured out his bowl" upon the throne of the beast, so that its "kingdom" became darkened (16:10a). But the sixth "poured out his bowl upon the great river the Euphrates, and its water was dried up, so that there was prepared the way for the kings from east of the sun" (16:12). The angel with the sixth trumpet was told to release the four angels who are bound at the "great river Euphrates" (9:14). And now, the angel with the sixth bowl poured it out upon the "great river the Euphrates." Just as the harvest of the earth is "dried up" (14:15), so the water of the great river was similarly "dried up" for the divine judgment against false worship.[16]

The four angels released at the great river Euphrates had been "prepared" by God (divine passive) for this time, so that they may kill a third of the human beings (9:15) as part of the divine judgment against idolatrous worship. And now, the water of the great river the Euphrates was dried up, so that there was "prepared" by God, the God whose "ways" are righteous and true and who is the "king" of the nations (15:3), the "way" for the "kings" from east of the sun (16:12). The way has thus been prepared by God for the kings "from east of the sun" to play their role in the divine judgment against idolatrous worship. But the audience are to identify themselves as among the servants of our God (7:3) who have been sealed by the angel who ascended "from east of the sun" (7:2) to protect them from the destruction of the divine judgment against idolatrous worship. They have been sealed with the seal of the living God to participate in the true heavenly worship for eternal life in the Spirit of prophecy.

---

16. "The kings coming from the east and from the vicinity of the Euphrates in Rev. 16:12 evokes the OT prophecy of a northern enemy beyond the Euphrates, whom God will bring to judge sinful Israel" (Beale, *Revelation*, 827).

5b′) Vision of Three Unclean Spirits Who Assemble Kings for Harmagedon (16:13–16)

A   a) ¹³ᵃ Then I saw from the mouth of the dragon and from the mouth of the beast and from the mouth of the false prophet three unclean ***spirits***

      b) ¹³ᵇ as frogs.

   a′) ¹⁴ For they are ***spirits*** of demons making signs, which are going out upon the kings of the whole world to **assemble** them for the battle of the great day of God, the Almighty.

B ¹⁵ᵃ "Behold, I am coming as a thief. Blessed is the one who watches and keeps **his** garments,

B′ ¹⁵ᵇ so that he does not walk naked and they observe **his** shamefulness."

A′ ¹⁶ Then they **assembled** them to the place that is called in Hebrew Harmagedon.

The earth helped the woman when it opened its mouth and swallowed the river the "dragon" threw "from his mouth" (12:16). But now John reports that he saw "from the mouth of the dragon and from the mouth of the beast and from the mouth of the false prophet three unclean spirits as frogs" (16:13). The first beast (from the sea) and the false prophet, the second beast (from the earth), have been closely aligned with the dragon at the center of idolatrous worship. The "dragon" gave the beast from the sea his power and his throne and great authority (13:2). The whole earth worshiped the "dragon" and they worshiped the beast (13:4). The second beast was speaking as a "dragon" (13:11). It activates the earth and those inhabiting on it so that they will worship the first beast (13:12), thus functioning as a false prophet.

    Divine grace and peace come from the seven "Spirits" before God's throne in heaven (1:4), the seven "Spirits" of God (3:1; 4:5) sent into all the earth (5:6). They are equivalent to the divine Spirit of true prophecy that inspires the heavenly worship of God and the Lamb. In contrast, out of the mouths of the dragon, beast, and false prophet come three unclean "spirits" as frogs (16:13).[17] They are "spirits" of "demons" (16:14), recalling that "demons" are an object of idolatrous worship (9:20). And that they are "making signs" (16:14) further associates them with idolatrous worship. It recalls that the second beast, the false prophet, "activates" or "makes" great "signs" (13:13). It misleads those inhabiting upon the earth on account of the "signs" that are given to it to "make" before the beast, telling those who inhabit upon the earth to "make" an image for the beast (13:14), which serves as an object of idolatrous worship (13:15).

At the sixth trumpeting, from the mouths of the horses was "going out" fire and smoke and sulfur to execute divine judgment upon idolaters (9:17). Indeed, from these three plagues were killed a third of the human beings engaged in idolatrous worship, from the fire and the smoke and the sulfur "going out" from their mouths (9:18). If anyone wishes to harm the two prophetic witnesses against idolatrous worship, fire "goes out" from their mouth and devours their enemies as divine judgment (11:5). And now, the demonic spirits from the mouths of the dragon, the beast, and the false prophet (16:13) are "going out upon the kings of the whole world to assemble them for the battle of the great day of God, the Almighty" (16:14).

After John reported that after these things "I saw" (15:5), seven angels having the seven plagues "came out" from the temple (15:6) to execute divine judgment (15:7). The next time John reported that "I saw," demonic spirits are "going out" (16:14), implicitly and ironically for the purpose of divine judgment against idolatry. This resonates with the sharp two-edged sword symbolic of the word of God "going out" from the mouth of the exalted Jesus to execute divine judgment (1:16).

At the outpouring of the sixth bowl there was prepared by God the way for the "kings" from east of the sun (16:12) to play their role in divine judgment against idolatry. And now, the demonic spirits of idolatrous worship are going out upon the "kings" of the "whole world"

---

17. "As a further motif from the Egyptian plagues, frogs (Exod. 8:2) now appear" (Roloff, *Revelation*, 190). On the metaphorical connotations of frogs, mostly connected with silliness and loquaciousness, meant to ridicule the dragon and the beasts, see Witetschek, "Dragon Spitting Frogs," 557–72.

(16:14).[18] This recalls that the dragon misleads the "whole world" to engage in idolatrous worship (12:9), and that the testing is about to come upon the "whole world" to test those inhabiting upon the earth (3:10), those engaged in idolatrous worship.

When the two prophetic witnesses have completed their witness against idolatrous worship, the beast ascending from the abyss will make against them a "battle" and will conquer and kill them (11:7). The dragon, angered at the woman, went forth to make a "battle" against the rest of her offspring who keep the commandments of God and maintain the witness of Jesus against idolatrous worship (12:17). It was given to the beast to do "battle" against the holy ones, those engaged in true worship, and to conquer them (13:7). And now, the three demonic spirits from the dragon, beast, and false prophet are going out upon the kings of the whole world to assemble them for "*the* battle" of the great day of God, the Almighty (16:14).

The "great day" of the anger of God and the Lamb as the day of divine judgment against idolatry has come (6:17). Accordingly, the kings of the whole world are being assembled for the decisive battle of the "great day" of God, the Almighty (16:14). This climactic and emphatic reference to the great day as that of "God the Almighty" underscores the divinely sovereign judgment against idolatrous worship, as it reverberates with the true heavenly worship of "God the Almighty" (4:8; 11:17; 15:3; 16:7).[19]

After exhorting the church in Sardis to become "watching" (3:2), the exalted Jesus urged, "Remember then how you received and heard and keep and repent. If then you do not watch, I will come as a thief and you will never know at what hour I will come upon you" (3:3) for judgment. There are some in Sardis who have not defiled their "garments" and they will "walk" with Jesus in white (3:4). Indeed, the one who conquers idolatrous worship will be clothed in white "garments"

---

18. "The 'kings' themselves are best understood as equivalent to the 'kings from the east' in verse 12, but now represented from a world-wide perspective" (Smalley, *Revelation*, 410).

19. "The nations are deceived into thinking that they are gathering to exterminate the saints, but they are gathered together ultimately by God only in order to meet their own judgment" (Beale, *Revelation*, 835).

to participate in the eternal life and worship in heaven (3:5). And now, with a sudden interjection illustrating the manner of his coming, the exalted Jesus similarly exhorts the audience, "Behold, I am coming as a thief. Blessed is the one who watches and keeps his garments, so that he does not walk naked and they observe his shamefulness" (16:15).

After accusing the church in Laodicea of being metaphorically "naked" (3:17), the exalted Jesus advised it to acquire from him white "garments" so that its "shame of nakedness," disqualifying it for true heavenly worship, not be manifested (3:18). And now, the exalted Jesus similarly exhorts every individual in the audience to be blessed by "keeping" their metaphorical "garments," so that they do not walk "naked," and others observe their "shamefulness" (16:15), that is, their not being properly "clothed" for true heavenly worship." That the one who "keeps" his garments for true worship is divinely "blessed" resonates with the promise that "blessed" is the one who reads aloud and those who "keep" the prophecy for true worship written in the book of Revelation (1:3). For people to "observe" such shamefulness would contradict those who "observe" the corpse of the two prophetic witnesses against idolatrous worship (11:9).[20]

The three demonic spirits of idolatry going out to "assemble" the kings of the whole world for the battle of the great day of God, the Almighty (16:14) "assembled them to the place that is called in Hebrew Harmagedon" (16:16). The heavenly woman representative of the audience has a "place" prepared for her by God as protection from the dragon during her time of prophetic witness against false worship (12:6, 14). But the demonic spirits of idolatry from the dragon, beast, and false prophet assembled the kings to the "place" called Harmagedon.

References to proper names of certain entities by how they are "called" indicate that they have a key role to play in the divine plan against idolatry. John was on the island "called" Patmos on account of his prophetic witness against idolatrous worship (1:9). The corpse of the two prophetic witnesses against idolatry is on the main street of the great city, which is "called" spiritually Sodom and Egypt (11:8). The

---

20. "In the context of the Apocalypse and specifically ch. 16 to 'watch' and 'keep one's garments' is to refuse to concede to the idolatrous demands of beast worship" (Beale, *Revelation*, 837).

dragon is "called" Devil and the Satan, who misleads the whole world to engage in idolatrous worship (12:9). And now, the place to which the kings of the whole world are assembled for divine judgment against idolatry is "called" in Hebrew Harmagedon (16:16).

At the fifth trumpeting the name of the angel of the abyss, the king over the destructive locusts, "in Hebrew" is Abaddon, meaning destruction (9:11). Similarly, the place for the battle of the great day of God's judgment (16:14) against idolatry is called "in Hebrew" Harmagedon (16:16), a name alliterative with Abaddon and a place traditionally associated with decisive battles of great destruction.[21] This dramatic and ominous setting of the stage for *the* battle of the great day of divine judgment against idolatrous worship reinforces the exhortation for everyone in the audience to keep the metaphorical "garments" (16:15) requisite for participation in true heavenly worship. The audience are thus to keep and maintain the prophetic witness against idolatrous worship in favor of the true heavenly worship for eternal life in the Spirit of prophecy.

6a') Seventh Bowl: Great Earthquake and Hail and They Blasphemed God (16:17–21)

A ¹⁷ The seventh poured out his bowl upon the air, then a **great** sound came out, out of the temple, from the throne, saying, "It has come to be!"

   B ¹⁸ᵃ Then there came to be lightnings and sounds and thunders and a **great earthquake** came to be,

   B' ¹⁸ᵇ such as has not come to be—since a human being came to be—upon the earth, an **earthquake** so large, so **great**.

A' a) ¹⁹ Then the *great* city came to be into three parts and the cities of the nations fell. And Babylon the *great* was remem-

---

21. "Harmagedon" in Hebrew means "mount of Megiddo." "The battles of Israel associated with Megiddo and the nearby mountain become a typological symbol of the last battle against the saints and Christ, which occurs throughout the earth" (Beale, *Revelation*, 838). For other suggestions of the meaning, see Jauhiainen, "OT Background to *Armageddon*," 381–93.

bered before God to give her the cup of the wine of the fury of his anger.

> b) [20] Then every island fled and mountains were not found.

a') [a] [21a] Then great *hail* as huge weights descended out of heaven

> [b] [21b] upon the *human beings*,
>
> [b'] [21c] and the *human beings* blasphemed God
>
> [a'] [21d] from the plague of the *hail*, for exceedingly **great** was its plague.

Each of the first six angels "poured out his bowl" (16:2, 3, 4, 8, 10, 12), the first three "on" something and the previous three "upon" something. And now, the seventh "poured out his bowl upon" the "air" (16:17a). This recalls that at the fifth trumpeting the sun and the "air" were darkened from the smoke that ascended from the shaft of the abyss as part of the destructive judgment upon those engaged in idolatrous worship (9:2).[22]

An angel "came out from the temple," crying out with a "great sound," calling for the one like a Son of Man to execute judgment (14:15). Another angel "came out from the temple" having a sharp sickle for judgment (14:17). The seven angels "came out" having the seven plagues of divine judgment "from the temple" (15:6). John heard a "great sound out of the temple" telling the seven angels to pour out the seven bowls of the fury of God's judgment on the earth (16:1). And now, at the outpouring of the seventh bowl a "great sound came out, out of the temple" from the "throne," saying, "It has come to be!" (16:17). This recalls and resonates with the warning of Jesus, the Lamb in the midst of the "throne" (5:6; 7:17), that "I am coming as a thief" (16:15) to execute divine judgment upon idolatrous worship.

The dramatic pronouncement that "it has come to be" decisively and definitively (perfect tense) within the divine plan is emphatically

---

22. "The bowl being poured out on the 'air' is best understood as part of the exodus plague imagery present in the trumpets and the preceding bowls and alluded to in 'the plague of hail' in 16:21" (Beale, *Revelation*, 841).

John's Visions of the Seven Angels Pouring out Their Seven Bowls

elaborated through verbal repetition: "Then there came to be lightnings and sounds and thunders and a great earthquake came to be." It was "such as has not come to be—since a human being came to be—upon the earth, an earthquake so large, so great" (16:18).

John saw that from the throne of God were going out "lightnings and sounds and thunders" (4:5). Then there "came to be thunders and sounds and lightnings and an earthquake" (8:5) in answer to the prayers of the holy ones (8:3-4), including the prayer of the slaughtered souls for judgment (6:10). At the seventh trumpeting "there came to be lightnings and sounds and thunders and an earthquake and great hail" (11:19) in accord with the notice that the time for judgment has come (11:18). And now, at the outpouring of the seventh bowl similarly "there came to be lightnings and sounds and thunders and a great earthquake came to be" (16:18a).

At the opening of the sixth seal a "great earthquake came to be" (6:12) as part of the judgment of God and the Lamb (6:16). When the two prophetic witnesses against idolatrous worship ascended to heaven (11:12), similarly "there came to be a great earthquake" in divine judgment (11:13). But then a "great earthquake came to be" (16:18a), such as has not come to be—since a human being came to be—upon the earth, an "earthquake" so large, so "great" (16:18b). This emphatically indicates to the audience the major significance of this uniquely great earthquake for the divine judgment against idolatry.

Continuing the elaboration of the pronouncement that "it has come to be" (16:17), then the great city "came to be into three parts and the cities of the nations fell. And Babylon the great was remembered before God to give her the cup of the wine of the fury of his anger" (16:19). The "great city" that came to be into three parts refers to the "great city," which is called spiritually Sodom and Egypt, where the two prophetic witnesses against idolatry and their Lord were killed (11:8). Another name for this "city" is Babylon the "great" (14:8; 16:19). The great city came to be into "three" parts in ironic contrast to the "three" unclean, demonic spirits (16:13) of idolatrous worship that were going out of the mouths of the dragon, the beast, and the false prophet (16:14).

When the two prophetic witnesses against idolatry ascended to heaven (11:12), there came to be a great earthquake and a tenth of the

PART TWO—*Shown What Must Happen after These Things (4:1—16:21)*

"city fell" (11:13) in divine judgment. And now, similarly, after the greatest of earthquakes (16:18) the great "city" came to be into three parts and the "cities" of the nations "fell" (16:19) because of their idolatrous worship, in ironic contrast with those who "fell" down in true worship of God and the Lamb (5:8, 14; 7:11; 11:16). This also resonates with the pronouncement that, since the hour of divine judgment against idolatry has come (14:7), "fallen, fallen" has Babylon the great (14:8). Indeed, the cities of the "nations" fell because Babylon made all the "nations" drink from the wine of the fury of her "prostitution"—her idolatrous worship (14:8).

The cities of the "nations" engaged in idolatry fell and Babylon was remembered "before" God to give her divine judgment for her idolatrous worship (16:19). This opens the way for the fulfillment of the promise that all the "nations" will come and worship "before" God (15:4), the king of the "nations" (15:3). If anyone worships the beast and its image (14:9), he will drink from the "wine of the fury" of God that has been mixed undiluted in the "cup" of "his anger" (14:10), his divine judgment. Accordingly, Babylon, who made all the nations drink from the "wine of the fury" of her idolatrous "prostitution" (14:8), was remembered before God to give her the "cup of the wine of the fury of his anger" (16:19).

The heavenly woman "fled" into the wilderness, where she had a place of refuge and protection prepared by God (12:6, 14). But at the opening of the sixth seal, a scene of divine judgment, "every mountain" and "island" that could serve as refuge and protection were moved from their places (6:14). And now, similarly and ironically, "every island fled" and "mountains" were not found to serve as refuge and protection at the outpouring of the seventh bowl (16:20). There was "not" a place "found" for the dragon and his angels in heaven (12:8). Similarly, mountains were "not found" for refuge on earth after this greatest of earthquakes.

After the announcement that the time for divine judgment has come (11:18), there came to be "great hail" (11:19; cf. 8:7). And now "great hail as huge weights descended out of heaven upon the human beings, and the human beings blasphemed God from the plague of the hail, for exceedingly great was its plague" (16:21). The second beast (from the earth), the false prophet (16:13), could make fire "descend

John's Visions of the Seven Angels Pouring out Their Seven Bowls

out of heaven" to the earth before "the human beings" (13:13), as one of the signs misleading them to worship the image of the beast (13:14-15). In ironic contrast, great hail "descended out of heaven upon the human beings," that is, "upon the human beings" who have the mark of the beast and who worship its image (16:2).

At the outpouring of the fourth bowl the "human beings" were burned with a great burning and they "blasphemed" the name of God and they did not repent to give him glory (16:9). At the outpouring of the fifth bowl they "blasphemed" the God of heaven but did not repent (16:11). And now, at the outpouring of the seventh bowl the "human beings" upon whom the great hail descended out of heaven also "blasphemed," instead of repenting and worshiping, God (16:21).

The human beings blasphemed God from the plague of the "hail," the "great hail," for exceedingly "great" was its plague (16:21), like the "great" earthquake that was so large, so "great" (16:18). In correspondence to this destructive "greatness" of divine judgment, ironically the "great" city came to be in three parts and Babylon the "great" was remembered before God to give her the destruction of divine judgment in return for her idolatrous worship (16:19). The outpouring of the seventh bowl, then, dramatically reinforces the ongoing exhortation for the audience to avoid the destructive blasphemy of idolatrous worship and witness to the true heavenly worship for eternal life in the Spirit of prophecy.

Summary on 15:1—16:21

The audience hear the six units of this subsection (15:1—16:21) in a chiastic pattern centering around the theme of divine judgment resulting in a failure to repent of idolatrous worship on earth in order to participate in a true and universal worship in heaven. When the audience hear the (c') unit (16:10-12), they hear a chiastic progression of the (c) unit (16:1-9). At the outpouring of the fourth bowl the human beings who were burned "blasphemed" rather than worshiped the name of God (16:9). Those biting their tongues from the pain of the fifth bowl (16:10) likewise "blasphemed" rather than worshiped the God of heaven (16:11). Those who blasphemed rather than worshiped the

PART TWO—*Shown What Must Happen after These Things (4:1—16:21)*

God of heaven "did not repent from their works" of idolatry (16:11) at the outpouring of the fifth bowl. Indeed, like the human beings who blasphemed the name of God at the outpouring of the fourth bowl, they "did not repent" to give him glory (16:9) by engaging in true heavenly worship rather than the blasphemy of idolatrous worship.

When the audience hear the (b') unit (16:13-16), they hear a chiastic progression of the (b) unit (15:5-8). After John reported that after these things "I saw" (15:5), seven angels having the seven plagues "came out" from the temple (15:6) to execute divine judgment (15:7). The next time John reported that "I saw," demonic spirits are "going out" (16:14), implicitly and ironically for the purpose of divine judgment against idolatry.

When the audience hear the (a') unit (16:17-21), they hear a chiastic progression of the (a) unit (15:1-4). The cities of the "nations" engaged in idolatry fell and Babylon was remembered "before" God to give her divine judgment for her idolatrous worship (16:19). This opens the way for the fulfillment of the promise that all the "nations" will come and worship "before" God (15:4), the king of the "nations" (15:3). The blaspheming associated with idolatrous worship and failure to repent and engage in true heavenly worship despite dramatic acts of divine judgment encourage the audience to play their part in the fulfillment of the promise of a universal heavenly worship. They are to witness against idolatrous worship and maintain their true worship so that all nations will engage in the true worship of God and the Lamb for eternal life in the Spirit of prophecy.

Once the audience have heard this (e') subsection (15:1—16:21), they have experienced a chiastic progression from the (e) subsection (12:1—14:20) within the overall macrochiastic structure of the book of Revelation. The (e) subsection centers around the theme of divine judgment against idolatrous worship on earth in favor of a true and universal worship in heaven. This progresses to the theme of divine judgment resulting in a failure to repent of idolatrous worship and participate in true and universal heavenly worship in the (e') subsection.

The dragon, "another sign in heaven" (12:3), misleading the "whole world" into idolatry (12:9) progresses to the dragon's demonic spirits assembling the kings of the "whole world" for the judgment of idolaters

(16:14) that comes from "another sign in heaven," seven angels with the seven last plagues of divine judgment (15:1). The beast who spoke "blasphemies" and "blasphemed" God (13:5–6) progresses to the human beings who "blasphemed" rather than worshiped God despite suffering the pains of divine judgment (16:9, 11, 21). And despite the everlasting good news for those on earth from the angel flying in midheaven, inviting those from every nation to participate in universal worship—to fear God and "give him glory" (14:7)—the human beings who were burned in divine judgment blasphemed God and did not repent to "give him glory" (16:9).

The scene of heavenly worshipers "singing a new song" before God's throne (14:3) as those who follow the Lamb (14:4) progresses to those conquering idolatrous worship "singing the song" of Moses and of the Lamb (15:3). They proclaim that all the nations will worship before God (15:4). Those who blasphemed God did not repent of "their works" of idolatry (16:11). But the Spirit's promise that those who die in the Lord will rest from their labors, for "their works" against idolatry follow them (14:13) encourages the audience to endure in their struggle against idolatrous worship in order to participate along with all the nations in the true heavenly worship for eternal life in the Spirit of prophecy.

PART THREE

Carried in Spirit to Wilderness, John Shown Prostitute and Wife of Lamb (17:1—21:8)

8

Vision and Downfall of the Idolatrous Prostitute Babylon

Revelation 17:1—18:24

1a) An Angel Will Show the Judgment of the Great Prostitute (17:1–5)

    A ¹⁷:¹ᵃ Then came one of the seven angels having the seven bowls and spoke with me, saying,

        a) ¹ᵇ "Here, I will show you the judgment of the **great *prostitute*** who sits upon many waters,

            b) ²ᵃ with whom the kings of ***the earth*** engaged in prostitution

            b′) ²ᵇ and those inhabiting ***the earth*** were made drunk

        a′) ²ᶜ from the wine of her ***prostitution***."

    B ³ᵃ Then he carried me into a wilderness in Spirit. Then I saw a **woman** sitting upon a **scarlet** beast,

        C ³ᵇ filled with names of blasphemy, having seven heads and ten horns,

PART THREE—*Shown Prostitute and Wife of Lamb (17:1—21:8)*

        B' ⁴ᵃ and the **woman** was clothed with purple and **scarlet** and adorned with gold and a precious stone and pearls,

A' a) ⁴ᵇ having a golden cup in her hand filled with ***abominations***

      b) ⁴ᶜ and the unclean things of her ***prostitution***

          c) ⁵ᵃ and upon her forehead a name written, a mystery, "Babylon the **great**,

    b') ⁵ᵇ the mother of ***prostitutes***

a') ⁵ᶜ and of the ***abominations*** of **the earth**."

One of the four living creatures gave to the seven angels "seven golden bowls" filled with the fury of the eternally living God for judgment against idolatry (15:7). Then John heard a great sound out of the temple in heaven telling the seven angels to pour out the "seven bowls" of the fury of God against idolatry on the earth (16:1). And now one of the seven angels having the "seven bowls" came and told John, "Here, I will show you the judgment of the great prostitute who sits upon many waters, with whom the kings of the earth engaged in prostitution and those inhabiting the earth were made drunk from the wine of her prostitution" (17:1–2).

After John saw a door opened in heaven, he heard the sound as a trumpet "speaking with me, saying," "Ascend here, and I will show you the things it is necessary to happen after these things" (4:1). John was then shown dramatic scenes of heavenly worship of God and the Lamb (4:2–5:14). And now John reports that one of the seven angels "spoke with me, saying," "Here, I will show you the judgment of the great prostitute who sits upon many waters" (17:1). The angel will show John the divine "judgment" of the great prostitute responsible for idolatrous worship on earth. This continues to answer the prayer of the slaughtered souls, who ask how long until "you judge and vindicate our blood from those inhabiting upon the earth?" (6:10), those engaged in idolatrous worship.

The "great" prostitute to be judged (17:1) refers to the "great" city, Babylon the "great," who "was remembered before God to give her the cup of the wine of the fury of his anger" (16:19), the divine judgment for her idolatrous ways.[1] In ironic correspondence to her greatness on earth, "great" hail descended out of heaven as an exceedingly "great" plague of divine judgment upon the human beings engaged in idolatrous worship, but they blasphemed rather than worshiped God (16:21). The great prostitute "sits upon many waters" (17:1), a position from which she instigates idolatrous worship on earth. In a notably ironic contrast, as the object of true worship, God "sits upon" a throne in heaven (4:2, 9, 10; 5:1, 7, 13; 7:10, 15), the source of a divine sound as the sound of "many waters" (1:15; 14:2).

The kings of the earth "engaged in prostitution" (17:2a), that is, they engaged in idolatrous worship, with the great prostitute (17:1), like those in the churches who were taught to "engage in prostitution" (2:14, 20). The "kings of the earth" who engaged in the prostitution of false worship include the "kings" of the whole world who are to be gathered for divine judgment (16:14), and the "kings of the earth" who hid from divine judgment at the opening of the sixth seal (6:15). But, ironically, Jesus, as an object of true heavenly worship, is the ruler of the "kings of the earth" (1:5).

Not only were the kings of the "earth" engaged in the "prostitution" of idolatry (17:2a), but those inhabiting the "earth" were made metaphorically drunk (17:2b) from the wine of the "prostitution" (17:2c) of the great "prostitute" (17:1), contradicting the eucharistic dining with Jesus (3:20). Those "inhabiting the earth" include all those "inhabiting upon the earth" as those engaged in idolatrous worship (3:10; 6:10; 8:13; 11:10; 13:8, 12, 14). Those inhabiting the earth were made drunk from the "wine of her prostitution," since Babylon the great made all the nations drink from the "wine of the fury of her prostitution" (14:8). But anyone who worships the beast (14:9) will drink from the "wine" of the fury of God (14:10). And Babylon the great is to be given the cup of the "wine" of the fury of God's anger (16:19).

The heavenly woman fled "into the wilderness," to a specific place where she was divinely nourished during the time of her prophetic wit-

---

1. "The picture of the harlot is not at all surprising and ties into the familiar Old Testament designation of idolatry and apostasy as harlotry" (Roloff, *Revelation*, 196). On the characterization of the Roman empire as a prostitute, see Glancy and Moore, "Roman Prostitute," 551–69.

ness against idolatry (12:6, 14). But now an angel carried John "into a wilderness," a more general place on earth, in Spirit (17:3a).[2] John was "in Spirit," that is, under the influence of God's holy Spirit, on the Lord's day (1:10) on the island called Patmos on account of his prophetic witness against idolatry (1:9) for his vision of the exalted Jesus in heaven (1:11–20). After he ascended to heaven through the opened door (4:1), John was again "in Spirit" for his visions of the heavenly worship of God and the Lamb (4:2—5:14). But now an angel carried John "in Spirit" into a wilderness on the earth to be shown the divine judgment of the great prostitute (17:1), who has involved the kings of the earth and those inhabiting the earth in her intoxicating "prostitution" of idolatrous worship (17:2).

The great prostitute who "sits upon" many waters (17:1) John saw as a woman "sitting upon" a scarlet beast (17:3a).[3] The scarlet "beast" is filled with "names of blasphemy," having "seven heads and ten horns" (17:3b). This identifies it as the "beast" John saw from the sea, having "ten horns and seven heads" and upon its heads "names of blasphemy" (13:1). The scarlet beast is "filled" with names of the blasphemy of idolatrous worship. But the seven golden bowls of the seven last plagues are "filled" with the fury of the eternally living God for judgment against idolatrous worship (15:7). And the golden bowls for heavenly worship are "filled" with incense, which are the prayers of the holy ones (5:8), including the prayer of the slaughtered souls for judgment against idolatry on earth (6:10).

The heavenly "woman" is "clothed" with majestic heavenly characteristics involving the sun, moon, and stars (12:1). But the earthly "woman" sitting upon a scarlet beast (17:3a) is the "woman" who was "clothed" with dazzling earthly characteristics—purple and "scarlet," underlining her alignment with the "scarlet" beast on earth, "and adorned with gold and a precious stone and pearls" (17:4a).[4] That this

2. "The desert is the place of demons; according to prophetic announcement, Babylon is to become a desert (Isa. 13:21; 14:23; Jer. 51:26, 29, 43). Precisely this destiny is also in store for the empire and its powerful capital" (Roloff, *Revelation*, 196).

3. Duff, *Who Rides the Beast?*, 83–96.

4. "The scarlet color of the beast refers to luxury. Scarlet was an extremely precious pigment that was often used to dye expensive textiles" (Roloff, *Revelation*, 197).

earthly woman is adorned with "gold" and a precious "stone" adds to her deceptiveness as a seductress of idolatrous worship. It deceitfully likens her to the exalted Jesus as the source of true heavenly "gold" (3:18) and to the God of true heavenly worship whose vision is like a "stone" of jasper and carnelian (4:3).

The earthly woman, Babylon the great prostitute, is seen also "having a golden cup in her hand filled with abominations and the unclean things of her prostitution" (17:4bc). But, in ironic contrast, Babylon the great is to be given the "cup" of the wine of the fury of God's anger for judgment (16:19). And anyone who worships the beast and its image (14:9) will likewise drink from the "cup" of God's anger (14:10). She is seen "having" a "golden" cup "in her hand," but the exalted Jesus is seen "having" a "golden" crown and "in his hand" a sharp sickle for divine judgment (14:14). Her cup is "filled" with the abominations associated with the names of the blasphemy of idolatrous worship with which the scarlet beast is "filled" (17:3). And the "unclean things" of her idolatrous prostitution associate her with the "unclean" spirits that inspire the idolatry that leads to divine judgment (16:13).

The one hundred forty-four thousand standing with the Lamb on the heavenly Mount Zion have his "name" and the "name" of his Father "written upon their foreheads" (14:1), designating them as participants in true heavenly worship. But the great woman prostitute of idolatrous worship has "upon her forehead a name written," which is a mystery: "Babylon the great, the mother of prostitutes and of the abominations of the earth" (17:5). This is a "mystery" within the divine plan, like the "mystery" of God to be completed at the seventh trumpeting (10:7) and the "mystery" of the seven stars in the hand of the heavenly exalted Jesus (1:20).[5]

Babylon the "great" is the identity of the "great prostitute" (17:1), who made those inhabiting the earth drunk from the wine of her "prostitution" (17:2), from the unclean things of her "prostitution" (17:4). She is also the mother of "prostitutes" (17:5) and of the abominations of the earth with which her golden cup is filled (17:4) and by which she se-

---

5. "The name is a 'mystery' not because it gives rise to conjecture but rather because it exposes the essence that the phenomenon has in the sight of God and his end-time plan of salvation" (Roloff, *Revelation*, 197).

duced not only the kings of the "earth" but those inhabiting the "earth" to engage in idolatrous worship (17:2).[6] But Babylon the "great," who made all the nations drink from the wine of the fury of her idolatrous prostitution, has fallen (14:8). Accordingly, Babylon the "great" is to be given the cup of the wine of the fury of God's anger (16:19) as judgment against the idolatrous worship that contradicts the true heavenly worship for eternal life in the Spirit of prophecy.[7]

2b) Vision of Woman and Angel's Explanation of Marveling at Beast (17:6–8)

A a) [6a] Then I **saw *the woman*** drunk from the blood of the holy ones, that is, from the blood of the witnesses of Jesus.

    b) [6b] And seeing her I ***marveled***, a great ***marvel***.

      c) [7a] Then the angel said to me,

    b') [7b] "Why do you ***marvel***?

  a') [7c] I am the one who will tell you the mystery of ***the woman*** and of **the beast**

B [7d] who bears her having **the** seven heads

B' [7e] and **the** ten horns.

A' a) [8a] ***The beast*** whom you **saw *was and is not*** but is about to ascend from the abyss and is going into destruction,

    b) [8b] and those inhabiting ***upon*** the earth will be **marveling**,

    b') [8c] whose name has not been written ***upon*** the scroll of the life from the foundation of the world,

  a') [8d] who observe ***the beast*** who ***was and is not*** but is to be present.

---

6. "The additional reference to 'abominations' in 17:4 establishes beyond doubt the connection with idolatry, since this is one of the common words for idol or idolatrous sacrifice in the LXX" (Beale, *Revelation*, 856).

7. "Babylon is not Rome; rather Rome represents the latest incarnation of the oppressive and idolatrous city, 'the great city', which originally bore the features of Mesopotamian Babylon" (Boxall, *Revelation*, 244).

Those inhabiting the earth were "made drunk" from the wine of the idolatrous prostitution (17:2) of the "woman" having a golden cup in her hand filled with abominations (17:4). But John saw the "woman" herself "drunk from the blood of the holy ones, that is, from the blood of the witnesses of Jesus" (17:6a), a travesty of the eucharistic dining with Jesus (3:20).[8] Since those who worship the image of the beast (16:2) poured out the "blood of holy ones" and prophets, the "blood" that came to be at the outpouring of the third bowl (16:4) was given them to drink (16:6). And now the woman is drunk from the "blood of the holy ones," that is, the "blood" of those killed as prophetic "witnesses" of Jesus. These include the prophetic "witness" Antipas (2:13), the two prophetic "witnesses" (11:3) the beast kills (11:6), and the souls slaughtered on account of the "witness" they had (6:9), who prayed that their "blood" be divinely vindicated (6:10).

John reports that seeing her, "I marveled, a great marvel" (17:6b), at the "great" prostitute (17:1), Babylon the "great" (17:5). But it is the works of God that are truly "great and marvelous" (15:3). This recalls that the whole earth mistakenly "marveled" after the beast (13:3). The angel said to John (17:7a), "Why do you marvel?" (17:7b), and then discloses that he is the one who will tell John the "mystery" of the "woman" (17:7c), the "mystery" of Babylon the great (17:5), the "woman" John saw drunk from the blood of the prophetic witnesses against idolatry (17:6). It is also the mystery "of the beast who bears her having the seven heads and the ten horns" (17:7). This is the scarlet "beast," filled with names of the blasphemy of idolatry, "having seven heads and ten horns," upon which the woman is sitting (17:3).

In ironic contrast to God, the object of true worship, who "was and who is" (4:8; cf. 1:4, 8; 11:17; 16:5), the beast whom John saw, the object of idolatrous worship, "was and is not but is about to ascend from the abyss and is going into destruction" (17:8a). That the "beast" is about to "ascend from the abyss" recalls and resonates with the "beast ascending from the abyss" who will kill the two prophetic witnesses against idolatrous worship (11:7). But in ironic contrast to anyone who is to

---

8. For the view that the woman drinking blood is a travesty of a eucharistic gesture, see King, "Travesty," 303–25.

"go" into captivity or is to be killed for witnessing against idolatry, the beast is "going" into destruction.

Those inhabiting "upon" the earth will be "marveling" (17:8b), like John who reported that when he saw the woman "I marveled, a great marvel" (17:6). But their name has not been written "upon" the scroll of the life in heaven from the foundation of the world (17:8c). All those "inhabiting upon the earth," each of whose "name has not been written in the scroll of the life" of the Lamb who has been slaughtered "from the foundation of the world" (13:8) will worship the beast." Resonating with this, "those inhabiting upon the earth" will be marveling, whose "name has not been written upon the scroll of the life from the foundation of the world." But for the one who conquers idolatry, Jesus will never wipe away "his name from the scroll of the life" (3:5), the eternal life of heaven.

Those inhabiting upon the earth, those engaged in idolatrous worship, are those who observe "the beast" who "was and is not" but is to be present (17:8d). This is "the beast" John saw who "was and is not" but is to be present as one about to ascend from the abyss (17:8a) and kill those witnessing against idolatry (11:7). But that the beast is going into destruction (17:8a) warns the audience not to be among those who marvel after and worship the beast, but rather to be among those who witness prophetically against such idolatrous worship and engage in true heavenly worship for eternal life in the Spirit of prophecy.

3c) Explanation of Vision of Seven Heads and Ten Horns (17:9–14)

> **A** [9] Here is the mind that **has** wisdom. The seven heads are seven mountains, where the woman sits on them. And they are seven **kings**.
>> **B** [10a] Five have fallen, one **is**,
>>> **C** [10b] the other has not yet **come**,
>>> **C'** [10c] but whenever he **comes** it is necessary that he remain a little while.

B' ¹¹ The beast who was and **is not is** himself an eighth but **is** from the seven, and is going into destruction.

A' a) ¹² And the ten horns that you saw are ten **kings**, who have not yet received a **kingdom**, but will receive authority as **kings** for one hour with the beast.

    b) ¹³ᵃ ***These*** **have** one purpose

        c) ¹³ᵇ and their power and authority they give to the beast.

    b') ¹⁴ᵃ ***These*** against the Lamb will battle but the Lamb will conquer them,

    a') ¹⁴ᵇ for Lord of lords is he and **King** of **kings** and those with him are called and chosen and faithful."

John disclosed the inferior status of the beast when he asserted that "here" is the "wisdom," let one "having" a "mind calculate the number of the beast, for it is a number of a human being, and its number: six hundred sixty-six" (13:18), a symbolic indication of the beast's emphatically human imperfection. And now, similarly, John asserts that "here" is the "mind" that "has wisdom": "the seven heads are seven mountains, where the woman sits on them, and they are seven kings" (17:9). The "seven heads" refer to the "seven heads" the beast who bears the woman has (17:7). That they represent seven "mountains" on earth belies their instability in the face of divine judgment, recalling that at the outpouring of the seventh bowl "mountains" were not found (16:20; cf. 6:14–16).[9] That the woman "sits" upon these earthly mountains corresponds to her "sitting" upon the scarlet beast (17:3) in ironic contrast to the Lamb "standing" upon the heavenly "Mount" Zion (14:1).

The seven heads of the beast represent not only seven earthly mountains but also seven earthly "kings" (17:9) among the "kings" of the earth who are engaged in the prostitution of idolatrous worship (17:2) with the great prostitute (17:1), the woman who sits upon the beast. Five of the kings have "fallen" (17:10a) in accord with the fact

---

9. "There is little doubt that a first-century reader would understand this reference in any way other than as a reference to Rome, the city built upon seven hills" (Mounce, *Revelation*, 315).

that "fallen, fallen" has Babylon the great (14:8), and that the cities of the nations "fell" at the outpouring of the seventh bowl in divine judgment against idolatry (16:19). Although five of the seven kings have fallen, "one is, the other has not yet come, but whenever he comes it is necessary that he remain a little while" (17:10). That it is necessary that the seventh earthly king remain a "little" while is ominous for the audience, as it resonates with the "little" time the devil has on earth (12:12). But that "it is necessary" means that it is a divine necessity which is part of God's plan of salvation (cf. 1:1; 4:1; 10:11; 11:5).

The beast is yet an eighth earthly king: "The beast who was and is not is himself an eighth but is from the seven, and is going into destruction" (17:11). The "beast" who "was and is not" recalls that the "beast" whom John saw "was and is not," but is about to ascend from the abyss to kill the prophetic witnesses against idolatrous worship (11:7) and yet is going into destruction (17:8). Although the beast ultimately "is" not, presently he "is" an eighth king but "is" from the seven, like the sixth king yet to fall with the previous five, who still "is" (17:10a). But the beast who is an eighth earthly king "is going into destruction." This reinforces that the beast who will kill some of those in the audience who witness against idolatry ultimately "is going into destruction" (17:8).[10]

Whereas the seven heads of the beast are seven "kings" (17:9), the "ten horns" that John saw, the "ten horns" that the beast who bears the woman has (17:7), "are ten kings, who have not yet received a kingdom, but will receive authority as kings for one hour with the beast" (17:12).[11] That these additional ten earthly kings have not yet "received" a "kingdom," but "will receive" authority as kings for the short period of only one hour stands in stark contrast with the divine kingdom. God is worshiped as the one "who is and who was, for you have received your great power and have reigned" (11:17). Indeed, "there has come to be the kingdom of the world of our Lord and of his Christ, and it will reign for the ages of the ages" (11:15).

---

10. Hitchcock, "Revelation 17:9–11," 472–85.

11. "The number ten is symbolic and indicates completeness. It does not point to ten specific kings nor to ten European kingdoms of a revived Roman empire" (Mounce, *Revelation*, 319).

Vision and Downfall of the Idolatrous Prostitute Babylon

These ten kings "have one purpose and their power and authority they give to the beast" (17:13). United with each other, these kings are also united with the dragon, who likewise "gave" the beast his "power" and his throne and great "authority" (13:2). But the superiority of heavenly power and authority to this earthly power and authority has already been indicated. After the dragon was thrown from heaven to earth (12:9), a great sound in heaven declared that "now there has come to be the salvation and the power and the kingdom of our God and the authority of his Christ" (12:10). Although the ten kings "have" one purpose in union with the beast and the dragon, the mind that "has" wisdom (17:9) knows they are doomed.

"These," that is, "these" ten kings who have one purpose (17:13a), "against the Lamb will battle but the Lamb will conquer them" (17:14a). The whole earth worshiped the dragon who gave the authority to the beast, and they worshiped the beast saying, "Who is like the beast and who is able to battle against it?" (13:4). Accordingly, the ten kings in union with the beast "will battle" against the Lamb. When the prophets have completed their witness against idolatrous worship, the beast will make a "battle" against them and "will conquer" and kill them (11:7). And it was given to the beast to do "battle" against the holy ones and to "conquer" them (13:7). But the Lamb who "conquered" to open the scroll (5:5) "will conquer" the ten kings in union with the beast. Consequently, those the beast killed are those John saw in heaven "conquering" from the beast (15:2), those who "conquered" the dragon on account of the blood of the Lamb and their witness against idolatry (12:11).

The Lamb will conquer them (17:14a), "for Lord of lords is he and King of kings" (17:14b)—of the ten "kings" in union with the beast (17:12) as well as of the seven "kings" prior to the beast (17:9) as the eighth who is going into destruction (17:11). And those "with him"— with the Lamb—"are called and chosen and faithful" (17:14b). These are the same as the one hundred forty-four thousand standing "with him" upon the heavenly Mount Zion to participate in heavenly worship (14:1). That they are "faithful" like both Jesus and Antipas, each of whom was "faithful" unto death in their prophetic witness (1:5; 2:10, 13; 3:14), encourages the audience likewise to be faithful in their prophetic

PART THREE—*Shown Prostitute and Wife of Lamb (17:1—21:8)*

witness against idolatrous worship in order to participate in the true heavenly worship for eternal life in the Spirit of prophecy.

4d) Explanations of Visions of Waters, Ten Horns and Beast, and Woman (17:15–18)

   A a) ¹⁵ᵃ Then he said to me, "The waters that *you saw* where the ***prostitute*** sits

          b) ¹⁵ᵇ are peoples and crowds and nations and tongues.

      a′) ¹⁶ And the ten horns that *you saw* and the **beast**—these will hate the ***prostitute*** and make her desolated and naked and they will eat her flesh and burn her up with fire.

   B ¹⁷ᵃ For God gave it into their hearts to do his **purpose**

   B′ ¹⁷ᵇ and to do one **purpose**

A′ ¹⁷ᶜ and to give their kingdom to the **beast** until will be completed the words of God. ¹⁸ And the woman whom *you saw* is the great city which has a kingdom over the kings of the earth."

The angel then said to John, "The waters that you saw where the prostitute sits are peoples and crowds and nations and tongues" (17:15). This recalls the angel saying that he will show "the judgment of the great prostitute who sits upon many waters" (17:1). That where the prostitute sits, who is the woman John saw "sitting" upon a scarlet beast (17:3), are "peoples and crowds and nations and tongues" indicates her universal influence for idolatrous worship.¹² This accords with the fact that authority was given to the beast similarly "over every tribe and people and tongue and nation" (13:7), so that all those inhabiting upon the earth will worship it (13:8).¹³

But the angel flying in midheaven has good news with a universal influence for true worship for "every nation and tribe and tongue and people" (14:6), inviting all to worship the God who made everything (14:7). Both John, who is to prophesy "about many peoples and nations

    12. "This fourfold grouping stresses universality" (Mounce, *Revelation*, 320).
    13. "The multitudes of humanity that the waters now represent are the basis for Babylon's economic trade and her economic security" (Beale, *Revelation*, 882).

and tongues and kings" (10:11), and the prophetic witnesses have a role to play in the universal influence for true worship. Those "from the peoples and tribes and tongues and nations" observe the corpse of the two prophets (11:9) killed for their witness against false worship. The goal of this witness is the universal heavenly worship John saw as a large, numberless crowd "from every nation and tribes and peoples and tongues" (7:9) engaged in the worship of God and the Lamb (7:10). This accords with the heavenly worship of the Lamb as the one who bought for God with his blood those "from every tribe and tongue and people and nation"(5:9).

The angel had told John that the "ten horns that you saw" are ten kings, who will receive authority as kings for one hour with the beast (17:12). And now the angel tells him that the "ten horns that you saw" and the beast "will hate the prostitute and make her desolated and naked and they will eat her flesh and burn her up with fire" (17:16). The exalted Jesus told the church at Ephesus that "you hate" the idolatrous works of the Nicolaitans, which also "I hate" (2:6). But now the ten kings in union with the beast "will hate" the idolatrous "prostitute," the "prostitute" with a universal influence for idolatry (17:15).

They will make the idolatrous prostitute desolated and "naked" (17:16), like one without the proper moral "clothing" necessary for true worship is "naked" (3:17; 16:15). Ironically, they "will eat" the flesh of the one drunk from the blood of the holy ones (17:6), a travesty of the eucharistic dining with Jesus (3:20). Her idolatrous "prostitution" includes "eating" food sacrificed to idols (2:14, 20), against which John, who reported that "I had eaten" the small scroll containing the divine plan (10:10), is to prophesy (10:11). But Jesus promises that he will give the one who conquers idolatry "to eat" from the tree of eternal life (2:7). And the idolatrous prostitute they "will burn up" with "fire" (17:16) in accord with the divine judgment at the first trumpeting in which "fire" thrown to earth caused a third of the earth, trees, and all green grass to be "burned up" (8:7).[14]

---

14. "This is an allusion to Ezek 23:26–29, where Jerusalem is compared to a woman stripped naked, and to Ezek 23:25, where the survivors of Jerusalem will be burned with fire" (Aune, *Revelation 17–22*, 956–57).

PART THREE—*Shown Prostitute and Wife of Lamb (17:1—21:8)*

The ten kings have "one purpose" and their power and authority they "give" to the "beast" (17:13). But God gave it into their "hearts," recalling that, as the divine judge, Jesus searches "hearts" (2:23), to do his "purpose." And the ten kings are to act with "one purpose" and to "give" their kingdom they are yet to receive (17:12) to the "beast until are completed the words of God" (17:17). The ten kings will give their kingdom to the beast "until will be completed" the "words" of God's judgment against idolatry, the "words" of the prophecy in Revelation that the audience are to hear and keep (1:3). This resonates with no one being able to come into the temple "until were completed" the seven plagues of judgment (15:8), for in them is "completed" the fury of God's judgment (15:1), when is "completed" the mystery of God's plan of salvation (10:7).

The angel then tells John that the woman whom "you saw," the prostitute sitting upon the waters that "you saw" (17:15), "is the great city which has a kingdom over the kings of the earth" (17:18). The woman is the "great city," that is, the "great city" on whose main street is the corpse of the prophetic witnesses against idolatry (11:8). But the "great city" was dispersed into three parts in the divine judgment at the outpouring of the seventh bowl (16:19).

The great city that is the woman has a "kingdom" over the "kings of the earth" (17:18).[15] But the ten kings are to give their "kingdom" to the beast (17:17) for the destruction of the idolatrous woman (17:16). Furthermore, as "King of kings" (17:14b) and ruler of the "kings of the earth" (1:5), the Lamb will conquer them (17:14a). Indeed, the "kings of the earth" have engaged in idolatry with the great prostitute (17:2), but the "kings of the earth" hid from divine judgment against them at the opening of the sixth seal (6:15). Consequently, the audience are further warned not to engage in the idolatrous worship associated with the great city, the great woman prostitute doomed to be destroyed by those under her influence (17:16). They are thus encouraged to continue their prophetic witness against idolatry in order to participate in the true heavenly and universal worship of God and the Lamb for eternal life in the Spirit of prophecy.

---

15. "She includes the entire evil economic-religious system of the world throughout history" (Beale, *Revelation*, 888).

5c′) The Fall and Divine Judgment of Babylon the Great (18:1–8)

A   a) ^{18:1} After these things I **saw *another*** angel descending ***out of heaven*** having great authority, and ***the earth*** was illumined from his **glory**. ^{2a} Then he cried out in a **mighty *sound*** saying, "Fallen, fallen has Babylon the great, and she has become a dwelling-place of demons

    b) ^{2b} and a ***prison*** for ***every unclean*** spirit

    b′) ^{2c} and a ***prison*** for ***every unclean*** bird and a ***prison*** for ***every unclean*** and hated beast,

   a′) ³ for from the wine of the fury of her prostitution have drunk all the nations and the kings of ***the earth*** engaged in prostitution with her and the merchants of ***the earth*** became rich from her power and **luxury**. ^{4a} Then I heard ***another sound out of heaven*** saying,

B ^{4b} "Come out, my people, from her [LXX Jer 27:8; Isa 48:20] so that you may not share in **her sins**,

  C ^{4c} and may not receive from her plagues,

B′ ^{5a} for **her sins** have been piled up to heaven

A′   a) ^{5b} and **God** has remembered her ***injustices***.

    b) ⁶ Give out to her as she also has given out and double the double things according to her works, in the cup in which she mixed, mix for her double, ^{7a} as much as she **glorified** herself and **lived in luxury**, so much give to her torment and ***grief***,

    c) ^{7b} for in her heart she says, 'I sit as queen

    b′) ^{7c} and I am no widow and I will never **see *grief***.' ^{8a} Therefore in one day her plagues will come, death and ***grief*** and famine [Isa 47:8–9], and with fire she will be burned up,

   a′) ^{8b} for **mighty** is the Lord **God** who ***judges*** her."

PART THREE—*Shown Prostitute and Wife of Lamb (17:1—21:8)*

John saw "another mighty angel descending out of heaven clothed with a cloud, and a rainbow upon his head and his face as the sun and his feet as pillars of fire" (10:1). And now he saw "another angel descending out of heaven having great authority, and the earth was illumined from his glory" (18:1). The dragon gave the beast "great authority" for idolatry (13:2). But the angel is "having great authority," like that of God who "has the authority" over the plagues of judgment against idolatry (16:9), and over the "authority" the ten kings give to the beast as an object of idolatrous worship (17:12–13). The earth over whose kings the woman who is the great city has a kingdom associated with earthly idolatry (17:18) was illumined from the angel's heavenly "glory," resonating with the "glory" of God that filled the temple in heaven (15:8).

The other "mighty" angel John saw (10:1) "cried out with a great sound" (10:3). But now the other angel "cried out in a mighty sound" saying, "Fallen, fallen has Babylon the great, and she has become a dwelling-place of demons and a prison for every unclean spirit and a prison for every unclean bird and a prison for every unclean and hated beast" (18:2). That "fallen, fallen has Babylon the great" reinforces the previous angelic declaration that "fallen, fallen has Babylon the great," who made all the nations drink from the wine of the fury of her idolatry (14:8).[16] Indeed, already there have "fallen" five of the kings (17:10) who engaged in idolatrous worship with Babylon (17:2).

Babylon has become a dwelling-place of "demons" (18:2a), which are an object of idolatrous worship (9:20). In ironic contrast to the "prison" in which the Devil is about to throw some to be tested regarding idolatry (2:10), Babylon has become a "prison" (18:2b) of the "unclean things" of her idolatry (17:4). She has become a prison for every "unclean spirit" (18:2b), recalling the "three unclean spirits" from the mouths of the dragon, beast, and false prophet (16:13), which are the "spirits of demons" of idolatry (16:14). Babylon has become a prison also for every "unclean" bird and every "unclean" and "hated" beast (18:2c), ironically recalling that the ten kings and the beast who engaged in idolatry with her "will hate" the idolatrous Babylon whom they will then destroy (17:16).

---

16. "The future is so certain that it can be spoken of in the past tense" (Blount, *Revelation*, 324).

Vision and Downfall of the Idolatrous Prostitute Babylon

Babylon has fallen, who "from the wine of the fury of her prostitution made drink all the nations" (14:8). Accordingly, "from the wine of the fury of her prostitution have drunk all the nations," a further metaphorical contradiction to the eucharistic dining with Jesus (3:20). And "the kings of the earth engaged in prostitution with her and the merchants of the earth became rich from her power and luxury" (18:3).[17] That the "kings of the earth engaged in prostitution with her" reinforces that Babylon is the great prostitute of idolatrous worship "with whom the kings of the earth engaged in prostitution" (17:2).

The "earth" was illumined from the heavenly glory of the angel with great divine authority (18:1). But the kings of the "earth" and the merchants of the "earth" nevertheless preferred the earthly idolatry and power of Babylon (18:3). The merchants of the earth "became rich" from her earthly power and luxury (18:3). Similarly, the church in Laodicea boasted that "I am rich and have become rich and I have need of nothing" (3:17). But the exalted Jesus advised the church and thus the audience to follow him and his prophetic witness against earthly and idolatrous wealth so that truly "you may become rich" (3:18).

John saw "another" angel descending "out of heaven" (18:1), who cried out with a mighty "sound" (18:2a). And now he heard "another sound out of heaven" saying, "Come out, my people, from her [LXX Jer 27:8; Isa 48:20] so that you may not share in her sins, and may not receive from her plagues" (18:4). The exalted Jesus promised that the one who conquers idolatrous worship on earth will never "come out from" the temple of heavenly worship (3:12). In ironic contrast, "my people," the people of God, are now exhorted to "come out from" idolatrous Babylon. They are not to share in her "sins," especially those of idolatry, since Jesus has released us from our "sins" by his sacrificial blood (1:5). As a consequence, they may not receive from her "plagues," that is, the seven last "plagues" in which is completed the fury of God against idolatrous worship (15:1, 6, 8; 16:9).

The people of God, with whom the audience are to identify, are not to share in "her sins," especially those of idolatry (18:4b), "for her sins have been piled up to heaven and God has remembered her injustices"

---

17. "Economic security would be removed from Babylon's subjects if they did not cooperate with her idolatry" (Beale, *Revelation*, 896).

(18:5). That God has "remembered" her injustices recalls that Babylon the great was "remembered before God to give her the cup of the wine of the fury of his anger" in divine judgment against her (16:19). And that God has remembered the "injustices" of idolatrous Babylon further answers the prayer of the souls slaughtered for their prophetic witness against idolatry. They asked how long until "you judge and vindicate our blood?" (6:10).

In coming out of Babylon and refusing to engage in her idolatry, the people of God will thus play their role in fulfilling the divine command to "give out to her as she also has given and double the double things according to her works, in the cup in which she mixed, mix for her double" (18:6).[18] That they are to "give out" to her "according to her works" is part of the divine judgment against her, in accord with the promise of Jesus that "I will give to you, to each one, according to your works" (2:23). And in the "cup" in which she "mixed" (cf. 17:4) they are to "mix" for her double. This accords with the divine judgment that anyone who worships the beast and its image (14:9) will drink from the wine of the fury of God that has been "mixed" undiluted in the "cup" of his anger (14:10).

The sound out of heaven (18:4) continues to exhort the people of God: "As much as she glorified herself and lived in luxury, so much give to her torment and grief, for in her heart she says, 'I sit as queen and I am no widow and I will never see grief'" (18:7).[19] That idolatrous Babylon "glorified" herself contradicts the true worship according to which one "will glorify" the name of God (15:4). They are to give to her "torment" in accord with the divine judgment that anyone who worships the beast and its image "will be tormented with fire and sulfur before holy angels and before the Lamb" (14:10), and the smoke of their "torment" ascends forever (14:11). In her "heart" she boasts that she will never see the grief of divine judgment. But God gave it into the "hearts" (17:17) of the ten kings and the beast to execute his judgment, as "they

---

18. "Babylon will now have to endure the twofold measure of torment and suffering in conformity with the divine legal maxim that the sin is to be punished twofold (Jer. 16:18; Isa. 40:2)" (Roloff, *Revelation*, 205).

19. Elliott, "Revelation 18:6–7," 98–113.

will hate the prostitute and make her desolated and naked and they will eat her flesh and burn her up with fire" (17:16).

Although in her heart Babylon, the great prostitute of idolatry, says that "I sit" as queen and will never see the grief of judgment (18:7), the angel will show the judgment of the great prostitute who "sits" upon many waters (17:1; cf. 17:3, 9, 15).[20] In accord with this judgment, "in one day her plagues will come, death and grief and famine [Isa 47:8–9], and with fire she will be burned up, for mighty is the Lord God who judges her" (18:8). That in the suddenness of one "day" her plagues of judgment will come resonates with the great "day" of the anger of God and the Lamb (6:17), and the battle of the great "day" of God's judgment (16:14). In ironic contrast to all of those who "will come" and offer true worship to God (3:9; 15:4), in one day her plagues of divine judgment for her idolatrous worship "will come."

During the judgment at the fifth trumpeting human beings will seek "death," but "death" will flee from them (9:6). Now, however, "death" and "famine" will come to Babylon (18:8a), so that she will experience the divine authority given to personified "Death" to kill with "famine" and with "death" (6:8). The "grief" of judgment will come to the Babylon (18:8a) who boasted that she will never see "grief" (18:7c), in accord with the divine command to give her torment and "grief" (18:7a). And in accord with God's purpose that the ten kings and the beast "will burn up with fire" the great prostitute (17:16), Babylon "with fire will be burned up" (18:8a).

In accord with the "mighty" sound of the angel out of heaven (18:2), Babylon will suffer this divine judgment, "for mighty is the Lord God who judges her" (18:8b). That mighty is the "Lord" God who judges Babylon for her idolatrous worship resonates with the Lamb being the "Lord" of lords who will conquer the beast as the object of idolatrous worship (17:14). The God who has remembered the "injustices" of Babylon (18:5b) is the Lord God who "judges" her. This recalls that God is "righteous" because of the things "you have judged" (16:5). Indeed, true and "righteous" are God's "judgments" (16:7). And it reinforces the

---

20. "As with the Babylon of history, the eschatological Babylon sees herself as both in control and perpetually surrounded by her equally corrupt offspring ('not a widow', and 'never mourning')" (Smalley, *Revelation*, 449).

PART THREE—*Shown Prostitute and Wife of Lamb (17:1—21:8)*

answer to the prayer of the slaughtered souls as to when will "you judge" those inhabiting upon the earth (6:10), those engaged in the idolatrous worship that contradicts the true heavenly worship for eternal life in the Spirit of prophecy.

6b') Kings and Merchants Pronounce Woes of Divine Judgment on Babylon (18:9–19)

A a) ⁹ Then will **weep** and lament over her the kings of ***the earth*** who engaged in prostitution with her and lived in luxury, whenever they **observe the smoke of her burning**,

¹⁰ᵃ **from afar standing on account of the fear of her torment**, saying,

  b) ¹⁰ᵇ "**Woe, woe, the great *city*,**

   c) ¹⁰ᶜ **Babylon**,

  b') ¹⁰ᵈ the mighty ***city***, for **in one hour** has come your judgment."

 a') ¹¹ᵃ Then **the merchants** of ***the earth*** are **weeping and grieving** over her,

B ¹¹ᵇ for no one buys their cargo **any longer**,

 C ¹²ᵃ cargo of gold and of silver and of **precious** stone and of pearls and of fine linen and of purple and of silk and of scarlet, and **every** citron **tree** and **every** ivory **vessel**

  C' a) ¹²ᵇ and ***every* vessel** from a **most precious tree** and of bronze and of iron and of marble, ¹³ᵃ and cinnamon and spice and incense and perfume and frankincense and wine and olive oil and fine flour and wheat and cattle and sheep, and of horses and of chariots and of bodies,

   b) ¹³ᵇ even ***souls*** of human beings,

   b') ¹⁴ᵃ but the fruit of the desire of your ***soul*** has gone away from you,

Vision and Downfall of the Idolatrous Prostitute Babylon

> > a') ¹⁴ᵇ and ***all*** the costly and bright things have perished away from you
>
> B' ¹⁴ᶜ and these very things will not be found **any longer**.
>
> A' a) ¹⁵ **The merchants** of these things, who ***became rich*** from her, ***from afar will stand*** on account of the fear of her torment, ***weeping and grieving***, ¹⁶ saying, "**Woe, woe, the great city**, clothed with fine linen and purple and scarlet and adorned with gold and precious stone and pearl, ¹⁷ᵃ ***for in one hour has been desolated*** such great wealth."
>
> > b) ¹⁷ᵇ Then ***every*** shipmaster
> >
> > b') ¹⁷ᶜ and ***everyone*** who sails to a place and sailors and as many as work with regard to the sea,
>
> a') ¹⁷ᵈ ***from afar stood*** ¹⁸ and cried out, **observing the smoke of her burning**, saying, "Who is like ***the great city***?" ¹⁹ And they threw dust upon their heads and cried out, ***weeping and grieving***, saying, "**Woe, woe, the great city**, in which all having ships on the sea ***became rich*** from her prosperity, ***for in one hour she has been desolated***.

John reported that "I was weeping" when no one was found worthy to open the scroll (5:4). But he was told not to "weep," since Jesus has conquered to open the scroll containing the divine plan (5:5). All the tribes of the earth "will lament over him," over Jesus, coming with the clouds for divine judgment (1:7). But now "will weep" and "lament over her," over Babylon, "the kings of the earth who engaged in prostitution with her and lived in luxury, whenever they observe the smoke of her burning" (18:9).²¹ The angel told John that he will show the divine judgment of the great prostitute of idolatry "with whom the kings of the earth engaged in prostitution" (17:2; cf. 18:3). In accord with this divine judgment, then "the kings of the earth who engaged in prostitution with

---

21. "The series of lamenting onlookers who observe the fall of the city from a distance opens with the kings of the earth. John sees no conflict here with earlier statements indicating that the kings of the world themselves had participated in the catastrophe (16:14, 16), or had even led it (17:16f.). For him the kings are not real, identifiable individuals, but rather types. They represent one of the groups of persons who have profited from the godless city" (Roloff, *Revelation*, 206).

her" and "lived in luxury," as Babylon "lived in luxury" (18:7), will weep and lament over Babylon, the great prostitute.[22]

Those inhabiting upon the earth, who "observe" the beast, an object of their idolatrous worship, but who is going into the destruction from divine judgment, will be marveling (17:8). But the kings of the earth will weep and lament over Babylon with whom they engaged in idolatrous worship of the beast, whenever they "observe" the smoke of her burning from divine judgment (18:9). The "smoke" they observe of her burning for idolatrous worship stands in contrast to the "smoke" from the glory of God with which the temple of heavenly worship was filled (15:8), but in accord with the "smoke" of the torment of divine judgment against idolatrous worship (14:11).[23] The kings of the earth will observe the smoke of the "burning" of Babylon, since the ten kings and the beast will burn her up with "fire" (17:16), so that with "fire" she will be burned up in accord with the divine judgment against her idolatry (18:8).

When the kings of the earth weep and lament over Babylon (18:9), they will be "standing from afar on account of the fear of her torment, saying, 'Woe, woe, the great city, Babylon, the mighty city, for in one hour has come your judgment'" (18:10). John saw those conquering from the beast of idolatrous worship "standing" upon the glassy sea (15:2) and proclaiming in their heavenly worship of God, "Who will not fear you, Lord?" (15:4). But now the kings of the earth from afar will be "standing" on account of the "fear" of the torment to be given Babylon in divine judgment against her idolatry (18:7).

Echoing the "woe, woe, woe" of divine judgment against the idolatry of those inhabiting upon the earth (8:13), the kings of the earth are

---

22. "The close connection between idolatry and economic prosperity was a fact of life in Asia Minor of John's time, where allegiance to both Caesar and the patron gods of the trade guilds was essential for people to maintain good standing in their trades" (Beale, *Revelation*, 905).

23. "In this book there is a contrast between smoke as incense and prayer (8:2–3) and smoke as a symbol of final judgment (9:17–18; 18:9, 18). The two aspects are combined in 14:11, where the 'smoke of their torment rises [to God as incense] forever and ever.' This is part of the motif that says the judgment of the sinners is God's answer to the prayers of his saints for vengeance and vindication" (Osborne, *Revelation*, 645).

Vision and Downfall of the Idolatrous Prostitute Babylon

pronouncing the "woe, woe" of divine judgment against the "great city" (18:10b). This is the "great city" that has a kingdom over the kings of the earth (17:18), that is, Babylon (18:10c). Although this great city Babylon is also the "mighty" city, in one hour has come her "judgment" (18:10d), for "mighty" is the Lord God who "judges" her (18:8). In the sudden and short span of "one hour," recalling that the ten kings will receive authority as kings for only "one hour" with the beast (17:12), divine judgment has come for Babylon. This further reinforces the answer to the prayer of the slaughtered souls in heaven calling for divine judgment against the idolaters who slaughtered them on earth (6:10).

The kings of the earth who engaged in idolatrous worship with her "will weep" and lament over Babylon (18:9). But also the "merchants of the earth," the "merchants of the earth" who became rich from her power and luxury (18:3), "are weeping and grieving over her, for no one buys their cargo any longer" (18:11). That the merchants are "grieving" over her accords with the divine judgment that in one day her plagues will come, death and "grief" and famine (18:8). Although she boasted of never seeing "grief," torment and "grief" is given to her (18:7).

As the great prostitute and idolatrous woman, Babylon "was clothed with purple and scarlet and adorned with gold and a precious stone and pearls" (17:4). But now no one any longer buys the merchants' "cargo of gold and of silver and of precious stone and of pearls and of fine linen and of purple and of silk and of scarlet, and every citron tree and every ivory vessel and every vessel from a most precious tree and of bronze and of iron and of marble" (18:12). The climactic conclusion to the additional long list of items no longer bought (18:13a) is even "souls" of human beings (18:13b).[24] But, ironically and with a shift to direct address, the fruit of the desire of "your soul" has gone away from "you" (18:14a).[25]

---

24. Koester, "Roman Slave Trade," 766–86. "Fifteen of the twenty-nine commodities listed in Rev 18:12–13 are also found in Ezek 27:12–22. The same three groups of mourners are all referred to in the Ezekiel passage" (Mounce, *Revelation*, 331).

25. "The phrase 'the fruit your soul desires' expresses that the core of Babylon's being is committed to satisfying herself with economic wealth instead of desiring God's glory" (Beale, *Revelation*, 910).

Not only "every" vessel (18:12b) but "all" the costly and bright things have perished away from "you" (18:14b). That all "the costly and bright things" on earth have perished away from her stands in ironic contrast to the seven angels in heaven dressed in pure "bright" linen and having the seven plagues of divine judgment against idolatry (15:6). These very things of glamorous but ephemeral luxury on earth will not be found "any longer" (18:14c), for no one buys the merchants' cargo "any longer" (18:11b).

The "merchants" of these things, who "became rich" from Babylon (18:15), are the "merchants" of the earth who "became rich" from her power and luxury (18:3). Like the kings of the earth "from afar standing on account of the fear of her torment" (18:10), the merchants "from afar will stand on account of the fear of her torment" (18:15). That they are "weeping and grieving" (18:15) recalls that they are "weeping and grieving" over her, "for no one buys their cargo any longer" (18:11).

Echoing the kings of the earth saying, "Woe, woe, the great city" (18:10), the merchants of the earth are saying, "Woe, woe, the great city" (18:16). The woe of divine judgment is for the great city "clothed with fine linen and purple and scarlet and adorned with gold and precious stone and pearl" (18:16). Ironically, the great city is clothed with many of the same costly and bright things—the cargo of "gold" and of "precious stone" and of "pearls" and of "fine linen" and of "purple" and of "scarlet" (18:12; cf. 17:4), which no one any longer buys from the merchants (18:11).[26]

The kings pronounced woe upon Babylon, "for in one hour has come your judgment" (18:10). And now the merchants do the same, "for in one hour has been desolated such wealth" (18:17a). That in one hour such wealth has been "desolated" accords with the divine judgment that the ten kings and the beast will hate the prostitute and make her "desolated" (17:16). The great earthly but ephemeral "wealth" of the Babylon engaged in false worship stands in contrast to the heavenly, eternal "wealth" of the Lamb, an object of true worship (5:12; cf. 3:17–18).

Complementing the kings and merchants of the earth "from afar standing" (18:10, 15), "then every shipmaster and everyone who sails to

26. Ruiz, *Ezekiel*, 440.

Vision and Downfall of the Idolatrous Prostitute Babylon

a place and sailors and as many as work with regard to the sea, from afar stood" (18:17). They "cried out, observing the smoke of her burning, saying, 'Who is like the great city?'" (18:18). That they are "observing the smoke of her burning," just as the kings "observe the smoke of her burning" (18:9), reinforces the destruction from the divine judgment against her. Their question of "who is like" the great city echoes that of those who worshiped the beast saying, "Who is like the beast?" (13:4). But it stands in ironic contrast to the question of those who worship the true God: "Who will not fear you, Lord, and glorify your name?" (15:4).

At the fifth trumpeting the destructive locusts of divine judgment had "upon their heads" crowns like gold (9:7), in contrast to the twenty-four elders engaged in true heavenly worship who have "upon their heads" actual golden crowns (4:4). But the ship merchants threw dust "upon their heads and cried out, weeping and grieving, saying, 'Woe, woe, the great city, in which all having ships on the sea became rich from her prosperity, for in one hour she has been desolated'" (18:19).[27] That they are "weeping and grieving, saying, 'Woe, woe, the great city'" serves as an emphatic verbatim echo of the merchants of the earth, who are likewise "weeping and grieving, saying, 'Woe, woe, the great city'" (18:15–16; cf. 18:11).

All having ships on the sea "became rich" from her prosperity (18:19), just as the merchants of the earth "became rich" from her (18:15), "became rich" from her earthly power and luxury (18:3). The woe of divine judgment is pronounced against her "for she in one hour has been desolated" (18:19). This climactically and emphatically reinforces "for in one hour has been desolated such great wealth" (18:17a). These woes of divine judgment pronounced by the kings of the earth and by the merchants of the earth and of the sea thus warn the audience not to become overly dependent upon an ephemeral economic system entangled with idolatrous worship on earth and doomed to self-destruction. Rather, they are to focus upon an everlasting and real wealth based on the true heavenly worship for eternal life in the Spirit of prophecy.

---

27. "The custom of throwing dust on one's head was an act of mourning or sorrow" (Aune, *Revelation 17–22*, 1006).

PART THREE—*Shown Prostitute and Wife of Lamb (17:1—21:8)*

7a′) Babylon Not Found Again as in Her Was Found Blood of Those Slaughtered (18:20-24)

A [20] Celebrate over her, heaven, and the **holy ones** and the apostles and the **prophets**, for God has judged your judgment from her."

  B a) [21a] Then raised one mighty angel a stone as a *great* millstone

      b) [21b] and *threw* it into the sea saying,

          c) [21c] "With such violence

      b′) [21d] will be *thrown* down

  a′) [21e] the *great* city Babylon

  C a) [21f] and *may never be found* again!"

      b) [22a] And a sound of harpists and of musicians and of flutists and of trumpeters **may never be heard in you again**,

      a′) [22b] and any craftsman of any craft *may never be found* in you again,

  C′ a) [22c] and a *sound* of the mill *may never be heard* **in you again**,

      b) [23a] and a light of a lamp may never appear in you again,

      a′) [23b] and a *sound* of a bridegroom and bride *may never be heard* **in you again**,

  B′ [23c] for your merchants were the **great ones** of the earth, for by your sorcery were misled all the nations,

A′ [24] and in her the blood of **prophets** and **holy ones** was found and of all those slaughtered upon the earth.

After the devil was thrown to the earth, John heard a great sound in heaven saying (12:9-10), "Celebrate, you heavens and those dwelling in them" (12:12). And now after the fall of Babylon the angel declares, "Celebrate over her, heaven" (18:20). The "holy ones" and the apostles and the "prophets" are invited to join this celebratory act of worship in heaven of the fall of idolatrous Babylon, "for God has judged your judgment from her" (18:20). This resonates with the angel of the waters declaring that God is righteous for the things "you have judged" (16:5), for the blood of "holy ones" and "prophets" the idolaters poured out (16:6). The personified heavenly altar added that true and righteous are God's "judgments" against idolatry (16:7). And the worshipers in heaven announced that the time has come for the dead to be "judged" and to give the reward to God's servants the "prophets" and to the "holy ones" (11:18).

God has "judged" Babylon the great for her idolatrous worship (18:20), "for mighty is the Lord God who judges her" (18:8). This continues to answer the prayer of the slaughtered souls in heaven as to when will you "judge and vindicate our blood from those inhabiting upon the earth?" (6:10), those engaged in idolatrous worship with Babylon, the great prostitute. And that "God has judged your judgment from her" (18:20) reaffirms the divine "judgment" of the great prostitute of idolatrous worship that the angel promised to show (17:1).

The "mighty angel" (10:1) John saw standing upon the sea and upon the earth, "raised" his right hand to heaven (10:5) and swore by the eternally living God (10:6) that at the seventh trumpeting "is completed the mystery of God, as he brought good news to his own servants the prophets" (10:7). In accord with this, one "mighty angel raised" a stone as a "great" millstone, appropriate for the woe of divine judgment for the "great" city (18:19), and threw it into the sea saying, "With such violence will be thrown down the great city Babylon and may never be found again" (18:21).[28] There was no place "found" for the dragon "still" in heaven (12:8), so that the "great" dragon "was thrown" by God (divine passive) to the earth (12:9). Similarly, the "great" city Babylon "will be thrown" down in divine judgment for her idolatry and may never be "found again."

John previously reported that the "sound" that "I heard" out of heaven was like "harpists" harp-playing with their harps as part of

---

28. "The scene is no doubt inspired by Jer. 51:63–64, where a scroll containing the disasters prophesied against Babylon is tied to a stone and thrown into the Euphrates, as a sign of Babylon's own fall" (Boxall, *Revelation*, 263).

heavenly worship (14:2). But now as part of the divine judgment against Babylon's idolatrous worship a "sound of harpists and of musicians and of flutists and of trumpeters may never be heard in you again" (18:22a). That a sound of "trumpeters" may never be heard in Babylon again stands in ironic contrast to the great "sounds" in heaven that there came to be when the seventh angel with a seventh plague of divine judgment "trumpeted" (11:15).

Since Babylon "may never be found" again (18:21–22), "any craftsman of any craft may never be found in you again" (18:22b). The divine judgment that a "sound" of music "may never be heard in you again" is emphatically intensified through repetition as also "a sound of the mill may never be heard in you again" (18:22c). Whereas at the fourth trumpeting the day did not "appear" (8:12), a light of a lamp may never "appear" in idolatrous Babylon again (18:23a). "And a sound of a bridegroom and bride may never be heard in you again" (18:23b).

Babylon's merchants were the "great ones" of the earth (18:23c), further justifying the "great" millstone (18:21a) depicting the divine judgment against the "great" city Babylon (18:21e). That by her "sorcery," recalling the idolatrous "sorceries" from which human beings did not repent (9:21), were "misled" all the nations (18:23c) likens Babylon to the beast from the earth, the false prophet (16:13). It "misleads" those inhabiting upon the earth into idolatrous worship (13:14). Likewise the dragon "misleads" the whole world (12:9). That by her sorcery were misled "all the nations" recalls that "all the nations" have drunk from the wine of the fury of her idolatrous worship (14:8; 18:3). But Jesus, the son of the heavenly woman, is about to shepherd "all the nations" with an iron staff (12:5), so that ultimately "all the nations" will come and participate in the universal heavenly worship of God (15:4).

The "holy ones" and the "prophets" were appropriately invited to celebrate the divine judgment against idolatrous Babylon (18:20), since "in her the blood of prophets and holy ones was found and of all those slaughtered upon the earth" (18:24). The "blood" of all those "slaughtered" upon the earth includes the "blood" (6:10) of the souls "slaughtered" for their prophetic witness against idolatry (6:9), as well as the "blood" of Jesus, the "slaughtered" Lamb who is an object of true heavenly worship (5:6, 9, 12). Called to be prophetic witnesses against

Vision and Downfall of the Idolatrous Prostitute Babylon

idolatrous worship, the audience are likewise invited to share in the heavenly worship celebrating the divine judgment against the false worship of Babylon, as it is the true worship of God and the Lamb for eternal life in the Spirit of prophecy.[29]

Summary on 17:1—18:24

The audience hear the seven units of this subsection (17:1—18:24) in a chiastic pattern centering around the theme of the divine judgment of Babylon for the false worship that contradicts true heavenly worship. In the unparalleled central (d) unit (17:15-18) of this subsection the audience hear that God gave it into the hearts of the ten kings to give their kingdom to the beast, the object of idolatrous worship, until will be completed the prophetic words of God's judgment against idolatry (17:17). Consequently, the ten kings and the beast will carry out this divine judgment, as they will hate the idolatrous prostitute Babylon "and make her desolated and naked and they will eat her flesh and burn her up with fire" (17:16).

When the audience hear the (c') unit (18:1-8), they hear a chiastic progression of the (c) unit (17:9-14). Five kings have already "fallen" in divine judgment (17:10), since "fallen, fallen" has Babylon the great (18:2; 14:8). That the ten kings will give their "authority," the ephemeral "authority" they are yet to receive for only one hour (17:12), to the beast (17:13) progresses to the great "authority" the angel has to execute divine judgment against idolatry (18:1). And that, as "Lord of lords," the Lamb will conquer the ten kings and the idolatrous beast (17:14) progresses to the might of the "Lord" God who judges idolatrous Babylon (18:8).

When the audience hear the (b') unit (18:9-19), they hear a chiastic progression of the (b) unit (17:6-8). Those inhabiting upon the earth will be marveling as they "observe" the beast whom they worship going into destruction (17:8). This progresses to the kings of the earth who "observe" Babylon burning from the divine judgment against her idolatry (18:9), and to the merchants of the sea likewise "observing" the smoke of her burning (18:18).

---

29. Biguzzi, "Babylon," 371–86.

PART THREE—*Shown Prostitute and Wife of Lamb (17:1—21:8)*

When the audience hear the final (a') unit (18:20–24), they hear a chiastic progression of and inclusion with the initial (a) unit (17:1–5). One of the seven angels having the seven bowls told John that he will show him the divine "judgment" against the idolatry of the great prostitute Babylon (17:1). This progresses to the invitation to participate in the heavenly worship that celebrates the fall of Babylon as a consequence of God's "judgment" against her idolatrous worship (18:20). This is part of the true heavenly worship for eternal life in the Spirit of prophecy.

Once the audience have heard this (d') subsection (17:1—18:24), they have experienced a chiastic progression from the (d) subsection (8:1—11:19) within the overall macrochiastic structure of the book of Revelation. The (d) subsection centers around the theme of the ongoing divine response to the prayer of the souls slaughtered because of their prophetic witness against idolatrous worship (6:9–11). This progresses to the theme of the divine judgment of the great prostitute Babylon for the idolatrous worship that contradicts true heavenly worship in the (d') subsection.

At the first trumpeting "fire" caused a third of the earth, trees, and all green grass to be "burned up" (8:7). This progresses to the divine judgment that the ten kings and the beast "will burn up" the idolatrous prostitute Babylon with "fire" (17:16), indeed with "fire" she will be "burned up" (18:8). That a third of the "ships" was destroyed (8:9) progresses to all having "ships" witnessing the destruction of Babylon through divine judgment (18:19). Whereas at the fourth trumpeting the day did not "appear" (8:12), a light of a lamp may never "appear" in idolatrous Babylon again (18:23). That during the divine judgment at the fifth trumpeting human beings will seek "death," but "death" will flee from them (9:6) progresses to the "death" that will come to Babylon (18:8). At the fifth trumpeting the destructive locusts of divine judgment had "upon their heads" crowns like gold (9:7). But the ship merchants threw dust "upon their heads" as they wept and grieved over the fall of Babylon (18:19).

The idolatrous "sorceries" from which human beings did not repent (9:21) progress to the "sorcery" by which Babylon misled all the nations into idolatry (18:23). The "mighty angel" (10:1) John saw standing upon the sea and upon the earth, "raised" his right hand to heaven

(10:5) and swore by the eternally living God (10:6) that at the seventh trumpeting is completed the "mystery" of God (10:7). This progresses to the "mystery" of Babylon (17:5, 7) and one "mighty angel" who "raised" a stone as a great millstone and threw it into the sea saying, "With such violence will be thrown down the great city Babylon and may never be found again" (18:21). That the two prophets were killed as "witnesses" against idolatry (11:3) progresses to the idolatrous woman Babylon made drunk from the blood of the "witnesses" of Jesus (17:6). And the "beast ascending from the abyss" who will kill the two prophetic witnesses against idolatrous worship (11:7) progresses to the "beast" who is about to "ascend from the abyss," yet is going into destruction from divine judgment (17:8).

God is worshiped as the one who is and who was, for he has "received" his great power and has "reigned" (11:17). Indeed, there has come to be the "kingdom" of the world of our Lord and of his Christ, and it "will reign" for the ages of the ages (11:15). This progresses to the ten earthly "kings" who have not yet "received" a "kingdom," but "will receive" authority as "kings" for the short period of only one hour with the beast (17:12), the object of idolatrous worship. But the Lamb will conquer them, for Lord of lords is he and "King of kings" and those with him are called and chosen and faithful (17:14). Consequently, as those with the Lamb, the audience are exhorted and encouraged to resist idolatrous worship through their prophetic witness in favor of the true heavenly worship of God and the Lamb for eternal life in the Spirit of prophecy.

9

Heavenly Worship and Final Judgment

Revelation 19:1—21:8

1a) Hearing Worship of God in Heaven for Judgment of Great Prostitute (19:1–5)

   A a) ¹⁹:¹ After these things I heard what was as a **great** sound of a large crowd in heaven saying, "***Hallelujah***! The salvation and the glory and the power of our **God**,

        b) ²ᵃ for true and ***righteous*** are his judgments, for he has judged

           c) ²ᵇ the **great** *prostitute*

              d) ²ᶜ who corrupted the earth

           c′) ²ᵈ with her ***prostitution***,

        b′) ²ᵉ and he has ***vindicated*** the blood of **his servants** from her hand."

      a′) ³ Then a second time they said, "***Hallelujah***! And her smoke ascends for the ages of the ages."

   B ⁴ᵃ Then fell the elders, the twenty-**four**,

> **B′** ⁴ᵇ and the **four** living creatures
>
> **A′** a) ⁴ᶜ and they worshiped **God**,
>
> > b) ⁴ᵈ the one sitting upon the ***throne***, ***saying***,
> >
> > > c) ⁴ᵉ "**Amen**! **Hallelujah**!"
> >
> > b′) ⁵ᵃ Then a sound from the ***throne*** came out, ***saying***,
>
> a′) ⁵ᵇ "Praise our **God** all **his servants** and those who fear him, the small and the **great**."

A "sound" may never be "heard" in Babylon again (18:22a, 22c, 23b). But John reports that after these things "I heard" what was as a "great sound" of a "large crowd in heaven" performing an act of worship, saying, "Hallelujah! The salvation and the glory and the power of our God" (19:1).[1] This resonates with John's report that "I heard a great sound in heaven" saying, "Now there has come to be the salvation and the power and the kingdom of our God" (12:10). It also recalls the "large crowd" John saw in heaven (7:9), crying out with a "great sound" saying, "The salvation to our God" (7:10). The other heavenly worshipers conclude this act of worship saying, "Amen! The blessing and the glory and the wisdom and the thanksgiving and the honor and the power and the strength to our God for the ages of the ages. Amen!" (7:12).

The large crowd in heaven declare that the motivation for this act of worship is God's judgment of the great prostitute for her idolatrous worship, "for true and righteous are his judgments, for he has judged the great prostitute who corrupted the earth with her prostitution, and he has vindicated the blood of his servants from her hand" (19:2). This recalls that at the outpouring of the third bowl of divine judgment against idolatrous worship the personified altar in heaven was saying, "Yes Lord God, the Almighty, true and righteous are your judgments" (16:7). It also resonates with the true worship of God by those who conquered the idolatrous worship of the beast saying, "Righteous and true are your ways" (15:3).

---

1. "The Hallelujah with which they begin is a familiar term in Old Testament prayer language that is documented here in a Christian sense for the first time. Its original meaning was that of a call to praise God (Heb. *hallelujah* = praise Yahweh), which the worshiping community answers with its praise" (Roloff, *Revelation*, 210).

PART THREE—*Shown Prostitute and Wife of Lamb (17:1—21:8)*

One of the seven angels having the seven bowls of divine judgment told John that he will show the "judgment" of the "great prostitute" (17:1). The kings of the "earth engaged in the prostitution" of idolatrous worship with her and those inhabiting the "earth" were made drunk from the wine of "her prostitution" (17:2; cf. 14:8). Indeed, all the nations and the kings of the "earth engaged in prostitution" with her (18:3) have drunk from the wine of the fury of "her prostitution." But because God has "judged" your "judgment" from her, an invitation to celebrate over her was issued (18:20). And now in response to that invitation the large crowd in heaven perform an act of celebratory worship of the God who has "judged" the "great prostitute" who corrupted the "earth" with "her prostitution" of idolatrous worship (19:2).

The large crowd's heavenly worship of the God whose judgments are "true" and "righteous" (19:2a), so that he has "vindicated" the "blood" of his servants from her hand (19:2e) continues to answer the prayer of the souls slaughtered for their prophetic witness against idolatry (6:9). They asked when the "true" Master will "judge" and "vindicate" their "blood" (6:10). Now God has vindicated the blood of his "servants" from the hand of the great prostitute who "corrupted the earth" with her idolatry, but whom God has "judged" (19:2). This recalls that the time for the dead to be "judged" has come and to give the reward to God's "servants" the prophets and holy ones, and to destroy those "destroying the earth" with idolatrous worship (11:18; cf. 7:3; 10:7). God has vindicated the blood of his servants from "her hand," since in "her hand" she has a golden cup filled with the unclean things of her idolatrous worship (17:4).

Then a second time the large crowd in heaven said, "Hallelujah! And her smoke ascends for the ages of the ages" (19:3; cf. 19:1). Her "smoke" refers to the "smoke" of the burning of Babylon in divine judgment against her idolatrous worship (18:9, 18). That it "ascends for the ages of the ages" resonates with the "smoke" of the torment of those worshiping the beast and its image that "ascends for ages of ages" (14:11). And at the fifth trumpeting "smoke ascended" from the shaft of the abyss (9:2) from which the destructive locusts of divine judgment against idolatry came out (9:3). This ironically corresponds to the "smoke" of the incense that "ascended" with the prayers of the holy ones

(8:4), which include the prayer of the slaughtered souls in heaven for divine judgment against the idolaters on earth (6:10).

When the Lamb received the scroll, the "four living creatures" and the "twenty-four elders fell" in an act of heavenly worship before the Lamb (5:8). To the "one sitting upon the throne" and the Lamb (5:13) the "four living creatures" were saying, "Amen!" And the "elders fell down and worshiped" (5:14; cf. 7:10–12). Then at the seventh trumpeting of divine judgment against idolatrous worship the "twenty-four elders fell" upon their faces and "worshiped God" (11:16). And now, for the divine judgment of the great prostitute and with a climactic addition of a celebratory "Hallelujah!," the "elders," the "twenty-four," and the "four living creatures," "fell." They exuberantly "worshiped God," the "one sitting upon the throne," saying, "Amen! Hallelujah!" (19:4).

Adding to the great "sound" John heard of a large crowd in heaven (19:1), a "sound from the throne," the "throne" upon which God sits (19:4d), "came out" (19:5a). This recalls that at the outpouring of the seventh bowl of divine judgment against idolatrous worship a great "sound came out from the throne" in heaven saying, "It has come to be!" (16:17). Now the sound is saying, "Praise our God all his servants" (19:5b), including "his servants" on earth whose blood God has vindicated from the hand of the great prostitute of idolatrous worship (19:2).

With their praise to "God" (19:5b), God's servants on earth are thus to join the elders and living creatures who worshiped "God" (19:4c) in heaven. Those who "fear" him, "the small and the great" are also to praise God (19:5a). This accords with the arrival of the time to reward God's "servants" the prophets who witness against false worship and those who "fear" his name, "the small and the great" (11:18).[2] This heavenly celebration of the divine judgment against the great prostitute thus continues the ongoing exhortation for the audience to maintain their prophetic witness against idolatry, as it engages them in the true heavenly worship for eternal life in the Spirit of the prophecy that pronounces divine judgment against idolatrous worship.

---

2. "Fearing God is not to be understood in the negative sense of that word, but in the positive biblical sense of joyful, reverential awe towards the one who is worthy of worship (cf. 11:18; 14:7; 15:4)" (Boxall, *Revelation*, 268).

PART THREE—*Shown Prostitute and Wife of Lamb (17:1—21:8)*

2b) The Wedding Feast of the Lamb and Worship of God (19:6–10)

A ⁶ Then I heard what was as a sound of a large crowd and what was as a sound of many waters and what was as a sound of mighty thunders **saying,** "Hallelujah! For reigns a Lord, our **God,** the Almighty. ⁷ Let us rejoice and exult and give the glory to him, for has come **the wedding feast of the Lamb** and his woman has prepared herself

    B ⁸ᵃ and it was given to her that she be clothed with **fine linen,**

        C ⁸ᵇ bright, pure,

    B' ⁸ᶜ for the **fine linen** is the righteous deeds of the holy ones."

A' a) ⁹ *Then he said to me,* "Write: Blessed are those who have been called to the supper of **the wedding feast of the Lamb.**" *Then he said to me,* "These *are* the true words of *God.*"

    b) ¹⁰ᵃ Then I fell before his feet to worship him.

  a') ¹⁰ᵇ *Then he said to me,* "See that you don't!

[a] ¹⁰ᶜ A fellow servant *am* I of you and of the brothers of you

    [b] ¹⁰ᵈ who have *the witness of Jesus.*

        [c] ¹⁰ᵉ Worship **God,**

    [b'] ¹⁰ᶠ for *the witness of Jesus*

[a'] ¹⁰ᵍ *is* the Spirit of prophecy."

After the "sound" that came out from the throne in heaven with its invitation to worship God with praise (19:5), John reports that "I heard what was as a sound of a large crowd" (19:6). This resonates with his previous report that "I heard what was as a great sound of a large crowd" in heaven (19:1), worshiping God for his judgment of the great prostitute of idolatrous worship (19:2). What John heard was also "as a sound of many waters and what was as a sound of mighty thunders" performing another act of heavenly worship saying, "Hallelujah! For reigns a Lord, our God, the Almighty" (19:6). This resonates with his report that "I heard a sound" out of heaven "as a sound of many waters [cf. 1:15] and as a sound of great thunder" as harpists (14:2). And they are singing a new song of heavenly worship as followers of the Lamb (14:3–4).

The large crowd in heaven with an intense thunderous sound exclaim, "Hallelujah! For reigns a Lord, our God, the Almighty" (19:6). This adds to the previous threefold "Hallelujah" (19:1, 3, 4), further accentuating and magnifying the crowd's heavenly worship that acknowledges the salvation and the glory and the power of "our God" (19:1). It also resonates with the heavenly worship of the twenty-four elders (11:16) who exclaim, "We give thanks to you, Lord God, the Almighty, who is and who was, for you have received your great power and have reigned" (11:17).

In ironic contrast to those inhabiting upon the earth who "rejoice" over the two prophets killed for their witness against false worship (11:10), the large crowd in heaven continue their true worship of God with the proclamation, "Let us rejoice and exult and give the glory to him" (19:7). This reinforces the angelic invitation for all those on earth (14:6) to fear God and "give him glory" for his judgment against idolaters, and to worship the God who made everything (14:7). They are thus to join not those idolaters who did not repent "to give him glory" (16:9), but those who repented, became fearful, and "gave glory to the God" of heaven (11:13).

The large crowd in heaven, who worshiped God "for he has judged the great prostitute who corrupted the earth with her prostitution" (19:2) of idolatrous worship, now worship God "for has come the wedding feast of the Lamb and his woman has prepared herself" (19:7). The "woman" of the "Lamb" refers to the heavenly "woman" who is the corporate representative of the people of God (12:1–17). As a communal figure, she includes the one hundred forty-four thousand standing with the "Lamb" on the heavenly Mount Zion (14:1) to participate in heavenly worship (14:2–3), those who follow the "Lamb" wherever he may go, those bought as first fruits for God and the "Lamb" (14:4). The communal "woman" who fled into the wilderness, where she has a place "prepared" by God for the time of her prophetic witness against idolatry on earth (12:6; cf. 11:3), has now "prepared" herself for the wedding feast of the Lamb in heaven.[3]

---

3. Tavo, *Woman*, 339.

PART THREE—*Shown Prostitute and Wife of Lamb (17:1—21:8)*

The two wings of the great eagle were "given" by God to the woman, so that she could fly into the wilderness to her place of nourishment during the time of her prophetic witness against idolatry (12:14). Similarly, it was "given" to her, to the Lamb's woman (19:7), "that she be clothed with fine linen" (19:8a), "bright, pure" (19:8b). Whereas the heavenly woman initially appeared "clothed" with the sun (12:1), now she is divinely privileged to be "clothed" with fine linen, bright, pure. "Clothed" with earthly wealth was the "woman," the great prostitute Babylon (17:4), who, as the great city, was "clothed" with the earthly wealth that included "fine linen" (18:16). But in a striking contrast, the "woman" who is the bride of the wedding feast of the Lamb (19:7) is to be clothed with "fine linen" that is "bright, pure," in other words with heavenly clothing like the "pure bright" linen in which the seven angels are dressed (15:6).

The "fine linen," that is, the "fine linen" with which the Lamb's communal woman is to be clothed (19:8a), "is the righteous deeds of the holy ones" (19:8c). The "righteous deeds" of the holy ones recall and correspond to the "righteous deeds" that have been manifested by the God who is the proper object of a true and universal worship (15:4). The righteous deeds of the "holy ones" include the endurance and faith of the "holy ones" as "those keeping the commandments of God and the faith of Jesus" (14:12) through their prophetic witness against idolatry, whether they are imprisoned and/or killed (13:10). These righteous deeds are epitomized by the pouring out of the blood of the "holy ones" as prophetic witnesses of Jesus (16:6; 17:6; 18:24). That the Lamb's woman is to be "clothed" with the bright, pure, fine linen which is the righteous deeds of the holy ones relates her to the vast crowd of heavenly worshipers "clothed" with white robes (7:13) whitened in the blood of the Lamb (7:14).[4]

John previously heard a sound out of heaven saying, "Write: Blessed are the dead, the ones who die in the Lord from now on!" (14:13). Closely corresponding to this, the angel (17:1), who previously "said to me" (17:15), now "said to me," "Write: Blessed are those who have been called to the supper of the wedding feast of the Lamb" (19:9).[5]

---

4. McIlraith, "Fine Linen," 512–29.

5. "Note that in vv 7–9 the church is pictured both as the bride and as the guests

They have been "called" to the supper because, as those with the Lamb who will conquer the idolaters on earth, they are "called" and "chosen" and faithful (17:14) as prophetic witnesses against idolatry. They have been called to the "supper" or "dinner" of the wedding feast of the Lamb that is anticipated in their eucharistic liturgy.[6] Indeed, this recalls and reinforces the exalted Jesus' promise that if anyone hears the sound of his knocking and opens the door, "I will come in to him and I will dine with him and he with me" (3:20), a promise realized for everyone in the audience who participates in the eucharistic liturgy.

The angel then said to John, "These are the true words of God" (19:9). As the "true" words of God, they correspond to the "true" and righteous ways and judgments of God against idolatrous worship (15:3; 16:7; 19:2). And as the "words" true "of God," they correspond to the "words of God" to be completed when the ten kings do God's purpose (17:17) by destroying the prostitute for her idolatrous worship (17:16). The true "words of God" refer preeminently to the words "blessed are those called to the supper of the wedding feast of the Lamb" (19:9). They reinforce the promise that "blessed" is the lector who reads aloud as well as the audience who hear the "words" of the prophecy, the prophetic "word of God" (1:2), and keep the things written in the book of Revelation (1:3). Those called to the supper of the Lamb are those who have kept the words of the prophecy by witnessing against idolatrous worship and maintaining the true worship of God and the Lamb.[7]

John previously reported that "I fell toward the feet" of the exalted Jesus in worshipful submission (1:17). He now reports that "I fell before the feet" of the angel to "worship" him (19:10a). This surprisingly and strikingly contradicts the invitation to "praise our God" (19:5) by joining the elders and living creatures who "worshiped" God (19:4). But the angel, who emphatically assured John that these "are" the true words of God (19:9), said to him, "See that you don't! A fellow servant am I of you

---

who are invited to the wedding" (Mounce, *Revelation*, 348).

6. "It is a saying that has found its place within the Christian Eucharist, reflecting an understanding of that sacrament as a foreshadowing of the messianic banquet" (Boxall, *Revelation*, 269).

7. The statement that "these are the true words of God" thus "authenticates the whole of the book of Revelation" (Smalley, *Revelation*, 485).

and of the brothers of you who have the witness of Jesus. Worship God, for the witness of Jesus is the Spirit of prophecy" (19:10).

The angel affirms that he is a "fellow servant" of John and of his "brothers" who "have the witness of Jesus" (19:10). These include the audience, of whom John, who witnessed to the "witness of Jesus Christ" (1:2), is a "brother" on Patmos on account of the "witness of Jesus" (1:9). The dragon went forth to make a battle against the rest of the offspring of the Lamb's woman who "have the witness of Jesus" (12:17). And the "fellow servants" and "brothers" of the slaughtered souls are about to be killed even as they (6:11), on account of the "witness that they had" (6:9). But the audience are to be encouraged in their prophetic witness regarding true and false worship, because the accuser of "our brothers" was thrown down (12:10) and they have conquered the dragon on account of the blood of the Lamb and on account of the word of their "witness" against idolatrous worship (12:11).

Instead of trying to "worship" him (19:10a), the angel tells John to "worship" God (19:10e), like the elders and living creatures who "worshiped" God (19:4). John is to worship God, for the "witness of Jesus" (19:10f), the "witness of Jesus" that the audience as his brothers have (19:10d), "is the Spirit of prophecy" (19:10g) regarding the true worship of God. But the angel insists that "I am" only a fellow servant (19:10c).[8]

The witness to God that Jesus gave through his sacrificial death as the Lamb once slaughtered but now standing in heaven (5:6) and that the audience are to give in their witness regarding the true worship of God is the divine Spirit of "prophecy" (19:10). This Spirit inspires the words of the "prophecy" written in the book of Revelation (1:3). It is divinely necessary that not only John but the audience "prophesy" about the universal worship of the true God (10:11), like the two witnesses who "will prophesy" (11:3) with divine authority during the days of their "prophecy" (11:6).

The witness of Jesus for the true worship of God is the divine prophetic "Spirit" (19:10), the singular representative of the complete seven "Spirits" of God before the throne in heaven (1:4; 4:5), which, as

---

8. This is a warning "not merely against worship of angels in particular, but against idolatry of any form in general . . . This passage presents an example of how easy it is to fall into idolatry" (Beale, *Revelation*, 946).

the seven eyes of the Lamb, are sent into all the earth (3:1; 5:6). In this divine "Spirit" John has received the words of the prophecy written in the book of Revelation (1:10; 4:2; 17:3; 21:10). This is the divine "Spirit" challenging, encouraging, and inspiring the churches to a prophetic witness regarding true and false worship (2:7, 11, 17, 29; 3:6, 13, 22). Indeed, this divine "Spirit" emphatically affirms that blessed are those who die in the Lord from now on, for their works, preeminently their prophetic witness to the true and universal worship of God for eternal life in the divine Spirit of prophecy, follow with them (14:13).

3c) Vision of the Faithful and True Rider on a White Horse (19:11–16)

A   a) ¹¹ᵃ Then I saw the *heaven* opened, and behold a *white horse*

    b) ¹¹ᵇ and the one sitting upon it *called* faithful and true, and in righteousness he judges and battles, ¹² his eyes as a flame of fire, and upon his head many diadems, having a *name* *written* that no one knows except himself,

      c) ¹³ᵃ and clothed with a *garment* dipped in blood,

    b′) ¹³ᵇ and his *name* is *called* the word of God.

  a′) ¹⁴ And the armies that are in *heaven* were following him on *white horses*, dressed with fine linen, *white*, pure,

B ¹⁵ᵃ and from his mouth is going out a sharp sword, so that with it he may strike the nations, and **he himself** will shepherd them with an iron staff,

B′ ¹⁵ᵇ and **he himself** will trample the winepress of the wine of the fury of the anger of God, the Almighty,

A′ ¹⁶ and he has upon the *garment* and upon his thigh a *name* *written*: King of kings and Lord of lords.

Previously John saw a door "opened" and the temple of God "opened" in "heaven" (4:1; 11:10; 15:5). But now he saw the "heaven" itself "opened" (19:11a). At the opening of the first seal John reported that "I saw, and behold a white horse, and the one sitting upon it" (6:2). And now John reports that similarly "I saw" the heaven opened, "and behold a white horse and the one sitting upon it" (19:11). But there is only a deceptively apparent similarity. The rider of a white horse at the opening of the first seal "came out conquering even so that he might conquer" with a bow, a human weapon of war (6:2). But, in a noteworthy contrast, the rider of a white horse in the opened heaven "judges and battles," not with a human weapon of war, but with a divine attribute of righteousness (19:11).

In contrast to the ancient serpent, the one "called" Devil and the Satan, who misleads the whole world into idolatry (12:9), this second rider of a white horse is "called faithful and true" (19:11). This confirms his identity as the exalted Jesus, "the faithful and true one" (3:14), and associates him with the "true" words of God (19:9). That in "righteousness he judges" (19:11) links him to the God worshiped because "true and righteous are his judgments," for he has "judged" the great prostitute who corrupted the earth with her prostitution of idolatrous worship (19:2; cf. 18:8, 20). Indeed, God is worshiped as "righteous," for these things "you have judged" (16:5), and "true and righteous are your judgments" (16:7). And it further answers the prayer of the slaughtered souls to the "true" Master, as to when "do you judge and vindicate our blood" from the idolaters (6:10).

"His eyes as a flame of fire" (19:12) further confirms the identity of the second rider of a white horse (19:11) as the exalted Jesus, who has "his eyes as a flame of fire" (2:18; cf. 1:14). In contrast with the dragon upon whose seven "heads" are seven "diadems" (12:3), and with the beast upon whose ten horns are ten "diadems" (13:1), Jesus has upon his "head" many "diadems" (19:12). The prostitute has a "name written," known as a mystery within God's plan, "Babylon the great, the mother of prostitutes and of the abominations of the earth" (17:5). But Jesus on a white horse has a unique "name written that no one knows except himself" (19:12).[9] This reinforces his promise that to the one who conquers idolatry he will give a white stone upon which is a "new name written which no one knows except the one receiving it" (2:17).

---

9. "It is his unique status and autonomy as Lord rather than any interest in deciphering his name that John wants most to impress upon his readers here" (Blount, *Revelation*, 352).

Heavenly Worship and Final Judgment

The exalted Jesus on a white horse in heaven is "clothed with a garment dipped in blood" (19:13a). The garment is dipped in his own blood as the sacrificial Lamb.[10] This is the "blood" by which he released us from our sins (1:5), the "blood" with which he bought those participating in the universal worship of God (5:9), the "blood" in which are whitened the robes of the vast crowd participating in heavenly worship (7:14). And it is the "blood" on account of which heavenly worshipers conquered the great dragon of idolatrous worship (12:11). But it is by the blood of the Lamb that God vindicated the "blood" of the slaughtered souls (6:10), of the holy ones and prophets (16:6; 18:24), of the holy ones and witnesses of Jesus (17:6), and of God's servants (19:2). Furthermore, it is the blood of the Lamb that brings about the destructive deadly "blood" of judgment against idolaters (6:12; 8:7–8; 11:6; 14:20; 16:3, 4), "for the blood of holy ones and prophets they poured out and blood to them you have given to drink" (16:6).[11]

On a "white" horse in heaven the exalted Jesus is "clothed" with a "garment" dipped in his own sacrificial "blood" as the Lamb (19:13a). This makes it possible for the vast crowd of heavenly worshipers to be "clothed" with the "white" robes (7:13) that they have washed and "whitened" in the "blood" of the Lamb (7:14). It is why the twenty-four elders are sitting "clothed" in "white garments" (4:4) for their heavenly worship (5:8) of the Lamb who bought for God with his "blood those from every tribe and tongue and nation" (5:9) to participate in the universal worship of God. And it makes possible the acquisition from the exalted Jesus of "white garments" for each member of the audience, so that "you may be clothed" properly (3:18) for heavenly worship of God and the Lamb.

The "name" of the exalted Jesus, who has a "name" written by God (divine passive), which no one knows except himself, so that it is uniquely his (19:12), is called the word of God (19:13b). That his name

---

10. "Almost certainly it is his own blood, that of the slaughtered Lamb, by which he sets his people free from their sins (1:5)" (Boxall, *Revelation*, 274).

11. "In this climactic setting, the imagery of blood comes full circle, tied up as it is with the person of Christ, who with the saints (12:11) brings victory through his blood for the blood of the saints by drawing the blood of the enemy" (Blount, *Revelation*, 353).

has been and still is "called" by God definitively and finally (perfect passive) the word of God climactically and emphatically indicates that Jesus, as the one "called" by God faithful and true (19:11b), uniquely embodies and personifies the very prophetic "word of God." As such, Jesus, the slaughtered but divinely exalted Lamb (5:6), represents the "word of God" on account of which the souls were slaughtered for their prophetic witness against idolatrous worship (6:9). Jesus himself epitomizes the "word of God" on account of which John was on the island called Patmos (1:9) as the servant who prophetically witnessed, for the sake of his audience as fellow prophetic servants (1:1), to the "word of God," which is correlative with the witness of Jesus Christ (1:2).

At the sixth trumpeting angelic "armies" of "horsemen" (9:16) were released by God to kill a third of the human beings (9:15). In contrast, the "armies" that are in "heaven" were following the exalted Jesus on "white horses," just as he appeared in the opened "heaven" on a "white horse" (19:11a), and they are "dressed with fine linen, white, pure" (19:14). That the armies are "following him" identifies them with the one hundred forty-four thousand worshipers in heaven, who are "following the Lamb" wherever he may go (14:4). And that the armies are "dressed" with "fine linen," white, "pure," identifies them with the heavenly woman of the Lamb to whom it was given that she be clothed with "fine linen," bright, "pure" (19:8). It also likens them as heavenly figures to the seven angels with the seven plagues, who came out of the heavenly temple "dressed" in "pure" bright linen (15:6).

Not only is the name of the one sitting upon a white horse in heaven called the word of God (19:13), but he speaks the prophetic word of God symbolized by the "sharp sword" that is "going out from his mouth" (19:15a). This further identifies him with the exalted Jesus, who has a "sharp" two-edged "sword going out from his mouth" (1:16; cf. 2:12). He called for the church to repent from idolatry and promised that he will battle against those engaged in idolatrous worship with the "sword" of "my mouth" (2:16).

Accordingly, similar to the two prophetic witnesses who have divine authority to "strike" the earth with every plague (11:6), with the sword which is the prophetic word of God Jesus may "strike" the nations engaged in idolatrous worship (19:15a). And he himself "will shepherd"

Heavenly Worship and Final Judgment

the "nations" with an "iron staff" (19:15a). This recalls that Jesus, as the son of the heavenly woman, is about to "shepherd" all the "nations" with an "iron staff" (12:5). Indeed, as the Lamb, he "will shepherd" those engaged in heavenly worship from every "nation" (7:9) and lead them to eternal life with God (7:17).

With an emphatic accentuation, "he himself," who has a name written which no one knows except "himself" (19:12), will shepherd the nations with an iron staff (19:15a). This reinforces his promise that he will give the one who conquers idolatrous worship divine authority over the "nations" (2:26). Such a one will play his role in bringing about a universal heavenly worship for eternal life, as he "will shepherd" them with an "iron staff" (2:27).

An angel declared that if anyone worships the beast and its image (14:9), then he will drink from the "wine" of the "fury of God" that has been mixed undiluted in the cup of his "anger" and will be tormented with fire and sulfur before holy angels and the Lamb (14:10). Another angel threw the vine of the earth engaged in idolatrous worship into the "winepress" of the "fury of God," the great one (14:19). And, as divine judgment against idolatrous worship, the "winepress" was "trampled" outside of the city and blood came out from the "winepress" up to the bridles of the horses for one thousand six hundred stadia (14:20).

And now, "he himself," the Jesus who "may strike" the nations and will shepherd them with an iron staff (19:15a), "he himself will trample" the "winepress" of the "wine" of the "fury of the anger of God," the "Almighty" (19:15b). This is in divine judgment against those engaged in idolatrous worship rather than the true worship of God as the "Almighty" (1:8; 4:8; 11:17; 15:3; 16:7; 19:6). It accords with the gathering of the kings of the whole world for the battle of the great day of the judgment of God, the "Almighty" (16:14).

The exalted Jesus, as the one sitting on a white horse in heaven (19:11), has upon the garment dipped in his sacrificial blood as the Lamb and upon his thigh a "name written": "King of kings and Lord of lords" (19:16). This is the "name written" that no one knows except himself, so that he alone possesses it (19:12). It adds to the "name" that is called the word of God of the one (19:13) who uniquely embodies and personifies the prophetic word of God against idolatrous worship on earth for the sake of a true universal worship of God in heaven.

The exalted Jesus in heaven with a "name written" upon his "thigh" (19:16) thus stands in striking contrast to the great woman prostitute of idolatrous worship on earth. She has upon her "forehead" a "name written," a mystery in God's plan, "Babylon the great, the mother of prostitutes and of the abominations of the earth" (17:5). That his name is "King of kings" and "Lord of lords" (19:16) recalls that the Lamb will conquer the beast of idolatrous worship and the kings aligned with it, for "Lord of lords" is he and "King of kings" and those with him are called and chosen and faithful (17:14). As those called and chosen to be faithful to the true worship of God on earth, the audience are to see themselves as belonging to the armies in heaven following the Lamb on white horses and dressed in the white that makes them participants in the heavenly worship of God and the Lamb for eternal life in the Spirit of prophecy.

4d) Great Supper of God and Beast and False Prophet Thrown into Lake of Fire (19:17-21)

A ¹⁷ Then I saw one angel standing in the sun and he cried out in a great sound saying to **all the birds** flying in midheaven, "Come here, assemble for the great supper of God ¹⁸ so that you may eat **flesh** of kings and **flesh** of commanders and **flesh** of mighty ones and **flesh** of horses and of those sitting upon them and **flesh** of all, of free as well as of slaves, of small and great."

B ¹⁹ᵃ Then I saw **the beast** and the kings of the earth and their **armies** assembled to do the battle

B' a) ¹⁹ᵇ against *the one sitting on the horse* and against his **army**,

  b) ²⁰ᵃ but seized was *the beast*

    c) ²⁰ᵇ and with it the false prophet who made the signs before it,

> **b′)** ²⁰ᶜ by which he misled those who received the
> mark of ***the beast*** and those worshiping its image.
> Living, the two were thrown into the lake of fire
> burning with sulfur,
>
> **a′)** ²¹ᵃ and the rest were killed with the sword of ***the one
> sitting on the horse***, one coming out from his mouth,
>
> **A′** ²¹ᵇ And **all the birds** gorged themselves from their **flesh**.

John previously saw another angel (18:1) who "cried out in a mighty sound," announcing that Babylon the great has fallen as a result of divine judgment against her idolatrous worship (18:2). And he previously saw a mighty angel "standing" upon the sea and upon the earth (10:5) with his face as the "sun" (10:1). He "cried out with a great sound" (10:3) and announced the imminent completion of the mystery of God's plan (10:6–7). John also saw and heard "one" eagle "flying in midheaven" announcing with a "great sound" the coming woes of divine judgment against those engaged in idolatry on earth (8:13). And now, accordingly and similarly, he saw "one" angel "standing" in the "sun" and he "cried out in a great sound" saying to all the birds "flying in midheaven," "Come here, assemble for the great supper of God" (19:17).

Babylon, the great prostitute of idolatrous worship, has become a prison for every unclean spirit and for "every bird" that is unclean (18:2). Unclean spirits of demons are going out upon the kings of the whole world to "assemble" them for the battle of the great day of God's judgment against idolaters (16:13; cf. 16:16). And now an angel invites "all the birds" to "assemble" for the great supper of God's judgment (19:17). The invitation "to the supper" of God thus stands in stark contrast "to the supper" of the wedding feast of the Lamb (19:9), to which the audience are invited to participate, and anticipate in their eucharistic suppers, as those engaged in the true worship of God and the Lamb.

This alternate supper, the "great one," of "God" (19:17) is closely related to the winepress of the wine of the fury of the anger of "God" (19:15). Indeed, it recalls that the angel threw the vine of the earth engaged in idolatrous worship into the winepress of the fury of "God," the "great one" (14:19). The deadly blood that came out from the great winepress (14:20) was given ironically as drink to the idolaters who

PART THREE—Shown Prostitute and Wife of Lamb (17:1—21:8)

poured out the blood of holy ones and prophets (16:6). The drinking of blood from the great winepress and the eating of flesh (19:18) at the great "supper" or "dinner" of God as judgment against idolaters thus stand in sharp contrast to the eucharistic dinner promised to the one who hears the sound of Jesus knocking and opens the door: "I will dine with him and he with me" (3:20).

As part of divine judgment against idolatry, the ten kings and the beast "will eat" the "flesh" of the great prostitute (17:16). And now all the birds are invited to the great supper of God (19:17), "so that you may eat flesh of kings and flesh of commanders and flesh of mighty ones and flesh of horses and of those sitting upon them and flesh of all, of free as well as of slaves, of small and great" (19:18).[12] At the opening of the sixth seal divine judgment came to "kings" and "commanders" and the "mighty and everyone, slave and free" (6:15). Those engaged in the idolatry of the beast include the "small and the great" and the "free and the slaves" (13:16). And now the birds may eat flesh of "kings" and of "commanders" and of "mighty ones" and "of all, of free as well as of slaves, of small and great."

The birds flying between earth and heaven (19:17) may eat flesh of earthly "horses" and of "those sitting upon them" (19:18). This thus includes each "horse" and "the one sitting upon it," those responsible for the violent destruction and death on earth at the opening of the first four seals (6:2, 4, 5, 8). It also includes the "horses" John saw and "those sitting upon them" (9:17), who killed a third of the human beings on earth (9:15, 18) at the sixth trumpeting. But in contrast to this destruction of horses and riders on earth, in heaven is a white "horse" and the exalted Jesus is "the one sitting upon it" (19:11). And armies in heaven were following him on white "horses," dressed in white to participate in heavenly worship (19:14).

The birds may also eat flesh of "small and great" (19:18), the "small and the great" involved in idolatrous worship of the beast on earth (13:16). But God's servants the prophets, the holy ones, and those

---

12. "This image is drawn from Ezek. 39:17–20, where the judgment against Gog is punctuated by an invitation to the birds and wild animals to 'come together' for 'the great sacrifice on the mountains of Israel,' where they will 'eat the flesh of mighty men and drink the blood of the princes of the earth'" (Osborne, *Revelation*, 687).

Heavenly Worship and Final Judgment

who fear God's name through true and proper worship also include the "small and the great" (11:18). Indeed, the "small and the great" are included among all God's servants and those who fear God, who are invited to praise our God in true and universal heavenly worship (19:5).

John previously saw from the mouth of the "beast" (16:13) unclean spirits of demons going out upon the "kings" of the whole world to "assemble" them for "the battle" of the day of God's judgment (16:14). But the "kings" who give their authority to the "beast" (17:12–13), so that together they "will battle" against the Lamb, the Lamb will conquer (17:14). And so now John saw the "beast" and the "kings" of the earth and their "armies assembled" to do "the battle" against the one sitting on the horse and against his "army" (19:19). This refers to the exalted Jesus, the Lamb, sitting on a white horse in heaven (19:11) and the "armies" that are in heaven following him on white horses (19:14).

But the "beast" (19:20a) John saw with the kings of the earth assembled to do the battle (19:19a) was seized by God (divine passive). And with it was seized the false prophet, the second beast, the one from the earth (13:11–12; cf. 16:13), who "made the signs before it," by which he "misled" those who received the "mark" of the "beast" and those "worshiping" its "image" (19:20). This recalls that the second beast, the false prophet, "misleads" those inhabiting upon the earth on account of the "signs" which are given to it "to make before the beast" (13:14). Accordingly, those on earth are given the "mark" (13:16, 17; 14:9, 11; 16:2) and may "worship the image of the beast" or be killed (13:15).

It is emphatically while "living" that the two, that is, the beast and the false prophet, "were thrown into the lake of fire burning with sulfur" (19:20). Their lives on earth having been brought to an end, they thus stand in notable contrast to the eternally "living" God (15:7; cf. 4:9, 10; 10:6) and the eternally "living" Jesus (1:18) as the objects of true heavenly worship. At the second trumpeting of divine judgment something as a great mountain with "fire burning was thrown" into the sea (8:8). And now, as an act of divine judgment against their idolatry, the beast and the false prophet "were thrown" by God (divine passive) into the lake of "fire burning with sulfur." This reinforces the warning that anyone who engages in idolatrous worship of the beast (14:9) will be tormented with "fire and sulfur" before holy angels and before the Lamb (14:10) eternally (14:11).[13]

At the sixth trumpeting of divine judgment the "rest" of the human beings, those who were not "killed" by the plagues, did not repent of their idolatrous worship (9:20). But now the "rest," those whom the false prophet misled to worship the image of the beast (19:20), were "killed" with the sword of "the one sitting on the horse" (19:21a). This is the exalted Jesus, "the one sitting on the horse" against whom the beast and the kings assembled to do the battle (19:19). The rest were killed with the "sword" of the one sitting on the horse, a sword coming out "from his mouth" (19:21a). This accords with his striking the nations with a sharp "sword," symbol of the prophetic word of God, that is going out "from his mouth," so that he himself will shepherd them with an iron staff (19:15), leading them to the true universal worship of God (14:6-7; cf. 7:17).

Not only were those engaged in idolatrous worship killed by the sword of the prophetic word of God coming out from the mouth of the exalted Jesus (19:21a), but "all the birds gorged themselves from their flesh" (19:21b). This refers to "all the birds" invited to assemble for the great supper of God's judgment against idolaters (19:17). They were invited so that "you may eat" the "flesh" of all the various groups involved in idolatrous worship of the beast on earth (19:18). But they did not merely eat, they "gorged themselves" from their "flesh," thus vividly underlining the magnitude of the ignominious death at the great supper of God's judgment against idolatrous worship. The audience are thus warned not to become involved in the idolatrous worship that leads to a gruesome end of life on earth. Rather, they are to dine with Jesus (3:20) in the supper of the wedding feast of the Lamb (19:9), as those engaged in true heavenly worship for eternal life in the Spirit of prophecy.

---

13. "Like the plagues, the lake of fire has repentance as its primary goal. John wants both to demonstrate the vulnerability of Babylon/Rome and to encourage believers to stop accommodating to it, or never to begin to do so" (Blount, *Revelation*, 358).

Heavenly Worship and Final Judgment

5c′) One Thousand Years and Final Defeat of Devil (20:1–10)

A   a) ²⁰:¹ Then I saw an angel **descending out of heaven**, having the *key* to the *abyss* and a great chain upon *his* hand,

      b) ² and he held the dragon, the ancient serpent, who is **Devil** and the **Satan** and bound *him* for a thousand years

    b′) ³ᵃ and **threw** *him*

  a′) ³ᵇ into the *abyss* and *closed* and sealed over *it*, so that he could not **mislead** again **the nations**

B   a) ³ᶜ *until the thousand years were completed*. After these things it is necessary that he be **released** for a little time.

      b) ⁴ᵃ Then I saw thrones and they sat upon them and judgment was given to them, and the souls of those who had been beheaded *on account of* the witness of Jesus

    b′) ⁴ᵇ and *on account of* the word of God.

  a′) ⁴ᶜ And whoever did not worship the beast or its image and did not receive the mark upon the forehead and upon their hand both lived and **reigned with Christ for a *thousand years*.** ⁵ᵃ The rest of the dead did not live *until the thousand years were completed*.

C ⁵ᵇ This is **the first resurrection**.

    D ⁶ᵃ Blessed and holy is

C′ ⁶ᵇ the one who has a part in **the first resurrection**.

B′ ⁶ᶜ Over them the second death does not have authority, but they will be priests of God and **of Christ and they will reign with him for a thousand years**. ⁷ᵃ And whenever **the thousand years are completed**, will be **released**

A′ a) ⁷ᵇ **Satan** from his prison, ⁸ᵃ and he will go out to *mislead* **the nations**

PART THREE—*Shown Prostitute and Wife of Lamb (17:1—21:8)*

> b) [8b] that are at the four corners **of the earth**,
>> c) [8c] Gog and Magog, to assemble **them** for the battle.
>> c') [8d] The number of **them** is as the sand of the sea,
> b') [9a] and they ascended to the breadth **of the earth** and encircled the camp of the holy ones, that is, the city, the one beloved,
>
> a') [a] [9b] but *fire* descended out of heaven
> [b] [9c] and devoured *them*,
> [b'] [10a] and the **Devil** who **misled** them
> [a'] [10b] was **thrown** into the lake of *fire* and sulfur where both the beast and the false prophet were, and they will be tormented day and night for the ages of the ages.

John previously saw another mighty angel "descending out of heaven" (10:1) and "having in his hand" a small scroll that had been opened (10:2), the scroll containing the prophetic word of God against idolatrous worship (10:3–11). He also saw another angel "descending out of heaven having great authority" (18:1), who announced the fall of idolatrous Babylon the great (18:2). And now John saw an angel "descending out of heaven," "having" the key to the abyss and a "great" chain "upon his hand" (20:1). The angel who has the "key" to the "abyss" recalls the angel of the "abyss" (9:11) and the angelic star fallen out of heaven to whom the "key" of the shaft of the "abyss" was given (9:1). It opened the shaft of the "abyss" (9:2) to release the scorpions that tormented the human beings engaged in idolatrous worship (9:3–10).

Resonating with the four angels "holding" the four winds of the earth (7:1), the angel with the key to the abyss and chain upon his hand (20:1) "held the dragon, the ancient serpent, who is Devil and the Satan and bound him for a thousand years" (20:2). This refers to the "great dragon, the ancient serpent, the one called Devil and the Satan," who misleads the whole world into idolatrous worship (12:9). Whereas the four angels "bound" by God at the great river Euphrates (9:14) were released to kill a third of the human beings engaged in idolatry (9:15), this angelic divine agent "bound" the dragon for a "thousand" years.

This extensive but limited period that symbolically includes the entirety of the present age greatly exceeds the much shorter and limited period of one "thousand" two hundred sixty days for the nourishing of the woman (12:6) during the time of prophetic witness against idolatrous worship (11:3).[14]

The angel who bound "him," the dragon (20:2), threw "him" (20:3a) into the abyss to which he had the "key" (20:1) with which he "closed" and sealed "over it" (20:3b) with the great chain "upon his hand" (20:1). This was so that the dragon could not "mislead" again the "nations" (20:3b), like the false prophet who "misled" many into worshiping the image of the beast (19:20), and like Babylon by whose sorcery all the "nations" were "misled" into idolatry (18:23). And this was "until were completed" the thousand years (20:3c) during which the dragon was bound (20:2). It corresponds to the divinely determined time "until will be completed" the prophetic words of God (17:17), and the time "until were completed" the seven plagues of divine judgment against idolatrous worship (15:8).

After these things "it is necessary," in accord with what "it is necessary" to take place within the divine plan (1:1; 4:1; 10:11; 11:5; 17:10), that the dragon be "released" for a little time (20:3c). This accords with the four bound angels having been "released" for a divinely specified time (9:15). And the "little time" for which the dragon will be released corresponds to the "little time" during which the slaughtered souls in heaven are to rest. This is the time of divine fulfillment when the fellow prophetic servants and brothers among the audience are about to be killed even as they (6:11)—for their prophetic witness against false worship.

The exalted Jesus promised that "I will give" the one who conquers by witnessing against idolatrous worship to "sit with me on my throne, as I also conquered and sat with my Father on his throne" (3:21). And now John saw "thrones" and they "sat" upon them and "judgment was given" to them (20:4a). In other words, those who conquered idolatrous worship are divinely authorized to share in the "judgment" of the great

---

14. "[T]he millennium in Rev. 20 is best interpreted as a symbol for the timeless reign of God in Christ, in heaven and on earth. This figurative period represents 'a long time'" (Smalley, *Revelation*, 504).

PART THREE—*Shown Prostitute and Wife of Lamb (17:1—21:8)*

prostitute of idolatrous worship (17:1), in accord with the proclamation that God has "judged" the "judgment" of the holy ones, apostles, and prophets from her (18:20).

John also saw the "souls" of those who had been beheaded "on account of the witness of Jesus" (20:4a) and "on account of the word of God" (20:4b). These are the "souls" John saw under the heavenly altar of those slaughtered "on account of the word of God and on account of the witness which they had" (6:9). That the name of the exalted Jesus on the white horse is called "the word of God" (19:13) underlines that the witness of Jesus is the prophetic witness of one who embodies the prophetic word of God against the idolatry for which the souls were killed. They prayed for the time when "you judge" the idolaters on earth (6:10) responsible for their brutal deaths as those who bore prophetic witness against idolatry. Their prayer is answered as God authorized those sitting upon the thrones to execute divine "judgment" against idolatrous worship (20:4a).[15]

The second beast, the false prophet, could make it so that as many as do not "worship the image of the beast" would be killed (13:15). The false prophet is responsible for a "mark upon their right hand or upon their forehead" for all those involved in the idolatrous economic system (13:16). But if anyone "worships the beast and its image and receives a mark upon his forehead or upon his hand" (14:9), he will be eternally tormented in divine judgment (14:10–11; cf. 16:2). And now the audience are exhorted that whoever did not "worship the beast or its image and did not receive the mark upon the forehead and upon their hand both lived and reigned with Christ for a thousand years" (20:4c).

With a poignant emphasis that they were still "living," the beast and the false prophet who misled those who "received the mark of the beast and those worshiping its image" were thrown into the lake of fire burning with sulfur (19:20). In ironic contrast, whoever did not "worship the beast or its image" and did not "receive the mark" both "lived" and "reigned" with Christ for a thousand years (20:4c). This fulfills the

---

15. The indefinite "they" who "sat" upon the thrones is not necessarily limited to the beheaded/slaughtered souls. Not everyone who conquers idolatry (3:21) need be killed. And note that the twenty-four elders have been depicted as "sitting" (11:16; 4:4) on thrones.

promise that those whom the Lamb made for our God a kingdom and priests "will reign" upon the earth (5:10). And it accords with the announcement that there has come to be the kingdom of the world of our Lord and of his Christ and it "will reign" for the ages of the ages (11:15). They lived and reigned with Christ for the "thousand years" during which the dragon, who is the Devil and Satan, was bound (20:2).

The "rest" of those engaged in idolatrous worship were killed with the sword of God's word coming out of the mouth of the exalted Lamb (19:21). But the "rest" of the "dead" (20:5a) refers to those not included among the souls already beheaded and who "lived" with the heavenly exalted Christ for a thousand years (20:4). They include those blessed "dead" who die (but are not necessarily killed) in the Lord from now on (14:13) for their prophetic witness against idolatrous worship. They did not yet "live" the eternal life of heaven "until were completed the thousand years" (20:5a). This recalls that the Devil was bound "until were completed the thousand years," and then it is divinely necessary that he be released for a little time to again mislead the nations into idolatrous worship (20:3).

That "this is the first resurrection" (20:5b) refers to the resurrection to eternal life of those prophetic witnesses against idolatrous worship who both lived and reigned with the risen Christ for a thousand years after their deaths (20:4c). The audience have heard the promise that each of them is "blessed" for keeping the words of the prophecy written in the book of Revelation through their witness against idolatry (1:3). "Blessed" are those who die in the Lord after that prophetic witness (14:13). "Blessed" is the one who watches and keeps his garments through that prophetic witness (16:15). "Blessed" are those who have been called to the supper of the wedding feast of the Lamb for that prophetic witness (19:9). And now the audience are again exhorted to maintain that prophetic witness, as "blessed" and "holy" (20:6a), like God and Christ who are "holy" (3:7; 4:8; 5:8), is the one who has a part in "the first resurrection" (20:6b) for the prophetic witness against idolatrous worship.[16]

---

16. "Everyone now should aspire, through the fact and manner of their testimony, to be a part of that first resurrection" (Blount, *Revelation*, 368).

Over "them," that is, those who have a part in the first resurrection after dying as prophetic witnesses against idolatry (20:6b), the "second death" does not have authority (20:6c). This reinforces the promise that the one who conquers idolatrous worship shall never be harmed by the "second death" (2:11), that is, the final death that deprives one of eternal life.[17] They will be "priests" of God and "of Christ and they will reign with him for a thousand years" (20:6b). This promise follows upon the assertion that those who did not engage in idolatrous worship both lived and "reigned with Christ for a thousand years" (20:4c). Indeed, the Christ who made us into a "kingdom," "priests" for his God and Father (1:6), made those from every nation (5:9) for our God a "kingdom" and "priests," and they "will reign" upon the earth (5:10).[18]

And whenever "are completed the thousand years" (20:7a), recalling that Satan was bound (20:2) "until were completed the thousand years" (20:3, 5), will be "released" (20:7a) Satan from his prison (20:7b). It is necessary that he be "released" for a little time (20:3). In ironic contrast to the warning that the Devil is about to "throw" some into "prison" (2:10), Satan, the Devil (20:2), will be released from the "prison" into which the angel "threw" him (20:3).[19]

Satan, who had been bound (20:2) so that he could not "mislead the nations" (20:3), will be released (20:7) and will go out to "mislead the nations" (20:8a) into idolatrous worship. In contrast to the four angels standing upon the "four corners of the earth" to protect it (7:1), Satan will mislead the nations that are at the "four corners of the earth" (20:8b). He will mislead the nations designated as Gog and Magog, symbols of all the idolatrous pagan nations (cf. Ezek 38:1—39:20), "to assemble them for the battle" (20:8c).[20] This recalls the demonic spirits

---

17. "John never speaks of a 'first death,' possibly because at the moment of death believers continue in eternal life" (Osborne, *Revelation*, 708).

18. Yates, "Resurrection," 453–66; Powell, "Progression," 95–109; Mathewson, "Re-Examination," 237–51; Giblin, "Millennium," 553–70.

19. Marshall, "Christian Millennium," 217–35. "The 'abyss' of vv 1–3 is now called a 'prison' to highlight the fact that the sphere in which the devil resides during the thousand years means that he is restrained in some significant manner, though not in every way" (Beale, *Revelation*, 1021).

20. "Gog and Magog are symbolic figures representing the nations of the world that band together for a final assault upon God and his people" (Mounce, *Revelation*, 372).

going out upon the kings of the whole world to "assemble" them for "the battle" of the great day of God, the Almighty (16:14). But when the beast and the kings of the earth and their armies "assembled" to do "the battle" (19:19), the beast and the false prophet who "misled" into idolatry were thrown into the lake of fire (19:20), and the rest were killed (19:21).

The "number of them," that is, the many angels involved in heavenly worship, "was ten thousands of ten thousands and thousands of thousands" (7:1). But the "number of them," that is, the "them" referring to the nations assembled for the battle (20:8c), is as the "sand of the sea" (20:8d) upon which the dragon, who is the Devil and Satan, stood (12:18). In contrast to the two prophetic witnesses against idolatry who "ascended" to heaven (11:12), the idolatrous nations "ascended" to the breadth "of the earth" (20:9a), emphasizing the great extensiveness of the number of them at the four corners "of the earth" (20:8b). Whereas Satan will go out to mislead the "nations" into idolatrous worship (20:8; cf. 20:3), the exalted Christ may metaphorically strike the "nations" with a sharp sword symbolic of the prophetic word of God, and thereby shepherd them into true worship and the eternal life of heaven (19:15).

The idolatrous nations encircled the camp of the "holy ones" (20:9a), which includes each one who is blessed and "holy" to have a part in the first resurrection (20:6). In contrast to the great idolatrous "city" Babylon, which will be thrown down by God (18:21), the nations encircled the camp of the holy ones, which is the "city" beloved by God (20:9a; cf. 1:5; 3:9).[21] Whereas the Devil "descended" out of heaven (12:7–11) to the earth and the sea, having great fury (12:12), "fire descended out of heaven" (20:9b) and "devoured" them, the idolatrous nations (20:9c). This recalls the angel "descending out of heaven" (20:1), who bound the Devil (20:2), and the "fire" that goes out from the mouth of the two prophetic witnesses against idolatry and "devours" their enemies (11:5).

The Devil "misled them" (20:10a), that is, the nations the released Satan will go out to "mislead" (20:8a) into idolatrous worship. Consequently, he "was thrown into the lake of fire and sulfur where

---

21. "The 'camp of the saints' is equated with 'the beloved city,' which further identifies the oppressed community of 20:9 as the church" (Beale, *Revelation*, 1027).

both the beast and the false prophet were, and they will be tormented day and night for the ages of the ages" (20:10b). This recalls that the false prophet and the beast "were thrown into the lake of fire burning with sulfur" (19:20). Anyone who worships the beast (14:9) "will be tormented with fire and sulfur" (14:10), and the smoke of their torment ascends "for the ages of the ages," and they do not have rest "day and night" (14:11). And now, not only the beast and false prophet but the Devil responsible for idolatrous worship "will be tormented day and night for the ages of the ages."

The angel "threw" the Devil only temporarily into the abyss until were completed the thousand years symbolic of the present age (20:3). But now, at the future and final battle at the end of the present age, the Devil responsible for idolatrous worship "was thrown" permanently into the lake of fire and sulfur for eternity (20:10). This further encourages the audience to maintain their prophetic witness against idolatrous worship and for the true worship of God and the Lamb for eternal life in the Spirit of prophecy.[22]

6b') Vision of Judgment and of Death and Hades Thrown into Lake of Fire (20:11–15)

A [11] Then I saw a great white throne and the one sitting upon it, from the face of whom fled the earth and the heaven, but a place was **not found** for them,

   B a) [12a] And I saw *the dead*, the great and the small, standing before the throne,

        b) [12b] and scrolls were *opened*,

        b') [12c] and another scroll was *opened*, which is of the life,

       a') [12d] and *the dead* were **judged** from the things written in the scrolls **according to their works**,

---

22. De Villiers, "Prime Evil," 57–85.

> **B′** ¹³ and the sea gave **the dead** that were in it and Death and Hades gave **the dead** that were in them, and they were **judged**, each **according to their works**,
>
> **A′ a)** ¹⁴ Then Death and Hades were *thrown* into *the lake of fire*. This is the second death, *the lake of fire*,
>
>   **b)** ¹⁵ᵃ and if anyone was **not found** written in the scroll of the life,
>
>   **a′)** ¹⁵ᵇ he was *thrown* into *the lake of fire*.

That John saw a great "white throne" and the one "sitting upon it" (20:11a) suggests the beginning of a scene of divine judgment executed by God and/or the Lamb. Before this a "white" horse and the one "sitting upon it," the Lamb, who judges in righteousness was similarly seen by John (19:11). And before that he saw a "white" cloud and "upon the cloud sitting" one like a Son of Man, the Lamb, with a sharp sickle (14:14) to harvest the earth in divine judgment (14:15). Salvation is attributed to both our God, the one "sitting upon the throne," and to the Lamb (7:10: cf. 5:13; 7:15).

A scene of divine judgment is further indicated as "from the face" of the one sitting on the great white throne "fled the earth and the heaven, but a place was not found for them" (20:11). This recalls those pleading to be hid from divine judgment—"from the face of the one sitting upon the throne and from the anger of the Lamb" (6:16). Whereas previously fire descended out of "heaven" and devoured the idolatrous nations (20:9), now both earth and "heaven fled." In a previous scene of divine judgment "heaven" was displaced and every mountain and island were moved from their "places" (6:14). At the outpouring of the seventh bowl for divine judgment every island "fled" and mountains "were not found" (16:20). And now, in ironic contrast to a "place was not found" for the dragon and his angels in "heaven" (12:8), a "place was not found" for earth and heaven, thus setting the stage for an even more dramatic scene of divine judgment.

In their worship of God the twenty-four elders declared that the time has come for the "dead" to be judged and to give the reward to God's servants the prophets, the holy ones, and those who fear God's name, "the small and the great" (11:18). And now John saw all the "dead," "the great and the small standing before the throne" (20:12a) in a position to be judged by the one sitting upon the great white throne (20:11). This parallels and complements the numberless crowd similarly "standing before the throne" and before the Lamb (7:9) in a position to participate in heavenly worship (7:10).

For the judgment of all the dead, scrolls "were opened" (20:12b) by God (divine passive), and another "scroll was opened," which is of "the life" (20:12c), that is, eternal life. This recalls that those inhabiting upon the earth will be marveling at the beast of idolatrous worship, those whose name has not been written upon the "scroll of the life" from the foundation of the world (17:8). And it recalls that all those inhabiting upon the earth will worship the beast, for each of whom his name has not been written in the "scroll of the life" of the Lamb who has been slaughtered from the foundation of the world (13:8). But the exalted Jesus, the Lamb, promises that he will never wipe away the name of the one who conquers idolatrous worship from the "scroll of the life" (3:5).

All the "dead," great and small (20:12a), "were judged" by the one sitting on the great white throne (20:11) "from the things written in the scrolls according to their works" (20:12d). This further answers the prayer of the slaughtered souls as to when "do you judge" (6:10), and reaffirms that the time has come for the "dead to be judged" (11:18). It recalls that the God who has remembered the injustices of idolatrous Babylon (18:5) is to give out to her "according to her works" (18:6). And it recalls that the exalted Jesus, the Lamb, as the one who searches minds and hearts, will give to each one "according to your works" (2:23).[23]

The sea gave the "dead" that were in it (cf. 8:9) and Death and Hades gave the "dead" that were in them, and they were "judged," "each according to their works" (20:13). This recalls that Death and Hades were given divine authority "over the fourth of the earth to kill with sword and with famine and with death and by the beasts of the earth" (6:8). But the exalted Jesus, the Lamb, has the keys of Death and of

---

23. "John obviously avoids speaking of a general resurrection of the dead at the judgment. The term 'second resurrection,' which one would expect here in parallel to the 'first resurrection' in v. 5, does not appear. Made alive in the sense of granting new corporeality are only those to whom the resurrection to salvation is imparted (cf. 20:4)" (Roloff, *Revelation*, 231).

Hades (1:18). It elaborates upon and emphatically underlines that the "dead" were "judged" from the things written in the scrolls "according to their works" (20:12). And it reaffirms that the exalted Jesus will give to "each one according to your works" (2:23). The sea "gave" and Death and Hades "gave" the dead to be judged. But the woman of the Lamb, representative of those clothed with the righteous deeds of the holy ones (19:8), may join in the heavenly worship that exclaims "let us give" the glory (19:7) to God (19:6).

The beast and the false prophet who misled people to worship the image of the beast were "thrown" by God (divine passive) "into the lake of fire burning with sulfur" (19:20). And the Devil who misled the nations into idolatrous worship was likewise "thrown into the lake of fire and sulfur" (20:10). And now Death and Hades, responsible for the deaths of those who witness prophetically against idolatrous worship, were also "thrown into the lake of fire" (20:14).

The lake of fire is the "second death" (20:14), the "second death" that does not have authority (20:6) over those who have a part in the first resurrection to eternal life through their prophetic witness against idolatrous worship (20:4–5). A place was "not found" for earth and heaven in the divine judgment (20:11). But if anyone in the divine judgment was "not found" written by God (divine passive) in the scroll of *the* (eternal) life (20:15a; cf. 20:12), he was "thrown into the lake of fire" (20:15b), like Death and Hades who were "thrown into the lake of fire" (20:14). This is the same "lake of fire" which is the second death that deprives one of the eternal life (20:14).

If anyone was not found "written" in the "scroll of the life" (20:15) further recalls that those inhabiting upon the earth will be marveling at the beast, those whose name has not been "written" upon the "scroll of the life" (17:8). And the name of each one who worships the beast has not been "written" in the "scroll of the life" (13:8). But the exalted Jesus will never wipe away the name of anyone who conquers idolatrous worship from the "scroll of the life" (3:5). The audience are thus exhorted to be found written in the scroll of *the* eternal life and to avoid the second, eternal and final death in the divine judgment by resisting the idolatrous worship which leads to it through their witness in the Spirit of prophecy to the true worship of God and the Lamb, which leads to *the* eternal life.

PART THREE—*Shown Prostitute and Wife of Lamb (17:1—21:8)*

7a') Vision of a New Heaven and a New Earth (21:1–8)

A a) [a] [21:1a] Then I saw a *new heaven* and a *new* earth, for the first *heaven* and the first earth have gone away (Isa 65:17; 66:22)

  [b] [1b] and the sea is no more,

 [a'] [2a] and the holy city, *new* Jerusalem, I saw descending out of *heaven*

  b) [2b] from *God*, prepared as a bride adorned for her husband. [3a] Then I heard a great sound out of the throne saying, "Behold the **dwelling** of *God* **with** human beings,

  b') [3b] and he will **dwell with** them, and they themselves **will be** his peoples, and *God* himself **will be** *with* them as their *God*,

 a') [4] and he will wipe away every tear from their eyes, and **death will be no more**, and grief and crying and pain **will be no more**, for the *first* things **have gone away**" (Isa 25:8; 35:10).

B [5] **Then said** the one sitting upon the throne, "Behold, new I am making all things [Isa 43:19]!" And he says, "Write, for these words **are** faithful and true."

B' [6] **Then said** he to me, "They have come to be! I **am** the Alpha and the Omega, the beginning and the end. To the one who is thirsting I will give from the spring of the water of the life freely.

A' a) [7] The one who conquers will inherit these things and I **will be** to him as *God* and he **will be** to me as son [cf. 2 Sam 7:14; Ps 2:7].

  b) [8a] But for the cowards and the unfaithful and the detestable and the murderers and the prostitutes and the sorcerers and the idolaters and all the lying their part is in *the* lake, b′) ⁸ᵇ ***the*** one burning with fire and sulfur,

a′) ⁸ᶜ which ***is*** the second **death**."

The audience have heard of several new things associated with the true heavenly worship that leads to a new and eternal life. The Jesus exalted to eternal life promised those who conquer false worship a "new" name (2:17; 3:12) and a "new" Jerusalem (3:12) appropriate for their share in his new, eternal life. As they share in the new and eternal life in heaven, heavenly worshipers appropriately sing a "new" song (5:9; 14:3). And now John saw a "new" heaven and a "new" earth, "for the first heaven and the first earth have gone away" (21:1a; cf. Isa 65:17; 66:22). And the sea that gave the dead in it to be judged (20:13) "is no more" (21:1b).[24]

The idolatrous nations will trample the "holy city" for forty-two months (11:2) on the first, former earth. But the "holy city," a "new" Jerusalem corresponding to a "new" heaven and a "new" earth (21:1), John saw "descending out of heaven" (21:2a) "from God" (21:2b). This reinforces the promise of the exalted Jesus to write upon the one who conquers idolatrous worship the "name of the city of my God, of the new Jerusalem that is descending out of heaven from my God" (3:12).

That this new city is "prepared as a bride adorned for her husband" (21:2b) resonates with the proclamation of the heavenly worshipers that "has come the wedding feast of the Lamb and his woman has prepared herself" (19:7). Her preparation is being clothed in the righteous deeds of the holy ones, the deeds of those engaged in true rather that false worship (19:8). In stark, alliterative contrast to the great idolatrous prostitute "adorned with gold" but without a husband (17:4), yet the mother of prostitutes as the great city Babylon (17:5), the people of God, the holy city, new Jerusalem, is prepared as a bride properly "adorned" for her husband.[25]

Death from divine judgment comes to the "human beings" who worship the image of the beast (16:2; cf. 16:8, 9, 21). John introduced it with his report that "I heard a great sound out of the temple say-

---

24. Mathewson, "New Exodus," 243–58; Moo, "Sea," 148–67. "The sea as a symbol of evil would best explain why it is added here" (Osborne, *Revelation*, 731).

25. "What is important for John is the rhetorical effect delivered both when the city is envisioned as a place for the people of God and then when it is envisioned as the people themselves" (Blount, *Revelation*, 379).

PART THREE—*Shown Prostitute and Wife of Lamb (17:1—21:8)*

ing" to the seven angels, "Go and pour out the seven bowls of the fury of God on the earth" (16:1). Eternal life comes to human beings from God's dwelling with them. It is similarly introduced by John's report that "I heard a great sound out of the throne"—the "throne" of divine judgment (20:11, 12)—saying, "Behold the dwelling of God with human beings" (21:3a). "And he will dwell with them" (21:3b). The great sound out of the throne announcing God's universal dwelling with human beings complements the "sound from the throne" with its invitation to a universal worship of God: "Praise our God all his servants and those who fear him, the small and the great" (19:5).

The "heavens" and those "dwelling" in them were exhorted to celebrate after the dragon was thrown out of heaven (12:12). The beast of idolatrous worship blasphemed God's "dwelling," that is, those in "heaven dwelling" (13:6). John saw that the temple of the "dwelling" of the testimony in "heaven" was opened (15:5). And now, corresponding to the new Jerusalem descending out of "heaven" (21:2), the heavenly "dwelling" of God is with human beings, and he "will dwell" with them (21:3). This reinforces the promise that God "will dwell" over all those who offer worship to him in heaven (7:15).

As for the human beings with whom God will dwell, "they themselves will be his peoples, and God himself will be with them as their God" (21:3). In a noteworthy contrast to the singular address of God's people as "my people" (18:4), the human beings with whom God will dwell will be "his peoples." The plural for peoples emphasizes that God is the God not merely of a single people but of all peoples who are to participate in heavenly worship and eternal life (cf. 5:9; 7:9; 10:11; 11:9; 13:7; 14:6; 17:15).[26]

The God who will be with his "peoples" as "their" God (21:3) "will wipe away every tear from their eyes" (21:4; cf. Isa 25:8). This reinforces the promise that the Lamb will shepherd the heavenly worshipers from all "peoples" (7:9) and lead them to eternal life's springs of waters, and "God will wipe away every tear from their eyes" (7:17). Not only the sea, a place for the dead (20:13), "is no more" (21:1), but death itself "will be

---

26. "This covenant language is significant because it is applied to all people universally, not just to a specific group" (Aune, *Revelation 17-22*, 1123).

no more" (cf. 20:14), and grief and crying and pain "will be no more" (21:4).

"Death" will be no more (21:4). This follows from and emphatically underlines that "Death" and Hades were thrown into the lake of fire, the second "death" (20:14). "Grief," like the "grief" that will come to idolatrous Babylon (18:7–8), and "pain," like the "pain" that came to idolaters (16:10–11), will be no more. For the "first" things "have gone away" (21:4; cf. Isa 35:10). This emphatically reaffirms that the "first" heaven and the "first" earth "have gone away" (21:1).

Recalling that the twenty-four elders and the four living creatures worshiped God, the "one sitting upon the throne" (19:4), then said the "one sitting upon the throne," "Behold, new I am making all things!" (21:5; cf. Isa 43:19). John saw a "new" heaven, a "new" earth (21:1), and a "new" Jerusalem (21:2). But now the God worshiped as the one sitting upon the throne himself declares that he is making all things completely and emphatically "new."[27]

An angel said to John, "Write: Blessed are those who have been called to the supper of the wedding feast of the Lamb." And he said, "These are the true words of God" (19:9). And now God himself similarly says, "Write, for these words are faithful and true" (21:5).[28] Not only are the prophetic words of God regarding those called as worshipers to participate in the heavenly supper of the wedding feast of the Lamb, those prepared as a bride adorned for her husband (21:2), true, but the prophetic words of God with regard to making all things new to facilitate that heavenly worship are faithful and true. And that the Lamb, whose name is called the "word of God" (19:13), is himself "faithful and true" (3:14; 19:11) underscores this.

At the outpouring of the seventh bowl a great sound from the "throne" dramatically and emphatically announced, "It has come to be!" (16:17). Then there came to be the greatest earthquake ever in divine

---

27. The term "new" is placed in a position of emphasis before the verb "I am making."

28. "This is the last of several commands to write that apparently have the entire composition in view (Rev 1:11, 19; 21:5; cf. 10:4) rather than just the partial texts that are the objects of the commands to write in 14:13 and 19:9" (Aune, *Revelation 17–22*, 1126).

judgment upon the idolatrous human beings who nevertheless continued to blaspheme God (16:18–21). And now, similarly, the one sitting upon the "throne" (21:5) dramatically and emphatically announced to John, "They have come to be!" (21:6). That is, the faithful and true prophetic words of God, especially including his making all things new (21:5) and dwelling with human beings (21:3), have definitively come to be within the divine plan of salvation.

The audience have already heard the Lord God proclaim, "I am the Alpha and the Omega, the one who is and who was and who is coming, the Almighty" (1:8). And now the similar pronouncement by God himself that "I am" the Alpha and the Omega, the beginning and the end (21:6), further establishes that these prophetic words of God "are" faithful and true (21:5).[29] The "one sitting upon the throne" will dwell over the worshipers in heaven who have conquered the idolatrous worship on earth (7:15), and they will not "thirst" again (7:16). Indeed, the Lamb who is in the middle of the throne will shepherd them and lead them to eternal "life's springs of waters" (7:17). And now the "one sitting upon the throne" (21:5) promises that to the one who is "thirsting" for it he will give from the "spring of the water of the life" freely (21:6). This is the eternal life that accords with the divine promise that death will be no more (21:4).

Echoing the promises to the one who "conquers" idolatrous worship (2:7, 11, 17, 26; 3:5, 12, 21), God now promises that the one who "conquers" will inherit "these" things (21:7), in accord with "these" faithful and true prophetic words of God (21:5). These things include all things God is making new (21:5), especially and preeminently the eternal life (21:6) that accords with death being no more (21:4). The promise pronounced by God himself that I "will be" to him as God and he "will be" to me as son (21:7; cf. 2 Sam 7:14; Ps 2:7) both personalizes and individualizes the promise that God will dwell with human beings, so that they "will be" his peoples, and God "will be" with them as their God (21:3). That the one who conquers idolatrous worship to partici-

---

29. "The figurative title 'Alpha and Omega,' using the first and last letters of the Greek alphabet, characterizes the Godhead as the origin and goal of all created and human existence" (Smalley, *Revelation*, 541).

pate in heavenly worship and eternal life will be to God as "son" likens that person to the exalted Jesus, the "Son" of God (2:18).

But for all those involved in idolatry—the cowards, unfaithful, detestable, "murderers," "prostitutes," "sorcerers," idolaters, and all the "lying," like those "lying" that they are apostles (2:2)—"their part is in the lake, the one burning with fire and sulfur, which is the second death" (21:8). This recalls the idolaters who did not repent of their "murders," "sorceries," and "prostitution" (9:21).[30] In contrast to the one who has a "part" in the first resurrection to eternal life (20:6), their "part" is in the "lake, the one burning with fire and sulfur." This reaffirms that if anyone was not found written in the scroll of eternal life, he was thrown into the "lake of fire" (20:15). All idolaters will thus join the beast and the false prophet in the "lake of fire burning with sulfur" (19:20), the Devil in the "lake of fire and sulfur" (20:10), and Death and Hades in the "lake of fire" (20:14).

In a poignant contrast to God's promise that to the one who conquers idolatrous worship "I will be" as God and "he will be" to God as son (21:7), the part of idolaters is in the lake of fire, which "is" the second death (21:8c). In contrast to the first, physical "death," which will be no more (21:4), the lake of fire for idolaters and for the personified power of "Death" itself is the second, the final and spiritual, "death" (20:14; 21:8) that deprives one of participating in heavenly worship and eternal life. But over those who do not engage in idolatrous worship (20:4) the second "death" does not have authority (20:6; cf. 2:11). Consequently, the audience are again exhorted not to be among the idolaters destined for the second, eternal death, but rather to be those thirsting for the water of the eternal life that God gives freely (21:6). As those engaged in the true, universal, and heavenly worship of God and the Lamb for eternal life in the Spirit of prophecy, they are to be among all the peoples with whom God promises to dwell and be with as their God (21:3).

---

30. "Such sins are either part of the activities surrounding idolatry, or they actually become acts of idolatry themselves (for idolatry involving murder, i.e., child-sacrifice, see also Ps. 106:36–38)" (Beale, *Revelation*, 1059).

PART THREE—*Shown Prostitute and Wife of Lamb (17:1—21:8)*

Summary on 19:1—21:8

The audience hear the seven units of this subsection (19:1—21:8) in a chiastic pattern centering around the theme of heavenly worship and final judgment. In the unparalleled central (d) unit (19:17-21) of this subsection the audience hear of the final divine judgment against the idolatrous beast, the false prophet, and those he misled into idolatrous worship: "But seized was the beast and with it the false prophet who made the signs before it, by which he misled those who received the mark of the beast and those worshiping its image. Living, the two were thrown in the lake of fire burning with sulfur, and the rest were killed" (19:20-21).

When the audience hear the (c') unit (20:1-10), they hear a chiastic progression of the (c) unit (19:11-16). That the name of the exalted Jesus on the white horse is called "the word of God" (19:13) underlines that the witness of Jesus is the prophetic witness of one who embodies the prophetic word of God against idolatrous worship. This progresses to the souls of those who had been beheaded on account of the witness of Jesus and on account of "the word of God" sharing in the divine judgment against idolatry (20:4; cf. 6:9-10). The exalted Christ may metaphorically strike the "nations" with a sharp sword symbolic of the prophetic word of God, and thereby shepherd them into true heavenly worship and eternal life (19:15). This progresses to Satan going out to mislead the "nations" into idolatrous worship (20:8; cf. 20:3), but then being thrown into the lake of fire and sulfur where both the beast and the false prophet were (20:10).

When the audience hear the (b') unit (20:11-15), they hear a chiastic progression of the (b) unit (19:6-10). The woman of the Lamb, representative of those clothed with the righteous deeds of the holy ones (19:8), may join in the heavenly worship that exclaims "let us give" the glory (19:7) to God (19:6). This progresses to the sea "gave" and Death and Hades "gave" the dead to be divinely judged, each according to their works (20:13). Then Death and Hades were thrown into the lake of fire, as well as anyone not found written in the scroll of the eternal life (20:14-15).

Heavenly Worship and Final Judgment

When the audience hear the final (a′) unit (21:1–8), they hear a chiastic progression of and inclusion with the initial (a) unit (19:1–5). The twenty-four elders and the four living creatures in heaven worshiped God as the "one sitting upon the throne" (19:4). This progresses to the "one sitting upon the throne" declaring, "Behold, new I am making all things!" (21:5). The "sound from the throne" in heaven called for a universal worship of God: "Praise our God all his servants and those who fear him, the small and the great" (19:5). This progresses to and is complemented by the "great sound out of the throne" announcing God's universal dwelling with human beings who will be his peoples (21:3).

Once the audience have heard this (c′) subsection (19:1—21:8), they have experienced a chiastic progression from the (c) subsection (4:1—7:17) within the overall macrochiastic structure of the book of Revelation. The (c) subsection centers around the theme of encouraging believers on earth to participate in heavenly worship. This progresses to the theme of the divine judgment that encourages believers on earth to participate in heavenly worship and eternal life in the (c′) subsection.

The twenty-four elders participating in heavenly worship (4:4, 10; 5:5, 6, 8, 11, 14; 7:11, 13) progresses to and is dramatically climaxed by their worship of God in heaven as the one sitting upon the throne, saying, "Amen! Hallelujah!" (19:4). The "number" of heavenly worshipers was "ten thousands of ten thousands and thousands of thousands" (5:11). This progresses to the "number" of the nations to be judged for their idolatrous worship is "as the sand of the sea" (20:8).

A "white horse and the one sitting upon it" who conquered with instruments of power and violence (6:2) progresses to a "white horse and the one sitting upon it" who is called faithful and true and judges in righteousness (19:11). The souls of those slaughtered on account of the word of God and on account of the witness they had against idolatrous worship (6:9) prayed for divine judgment (6:10). This progresses to the souls of those who had been beheaded on account of the witness of Jesus and on account of the word of God being associated with the divine judgment against idolatrous worship (20:4). They prayed to "vindicate our blood" from the idolaters on earth (6:10), and in response the heavenly worshipers proclaimed that God "has vindicated the blood of his servants" (19:2).

PART THREE—*Shown Prostitute and Wife of Lamb (17:1—21:8)*

The "large crowd" that John saw participating in heavenly worship (7:9) progresses to a "great sound of a large crowd" that he heard participating in heavenly worship (19:1, 6). The promise that the one sitting upon the throne "will dwell" over those worshiping in heaven (7:15) progresses to God "will dwell" with the human beings who will be his peoples (21:3). And the promise that God "will wipe away every tear from the eyes" of those participating in universal heavenly worship (7:17) progresses to God "will wipe away every tear from the eyes" of his universal peoples, so that death will be no more (21:4). Indeed, he will give to those thirsting for it the water of *the* eternal life freely (21:6). As those encouraged to participate in the true, universal, and heavenly worship of God and the Lamb for eternal life in the Spirit of prophecy, the audience are to be among all the peoples with whom God promises to dwell and be with as their God.

PART FOUR

Grace from John Carried in Spirit to Mountain and Shown Holy City (21:9—22:21)

10

Visions of the Heavenly City's Worship of God and the Lamb for Eternal Life

Revelation 21:9—22:5

1a) Angel Shows Bride of Lamb/Holy City Jerusalem from Heaven (21:9–14)

    A [9] Then came one of the seven **angels** having the seven bowls full of the seven last plagues and spoke with me saying, "Here, I will show you the bride, the woman of the **Lamb**."

        B [10a] Then he carried me in Spirit to a mountain **great and high**,

            C [10b] and showed me the holy city Jerusalem descending out of heaven from **God**,

            C' [11] having the glory of **God**, its brilliance like a most precious stone, as a crystal-clear jasper stone,

        B' [12a] having a wall **great and high**,

PART FOUR—*Shown Holy City (21:9—22:21)*

> **A'** **a)** ¹²ᵇ having *twelve* gates and upon the gates *twelve* **angels** and *names* inscribed, which are the *names* of the *twelve* tribes of the sons of Israel,
>
>   **b)** ¹³ᵃ from east *three gates* and from north *three gates*
>
>   **b')** ¹³ᵇ and from south *three gates* and from west *three gates*,
>
> **a')** ¹⁴ and the wall of the city has *twelve* foundations and on them the *twelve names* of the *twelve* apostles of the **Lamb**.

Previously John reported that "then came one of the seven angels having the seven bowls." The angel "spoke with me, saying, 'Here, I will show you the judgment of the great prostitute who sits upon many waters'" (17:1). And now he similarly reports its antithetical parallel: "Then came one of the seven angels having the seven bowls full of the seven last plagues." The angel "spoke with me saying, 'Here, I will show you the bride, the woman of the Lamb'" (21:9). This second report refers to the bowls as full of the "seven last plagues," recalling and thus underscoring that these are the "seven plagues, the last ones," "for in them is completed the fury of God" (15:1; cf. 15:7) against idolatrous worship.

In a poignant contrast to the divine judgment of the great prostitute responsible for idolatrous worship (17:1), the angel now will show John the "bride, the woman of the Lamb" (21:9). This refers to the new Jerusalem representative of the people of God prepared as a "bride" adorned for her husband (21:2). And the bride is the "woman" who has prepared herself to participate in the heavenly worship characterized as the wedding feast of the "Lamb" (19:7). The bride, the woman of the Lamb, is thus the same heavenly "woman" associated with true worship (12:1) in contrast to the great prostitute, Babylon the great (17:5), the earthly "woman" associated with idolatrous worship (17:4).

John reported that the angel who will show him the judgment of the great prostitute (17:1) "carried me" into an earthly wilderness "in Spirit" (17:3). And then John saw the great woman prostitute responsible for idolatrous worship on earth (17:3–5). And now he similarly reports that the angel who will show him the bride, the woman of the Lamb (21:9), "carried me in Spirit" to a heavenly mountain great and

Visions of the Heavenly City's Worship of God and the Lamb for Eternal Life

high (21:10a). At the second trumpeting of divine judgment against idolatry something as a "great mountain" with fire burning was thrown into the sea on earth (8:8). But now the angel carried John to a heavenly "mountain great and high."[1]

The "holy city, new Jerusalem," John saw "descending out of heaven from God" (21:2). Elaborating upon this, the angel showed John the "holy city Jerusalem descending out of heaven from God" (21:10b). This recalls and resonates with the divine promise that "I will be" to the one who conquers idolatrous worship on earth as "God" (21:7), the "God" whose dwelling (in the holy city) is with the human beings who will be his peoples (21:3). Indeed, the exalted Jesus promised that he will write upon the one who conquers idolatrous worship "the name of my God and the name of the city of my God, of the new Jerusalem that is descending out of heaven from my God" (3:12).

This holy city descending out of heaven from "God" (21:10b) has the "glory of God" (21:11a), the "glory of God" from which the temple for heavenly worship was filled with smoke (15:8). In contrast to the great woman prostitute, the idolatrous city Babylon, clothed with a "precious stone" (17:4; 18:16) on earth, the brilliance of this holy city from heaven is like a "most precious stone" (21:11b). And that its brilliance is as a crystal-clear "jasper stone" (21:11c) associates it with the vision of God like a "jasper stone" (4:3), the God who is the object of true heavenly worship.

The angel carried John in Spirit to a mountain "great and high" (21:10a), which associates it with the heavenly realm. The holy city Jerusalem descending out of heaven has a heavenly wall similarly "great and high" (21:12a). It has twelve gates and upon the gates "twelve angels" (21:12b), in distinction from the "seven angels" having the seven bowls full of the seven last plagues for the divine judgment against idolatrous worship (21:9). The "twelve angels" further associate the heavenly city with the heavenly woman who has upon her head a crown of "twelve stars" (12:1), symbolic of twelve angels (cf. 1:20). In contrast to the beast with "names" of the blasphemy of idolatrous worship (13:1; 17:3), the

---

1. "The high mountain to which the seer is led in an ecstasy effected by the Spirit is, like the desert in 17:3, not a real place, but a typical one; it belongs together with God's saving revelations (cf. also Ezek. 40:2)" (Roloff, *Revelation*, 242).

holy city has "names" inscribed, which are the "names" of the "twelve tribes of the sons of Israel" (21:12b). This associates the city with those sealed for heavenly worship from "every tribe of the sons of Israel" (7:4).[2]

The holy heavenly city can be universally entered by all peoples from every direction. It has "from east three gates and from north three gates and from south three gates and from west three gates" (21:13). In addition to the city's "twelve" gates, "twelve" angels, and "names" of the "twelve" tribes (21:12b), the wall of the city has "twelve" foundations and on them the "twelve names" of the "twelve apostles" of the "Lamb" (21:14). This includes the "apostles" invited to participate in heavenly worship (18:20), as part of and along with all the peoples of God represented by the bride, the woman of the "Lamb" (21:9). The audience are thus encouraged to identify with the apostles and woman of the Lamb destined to participate in the universal heavenly worship of God and the Lamb for eternal life in the Spirit of prophecy.[3]

2b) No Temple Seen in the Heavenly City (21:15–22a)

A a) [15a] Then the one speaking with me had a ***golden*** measure rod,

    b) [15b] so that he might ***measure*** the city and its **gates** and its **wall**, [16] and the city is laid out as a square and its length as great as its width, and he ***measured*** the city with the rod at twelve thousand stadia, its length and width and height are equal,

    b') [17] and he ***measured*** its **wall**, one hundred forty-four cubits, a measure of a human being, which is of an angel, [18a] and the material of its **wall** jasper

  a') [18b] and the city **pure gold** like **pure glass**.

B [19a] The **foundations** of the wall of the city are adorned with every precious stone—

---

2. "The juxtaposition of the twelve tribes and the twelve apostles shows the unity of ancient Israel and the NT church" (Mounce, *Revelation*, 391).

3. Mathewson, "Foundation Stones," 487–98.

Visions of the Heavenly City's Worship of God and the Lamb for Eternal Life

> **B′** ¹⁹ᵇ the first **foundation** jasper, the second sapphire, the third chalcedony, the fourth emerald, ²⁰ the fifth sardonyx, the sixth carnelian, the seventh chrysolite, the eighth beryl, the ninth topaz, the tenth chrysoprase, the eleventh hyacinth, the twelfth amethyst.
>
> **A′** ²¹ And the twelve **gates** twelve pearls, each one, each of the **gates**, was out of one pearl, and the main street of the city **pure gold** as transparent as **glass** [Tob 13:17; Isa 54:11–12].
> ²²ᵃ But a temple I did not see in it.

John reports that the one "speaking with me," that is, the angel who "spoke with me" about the bride, the woman of the Lamb (21:9), "has a golden measure rod" (21:15a). As part of heavenly worship an angel had a "golden" censer to offer incense upon the "golden" altar in heaven (8:3). As part of his heavenly status the one like a Son of Man sitting upon a white cloud had upon his head a "golden" crown (14:14). But as part of earthly idolatrous worship the great woman prostitute had a "golden" cup in her hand filled with the idolatrous abominations of the earth (17:4). And now the angel speaking with John had a "golden" measure rod, "so that he might measure the city and its gates and its wall" (21:15b).

As part of his divine commission to prophesy regarding true and false worship, John was given a "rod" like a staff and told to "measure" the heavenly temple of God and the altar and those worshiping in it (11:1). But he was not to "measure" the outer earthly courtyard of the temple, for with idolatrous worship the nations will trample the holy "city" for forty-two months (11:2). And now the angel had a golden measure "rod," so that he might "measure" the "city" and its "gates" and its "wall" (21:15b). This refers to the heavenly holy "city" Jerusalem (21:10) having a "wall" great and high and twelve "gates" (21:12), the "city" whose "wall" has twelve foundations (21:14).

Resonating with the throne that "was lying" in heaven (4:2), the heavenly city "is laid out" by God (divine passive) "as a square and its length as great as its width, and he measured the city with the rod at twelve thousand stadia, its length and width and height are equal" (21:16). The measurement of "twelve thousand stadia" for the city contrasts the measurement of "one thousand six hundred stadia" for the blood from the winepress in the divine judgment against earthly idolatrous worship (14:20). And it appropriately accords with the number of heavenly worshipers—"twelve thousand" from each of the twelve tribes of the sons of Israel (7:5, 6, 7, 8). This is further underlined as the angel who "measured" the city (21:16) and its "wall" (21:15b) "measured" its "wall" at "one hundred forty-four" cubits (21:17), corresponding to the "one hundred forty-four" thousand heavenly worshipers (7:4; 14:1, 3).

The number of the beast of idolatrous worship on earth "is" a number of a "human being"—the threefold imperfect number of six hundred sixty-six (13:18). But the measurement of the wall of the holy city for heavenly worship is the perfect number of one hundred forty-four cubits, a "measure," on the one hand, of a "human being," but that "is" also of an angel (21:17). Indeed, the angel who measured it had a golden "measure" rod (21:15) appropriate for measuring in human terms the holy city for divine heavenly worship.[4]

Recalling that the brilliance of the holy heavenly city is like "jasper" stone (21:11), the material of its wall is "jasper" (21:18a). The great woman prostitute of idolatrous worship was adorned with "gold" on earth (17:4; 18:16). But the holy city measured with a heavenly "golden" rod (21:15a) is "pure gold" like "pure" glass (21:18b). This accords not only with the "pure" clothing of the armies in heaven following the Lamb (19:14), but with the "pure" clothing that prepares the woman of the Lamb to participate in the heavenly worship that includes the wedding feast of the Lamb (19:8).

The foundations of the wall of the city are "adorned" with every "precious stone" (21:19a). This elaborates upon how the holy heavenly city is prepared as a bride "adorned" for her husband (21:2), and how its brilliance is like a "most precious stone" (21:11). A precious stone for each "foundation" (21:19b) of the twelve (21:14) "foundations" of the wall of the city (21:19a), beginning with "jasper" (21:19b), in accord

---

4. "John adds that this vision of 'human measurement' is to be understood more deeply according to its symbolic, heavenly, or 'angelic' meaning" (Beale, *Revelation*, 1077). "Human calculations merge here with angelic (verse 17), and the result is the unity of earthly and heavenly realities in a new cosmos" (Smalley, *Revelation*, 552).

with the city's brilliance being like "jasper" (21:11), is then enumerated (21:19b–20).

The twelve gates of the holy city measured for heavenly worship (21:12, 15) were twelve "pearls," each one, each of the "gates," was out of one "pearl" (21:21). This is a deliberately pointed contrast to the great woman prostitute of idolatrous worship on earth, who is said to be adorned with "pearls" (17:4; cf. 18:12) and with "pearl" (18:16). In contrast to the "main street" of the great earthly city of idolatrous worship on which is the corpse of the two prophetic witnesses against idolatry (11:8), the "main street" of the heavenly city is "pure gold" as transparent as "glass" (21:21). This emphatically reaffirms that the holy city for heavenly worship is "pure gold" like pure "glass" (21:18; cf. Tob 13:17; Isa 54:11–12).

The holy city that the nations will trample with their idolatrous worship (11:2) contains the "temple" of God for John to measure for heavenly worship (11:1). But now in this new holy heavenly city John surprisingly did not see an otherwise expected "temple" as a distinct and separate edifice (21:22a). Indeed, the entire city itself has been described as if it were in its totality a temple. The audience have thus been attracted to participate not in idolatrous worship that takes place in the earthly city of Babylon the great but in the true and universal worship for eternal life in the Spirit of prophecy that takes place in the heavenly holy city of a new and unique Jerusalem—one without the usually expected temple building.[5]

3b′) God and Lamb Are Temple of City for Glory and Honor of Nations (21:22b–27)

    A   a) [22b] For the Lord, the God, the Almighty, is its temple, as well as the ***Lamb***,

---

5. "John's words suggest that he was looking for a temple *in* the city, as one building among many, whereas it has already been revealed to him that the whole city is the sanctuary, built like Solomon's Holy of Holies as a perfect cube, and adorned with the precious stones of the high priest's breastplate" (Boxall, *Revelation*, 307–8; emphasis original).

> b) ²³ᵃ and the city does not have need of the sun nor of the moon that they *appear* in it,
>
> b') ²³ᵇ for the glory of God *illumines* it,
>
> a') ²³ᶜ and its lamp is the **Lamb**,
>
> B ²⁴ and the **nations** will walk by its light, and the kings of the earth **bring** their glory into it,
>
> C ²⁵ᵃ and its gates will **never** be closed during the day,
>
> C' ²⁵ᵇ for night will **not** be there,
>
> B' ²⁶ and they will **bring** the glory and the honor of the **nations** into it,
>
> A' ²⁷ and will never come into it any unclean thing or one doing an abomination or falsehood, but only those written in the scroll of the life of the **Lamb**.

The exalted Jesus promised to make the one who conquers idolatrous worship a pillar in the "temple" of God (3:12), but a "temple" John did not see in the new holy heavenly city Jerusalem (21:22a), "for the Lord, the God, the Almighty, is its temple, as well as the Lamb" (21:22b). That the "Lord, the God, the Almighty" himself is its temple underlines the presence of God in the city as an object of heavenly worship. It recalls how the "Lord God" who declared that he is "the Almighty" (1:8) has been repeatedly addressed by heavenly worshipers as the "Lord God, the Almighty" (4:8; 11:17; 15:3; 16:7; 19:6). The "Lamb" is likewise its temple as an object of heavenly worship. Just as the Lord God the creator is worthy to be worshiped (4:11), so is the slaughtered "Lamb" (5:12), the "Lord of lords" (17:14; 19:16). Indeed, God and the Lamb are the dual focus of universal heavenly worship (5:13; 7:9–10; 15:3).⁶

The materially wealthy church in Laodicea declared that "I have need of nothing" (3:17). But it needs to "buy" from Jesus heavenly "gold" (3:18). However, the heavenly "city of pure gold" (21:18; cf. 21:15, 16, 19, 21) "does not have need of the sun nor of the moon that they appear in it" (21:23a). "For the glory of God illumines it" (21:23b), like

---

6. "In the place of the indirect, cultically mediated presence of God appears a direct and actual presence of God" (Roloff, *Revelation*, 245).

the earth was "illumined" from the "glory" of an angel from heaven (18:1). And this accords with the fact that the countenance of the exalted Jesus, the Lamb, "appears" as the "sun" in its power (1:16), and the city has the "glory of God, its brilliance like a most precious stone" (21:11). Although a light of a "lamp" may never "appear" in the earthly city of idolatrous Babylon again (18:23), the heavenly city's "lamp" is the "Lamb" (21:23c), the "Lamb" whose presence in it is its temple for true worship (21:22b).

Some in Sardis "will walk" with the exalted Jesus, the Lamb, in white, for, as those who have resisted idolatrous worship, they are worthy to participate in heavenly worship (3:4). Similarly, the "nations will walk" by the "light" of the new holy city of heavenly worship (21:24), in contrast to the earthly idolatrous city of Babylon in which a "light" may never appear again (18:23). This accords with the proclamation of the heavenly worshipers who conquered idolatrous worship (15:2). They promised a universal heavenly worship—that "all the nations" will come and worship before God (15:4).

The "kings of the earth" who engaged in the prostitution of idolatrous worship with the city of Babylon (17:2; 18:3, 9) wanted to escape the divine judgment of God and the Lamb against idolatry (6:15; 19:19). But the Lamb, the "King of kings" (17:14; 19:16), is the ruler of the "kings of the earth" (1:5). And it is divinely necessary that John, as a model for his audience of fellow prophetic servants (1:1, 9), again prophesy about the many peoples and nations and tongues and "kings" who are to participate in universal heavenly worship (10:11; cf. 5:13). Consequently, the "kings of the earth" ultimately bring their "glory" into the new holy city as part of heavenly worship (21:24). This enables them to give the "glory" of heavenly worship to both God and the Lamb (1:6; 4:9, 11; 5:12, 13; 7:12; 11:13; 14:7; 16:9; 19:1, 7) as an appropriate response to the "glory" of God that illumines the holy heavenly city (21:23).[7]

The "gates" of the city, the twelve "gates" of pearl (21:21) and the "gates" to be measured (21:15) for an open access in all directions (21:12–13), "will never be closed" by God (divine passive) during the

---

7. "Participation in the new Jerusalem remains a possibility even for earth's kings, who up to this point have been marked out by their hostility to the Lamb and his followers" (Boxall, *Revelation*, 308).

day (21:25a). This permanently open access for universal worship in the holy heavenly city accords with the promise of the exalted Jesus, the Lamb, "who opens and no one will close" (3:7), to give a door opened, which "no one is able to close it" (3:8). This permanent openness is further emphasized as the gates will "never" be closed during the day or night, for night will "not" be there (21:25b).

The kings of the earth "bring" not only their own glory into the city (21:24) whose gates will never be closed (21:25), but they "will bring" the glory and the honor of the "nations," the "nations" who will walk by its light (21:24), into it (21:26). That they will bring the "glory and the honor" of the nations into the holy heavenly city will enable them to give the "glory and the honor" appropriate for the worship of both God (4:9, 11; 7:12) and the Lamb (5:12, 13). This will fulfill the promise of those singing the song of the Lamb for a universal heavenly worship as they worship the Lord God, the Almighty (15:3; cf. 21:22b), proclaiming that "all the nations will come and worship before you" (15:4).[8]

The holy heavenly city is permanently and completely open for all true worshipers but not for idolaters, as "will never come into it any unclean thing or one doing an abomination or falsehood" (21:27). "No one" was able "to come into" the heavenly temple filled with smoke from the glory of God (15:8). But now any ritually unclean thing "will never come into" the holy heavenly city whose temple is God and the Lamb. That one doing an "abomination" will never come into it refers to an idolater, as it recalls the idolatrous worship of the great woman prostitute and city of Babylon, who has a golden cup in her hand filled with the "abominations" of the earth (17:4, 5). And one doing "falsehood" will never come into it, since "falsehood" is not found in the mouth of true heavenly worshipers (14:5).[9]

The exalted Jesus never will wipe away the name of one who conquers idolatry from the "scroll of the life" (3:5). But the name of each

---

8. "The bringing of glory and honor to the eschatological city of God is surely a sign of the conversion of the nations and the kings of the earth, reflecting the Jewish hope for the eschatological conversion of the heathen" (Aune, *Revelation 17–22*, 1173).

9. "This is the same group described in 21:8. 'Unclean' is added to stress that these people have defiled themselves through the abomination of idolatry" (Beale, *Revelation*, 1101).

one who worships the beast has not been "written" in the "scroll of the life," the eternal life of the Lamb (13:8). And the name of those engaged in idolatrous worship has not been "written" upon the "scroll of the life" (17:8). Furthermore, if anyone was not found "written" in the "scroll of the life," he was thrown into the lake of fire (20:15), the second, eternal death (20:14). Accordingly, only those "written" in the "scroll of the life" of the Lamb will come into the holy city to participate in the universal worship and eternal life of heaven (21:27). As those who worship God and the Lamb for eternal life in the Spirit of prophecy, the audience will not be excluded idolaters but among those who enter the holy city to participate in its universal heavenly worship and eternal life as those written in the scroll of the life of the Lamb.

4a′) Angel Showed John the Worship for Eternal Life in the Heavenly City (22:1–5)

    A a) $^{22:1}$ Then he showed me the river of the water of life, bright as crystal, going out from **the throne of God and of the Lamb** (Ezek 47:1–12).

        b) ^{2a} In the midst of its main street and on each side of the river is the *tree* of life

            c) ^{2b} making twelve *fruits*,

            c′) ^{2c} during each month giving out its *fruit*,

        b′) ^{2d} and the leaves of the *tree* are for healing of the nations,

      a′) ^{3a} and any cursed thing **will be no more** and *the throne of God and of the Lamb* will be in it,

    B ^{3b} and **his** servants will offer worship to **him**

    B′ ^{4} and they will see **his** face, and **his** name will be upon their foreheads,

  A′ ^{5} and night **will be no more** and they do not have need of the light of a lamp or the light of the sun, for the Lord **God** will illumine over them, and they will reign for the ages of the ages.

PART FOUR—Shown Holy City (21:9—22:21)

The angel who "showed me," John, "the holy city Jerusalem descending out of heaven from God" (21:10) now "showed me the river of the water of life, bright as crystal, going out from the throne of God and of the Lamb" (22:1). The water of "life" from the throne of the "Lamb" refers to the eternal "life" of the "Lamb" destined for those written in the scroll, those who conquer idolatrous worship (21:27). The "rivers" and springs of the "waters" became blood for death in the divine judgment against idolatry (16:4; cf. 11:6). But this is the "river of the water" of eternal life. And this river of the "water of life" fulfills the divine promises of eternal "life's" springs of "waters" (7:17) and the spring of the "water of the life" (21:6) for those who conquer idolatrous worship (21:7).

The river of the water of life is "bright as crystal" (22:1). This underlines its heavenly character in contrast to the earthly "bright things" that have perished away from idolatrous Babylon (18:14). But it accords with the "bright" linen of angels (15:6) and of the heavenly woman (19:8), as well as with the glassy sea like "crystal" before the throne in heaven (4:6). From the heavenly "throne were going out" lightnings and sounds and thunders of divine judgment against idolatry (4:5; cf. 8:5; 11:19; 16:18). But the river of the water of eternal life is "going out from the throne" of God and of the Lamb (22:1; cf. Ezek 47:1–12), the dual objects of heavenly worship as the temple in the new holy city (21:22b).

In the midst of its "main street," the heavenly city's "main street" of pure gold (21:21), and on each side of the city's river of the water of "life" (22:1), is the "tree" of eternal "life" (22:2a). This recalls the exalted Jesus' promise to give the one who conquers idolatrous worship to eat from the "tree of the life" in the paradise of God (2:7). The tree is making twelve "fruits" (22:2b), during each month giving out its "fruit" (22:2c), so that it is always available, underlining that the life the tree provides is eternal. And the leaves of the city's "tree" of eternal life (22:2a) are for healing of the "nations" (22:2d). The medicinal leaves of the tree of life will thus heal the "nations" that have been misled to drink the poisonous wine of deadly idolatrous worship (14:8; 18:3, 23; 20:3, 8), so that they may receive eternal life as true heavenly worshipers in the holy city (21:24, 26).[10]

---

10. "Those nations who reject God's offer of repentance (9:20–21; 16:9, 11) will be destroyed (11:18; 16:5–7; 18:5–8, 20, 24; 19:19–21). But those who repent will enter the Holy City (21:24, 26) and be 'healed' (22:2)" (Osborne, *Revelation*, 772).

Anything cursed to eternal death by its association with idolatrous worship will be no more and the "throne of God and of the Lamb," the city's "throne of God and of the Lamb" from which the river of the water of eternal life is going out (22:1), will be in it (22:3a). In response to the invitation of the heavenly worshipers to "praise our God all his servants" (19:5), "his servants will offer worship to him" (22:3b).[11] This resonates with those before the throne of God who "offer worship to him" day and night in his heavenly temple (7:15).

In contrast to the earth and the heaven who fled from (20:11), and the idolaters on earth who wanted to hide from the "face" of the one sitting upon the throne (6:16), "his servants" (22:3b) will see "his face" (22:4). And "his name" will be "upon their foreheads" (22:4). This distinguishes them from Babylon with an idolatrous "name" written "upon her forehead" (17:5), and from those with the "name" of the idolatrous beast (13:17) "upon their forehead" (13:16; cf. 14:9). It identifies them as those who did not receive the mark of the beast "upon the forehead" and did not worship it (20:4). They are the heavenly worshipers with the "name" of the Lamb and of his Father written "upon their foreheads" (14:1), the "servants" of God sealed "upon their foreheads" for worship and eternal life in heaven (7:3; cf. 9:4).

Not only any cursed thing "will be no more" (22:3), but night "will be no more" (22:5), reaffirming that night "will not be" in the heavenly city (21:25). The servants "do not have need" of the light of a "lamp" or the light of the "sun," for the Lord God "will illumine" over them (22:5). This reaffirms that the city "does not have need" of the "sun," for the glory of God "illumines" it, and its "lamp" is the Lamb (21:23).

Heavenly worshipers declared that the Lamb bought for God those from every nation (5:9) and made them for our God a kingdom and priests, and they "will reign" upon the earth (5:10). Great sounds in heaven proclaimed that there has come to be the world of our Lord and of his Christ, and it "will reign for the ages of the ages" (11:15). Whoever did not worship the idolatrous beast both lived and "reigned" with Christ for a thousand years (20:4). Those who have part in the first

---

11. "That the Lamb is associated with God as the object of worship is stressed again here, both by the singular *throne* and by the singular pronoun *him* to describe the two" (Boxall, *Revelation*, 311; emphases original).

resurrection will be priests of God and of Christ and they "will reign" with him for a thousand years (20:6). And now, in accord with the heavenly city's water and tree for eternal life (22:1-2), those who worship in it "will reign for the ages of the ages" (22:5). This further encourages the audience to worship God and the Lamb in the Spirit of prophetic witness against the eternal death of idolatrous worship and for the eternal life available for all in the city of heavenly worship.

Summary on 21:9—22:5

The audience hear the four units of this subsection (21:9—22:5) in a chiastic pattern centering around the theme of the universal worship of God and the Lamb for eternal life in the heavenly city. When the audience hear the (b') unit (21:22b-27), they hear a chiastic progression of the (b) unit (21:15-22a). The heavenly "city" of pure gold like pure glass (21:18; cf. 21:15, 16, 19, 21) progresses to the heavenly "city" that does not have need of the sun nor of the moon that they appear in it, for the glory of God illumines it, and its lamp is the Lamb (21:23). The city's twelve "gates" of pearl (21:21), the "gates" to be measured (21:15) for an open access in all directions (21:12-13), progress to its "gates" that will never be closed during the day, for night will not be there (21:25). And a "temple" John did not see in the city (21:22a) progresses to the "temple" that is the Lord, the God, the Almighty, as well as the Lamb (21:22b).

When the audience hear the final (a') unit (22:1-5), they hear a chiastic progression of and inclusion with the initial (a) unit (21:9-14). An angel "showed" John the holy city Jerusalem descending out of heaven from God (21:10). This progresses to the angel "showed" John the river of the water of eternal life, bright as crystal, going out from the throne of God and of the Lamb (22:1). The audience are thus led to appreciate that the holy city is the place not only for a universal worship of God and the Lamb but for a share in their eternal life.

Once the audience have heard this (b') subsection (21:9-22:5), they have experienced a chiastic progression from the (b) subsection (2:1—3:22) within the overall macrochiastic structure of the book of Revelation. The (b) subsection centers around the theme of both encouraging the churches who encounter the deadly threat of idolatrous

Visions of the Heavenly City's Worship of God and the Lamb for Eternal Life

worship to withstand it and exhorting them to repent of any associations with it, so that they may participate in the worship and eternal life of heaven. This progresses to the theme of the universal worship of God and the Lamb for eternal life in the heavenly city in the (b') subsection.

The exalted Jesus promised to give the one who conquers idolatrous worship to eat from the "tree of the life" in the paradise of God (2:7). This progresses to the "tree of life" available on each side of the river (22:2) of the water of eternal life going out from the throne of God and of the Lamb in the holy city of true heavenly worship (22:1). Some in Sardis "will walk" with the exalted Jesus in white, for, as those who have resisted idolatrous worship, they are worthy to participate in heavenly worship (3:4). This progresses to the nations "will walk" by the light of the new holy city of heavenly worship (21:24). The exalted Jesus promised to make the one who conquers idolatrous worship a pillar in the "temple" of God (3:12). This progresses to John not seeing a "temple" in the new holy heavenly city Jerusalem, for the Lord, the God, the Almighty, is its "temple," as well as the Lamb (21:22).

The exalted Jesus promised that he will write upon the one who conquers idolatrous worship the name of his God and the name of the city of his God, of the "new Jerusalem that is descending out of heaven from my God" (3:12). This progresses to the angel showing John the "holy city Jerusalem descending out of heaven from God" (21:10) as the place for the universal worship of God and the Lamb. The materially wealthy church in Laodicea declared that "I have need of nothing" (3:17). But it needs to "buy" from Jesus heavenly gold (3:18). This progresses to the heavenly city of pure gold that "does not have need" of the light of sun or moon, for the glory of God illumines it (21:23), and to the worshipers in the city who "do not have need" of a lamp or sunlight, for the Lord God will illumine over them, and, as worshipers in the heavenly city of eternal life, who will reign for the ages of the ages (22:5). With the Spirit of prophetic witness against the eternal death of idolatrous worship the audience are to worship God and the Lamb for the eternal life available for all in the city of heavenly worship.

11

Epilogue: Exhortations about Words of This Prophecy for Worship of God

Revelation 22:6–21

1a) Keep the Faithful and True Words of the Prophecy of This Scroll (22:6–9)

A   a) [6a] Then he said to **me**, "These ***words*** are faithful and true, and the Lord, the **God** of the Spirits of the ***prophets***, sent his **angel**

      b) [6b] to **show** his servants the things it is necessary to happen ***soon***,"

      b′) [7a] and "Behold, I am coming ***soon***!

  a′) [7b] Blessed is the one who **keeps** the ***words*** of the ***prophecy of this scroll***."

B [8a] And it is I, John, who is **hearing and observing** these things,

Epilogue: Exhortations about Words of This Prophecy for Worship of God

    B' ⁸ᵇ and when I **heard and observed**,

A' a) ⁸ᶜ I fell to *worship* before the feet of the **angel** who **showed me** these things.

    b) ⁹ᵃ Then he said to **me**, "See that you don't! A fellow servant am I *of you*

    b') ⁹ᵇ and of the brothers *of you*, of the **prophets** and of those who **keep** the **words of this scroll**.

a') ⁹ᶜ *Worship* **God**."

The angel who showed "me," John, the river of the water of life in the heavenly city (22:1; cf. 21:9-10) said to "me," "These words are faithful and true, and the Lord, the God of the Spirits of the prophets, sent his angel to show his servants the things it is necessary to happen soon" (22:6). The God sitting upon the throne told John, "Write, for these words are faithful and true" (21:5b). This refers not merely to the immediately preceding words about making all things new (21:5a), but to the prophetic words of God in the entire book of Revelation that John has been divinely commissioned to write (1:3, 11, 19). And now the angel reaffirms that "these words are faithful and true."

The "Lord" God who will illumine over (22:5) "his servants" who offer worship to him in the heavenly city (22:3) is the "Lord," the God of the Spirits of the prophets, who sent his angel to show "his servants" the things it is necessary to happen soon (22:6). The book began by announcing the revelation of Jesus Christ that God gave him "to show his servants the things it is necessary to happen soon," and he signified it, "sending" it through "his angel" to his servant John (1:1). And now the angel reaffirms that God "sent his angel to show his servants the things it is necessary to happen soon." The "Spirits" of the "prophets" refers to the seven "Spirits" representative of *the* Spirit of God sent into all the earth (5:6; cf. 1:4; 4:5) to inspire prophetic witness against idolatry, for the witness of Jesus is the "Spirit" of "prophecy" (19:10).

Echoing and speaking on behalf of the exalted Jesus, the angel also said, "Behold, I am coming soon" (22:7a).[1] This assured final coming of

---

1. "It is to be understood almost as a demonstration for the fact that Revelation is the authentic word of God and/or Jesus, when the speech of the angel becomes a direct speech of Jesus" (Roloff, *Revelation*, 249).

PART FOUR—*Shown Holy City (21:9—22:21)*

Jesus will thus be a preeminent part of the things that it is divinely necessary to happen "soon" (22:6b). Its angelic announcement reinforces the exhortations of the exalted Jesus for the audience to maintain their witness against idolatrous worship for, "Behold, I am coming as a thief" (16:15) and "I am coming soon" (3:11). They are to repent of any association with idolatry for, "I am coming to you soon" (2:16) and "I am coming to you" (2:5) to execute final judgment and salvation.[2]

It was promised that "blessed" by God is the one who reads aloud (the lector for the liturgical performance of the book) and those who hear (its audience) the "words" of the "prophecy" and "keep" the things written in it—the book of Revelation, for the time is near (1:3). After warning that "behold, I am coming as a thief," the exalted Jesus promised that "blessed" is the one who watches and "keeps" his metaphorical garments, in order to be able to participate in true heavenly worship (16:15). And now, after announcing that "behold, I am coming soon," the angel adds that "blessed" is the one who "keeps" these "words" that are faithful and true (22:6a) of the "prophecy," inspired by the divine Spirits of the "prophets" (22:6a), of this scroll—the book of Revelation (22:7b).

John reported that "I, John" (1:9) was in Spirit on the Lord's day and "I heard behind me a great sound" (1:10). It told him to write what "you observe" and send it to the seven churches (1:11). Then he turned to "observe" (1:12) the heavenly exalted Jesus (1:12–16) toward whose "feet I fell" in a gesture of worship (1:17). But now, in a noteworthy contrast, he reports that "and it is I, John," who is "hearing and observing" these things (22:8a).[3] And when "I heard and observed" (22:8b), "I fell" to worship before the "feet" of the angel who "showed me" these things (22:8c), that is, the angel who "showed me" (22:1) the vision of worship for eternal life in the heavenly city (22:1–5).

But the angel said to John, "See that you don't! A fellow servant am I of you" (22:9a). The angel is also a fellow servant of the audience, the

---

2. "The coming here is primarily an urgent reference to Christ's final coming, though one should not rule out the intermediate 'comings' to the congregations gathered in worship (cf. 3:3, 20)" (Boxall, *Revelation*, 314).

3. "John names himself (the first time since 1:9), thus joining his authoritative witness to that of the angel, and of Christ himself" (Boxall, *Revelation*, 314).

brothers "of you" (cf. 1:9), of the "prophets" and of those who "keep the words of this scroll" (22:9b). This recalls and reaffirms that blessed is every member of the audience who, as a prophetic witness against idolatrous worship, "keeps the words of the prophecy of this scroll" (22:7). John fell to "worship" before the feet of the "angel" (22:8c). But the angel urged him instead to "worship God" (22:9c), the "God" of the Spirits of the "prophets" who sent his "angel" (22:6).

John reports that "I fell to worship before the feet of the angel who showed me these things" (22:8c). "Then he said to me, 'See that you don't! A fellow servant am I of you and of the brothers of you, of the prophets and of those who keep the words of this scroll. Worship God'" (22:9). This reinforces his previous report that "I fell before the feet" of an angel "to worship" him. "Then he said to me, 'See that you don't! A fellow servant am I of you and of the brothers of you who have the witness of Jesus. Worship God, for the witness of Jesus is the Spirit of prophecy'" (19:10). As prophets who have the witness of Jesus in the book itself, the audience are to be careful not to fall into any kind of idolatrous worship, even of angels.[4] They are rather to maintain the true heavenly worship of God for eternal life in the Spirit of prophecy.[5]

2b) Do Not Seal the Words of the Prophecy of This Scroll (22:10–15)

> A [10] Then he said to me, "Do not seal the words of the prophecy of this scroll, for the time is near. [11] Let the one who harms still harm and the one defiled still be defiled, but let the righteous one still **do** righteousness and the holy one still be made holy."
>
> B [12] "Behold, I am **coming** soon, and my reward with me to give out to each as to the work that **is** his.

---

4. "[T]he angel's prohibition is intended as a warning to Christians, not merely against worship of angels in particular, but against any form of idolatry" (Beale, *Revelation*, 1128).

5. Longenecker, "Rev 22.6–9," 105–17. "The angel's exhortation, 'Worship God!' puts in the most succinct form possible the theme of the entire book" (Mounce, *Revelation*, 405).

> C ¹³ I am the Alpha and the Omega, the first and the last, the beginning and the end."
>
> B' ¹⁴ Blessed are those who wash their robes, so that their authority **will be** over the tree of the life and by the gates they may **come into** the city.
>
> A' ¹⁵ Outside are the dogs and the sorcerers and the prostitutes and the murderers and the idolaters and everyone who loves and **does** falsehood.

A sound out of heaven curiously told John to "seal" the revelatory things the seven thunders spoke and do not write them for the audience (10:4). In contrast, the angel now tells John "do not seal," implicitly for the benefit of the audience, "the words of the prophecy of this scroll, for the time is near" (22:10). Not sealing them will make them available to the audience as those who are to keep the "words of this scroll" (22:9). Each member of the audience may thus be blessed as one who keeps the "words of the prophecy of this scroll" (22:7). The motivation for not sealing is "for the time is near." This reinforces the same motivation, "for the time is near," for the audience to be blessed as those who hear the "words of the prophecy" and keep—through their prophetic witness regarding true and false worship—the things written in the book of Revelation (1:3).⁶

"Let the one who harms, still harm" and the one defiled still be defiled by association with idolatry (22:11a; cf. 3:4). But if anyone wishes to "harm" prophetic witnesses against idolatrous worship, he will be destroyed (11:5). The audience then are exhorted to counter such threats to true worship: "Let the righteous still do righteousness and the holy one still be made holy" (22:11b). This will associate the members of the audience with the objects of true worship, with God who is "righteous" (16:5), and with the Lamb who judges in "righteousness" (19:11). And both God and the Lamb may be worshiped as "holy" (3:7; 4:8; 6:10) by

---

6. "The angel commands John not to 'seal up the words of the prophecy' so that God will be worshiped. If the revelation is sealed, the churches will not know its contents and will not be able to respond to its contents in obedience and worship (so 22:7, 9)" (Beale, *Revelation*, 1129).

the audience as those who are to be "holy ones " (18:20) and who offer prayers as the "holy ones" (5:8; 8:3, 4).

Reaffirming the angel who announced for him that "behold, I am coming soon" (22:7), the voice of Jesus himself declares and elaborates that "behold, I am coming soon, and my reward with me to give to each as to the work that is his" (22:12). This underscores his coming for the final judgment of each individual. It recalls that the dead were judged, "each according to their works" (20:13). It reaffirms that the time has come for the dead to be judged and to "give the reward" to God's servants the prophets and to the holy ones and to those who fear God's name through true worship (11:18). And it resonates with the exalted Jesus' promise that "I will give to you, to each one, according to your works" (2:23).

God himself proclaimed that "I am the Alpha and the Omega" as the one who is and who was and who is "coming," the Almighty (1:8). As once dead but now living eternally (1:18), the exalted Jesus declared that "I am the first and the last" (1:17; cf. 2:8). The God who promises to give to the one thirsting for it the water of eternal life freely proclaimed that "I am the Alpha and the Omega, the beginning and the end" (21:6). And now, to confirm his divine sovereignty as the one "coming" to reward each who maintains a prophetic witness for true heavenly worship (cf. 11:18), Jesus himself climactically declares that "I am the Alpha and the Omega, the first and the last, the beginning and the end" (22:13).[7]

"Blessed" is the lector who reads aloud and the audience who hear the words of the prophecy and keep the things written in the book of Revelation (1:3). "Blessed" are those who die in the Lord from now on (14:13). "Blessed" is the one who metaphorically keeps his garments so as not to walk naked (16:15) but be properly clothed for true worship. "Blessed" are those who have been called to the supper of the wedding feast of the Lamb (19:9). "Blessed" and holy is the one who has a part in the first resurrection to eternal life (20:6). "Blessed" is the one who keeps the words of the prophecy of this scroll—the book of Revelation (22:7). And now, "blessed" are those in the audience who metaphorically "wash their robes" (22:14) through their prophetic witness against idolatrous

---

7. "The emphasis of the bipolar names here at the end of the book is to underscore Christ's divine ability to conclude history at his coming" (Beale, *Revelation*, 1138).

worship, thus identifying with those enabled to offer heavenly worship because they have "washed their robes" and whitened them in the blood of the Lamb (7:14).

In accord with the reward to be given out to each as to the work that "is" his (22:12), for those blessed for washing their robes their authority "will be" over the "tree of the life" (22:14). This is the "tree of life" on each side of the river (22:2) of the water of eternal life going out from the throne of God and the Lamb in the heavenly city (22:1). And by the gates that will never be closed (21:25), they may "come into" the city (22:14), since only those written in the scroll of the life of the Lamb may "come into" it (21:27). They will thus be recipients of the reward promised to each of them by the exalted Jesus who declared that "I am coming" soon (22:12), and who promised that "I will come in" to and dine with the one who hears his sound and opens the door (3:20).

Outside of the heavenly city are those associated with idolatrous worship—the metaphorical dogs and the "sorcerers" and the "prostitutes" and the "murderers" and the "idolaters" and everyone who loves and "does falsehood" (22:15).[8] This is in contrast to each member of the audience who is to "do" righteousness (22:11), and in accord with no one "doing" an abomination or "falsehood" being able to come into the city (21:27). Indeed, in the mouth of heavenly worshipers is not found "falsehood" (14:5). It emphatically reaffirms that the part of the "murderers" and the "prostitutes" and the "sorcerers" and the "idolaters" and all the "lying" is in the lake burning with fire and sulfur, which is the second, eternal death (21:8). The audience are thus exhorted to come into the heavenly city to be rewarded with eternal life for their witness against idolatry and for the true worship of God and the Lamb in the Spirit of prophecy.

---

8. "The term 'dog' is used in Scripture for various kinds of impure and malicious persons" (Mounce, *Revelation*, 408). For the term's connotation of ritual impurity, see Smalley, *Revelation*, 574–75.

Epilogue: Exhortations about Words of This Prophecy for Worship of God

3a′) Witness to the Words of the Scroll of This Prophecy (22:16–21)

  A   **a)** [16] "I, **Jesus**, sent my angel to *witness* to you **these things** for the churches. I am the root and the descendant of David, the bright morning star."

      b) [17a] Then the Spirit and the bride say, "*Come!*"

      b′) [17b] And let the one who hears say, "*Come!*" And let the one who thirsts *come*, let the one who wishes receive water of life freely.

    a′) [18a] I am *witnessing* to **everyone** who hears

  B   **a)** [18b] the **words** of the *prophecy* of *this scroll*,

      b) [18c] if anyone *adds* to these things,

      b′) [18d] God *will add* to him the plagues

    a′) [18e] **written in** *this scroll*, [19a] and if anyone **takes away** from the **words** of the *scroll* of this *prophecy*,

  B′ [19b] God **will take away** his part from the tree of the life and out of the holy city, which are **written in this scroll** (Deut 4:2; 13:1).

A′ [20] Says the one who is **witnessing** to **these things**, "Yes, I am **coming** soon." Amen! **Come** Lord **Jesus**! [21] The grace of the Lord **Jesus** with **all**!

With an emphatic "I" Jesus proclaimed his divine sovereignty: "I am the Alpha and the Omega, the first and the last, the beginning and the end" (22:13). And now with a twofold emphatic "I" he declares that "I, Jesus, sent my angel to witness to you these things for the churches. I am the root and the descendant of David, the bright morning star" (22:16). That "I sent my angel" reaffirms the divine "sending" of the revelation of Jesus Christ through "his angel" (1:1). The angel sent "to witness to you these things for the churches" complements John who "witnessed" to the word of God and the witness of Jesus Christ (1:2). To the audience of the seven "churches," to "you," John offered a greeting of grace and peace (1:4). The angel was sent to witness to the audience "these things," referring to "these things" John is hearing and observing (22:8), which are included in the things written in the book of Revelation that the audience are to hear and keep (1:3).

That "I am the root and descendant of David" (22:16), the fulfillment of the promise for a Davidic Messiah, recalls and reaffirms that Jesus, the "root of David," conquered through his death to open the scroll and its seven seals (5:5) as the slaughtered Lamb (5:6). That Jesus is the "bright morning star" (22:16) reinforces his promise to give to the one who conquers idolatrous worship the "morning star," as Jesus himself received from his Father (2:28), a symbolic indication of resurrection to a new and eternal life. Indeed, the bright morning star resonates with the river of the water of eternal life, "bright" as crystal, which goes out from the throne of God and of the Lamb in the heavenly city (22:1).

The "Spirit" is the divine "Spirit" of prophecy (19:10) that inspires the true worship of the God of the "Spirits" of the prophets (22:6). And the "bride" is the "bride" shown as the woman of the Lamb (21:9), who is also the holy city, descending out of heaven from God, prepared as a "bride" adorned for her husband (21:2). Together they say, "Come!" (22:17a). With this exuberant invitation to "come," the Spirit and the bride welcome, not only for future judgment and salvation but also for their present eucharistic celebration of the supper of the wedding feast of the Lamb (19:9), the Jesus who announced that "I am coming" soon (22:12). They also welcome into their eucharistic liturgy each individual among those who may "come into" the heavenly city as a true worshiper (22:14) to participate in the eucharistic dinner with the Jesus who promised that "I will come in" to the one who hears his sound and opens the door, and "I will dine with him and he with me" (3:20).

Each individual in the audience who hears the invitation from the Spirit and the bride who say "come" (22:17a) is emphatically to reinforce it by likewise saying, "Come!" (22:17b).[9] The one who is "thirsting" for eternal life is to "come" (22:17b) to the eucharistic liturgy to be among those who may "come into" the holy city of heavenly worship

---

9. "In this cry, which every hearer of the reading of Revelation is to join, the entire fulfillment of salvation, which is promised for the future in 21:1—22:5, is transposed into the personal sphere and brought together with the present coming of Jesus in the Lord's Supper" (Roloff, *Revelation*, 252–53).

(22:14). And whoever wishes may receive "water of life freely" (22:17b) in accord with the divine promise that, to the one who is "thirsting" for it, "I will give from the spring of the water of the life freely" (21:6). By accepting the earnest invitation to come to the eucharistic supper, then, as among those who have been called to the heavenly supper of the wedding feast of the Lamb (19:9), everyone in the audience who thirsts for it may begin to drink the water of eternal life and eat from the tree of eternal life available in the heavenly city (2:7; 22:2, 14).[10]

Complementing the mission of the angel sent by Jesus to "witness" to the audience (22:16), John announces that "I am witnessing" to everyone who "hears" (22:18a) the "words of the prophecy of this scroll" (22:18b) as it is read aloud in their worship service. This refers to the "words of the prophecy of this scroll," which John was directed not to seal for the benefit of the audience (22:10). It recalls that blessed is the one who keeps the "words of the prophecy of this scroll" (22:7). And blessed are those in the audience who "hear" the "words of the prophecy" and keep the things written in the scroll which is the book of Revelation (1:3).

If anyone "adds" to these things written in the scroll (22:18c), God "will add" to him the "plagues" (22:18d) written in "this scroll" (22:18e) of the words of the prophecy regarding true and false worship (22:18b). This recalls the various "plagues" of divine judgment against idolatry previously depicted (9:18, 20; 15:1, 6, 8; 16:9, 21; 18:4, 8; 21:9). Whereas only those "written" in the "scroll" of the eternal life of the Lamb will come into the heavenly city (21:27), anyone who adds to it will suffer the plagues of divine judgment "written" in this "scroll."

John is witnessing to everyone who hears (22:18a) the "words" of the "prophecy" of this "scroll" (22:18b): If anyone "takes away" from the "words" of the "scroll" of this "prophecy" (22:19a), God "will take away his part from the tree of the life and out of the holy city, which are written in this scroll" (22:19b; cf. Deut 4:2; 13:1). Blessed and holy is the one who has a "part" in the first resurrection to eternal life (20:6). But the "part" of those involved in idolatrous behavior is in the lake, which is the second, eternal death (21:8). And now, God will take away from

---

10. "Here 'let him come' may also function as an invitation to participate in the Eucharist" (Aune, *Revelation 17–22*, 1228).

anyone who takes away from the words of the scroll of the prophecy against idolatry and for true worship his "part" from the tree of eternal life and out of the holy city. Just as the plagues of divine judgment against idolatry are "written in this scroll" (22:18), so the tree of eternal life and the holy heavenly city for true worshipers are "written in this scroll."[11]

Jesus sent his angel to "witness" to the audience "these things" (22:16). John declared that "I am witnessing" to everyone in the audience who hears the words of the prophecy of this scroll (22:18). And now, climactically, Jesus himself is "witnessing" to "these things" as he says, "Yes, I am coming soon" (22:20). This not only emphatically reaffirms his previous promises that "behold, I am coming soon" (22:7, 12), but serves as the affirmative answer to the exuberant invitation by the Spirit, the bride, and the hearer, who say, "Come!" (22:17).

John then emphatically reaffirms the pronouncement of Jesus that "yes," "I am coming" soon, with his words, "Amen! Come" Lord Jesus (22:20). This liturgical exchange recalls and resonates with the liturgical response of "Yes! Amen!" to the pronouncement that Jesus is "coming" with the clouds, and every eye will see him (1:7). John thus reinforces the invitations of the Spirit, the bride, and the hearer for Jesus to "come" (22:17) not only for future judgment and salvation at the end of time but also for their present and ongoing liturgical gatherings to celebrate the Eucharist, their anticipatory experience of "the supper of the wedding feast of the Lamb" (19:9), before the end of time.[12]

---

11. "[T]o 'add' to the words of John's prophecy is to promote the false teaching that idolatry is not inconsistent with faith in Christ. To 'take away from the words of the book of this prophecy' is also to advance such deceptive teaching, since this teaching would violate and vitiate the validity of Revelation's exhortations against idolatry" (Beale, *Revelation*, 1151).

12. "There seems, in conclusion, every reason to suppose that Revelation, which is in the basic literary form of a letter (1:4–11; 22:21), was designed to be read aloud (1:3) on the Lord's Day (1:10) in a setting which was both liturgical and eucharistic" (Smalley, *Revelation*, 585). "As the final section of the book is read out publicly, and visionary time prepares to give way to liturgical time, this urgent emphasis upon the Lord's return links his final coming to that coming which is about to take place in the eucharistic assembly" (Boxall, *Revelation*, 319–20).

Epilogue: Exhortations about Words of This Prophecy for Worship of God

Forming an inclusion with his opening greeting of "grace" to his audience (1:4), John concludes the book with the greeting, "the grace of the Lord Jesus with all!" (22:21). This verbless greeting serves as a prayer for "all," "everyone" in the audience who hears the words of the prophecy of this scroll (22:18), to receive renewed experiences of this divine grace in the future. It also reaffirms the grace all in the audience have already received from Jesus as "the one who loves us and has released us from our sins by his blood" (1:5). And it prays that the grace of the Lord Jesus may be experienced not only by all in the audience but by all peoples everywhere who are invited to participate in the true heavenly worship that is offered by all of creation (cf. 5:13; 14:6; 15:4; 19:5; 21:24–26).

It is the grace of the Lord "Jesus" (22:21), the Lord "Jesus" invited to come (22:20) now and in the future as the "Jesus" who is "the root and the descendant of David, the bright morning star" (22:16). And it is the grace of the "Lord" Jesus to be experienced at the coming of one addressed as the "Lord" Jesus (22:20), who, as the one who sent his angel to witness to the things written in the book (22:16), complements the "Lord" God who sent his angel to show the audience the things it is divinely necessary to happen soon (22:6). This closing liturgical dialogue thus prepares the audience to experience the divine grace of the Lord Jesus in and through their participation in the true heavenly and universal worship of God and the Lamb for eternal life in the Spirit of prophecy.[13]

Summary on 22:6–21

The audience hear the three units of this subsection (22:6–21) in a chiastic pattern centering around the theme of Revelation's words of prophecy witnessing to the true worship of the Lord God of the Spirits of the prophets and the Lord Jesus for eternal life. In the unparalleled (b) unit (22:10–15) at the center of this subsection the audience are exhorted to counter threats to true worship: "Let the righteous still do righteousness and the holy one still be made holy" (22:11). This will associate the members of the audience with the objects of true wor-

---

13. Biguzzi, "Chaos of Rev 22,6–21," 193–210.

ship, with God who is "righteous" (16:5), and with the Lamb who judges in "righteousness" (19:11). And both God and the Lamb may be worshiped as "holy" (3:7; 4:8; 6:10) by the audience as those who are to be "holy ones" (18:20) and who offer prayers as the "holy ones" (5:8; 8:3, 4).

When the audience hear the final (a') unit (22:16–21), they hear a chiastic progression of and inclusion with the initial (a) unit (22:6–9). The "Lord" God, the object of true worship (22:9), sent his angel to show his servants the things it is necessary to happen soon (22:6). This progresses to the prayer, "Come *Lord* Jesus!" (22:20) and the final greeting, "the grace of the *Lord* Jesus with all!" (22:21). The God of the "Spirits" of the prophets (22:6) progresses to the divine "Spirit" and the bride who say, "Come!" (22:17a). They thus welcome, not only for future judgment and salvation but also for their present eucharistic celebration, the Jesus who announced that "I am coming" soon (22:12). They also welcome into their eucharistic liturgy each individual among those who may "come into" the heavenly city as a true worshiper (22:14) who wishes to receive water of life freely (22:17) and thus to participate in the universal worship of God and the Lamb for eternal life in the Spirit of prophecy.

Once the audience have heard this concluding (a') subsection (22:6–21), they have experienced a chiastic progression from and inclusion with the introductory (a) subsection (1:1–20) within the overall macrochiastic structure of the book of Revelation. The (a) subsection introduces the theme of worship for the eternal life offered by the risen Jesus in the divine Spirit that inspires prophecy, the prophecy written in Revelation as the basis for the audience of servants to witness to the word of God and the witness of Jesus Christ together with their fellow prophetic servant, John. This progresses to the theme of Revelation's words of prophecy witnessing to the true worship of the Lord God of the Spirits of the prophets and the Lord Jesus for eternal life in the (a') subsection.

The book began by announcing the revelation of Jesus Christ that God gave him "to show his servants the things it is necessary to happen soon," and he signified it, "sending" it through "his angel" to his servant John (1:1). This progresses to the angel reaffirming that God "sent his angel to show his servants the things it is necessary to happen soon" (22:6). At the beginning of the book John reported that he "witnessed"

Epilogue: Exhortations about Words of This Prophecy for Worship of God

to the word of God and the witness of Jesus Christ (1:2). This progresses to the notice that the angel was sent to "witness" to the audience "these things" (22:16), that John is "witnessing" to everyone in the audience who hears the words of the prophecy of this scroll (22:18), and to Jesus himself "witnessing" to "these things" as he says, "Yes, I am coming soon" (22:20).

Blessed are those in the audience who "hear" the "words of the prophecy" and keep the things written in the scroll which is the book of Revelation (1:3). This progresses to blessed is the one who keeps the "words of the prophecy of this scroll" (22:7), to the "words of the prophecy of this scroll" that John was directed not to seal for the benefit of the audience (22:10), and to the "words of the prophecy of this scroll" to which John is witnessing to everyone who hears them (22:18). "For the time is near" motivates the blessing of the audience as those who hear and keep the words of the prophecy in the book of Revelation (1:3). This progresses to "for the time is near" as the motivation for John not to seal the words of the prophecy of this scroll (22:10).

The revelation of Jesus Christ was sent to God's servant "John" (1:1), this "John" sent the opening greeting of the book to the seven churches in Asia (1:4), and "John," the brother and fellow sharer of the audience, was on the island called Patmos on account of the word of God and the witness of Jesus (1:9). This progresses to "John" reaffirming that he is the one hearing and observing the things written in the book of Revelation (22:8). In his opening prayer greeting John prayed for "grace" to his audience and peace from God, the seven divine Spirits (1:4), and Jesus Christ (1:5). This progresses to his climactic closing prayer greeting of the "grace" of the Lord Jesus with all! (22:21). The audience and all others who hear and witness to Revelation's words inspired by the divine Spirit of prophecy against idolatrous and for true worship may experience this grace as those who participate in the universal and heavenly worship of the Lord God and the Lord Jesus, the Lamb, for eternal life.

12

Conclusion

THIS BOOK HAS PRESENTED a new analysis of the worship theme in the book of Revelation guided by a new illustration of its comprehensive chiastic structure. My introductory first chapter has provided an overview of Revelation's structure and a preliminary discussion of its main theme regarding worship. Each of the preceding ten chapters concludes with a substantial summary of the exegetical analysis conducted on each of the ten subsections comprising the structure of Revelation. Consequently, I will offer in this concluding chapter only a final succinct overview of Revelation's main worship theme, the subtitle of my book—"worship for life in the Spirit of prophecy."

The worship that Revelation exhorts and enables is in the divine Spirit of prophetic witness against all forms of idolatrous worship in favor of a true heavenly and universal worship. This accords with the division of Revelation into four main sections (1:1—3:22; 4:1—16:21; 17:1—21:8; 21:9—22:21) based on references to John being shown prophetic visions by the divine Spirit. John was "in Spirit" on the Lord's day of worship (1:10) when he was "shown" the revelation of Jesus Christ (1:1) as the eternally living one (1:18) toward whose feet John fell in worshipful submission (1:17). John was "in Spirit" (4:2) after he was invited to ascend to heaven to be "shown" (4:1) visions of true heavenly and universal worship and of divine judgment against idolatrous worship. John was carried into an earthly wilderness "in Spirit" (17:3) to be "shown" the judgment of the great idolatrous prostitute (17:1).

And John was carried "in Spirit" to a heavenly mountain (21:10) to be "shown" the bride, the communal woman of the Lamb (21:9; cf. 12:1), representative of the audience who are to engage in true worship (22:17, 20–21).

Revelation exhorts and enables a true worship of both the Lord God and the Lord Jesus Christ, the Lamb, which is heavenly, universal, and eternal. The audience are to join "every creature in heaven and upon the earth and under the earth and upon the sea and all the things in them" for a universal and eternal worship: "To the one sitting upon the throne and to the Lamb, the blessing and the honor and the glory and the might for the ages of the ages!" (5:13; cf. 7:9, 12). Although many did not repent of their idolatrous worship despite the prophetic witness of divine judgment against it (9:20–21; 16:9, 11), ultimately "all the nations will come and worship" before the Lord God, the Almighty (15:3–4; cf. 21:24, 26; 22:2, 21).

Revelation exhorts and enables a prophetic witness against false worship that leads to the second, eternal death (2:11; 20:6, 14; 21:8), and for true worship that leads to the heavenly and eternal life. The heavenly exalted Jesus promises to give to each member of the audience who conquers idolatrous worship the crown of *the* eternal life (2:10). In and through their true worship the audience demonstrate their heavenly destiny as those divinely written in the scroll of *the* eternal life (3:5; 13:8; 17:8; 20:12, 15; 21:27). The audience form part of the "bride," those blessed to have been called to the heavenly supper of the wedding feast of the Lamb (19:9), the Jesus who promised to dine with anyone in the audience who hears his sound and opens the door (3:20). In the eucharistic supper to which Revelation orients them, the audience anticipate eating from the tree of *the* eternal life (2:7; 22:2, 14, 19) and drinking the water of *the* eternal life in the heavenly city (7:17; 21:6; 22:1, 17) for a share in the eternal life of the Lord God and Lord Jesus who are living for the ages of the ages (1:18; 4:9, 10; 10:6; 15:7).

In sum, the book of Revelation exhorts and enables a worship for life in the Spirit of prophecy. More precisely, this refers to a worship inspired by the divine Spirit of prophetic witness against all forms of idolatrous worship on earth in favor of a true, heavenly and universal worship of the Lord God and the Lord Jesus Christ, the Lamb, for an eternal and heavenly life. The audience may begin this worship in the eucharistic supper into which Revelation leads them by inviting them to respond to the promise of Jesus, "Yes, I am coming soon," with "Amen! Come Lord Jesus!" (22:20). They thereby affirm and welcome the coming of the Lord Jesus, the exalted Lamb, to the eucharistic supper that anticipates his final coming and the divine grace, the gift of eternal life, of the Lord Jesus that is intended to be the destiny of all—"The grace of the Lord Jesus with all!" (22:21).

Bibliography

Aune, David E. *Revelation 1-5*. WBC 52A. Dallas: Word, 1997.
———. *Revelation 6-16*. WBC 52B. Nashville: Nelson, 1998.
———. *Revelation 17-22*. WBC 52C. Nashville: Nelson, 1998.
Bandy, Alan S. "The Layers of the Apocalypse: An Integrative Approach to Revelation's Macrostructure." *JSNT* 31 (2009) 469-99.
———. "Patterns of Prophetic Lawsuits in the Oracles to the Seven Churches." *Neot* 45 (2011) 178-205.
———. *The Prophetic Lawsuit in the Book of Revelation*. NTM 29. Sheffield, UK: Sheffield Phoenix, 2010.
Barr, David L. "The Apocalypse of John as Oral Enactment." *Int* 40 (1986) 243-56.
———. *Tales of the End: A Narrative Commentary on the Book of Revelation*. Santa Rosa, CA: Polebridge, 1998.
Bauckham, Richard. *The Climax of Prophecy: Studies on the Book of Revelation*. London: T. & T. Clark, 1993.
———. "Creation's Praise of God in the Book of Revelation." *BTB* 38 (2008) 55-63.
———. "The List of the Tribes in Revelation 7 Again." *JSNT* 42 (1991) 99-115.
———. *The Theology of the Book of Revelation*. Cambridge: Cambridge University Press, 1993.
Beale, Gregory K. *The Book of Revelation: A Commentary on the Greek Text*. NIGTC. Grand Rapids: Eerdmans, 1999.
Beale, Gregory K., and Sean M. McDonough. "Revelation." In *Commentary on the New Testament Use of the Old Testament*, edited by G. K. Beale and D. A. Carson, 1081-1161. Grand Rapids: Baker, 2007.
Biguzzi, Giancarlo. "The Chaos of Rev 22,6-21 and Prophecy in Asia." *Bib* 83 (2002) 193-210.
———. "Is the Babylon of Revelation Rome or Jerusalem?" *Bib* 87 (2006) 371-86.
Blount, Brian K. *Revelation: A Commentary*. NTL. Louisville: Westminster John Knox, 2009.
Boring, M. Eugene. "The Voice of Jesus in the Apocalypse of John." *NovT* 34 (1992) 334-59.
Bovon, François. "John's Self-presentation in Revelation 1:9-10." *CBQ* 62 (2000) 693-700.
Boxall, Ian. *The Revelation of Saint John*. BNTC. Peabody, MA: Hendrickson, 2006.
———. "'Who Rides the White Horse?': Truth and Deception in the Book of Revelation." *ScrB* 41 (2011) 76-88.
Brighton, Louis A. *Revelation*. Concordia Commentary. St. Louis: Concordia, 1999.

Bibliography

Brodd, Jeffrey, and Jonathan L. Reed, eds. *Rome and Religion: A Cross-Disciplinary Dialogue on the Imperial Cult*. Writings from the Greco-Roman World Supplement Series 5. Atlanta: SBL, 2011.

Charles, J. Daryl. "An Apocalyptic Tribute to the Lamb (Rev 5:1–14)." *JETS* 34 (1991) 461–73.

———. "Imperial Pretensions and the Throne-Vision of the Lamb: Observations on the Function of Revelation 5." *CTR* 7 (1993) 85–97.

Coutsoumpos, P. "The Social Implications of Idolatry in Revelation 2:14: Christ or Caesar?" *BTB* 27 (1997) 23–27.

Dalrymple, Rob. *Revelation and the Two Witnesses: The Implications for Understanding John's Depiction of the People of God and His Hortatory Intent*. Eugene, OR: Wipf and Stock, 2011.

———. "These Are the Ones . . . (Rev 7)." *Bib* 86 (2005) 396–406.

———. "The Use of καί in Revelation 11,1 and the Implications for the Identification of the Temple, the Altar, and the Worshippers." *Bib* 87 (2006) 387–94.

Dean, R. L. "Chronological Issues in the Book of Revelation." *BSac* 168 (2011) 217–26.

Den Dulk, Matthijs. "Measuring the Temple of God: Revelation 11.1–2 and the Destruction of Jerusalem." *NTS* 54 (2008) 436–49.

———. "The Promises to the Conquerors in the Book of Revelation." *Bib* 87 (2006) 516–22.

DeSilva, David A. "Out of Our Minds? Appeals to Reason (Logos) in the Seven Oracles of Revelation 2–3." *JSNT* 31 (2008) 123–55.

———. "Seeing Things John's Way: Rhetography and Conceptual Blending Revelation 14:6–13." *BBR* 18 (2008) 271–98.

———. "A Sociorhetorical Interpretation of Revelation 14:6–13: A Call to Act Justly toward the Just and Judging God." *BBR* 9 (1999) 65–117.

———. "X Marks the Spot?: A Critique of the Use of Chiasmus in Macro-Structural Analyses of Revelation." *JSNT* 30 (2008) 343–71.

De Villiers, P. G. R. "The Eschatological Celebration of Salvation and the Prophetic Announcement of Judgment: The Meaning of Revelation 8:1–6 in the Light of Its Composition." *Neot* 41 (2007) 67–96.

———. "Prime Evil and Its Many Faces in the Book of Revelation." *Neot* 34 (2000) 57–85.

———. "The Sixth Seal in Revelation 6:12–17." *AcT* Supplement 6 (2004) 1–30.

Duff, Paul B. "'I Will Give to Each of You as Your Works Deserve': Witchcraft Accusations and the Fiery-Eyed Son of God in Rev 2.18–23." *NTS* 43 (1997) 116–33.

———. "'The Synagogue of Satan': Crisis Mongering and the Apocalypse of John." In *The Reality of the Apocalypse: Rhetoric and Politics in the Book of Revelation*, edited by David L. Barr, 147–68. SBLSymS 39. Atlanta: SBL, 2006.

———. *Who Rides the Beast? Prophetic Rivalry and the Rhetoric of Crisis in the Churches of the Apocalypse*. Oxford: Oxford University Press, 2001.

Elliott, S. M. "Who Is Addressed in Revelation 18:6–7?" *BR* 40 (1995) 98–113.

Fee, Gordon D. *Revelation*. New Covenant Commentary Series 18. Eugene, OR: Cascade, 2011.

Frankfurter, David. "Jews or Not?: Reconstructing the 'Other' in Rev 2:9 and 3:9." *HTR* 94 (2001) 403–25.

Giblin, C. H. "From and before the Throne: Revelation 4:5–6a Integrating the Imagery of Revelation 4–16." *CBQ* 60 (1998) 500–513.

———. "The Millennium (Rev 20.4–6) as Heaven." *NTS* 45 (1999) 553–70.

Glancy, Jennifer A. and Stephen D. Moore, "How Typical a Roman Prostitute Is Revelation's 'Great Whore'?" *JBL* 130 (2011) 551–69.

Graves, D. E. "Local References in the Letter to Smyrna (Rv 2:8–11), Part 4: Religious Background." *Bible and Spade* 19 (2006) 88–96.

Hannah, D. D. "Of Cherubim and the Divine Throne: Rev 5.6 in Context." *NTS* 49 (2003) 528–42.

Harrington, Wilfrid J. *Revelation.* SP 16. Collegeville, MN: Liturgical, 1993.

Harris, Murray J. *Prepositions and Theology in the Greek New Testament.* Grand Rapids: Zondervan, 2012.

Heil, John Paul. "The Chiastic Structure and Meaning of Paul's Letter to Philemon." *Bib* 82 (2001) 178–206.

———. *Colossians: Encouragement to Walk in All Wisdom as Holy Ones in Christ.* SBLECL 4. Atlanta: SBL, 2010.

———. *Ephesians: Empowerment to Walk in Love for the Unity of All in Christ.* Studies in Biblical Literature 13. Atlanta: SBL, 2007.

———. "The Fifth Seal (Rev 6,9–11) as a Key to the Book of Revelation." *Bib* 74 (1993) 220–43.

———. *1 Peter, 2 Peter, and Jude: Worship Matters.* Eugene, OR: Cascade, 2013.

———. *Hebrews: Chiastic Structures and Audience Response.* CBQMS 46. Washington: Catholic Biblical Association, 2010.

———. *The Letter of James: Worship to Live By.* Eugene, OR: Cascade, 2012.

———. *The Letters of Paul as Rituals of Worship.* Eugene, OR: Cascade, 2011.

———. *Philippians: Let Us Rejoice in Being Conformed to Christ.* SBLECL 3. Atlanta: SBL, 2010.

Hemer, Colin J. *The Letters to the Seven Churches of Asia in Their Local Setting.* Grand Rapids: Eerdmans, 2001.

Herms, Ronald. *An Apocalypse for the Church and for the World: The Narrative Function of Universal Language in the Book of Revelation.* BZNW 143. Berlin: de Gruyter, 2006.

Hitchcock, M. L. "A Critique of the Preterist View of Revelation 17:9–11 and Nero." *BSac* 164 (2007) 472–85.

———. "A Critique of the Preterist View of the Temple in Revelation 11:1–2." *BSac* 164 (2007) 219–36.

Hurtado, Larry W. "Worship, NT Christian." In *The New Interpreter's Dictionary of the Bible S-Z Volume* 5, 910–23. Nashville: Abingdon, 2009.

Jauhiainen, Marko. "The Meaning of the Sanctuary Reconsidered (Rev 11,1–2)." *Bib* 83 (2002) 507–26.

———. "The OT Background to *Armageddon* (Rev. 16:16) Revisited." *NovT* 47 (2005) 381–93.

———. *The Use of Zechariah in Revelation.* WUNT 2/199. Tübingen: Mohr/Siebeck, 2005.

King, Fergus. "Travesty or Taboo?: 'Drinking Blood' and Revelation 17:2–6." *Neot* 38 (2004) 303–25.

Koenig, John. *The Feast of the World's Redemption: Eucharistic Origins and Christian Mission.* Harrisburg, PA: Trinity, 2000.

Koester, Craig R. "The Message to Laodicea and the Problem of Its Local Context: A Study of the Imagery in Rev 3.14–22." *NTS* 49 (2003) 407–24.

———. *Revelation and the End of All Things*. Grand Rapids: Eerdmans, 2001.

———. "Roman Slave Trade and the Critique of Babylon in Revelation 18." *CBQ* 70 (2008) 766–86.

Lambrecht, Jan. "Jewish Slander: A Note on Revelation 2.9–10." *ETL* 75 (1999) 421–29.

Lee, Margaret Ellen, and Bernard Brandon Scott. *Sound Mapping the New Testament*. Salem, OR: Polebridge, 2009.

Llewelyn, S. R. "The Use of Sunday for Meetings of Believers in the New Testament." *NovT* 43 (2001) 205–23.

Longenecker, Bruce W. "'Linked Like a Chain': Rev 22.6–9 in Light of an Ancient Transition Technique." *NTS* 47 (2001) 105–17.

Lupieri, Edmondo F. *A Commentary on the Apocalypse of John*. Grand Rapids: Eerdmans, 2006.

MacLeod, David J. "The Adoration of God the Creator: An Exposition of Revelation 4." *BSac* 164 (2007) 198–218.

———. "The Lion Who Is a Lamb: An Exposition of Revelation 5:1–7." *BSac* 164 (2007) 323–40.

Mangina, Joseph L. *Revelation*. Brazos Theological Commentary on the Bible. Grand Rapids: Brazos, 2010.

Marshall, I. H. "The Christian Millennium." *EvQ* 72 (2000) 217–35.

Mathews, M. D. "The Function of Imputed Speech in the Apocalypse of John." *CBQ* 74 (2012) 319–38.

Mathewson, D. "New Exodus as a Background for 'The Sea was No More' in Revelation 21:1c." *TJ* 24 (2003) 243–58.

———. "A Note on the Foundation Stones in Revelation 21.14, 19–20." *JSNT* 25 (2003) 487–98.

———. "A Re-Examination of the Millennium in Rev 20:1–6: Consummation and Recapitulation." *JETS* 44 (2001) 237–51.

Mayo, Philip L. *"Those Who Call Themselves Jews": The Church and Judaism in the Apocalypse of John*. Princeton Theological Monograph Series 60. Eugene, OR: Pickwick, 2006.

McIlraith, D. A. "'For the Fine Linen Is the Righteous Deeds of the Saints': Works and Wife in Revelation 19:8." *CBQ* 61 (1999) 512–29.

McKelvey, R. J. "Jews in the Book of Revelation." *IBS* 25 (2003) 175–94.

McLean, J. A. "The Chronology of the Two Witnesses in Revelation 11." *BSac* 168 (2011) 460–71.

McNicol, Allan J. *The Conversion of the Nations in Revelation*. LNTS 438. London: T. & T. Clark, 2011.

Moo, J. "The Sea that Is No More: Rev 21:1 and the Function of Sea Imagery in the Apocalypse of John." *NovT* 51 (2009) 148–67.

Morton, R. "Revelation 7:9–17: The Innumerable Crowd Before the One Upon the Throne and the Lamb." *ATJ* 32 (2000) 1–11.

Mounce, Robert H. *The Book of Revelation*. NICNT. Grand Rapids: Eerdmans, 1997.

Moyise, Steve. "Singing the Song of Moses and the Lamb: John's Dialogical Use of Scripture." *AUSS* 42 (2004) 347–60.

Olson, D. C. "'Those Who Have Not Defiled Themselves with Women': Revelation 14:4 and the Book of Enoch." *CBQ* 59 (1997) 492–510.
Osborne, Grant R. *Revelation*. BECNT. Grand Rapids: Baker, 2002.
Oster, Richard E. *Seven Congregations in a Roman Crucible: A Commentary on Revelation 1–3*. Eugene, OR: Wipf and Stock, 2013.
Parker, F. O. "'Our Lord and God' in Rev 4,11: Evidence for the Late Date of Revelation?" *Bib* (2001) 207–31.
Pataki, András Dávid. "A Non-Combat Myth in Revelation 12." *NTS* 57 (2011) 258–72.
Paul, Ian. "The Use of the Old Testament in Revelation 12." In *The Old Testament in the New Testament: Essays in Honour of J. L. North*, edited by Steve Moyise, 256–76. JSNTSup 189. Sheffield, UK: Sheffield Academic, 2000.
Peachey, B. F. "A Horse of a Different Colour: The Horses in Zechariah and Revelation." *ExpTim* 110 (1999) 214–16.
Perry, Peter S. *The Rhetoric of Digressions: Revelation 7:1–17 and 10:1–11:13 and Ancient Communication*. WUNT 2/268. Tübingen: Mohr/Siebeck, 2009.
———. "'Things Having Lives': Ecology, Allusion, and Performance in Revelation 8:9." *CurTM* 37 (2010) 105–13.
Powell, C. E. "Progression versus Recapitulation in Revelation 20:1–6." *BSac* 163 (2006) 94–109.
Resseguie, James, L. *The Revelation of John: A Narrative Commentary*. Grand Rapids: Baker, 2009.
Roloff, Jürgen. *The Revelation of John: A Continental Commentary*. Minneapolis: Fortress, 1993.
Ruiz, Jean-Pierre. "Betwixt and Between on the Lord's Day: Liturgy and the Apocalypse." In *The Reality of the Apocalypse: Rhetoric and Politics in the Book of Revelation*, edited by David L. Barr, 221–41. SBLSymS 39. Atlanta: SBL, 2006.
———. *Ezekiel in the Apocalypse: The Transformation of Prophetic Language in Revelation 16,17–19,10*. European University Studies 23/376. Frankfurt: Lang, 1989.
———. "Hearing and Seeing but Not Saying: A Rhetoric of Authority in Revelation 10:4 and 2 Corinthians 12:4." In *The Reality of the Apocalypse: Rhetoric and Politics in the Book of Revelation*, edited by David L. Barr, 91–111. SBLSymS 39. Atlanta: SBL, 2006.
———. "Praise and Politics in Revelation 19:1–10." In *Studies of the Book of Revelation*, edited by Steve Moyise, 69–84. Edinburgh: T. & T. Clark, 2001.
Ryan, Sean Michael. "*In Animate Praise*: The Heavenly Temple Liturgy of the Apocalypse and The Songs of the Sabbath Sacrifice." *ScrB* 42 (2012) 13–25.
Seal, David. "Sensitivity to Aural Elements of a Text: Some Acoustical Elements in Revelation." *Journal of Biblical and Pneumatological Research* 3 (2011) 38–51.
———. "Shouting in the Apocalypse: The Influence of First-Century Acclamations on the Praise Utterances in Revelation 4:8 and 11." *JETS* 51 (2008) 339–52.
Skaggs, Rebecca, and Thomas Doyle. "The Audio/Visual Motif in the Apocalypse of John through the Lens of Rhetorical Analysis." *Journal of Biblical and Pneumatological Research* 3 (2011) 19–37.
———. "Lion/Lamb in Revelation." *Currents in Biblical Research* 7 (2009) 362–75.
Smalley, Stephen S. *The Revelation of John: A Commentary on the Greek Text of the Apocalypse*. Downers Grove, IL: InterVarsity, 2005.

Bibliography

Smith, C. R. "The Portrayal of the Church as the New Israel in the Names and Order of the Tribes in Revelation 7.5–8." *JSNT* 39 (1990) 111–18.

———. "The Structure of the Book of Revelation in Light of Apocalyptic Literary Conventions." *NovT* 36 (1994) 373–93.

———. "The Tribes of Revelation 7 and the Literary Competence of John the Seer." *JETS* 38 (1995) 213–18.

Stefanovic, Ranko. "The Angel at the Altar (Revelation 8:3–5): A Case Study on Intercalations in Revelation." *AUSS* 44 (2006) 79–94.

———. "The Meaning and Significance of the ἐπὶ τὴν δεξιάν for the Location of the Sealed Scroll (Revelation 5:1) and Understanding the Scene of Revelation 5." *BR* 46 (2001) 42–54.

———. *Revelation of Jesus Christ: Commentary on the Book of Revelation*. Berrien Springs, MI: Andrews University Press, 2002.

Stevenson, Gregory M. "Conceptual Background to Golden Crown Imagery in the Apocalypse of John (4:4, 10: 14:14)." *JBL* 114 (1995) 257–72.

———. *Power and Place: Temple and Identity in the Book of Revelation*. BZNW 107. Berlin: de Gruyter, 2001.

Strawn, Brent A. "Why Does the Lion Disappear in Revelation 5? Leonine Imagery in Early Jewish and Christian Literatures." *JSP* 17 (2007) 37–74.

Streett, R. Alan. *Subversive Meals: An Analysis of the Lord's Supper under Roman Domination during the First Century*. Eugene, OR: Wipf and Stock, 2013.

Stuckenbruck, Loren T. "Revelation 4–5: Divided Worship or One Vision?" *Stone-Campbell Journal* 14 (2011) 235–48.

Tavo, Felise. "The Outer Court and Holy City in Rev 11:1–2: Arguing for a Positive Appraisal." *ABR* 54 (2006) 56–72.

———. *Woman, Mother and Bride: An Exegetical Investigation into the "Ecclesial" Notions of the Apocalypse*. BiTS 3. Leuven: Peeters, 2007.

Taylor, Deborah Furlan. "The Monetary Crisis in Revelation 13:17 and the Provenance of the Book of Revelation." *CBQ* 71 (2009) 580–96.

Thompson, Leonard L. *The Book of Revelation: Apocalypse and Empire*. Oxford: Oxford University Press, 1990.

———. "Lamentation for Christ as a Hero: Revelation 1:7." *JBL* 119 (2000) 683–703.

———. *Revelation*. ANTC. Nashville: Abingdon, 1998.

Tonstad, Sigve K. *Saving God's Reputation: The Theological Function of Pistis Iesou in the Cosmic Narratives of Revelation*. LNTS 337. London: T. & T. Clark, 2006.

Trebilco, Paul. *Self-designations and Group Identity in the New Testament*. Cambridge: Cambridge University Press, 2012.

Vanni, Ugo. "Liturgical Dialogue as a Literary Form in the Book of Revelation." *NTS* 37 (1991) 348–72.

Vassiliadis, Petros. "Apocalypse and Liturgy." *SVTQ* 41 (1997) 95–112.

Voorwinde, S. "Worship—The Key to The Book of Revelation?" *VR* 63 (1998) 3–35.

Wilson, Mark. *The Victor Sayings in the Book of Revelation*. Eugene, OR: Wipf and Stock, 2007.

Witetschek, S. "The Dragon Spitting Frogs: On the Imagery of Revelation 16:13–14." *NTS* 54 (2008) 557–72.

Wong, D. K. K. "The Hidden Manna and the White Stone in Revelation 2:17." *BSac* 155 (1998) 346–54.

———. "The Pillar and the Throne in Revelation 3:12, 21." *BSac* 156 (1999) 297–307.

———. "The Tree of Life in Revelation 2:7." *BSac* 155 (1998) 211–26.
Yarbro Collins, Adela. "Satan's Throne: Revelations from Revelation." *BAR* 32 (2006) 26–39.
Yates, R. S. "The Function of the Tribulation Saints." *BSac* 163 (2006) 215–33.
———. "The Resurrection of the Tribulation Saints." *BSac* 163 (2006) 453–66.
———. "The Rewards of the Tribulation Saints." *BSac* 163 (2006) 322–34.

Author Index

Aune, David E., 11n8, 11n13, 18n2, 23n14, 26n23, 43n17, 43n18, 54n35, 64n49, 71n2, 105n32, 108n34, 132n14, 152n33, 201n28, 206n1, 211n7, 214n10, 247n14, 259n27, 298n26, 299n28, 316n8, 331n10

Bandy, Alan S., 1n1, 19n7, 28n30, 36n3
Barr, David L., 1n2, 11n9, 11n10, 11n14
Bauckham, Richard, 12n15, 50n32, 102n30
Beale, Gregory K., 1n1, 10n5, 10n6, 11n13, 24n18, 36n4, 42n16, 44n21, 46n25, 48n29, 49n31, 64n50, 71n1, 71n2, 93n20, 96n24, 98n26, 107n33, 125n10, 128n12, 132n15, 143n25, 144n27, 166n5, 188n17, 195n21, 216n12, 217n14, 220n16, 223n19, 224n20, 225n21, 226n22, 240n6, 246n13, 248n15, 251n17, 256n22, 257n25, 274n8, 290n19, 291n21, 301n30, 312n4, 316n9, 325n4, 326n6, 327n7, 332n11
Biguzzi, Giancarlo, 263n19, 333n13
Blount, Brian K., 10n5, 10n6, 37n5, 44n20, 114n2, 120n6, 183n14, 187n16, 208n3, 250n16, 276n9, 277n11, 284n14, 289n16, 297n25
Boring, M. Eugene, 18n4, 27n28
Bovon, François, 25n22
Boxall, Ian, 25n20, 27n24, 29n31, 59n39, 75n6, 83n14, 88n17, 94n21, 109n35, 139n21, 143n23, 196n23, 210n6, 215n11, 240n7, 261n28, 269n2, 273n6, 277n10, 313n5, 315n7, 319n11, 324n2, 324n3, 332n12
Brighton, Louis A., 18n3
Brodd, Jeffrey, 10n7

Charles, J. Daryl, 80n11, 85n15
Coutsoumpos, P., 43n19

Dalrymple, Rob, 143n24, 144n27, 145n29
Dean, R. L., 152n34
Den Dulk, Matthijs, 65n51, 144n26
DeSilva, David A., 1n1, 38n7, 40n12, 44n22, 50n33, 60n42, 196n24
De Villiers, P. G. R., 88n17, 99n28, 116n3, 292n22
Doyle, Thomas, 1n2, 80n11
Duff, Paul B., 39n9, 49n30, 238n3

Elliott, S. M., 252n19

Fee, Gordon D., 46n24

Author Index

Frankfurter, David, 39n9

Giblin, C. H., 72n4, 290n18
Glancy, Jennifer A., 237n1
Graves, D. E., 38n8

Hannah, D. D., 80n10
Harrington, Wilfrid J., 10n5, 10n6, 44n22, 72n3
Harris, Murray J., 22n12
Heil, John Paul, 9n3, 11n12, 18n2, 95n23
Hemer, Colin J., 21n10, 35n1, 38n8, 41n13, 46n23, 51n34, 56n37, 61n43
Herms, Ronald, 22n13
Hitchcock, M. L., 144n26, 244n10
Hurtado, Larry W., 18n2

Jauhiainen, Marko, 24n18, 144n26, 225n21

King, Fergus, 241n8
Koenig, John, 11n14, 12n16
Koester, Craig R., 20n9, 62n45, 257n24

Lambrecht, Jan, 39n9
Lee, Margaret Ellen, 1n2
Llewelyn, S. R., 27n24
Longenecker, Bruce W., 325n5
Lupieri, Edmondo F., 37n6, 94n22, 135n17, 173n10, 177n13, 209n5

MacLeod, David J., 76n8, 81n12, 85n15
Mangina, Joseph L., 20n8, 23n14, 25n21
Marshall, I. H., 290n19
Mathews, M. D., 62n46
Mathewson, D., 290n18, 297n24, 310n3

Mayo, Philip L., 39n9, 58n38
McDonough, Sean M., 24n18
McIlraith, D. A., 272n4
McKelvey, R. J., 39n9
McLean, J. A., 152n34
McNicol, Allan J., 1n1
Moo, J., 297n24
Moore, Stephen D., 237n1
Morton, R., 109n35
Mounce, Robert H., 21n11, 27n25, 41n14, 50n32, 89n18, 102n29, 144n26, 156n35, 176n12, 185n15, 207n2, 218n15, 243n9, 244n11, 246n12, 257n24, 272n5, 290n20, 310n2, 325n5, 328n8
Moyise, Steve, 209n4

Olson, D. C., 188n19
Osborne, Grant R., 24n17, 27n24, 28n29, 35n2, 39n10, 47n27, 56n37, 59n40, 63n48, 73n5, 87n16, 113n1, 135n16, 136n18, 137n19, 138n20, 140n22, 170n8, 195n22, 198n25, 198n27, 213n8, 213n9, 256n23, 282n12, 290n17, 297n24, 318n10
Oster, Richard E., 35n1, 38n8, 41n13, 46n23, 51n34, 56n37, 61n43

Parker, F. O., 76n8
Pataki, András Dávid, 165n4
Paul, Ian, 174n11
Peachey, B. F., 90n19
Perry, Peter S., 109n35, 119n5
Powell, C. E., 290n18

Reed, Jonathan L., 10n7
Resseguie, James, L., 21n11, 25n19, 29n32, 31n33, 37n5

Roloff, Jürgen, 11n13, 24n16,
    39n11, 44n20, 47n28,
    129n13, 145n28, 146n30,
    148n31, 151n32, 162n1,
    163n2, 167n7, 172n9,
    188n18, 191n20, 198n26,
    217n13, 222n17, 237n1,
    238n2, 238n4, 239n5,
    252n18, 255n21, 267n1,
    294n23, 309n1, 314n6,
    323n1, 330n9
Ruiz, Jean-Pierre, 11n10, 11n11,
    137n19, 258n16
Ryan, Sean Michael, 11n10

Scott, Bernard Brandon, 1n2
Seal, David, 1n2, 76n8
Skaggs, Rebecca, 1n2, 80n11
Smalley, Stephen S., 27n26, 29n32,
    62n47, 75n7, 118n4, 120n7,
    126n11, 143n23, 215n11,
    223n18, 253n20, 273n7,
    287n14, 300n29, 312n4,
    328n8, 332n12
Smith, C. R., 102n30
Stefanovic, Ranko, 77n9, 116n3
Stevenson, Gregory M., 23n15,
    27n27, 72n3

Strawn, Brent A., 80n11
Streett, R. Alan, 64n49
Stuckenbruck, Loren T., 85n15

Tavo, Felise, 1n1, 109n35, 144n26,
    152n34, 165n3, 166n6,
    271n3
Taylor, Deborah Furlan, 183n14
Thompson, Leonard L., 11n10,
    24n18, 36n3
Tonstad, Sigve K., 11n11
Trebilco, Paul, 21n10

Vanni, Ugo, 11n10, 23n14
Vassiliadis, Petros, 11n9
Voorwinde, S., 10n7

Wilson, Mark, 1n1, 38n7, 40n12,
    44n22, 50n33, 60n42
Witetschek, S., 222n17
Wong, D. K. K., 37n6, 44n22,
    60n41

Yarbro Collins, Adela, 41n15
Yates, R. S., 109n35, 290n18

Scripture Index

OLD TESTAMENT

Genesis

2:8	100
2:9	35, 37
37:9	162
49:9	77–78
49:10	78

Exodus

12:6	80n11
12:7	82n13
15:1–18	205, 207
19:6	20, 23
19:13	27
19:16	27
19:19	27
20:18	27
25:31–40	26, 27
28:4	28
28:31	28
29:5	28

Numbers

25:1–3	42
31:16	42

Deuteronomy

4:2	329, 331
13:1	329, 331
32:43	170

2 Samuel

7:14	296, 300

2 Kings

9:22	46

1 Chronicles

5:25	43
29:11	84

Tobit

13:17	311, 313

1 Maccabees

10:89	28
11:58	28

Psalms

2:7	296, 300
2:8–9	45, 50
77:24 (LXX)	44
85:9 (LXX)	206, 208
141:2	81

Proverbs

3:11–12	63

Hosea

9:1	43
10:8	95, 97

Scripture Index

Joel

2:10–11	98n27

Nahum

1:5–6	98n27

Zechariah

4:1–3	141, 145
4:2	26, 27
4:10	80
4:11–14	141, 145
12:10	21, 24
12:12	21, 24

Isaiah

6:2	74
6:3	74
11:1	79
11:10	79
21:9	191
22:22	55, 57
25:8	104, 109, 296, 298
26:17	162
34:4	97n25
35:10	296, 299
43:19	296, 299
47:8–9	253
48:20	249, 251
49:10	104, 109
49:13	170
53:7	80n11
54:11–12	311, 313
61:6	20, 23
65:17	296, 297
66:7	165
66:22	296, 297

Jeremiah

3:6	43
10:7	206, 208
11:19	80n11
17:10	48
27:8	249, 251
31:31–34	23
51:7–8	191

Ezekiel

1:5–21	73, 74
1:23	28
2:8—3:3	134, 139
23:19	43
38:1—39:20	290
43:2	28
47:1–12	317, 318

Daniel

7:9	26, 28
7:13	21, 24, 26, 27
7:14	24
10:5–6	26, 28
10:13	167
10:21	167
12:1	167

~

NEW TESTAMENT

Matthew

26:27–18	23

Mark

14:23–24	23

Luke

22:20	23

Acts

5:30–31	38
10:39–40	38
13:29–30	38

Scripture Index

1 Corinthians

11:25–26	13
11:25	23
12:1–13	18n2
14:6	18n2
14:26	18n2

Galatians

3:13	38

1 Peter

2:24	38

Revelation

1:1—3:22	2, 4, 14, 336
1:1–20	2, 4, 12, 14, 17–33, 70, 334
1:1–3	4, 17–20, 91
1:1–2	13
1:1	2, 10, 10n4, 13, 17, 18, 18n2, 19–25, 30, 31, 33, 35, 37, 47, 70, 78, 81, 94, 101, 124, 136, 138–40, 176, 244, 278, 287, 315, 323, 329, 334–36
1:2	13, 17, 19, 20–22, 25, 26, 30, 31, 57, 92, 144, 147, 170, 174, 273, 274, 278, 329, 334–35
1:3	10, 10n4, 12, 13, 17, 20–24, 27, 30, 31, 37, 50, 53, 55, 57, 66, 77, 80, 85, 92, 138, 140, 144, 146, 155, 172, 173, 195, 196, 224, 248, 273, 274, 289, 323, 326, 327, 330, 331, 335
1:4–9	4, 12, 20–26
1:4–8	11, 23n14
1:4–6	32
1:4–5	22
1:4	10, 10n4, 12, 20–22, 24–27, 32, 37, 41, 52, 65, 71, 73, 75, 80–81, 87, 88, 215, 221, 241, 274, 323, 329, 333, 335
1:5–6	12, 23
1:5	12, 20, 22–24, 26, 29, 31, 32, 36, 37, 40, 42, 44, 58, 61, 78, 82, 93, 97, 105, 126, 129, 140, 144, 154, 155, 157, 195, 204, 216, 237, 245, 248, 251, 277, 291, 315, 333, 335
1:6–7	61
1:6	20, 24, 25, 28, 30, 32, 37, 39, 50, 52, 53, 55, 59, 65, 75, 81, 82, 85, 106, 107, 140, 154, 157, 186, 194, 219, 290, 315
1:7	21, 24, 25, 27, 32, 36, 49, 63, 85, 87, 106, 134, 151, 152, 197, 255, 332
1:8	21, 25, 29, 30, 32, 48, 75, 87, 107, 145, 154, 207, 215, 241, 279, 300, 314, 327
1:9	10, 13, 21, 25, 27, 32, 35, 36, 39, 57, 58, 92, 94, 97, 107, 140, 144, 147, 148, 168, 170, 174, 219, 224, 238, 274, 278, 315, 324, 325, 335
1:10–16	4, 26–28
1:10–11	32
1:10	2, 12, 18n2, 26–29, 32, 37, 64, 70–72, 78, 80, 83, 85, 114, 136, 151, 168, 238, 275, 324, 336
1:11–20	238
1:11–16	168
1:11	10, 26, 27, 30, 35, 63, 77, 78, 136, 149, 195, 323, 324
1:12–16	64, 324

353

Scripture Index

1:12–13	32
1:12	26–32, 63, 70, 72, 81, 136, 324
1:13	26–29, 31, 35, 46, 63, 71, 72, 74, 165, 175, 197, 198, 210
1:14–15	32, 46
1:14	26, 28, 44, 54, 63, 73, 74, 87, 125, 134, 276
1:15	26, 28, 29, 32, 63, 123, 134, 150, 175, 186, 237, 270
1:16	26–27, 28–30, 32, 35–37, 41, 43, 52, 62, 72, 76, 77, 89, 90, 96, 105, 130, 134, 135, 139, 198, 222, 278, 315
1:17–20	4, 28–31
1:17–18	30, 31
1:17	12, 28–29, 30–32, 38, 39, 46, 48, 70, 75, 77, 135, 151, 273, 324, 327, 336
1:18	12, 29, 30, 31, 33, 36–38, 40, 48, 52, 57, 58, 62, 75, 77, 80, 85, 90, 101, 122, 124, 126, 135, 138, 151, 154, 182, 194, 211, 216, 283, 294–95, 327, 336, 337
1:19	13, 29, 30, 33, 35, 70, 195, 323
1:20	29, 30, 31, 33, 35, 41, 52, 63, 72, 77, 81, 89, 96, 100, 105, 113, 122n8, 135, 138, 145, 162, 168, 239, 309
2:1—3:22	2, 4, 34–66, 70–71, 320
2:1–7	4, 34–38, 65
2:1	34–37, 41, 49, 52, 54, 63, 72, 77, 81, 100, 132, 195
2:2–3	58
2:2	34, 35–37, 39, 44, 46, 52, 57, 62, 196, 301
2:3	34, 36, 42, 44, 46, 52, 58, 90
2:4	34, 36, 37, 42, 46, 62
2:5	35–37, 43, 46–48, 53, 64, 65, 87, 97, 132, 152, 157, 165, 218, 324
2:6	35–37, 43, 48, 247
2:7	35, 37, 40, 43, 44, 48, 50, 52–55, 59, 60, 64–66, 79, 80, 88, 109, 148, 150, 170, 179, 196, 247, 275, 300, 318, 321, 331, 337
2:8	35, 46, 52, 151, 195, 327
2:8–11	4, 38–40, 65
2:8	38, 182
2:9	38, 39, 41, 44, 47, 49, 58, 62, 66, 107, 168, 175, 183
2:10–11	66
2:10	38–40, 42, 47–49, 52, 54, 58, 59, 64, 72, 87, 107, 109, 150, 151, 164, 168, 170, 245, 250, 290, 337
2:11	38, 40, 42, 43, 48, 50, 52, 53, 55, 58–60, 64–66, 79, 80, 88, 89, 148, 170, 179, 196, 275, 290, 300, 301, 337
2:12–17	4, 40–44, 66
2:12	40, 41, 43, 52, 90, 195, 198, 278
2:13	40–42, 44, 46, 48, 49, 52, 57, 59, 61, 65, 71, 90, 94, 124, 144, 148, 168, 176, 195, 241, 245
2:14	40–41, 42–44, 46, 47, 49, 54, 62, 102, 132, 157, 237, 247
2:15	41, 43, 49

2:16	41, 43, 47, 53, 59, 62, 64, 66, 87, 90, 132, 139, 152, 157, 167, 218, 278, 324	3:1	51–55, 57, 62, 73, 90, 195, 221, 275
2:17	41, 43, 44, 48, 50, 52–54, 55, 57, 59, 60, 64, 65, 66, 77, 79, 80, 81, 87, 88, 90, 148, 170, 179, 196, 275, 276, 297	3:2	51, 52, 54, 55, 59, 94, 223
		3:3	51, 53, 54, 58, 64, 66, 129, 132, 157, 218, 223
		3:4–5	94
		3:4	51, 54, 63, 64, 76, 78, 87, 151, 187, 216, 223, 315, 321, 326
2:18–29	4, 45–50, 53, 66	3:5	51, 54, 55, 59, 63–66, 71–72, 79, 87, 88, 90, 109, 144, 148, 150, 161, 170, 179, 194, 223–24, 242, 294, 295, 300, 316, 337
2:18	45, 46, 50, 52, 73, 74, 134, 150, 165, 175, 195, 276, 300–301		
2:19	45, 46, 52, 57, 58, 179–80		
2:20–23	180		
2:20–22	146, 188	3:6	51, 52, 55, 60, 65, 66, 80, 179, 196, 275
2:20	18n5, 45, 46, 47, 49, 62, 94, 101, 124, 125, 132, 138, 149, 157, 160, 168, 182, 187, 237, 247	3:7–13	4, 55–60, 66
		3:7	55–57, 60, 61, 74, 78, 79, 81, 93, 122, 146, 195, 208, 289, 316, 326, 334
2:21	45, 47, 48, 53, 57, 64, 66, 94, 132, 145, 157, 191	3:8	55–56, 57, 58, 60, 62, 64, 70, 76, 78, 90, 104, 146, 211, 316
2:22	45, 47–50, 53, 64, 66, 107, 132		
2:23	45, 48, 49, 54, 58, 64, 90, 93, 146, 164, 196, 198, 248, 252, 294, 295, 327	3:9	12, 56, 58, 59, 66, 75, 132, 143, 161, 168, 208, 253, 291
		3:10	56, 58, 59, 93, 96, 129, 150, 151, 164, 168, 223, 237
2:24	45, 49, 52, 54, 63, 168		
2:25	45, 49, 50, 52, 58, 59		
2:26–28	143	3:11	56, 59, 72, 87, 152, 324
2:26–27	50	3:12	56, 59, 60, 64, 66, 70, 79, 81, 87, 88, 90, 108, 134, 143, 144, 148, 155, 170, 181, 251, 297, 300, 309, 314, 321
2:26	45, 50, 53, 57, 59, 64, 79, 81, 88, 90, 144, 148, 165, 169, 170, 176, 208, 279, 300		
2:27–28	144	3:13	52, 56, 60, 65, 66, 80, 179, 196, 275
2:27	45, 50, 90, 109, 125, 142, 165, 279	3:14–22	4, 60–65, 66
2:28	45, 50, 53, 55, 63–66, 81, 330	3:14	60, 61, 62, 76, 84, 85, 106, 138, 144, 195, 204, 208, 245, 276, 299
2:29	45, 50, 52, 53, 55, 60, 65, 66, 80, 179, 196, 275	3:15–16	62
3:1–6	4, 51–55, 66	3:15	60, 62, 63

Scripture Index

Ref	Pages
3:16	60, 62, 64
3:17–18	258
3:17	61–63, 107, 183, 224, 247, 251, 314, 321
3:18	61, 63, 71, 73, 74, 82, 87, 94, 144, 161, 184, 208, 224, 239, 251, 277, 314, 321
3:19	61, 63, 64, 66, 132, 157, 218
3:20–21	65
3:20	61, 64, 65, 70, 80, 150, 191, 193, 216, 237, 241, 247, 251, 273, 282, 284, 328, 330, 337
3:21	61, 64–66, 71, 79, 88, 148, 170, 287, 300
3:22	52, 61, 65, 66, 80, 179, 196, 275
4:1—16:21	2, 3, 5, 14, 67–232, 336
4:1—7:17	3, 5, 69–111, 303
4:1–5a	5, 69–72, 104, 111
4:1–2	2
4:1	2, 69, 70–72, 83, 100, 104, 111, 114, 136, 140, 151, 156, 236, 238, 244, 275, 287, 336
4:2—5:14	151, 236, 238
4:2–3	77
4:2	2, 18n2, 69, 71, 75, 80, 85, 87, 237, 275, 311, 336
4:3	69, 71, 75, 130, 134, 239, 309
4:4	69–70, 71, 72, 75, 79, 87, 94, 105, 111, 125, 144, 154, 161–62, 163, 198, 259, 277, 303
4:5	70, 72, 73, 75, 80, 86–87, 115, 119, 136, 156, 221, 227, 274, 318, 323
4:5b–11	5, 72–76, 111
4:6	72–75, 77, 79, 80, 84, 206, 318
4:7	72–73, 74, 78, 98, 120, 125, 172, 175
4:8–11	79–80
4:8	73, 74, 76, 77, 80, 81, 87, 107, 108, 120, 125, 145, 154, 169, 172, 194, 207, 215, 223, 241, 279, 289, 314, 326, 334
4:9–11	11
4:9–10	77
4:9	73, 75, 76, 85, 87, 101, 106, 111, 138, 152, 154, 194, 211, 237, 283, 315, 316, 337
4:10	73, 75, 81, 85, 87, 97, 101, 105, 106, 111, 132, 138, 143, 154, 194, 211, 237, 283, 303, 337
4:11	73, 76, 78, 81–82, 84, 88, 106, 107, 138, 145, 169, 211, 216, 314, 315, 316
5:1–9	135
5:1–5	5, 76–79, 97, 110
5:1	76–78, 81, 87, 98, 100, 110, 134, 237
5:2	76, 77–78, 81, 84, 97, 98, 101, 110, 129, 134
5:3	76–77, 78, 84, 92, 98, 104, 110, 132, 161, 186, 211
5:4	77, 78, 107, 167, 255
5:5–6	187
5:5	77, 78, 80, 88, 101, 102, 107, 125, 136, 148, 169, 211, 245, 255, 303, 330
5:6–10	5, 79–83, 110
5:6	79, 80, 82, 87, 88, 89, 92, 97, 98, 104–5, 109, 128, 151, 163, 165, 176, 181, 182, 185, 221, 226, 262, 274, 275, 278, 303, 323, 330

Scripture Index

5:7	79, 81, 87, 98, 115, 139, 237	6:3	86, 88, 89, 91, 95, 101, 110, 135
5:8–9	97	6:4	86, 88–90, 92, 123, 163, 179, 282
5:8	11, 79, 81, 86, 93, 96, 105, 106, 110, 114, 117, 139, 154, 155, 186, 194, 207, 210, 215, 228, 238, 269, 277, 289, 303, 327, 334	6:5	86, 88–91, 95, 96, 105, 110, 135, 197, 198, 282
		6:6	86, 89, 101, 135, 198
		6:7	86, 89, 91, 95, 101, 110, 135
		6:8	86, 89–90, 93, 94, 101, 118, 119, 123, 124, 126, 147, 196, 197, 253, 282, 294
5:9–10	106		
5:9	79, 81, 82, 84, 86, 88, 90, 92, 93, 101, 102, 105, 108, 110, 139, 140, 149, 170, 178, 184, 186–88, 190, 197, 203, 204, 207, 216, 247, 262, 277, 290, 297, 298, 319	6:9–11	5, 91–95, 96, 110, 157, 264
		6:9–10	302
		6:9	91, 92, 93, 95, 96, 98, 101, 108, 110, 114–15, 118, 128, 135, 136, 143, 144, 147, 161, 170, 173, 190, 217, 241, 262, 268, 274, 278, 288, 303
5:9–14	11		
5:9–10	92, 150		
5:10	79, 82, 88, 91, 105, 108, 140, 154, 157, 169, 219, 289, 290, 319		
5:11–14	5, 83–85, 110	6:10	11, 91, 93, 94, 96–98, 101, 105, 108, 110, 114, 115, 117, 118, 120, 122, 123, 126, 128, 131, 134, 136, 150, 151, 155, 156, 158, 160, 162, 190, 199, 200–202, 208–11, 215, 217, 227, 236–38, 241, 252, 254, 257, 261, 262, 268, 269, 276, 277, 288, 294, 303, 326, 334
5:11	83, 84, 92, 102, 104, 106, 110, 130, 184, 303		
5:12	83, 84, 88, 92, 98, 106, 154, 165, 167, 169, 184, 211, 216, 258, 262, 314–16		
5:13	83–88, 90, 92, 99, 100, 106, 107, 113, 118, 135, 154, 161, 191, 194, 203, 237, 269, 293, 314–16, 333, 337		
		6:11	91, 93, 94, 101, 102, 105, 110, 114, 123, 124, 138, 148, 169, 170, 179, 183, 196, 198, 274, 287
5:14	83, 85, 86, 96, 106, 107, 110, 132, 143, 154, 228, 269, 303		
6:1–8	5, 85–91, 92, 96, 110	6:12–17	5, 95–99, 100, 110
6:1	85–89, 91, 95, 98, 101, 110, 113, 120, 135, 136, 165	6:12	95, 96, 97, 100, 101, 108, 113, 116, 119, 120, 122, 123, 135, 145, 151, 160, 227, 277
6:2	85, 87–90, 147, 197, 198, 275–76, 282, 303	6:13–14	97n25

357

Scripture Index

6:13	95–98, 100, 115, 119, 120, 122, 160
6:14–16	243
6:14	95, 97, 228, 293
6:15	95, 97, 110, 126, 140, 157, 183, 237, 248, 282, 315
6:16	95, 98, 99, 105, 108–9, 110, 172, 183, 193, 227, 293, 319
6:17	95, 98, 98n27, 100, 105, 111, 129, 155, 193, 223, 253
7:1–8	5, 99–102, 111
7:1	99, 100, 101, 104, 113, 114, 118, 129, 135, 137, 286, 290, 291
7:2	99, 100, 101, 111, 114, 124, 135, 147, 220
7:3	18n5, 99, 101, 102, 105, 114, 118, 124, 135, 137, 138, 183, 186, 220, 268, 319
7:4–17	124
7:4	99, 102, 104, 130, 137, 184, 186, 310, 312
7:5–8	102, 162
7:5	99, 102, 137, 312
7:6	99–100, 312
7:7	100, 312
7:8	100, 102, 137, 312
7:9–17	5, 103–9, 111
7:9–10	314
7:9	103–8, 111, 113–15, 140, 144, 145, 149, 161, 164, 165, 178, 183, 187, 190, 194, 211, 219, 247, 267, 279, 294, 298, 304, 337
7:10–12	269
7:10	103, 105, 108, 136, 140, 162, 169, 237, 247, 267, 293, 294
7:10–17	11, 164
7:11	103, 106–8, 113, 115, 132, 143, 154, 177, 228, 303
7:12	103, 106–7, 154, 167, 169, 184, 194, 211, 267, 315, 316, 337
7:13	103, 107, 111, 144, 161, 187, 272, 277, 303
7:14	13, 103, 107–9, 111, 145, 170, 187, 204, 216, 272, 277, 328
7:15	103, 108, 113, 115, 143, 169, 170, 237, 293, 298, 300, 304, 319
7:16	104, 109, 119, 217, 300
7:17	104, 109, 113, 119, 143, 144, 150, 165, 191, 216, 226, 279, 284, 298, 300, 304, 318, 337
8:1—11:19	3, 5, 112–58, 264
8:1–5	5, 112–16, 158, 160
8:1	112, 113, 116, 135, 153
8:2	112–15, 117, 164, 169
8:3–5	199, 209
8:3–4	136, 227
8:3	11, 112, 114, 115, 122, 128, 143, 155, 174, 215, 311, 327, 334
8:4	11, 112, 115, 117, 122, 128, 131, 155, 156, 158, 169, 194, 201, 211, 215, 268–69, 327, 334
8:5	113, 115, 117, 128, 131, 136, 143, 156, 158, 163, 199, 201, 202, 211, 227, 318
8:6–13	5, 116–20, 157
8:6	116, 117, 120, 124
8:7–12	129
8:7–8	277
8:7	116, 117–18, 119, 120, 123, 131, 168, 206, 228, 247, 264

358

Scripture Index

8:8	116, 118–20, 131, 147, 214, 283, 309	9:13	127, 128, 132, 143, 169
8:9	116, 118–20, 147, 156, 214, 264, 294	9:14	127–29, 220, 278, 282, 286
8:10	116, 119, 120, 122, 191, 214	9:15	127, 129, 130, 131, 165, 220, 278, 282, 286, 287
8:11	117, 119, 120, 123, 124, 140, 147, 214	9:16	127, 130, 184, 278
8:12	117, 120, 123, 160, 163, 218, 262, 264	9:17	127, 130, 131, 136, 145, 176, 193, 194, 222, 281, 282
8:13	117, 120, 122, 124–25, 126, 128, 129, 131, 138, 150, 157, 158, 171, 172, 189, 190, 237, 256, 281	9:18	127, 131, 145–47, 193, 222, 282, 331
		9:19	127, 131, 139, 163, 168
		9:20–21	157, 337
9:1–12	5, 121–26, 157	9:20	127–28, 131, 132, 135, 143, 146, 147, 149, 152, 182, 188, 217, 219, 250, 284, 331
9:1–2	123		
9:1	121, 122, 126, 134, 157, 286		
9:2	121, 122–23, 124, 126, 131, 135, 157, 194, 218, 226, 268, 286	9:21	128, 132, 191, 217, 219, 262, 264, 301
		10:1–11	6, 133–41, 157
9:3–10	286	10:1	133–35, 136–37, 151, 157, 161, 163, 171, 176, 181, 197, 198, 250, 261, 264, 281, 286
9:3	121, 123, 124, 126, 131, 134, 146, 268		
9:4	121, 123–24, 125, 126, 183, 214, 319		
9:5	121, 124, 126, 129, 130, 144, 150, 162, 193	10:2	133–37, 139, 157, 171–72, 198, 286
9:6	121, 124, 138, 165, 253, 264	10:3–11	286
		10:3–4	140
9:7–10	125	10:3	133, 136, 250, 281
9:7	121, 124–26, 129, 130, 134, 147, 162, 165, 167, 259, 264	10:4	133, 137, 139, 140, 186, 326
		10:5	133, 137, 183, 207, 261, 264–65, 281
9:8	121, 125, 136, 176	10:6–7	281
9:9	121–22, 125, 130, 147, 167, 172	10:6	133, 137, 138, 154, 194, 210–11, 261, 283, 337
9:10	122, 125, 129–31, 144, 145, 157	10:7	18n5, 133, 138–39, 147, 153, 155, 189, 206, 215, 239, 248, 261, 265, 268
9:11	122, 126, 140, 147, 157, 172, 225, 282, 286	10:8	133, 139, 140, 157, 207
9:12	122, 126, 128, 152, 157, 171, 173	10:9	133–34, 139, 140, 146, 164
9:13–21	5, 127–32, 157	10:10	134, 139, 146, 164, 247

Scripture Index

10:11	134, 140, 142–44, 146, 149, 157, 164, 178, 244, 246–47, 274, 287, 298, 315	11:16	153, 154, 169, 177, 228, 269, 271
11:1–14	6, 141–52, 157	11:17	153, 154, 169, 176, 195, 207–8, 215, 217, 223, 241, 244, 265, 271, 279, 314
11:1–2	143	11:18	18n5, 153, 155–56, 172, 173, 177, 180, 183, 190, 193, 196, 198, 215, 227, 228, 261, 268, 269, 282–83, 293, 294, 327
11:1	141–44, 156, 311, 313		
11:2	141, 143, 144, 146, 148, 155, 177, 202, 297, 311, 313		
11:3	141, 144, 146, 149, 161, 166, 172, 187, 241, 265, 271, 274, 287	11:19	153, 156, 158, 160, 198–99, 199–200, 209, 227, 228, 318
11:4	141, 145, 148–49, 154, 164, 187	12:1—14:20	3, 6, 159–204, 230
11:5	141, 145–48, 151, 164, 173, 179, 181, 222, 244, 287, 291, 326	12:1–17	271
		12:1–6	6, 159–66, 204
11:6	141, 146, 147, 149, 150, 241, 274, 277, 278, 318	12:1	159, 160, 161–63, 167, 206, 238, 272, 308, 309, 337
11:7	141, 147, 148, 150, 167, 169, 173, 175, 178, 223, 241, 242, 244, 245, 265	12:2	159, 162, 164
		12:3	159, 162, 163, 167, 175, 202, 206, 230, 276
11:8	141–42, 148, 149, 151, 168, 191, 224, 227, 248, 313	12:4–6	167
		12:4	160, 163–65, 167, 168, 199, 202, 204
11:9	142, 149, 150, 155, 178, 224, 247, 298	12:5	160, 165, 172, 176, 177, 192, 208, 262, 279
11:10	142, 149–50, 151, 157, 162, 170, 178, 215, 237, 271, 275	12:6	160, 165–66, 167, 172, 224, 228, 238, 271, 287
11:11	142, 150–52, 182	12:7–12a	6, 166–70, 204
11:12	142, 151, 182, 197, 213, 227, 291	12:7–11	291
		12:7	166–68, 177
11:13	142, 151–53, 155, 158, 190, 191, 218, 219, 227–28, 271, 315	12:8	166, 167, 168–69, 188, 228, 261, 293
		12:9–10	260
11:14	142, 152, 154, 171, 173	12:9	166–69, 172, 176, 177, 182, 200, 202, 204, 223, 225, 230, 245, 261, 262, 276, 286
11:15–19	6, 11, 152–56, 158		
11:15	152–54, 156, 169, 179, 194, 219, 244, 262, 265, 289, 319		
11:16–18	209	12:10–12	11, 171

Scripture Index

12:10	166, 169, 176, 196, 200, 204, 219, 245, 267, 274	13:11	180–82, 221
		13:12	180–83, 189, 190, 203, 206, 221, 237
12:11	167, 169, 170, 204, 245, 274, 277	13:13	180, 181, 184, 188, 222, 228–29
12:12b–18	6, 171–74, 204	13:14–15	187, 229
12:12	167, 170, 171, 173, 174, 178, 191, 202, 244, 260, 291, 298	13:14	180, 182, 187, 189–91, 203, 206, 222, 237, 262, 283
12:13	171–73	13:15	180, 182–83, 191, 193, 207, 222, 283, 288
12:14	171–73, 224, 228, 238, 272	13:16	180, 183, 186, 193, 203, 282, 283, 288, 319
12:15	171, 173	13:17	181, 183, 184, 186, 187, 193, 194, 203, 207, 283, 319
12:16	171, 173, 177, 221		
12:17	171, 173, 174, 178, 195, 204, 213, 223, 274	13:18	181, 184, 243, 312
12:18	171, 174, 175, 186, 291	14:1–5	6, 185–89, 203
13:1–10	6, 174–80, 203	14:1	185, 186, 188, 194, 197, 203, 239, 243, 245, 271, 312, 319
13:1	174–77, 181, 238, 276, 309		
13:2	174–77, 181, 218, 221, 245, 250	14:2–3	271
		14:2	185, 186, 207, 237, 261–62, 271
13:3	174, 176, 178, 179, 181, 182, 206, 241	14:3–4	271
13:4	174, 177–79, 181, 206–7, 209–10, 221, 245, 259	14:3	185–89, 197, 203, 207, 211–12, 231, 297, 312
		14:4	185, 187–89, 196, 203, 231, 271, 278
13:5–6	231	14:5	185, 188, 316, 328
13:5	174–75, 177, 178, 181, 182	14:6–8	6, 189–92, 203
13:6	175, 177, 179, 184, 188, 210, 217, 298	14:6–7	284
		14:6	189, 190, 191–92, 193, 198, 199, 201, 219, 246, 271, 298, 333
13:7	175, 178, 180, 181, 190, 203, 207, 223, 245, 246, 298		
		14:7	189–93, 199, 208, 218, 219, 228, 231, 246, 271, 315
13:8	175, 178, 179, 181, 184, 189, 190, 203, 237, 242, 246, 294, 295, 317, 337		
		14:8	189, 191, 193, 198, 199, 201, 202, 206, 208, 227, 228, 237, 240, 244, 250, 251, 262, 263, 268, 318
13:9–10	11		
13:9	175, 179		
13:10	175, 179, 182–84, 188, 195, 272		
13:11–18	6, 180–85, 203	14:9–13	6, 192–96, 204
13:11–12	283		

361

Scripture Index

14:9	192–94, 196, 198, 199, 201, 202, 206, 210, 214, 216, 217, 228, 237, 239, 252, 279, 283, 288, 292, 319	15:4	206, 208, 210, 215, 228, 230, 231, 252, 253, 256, 259, 262, 272, 315, 316, 333
14:10–11	288	15:5–8	7, 209–12, 230
14:10	192–95, 202, 206, 210, 214, 216, 217, 228, 237, 239, 252, 279, 284, 292	15:5	209, 222, 230, 275, 298
		15:6	209, 210, 212, 217, 222, 226, 230, 251, 258, 272, 278, 318, 331
14:11	192, 194, 211, 214, 252, 256, 268, 283, 284, 292	15:7	209, 210, 211, 213, 222, 230, 236, 238, 283, 308, 337
14:12–13	11		
14:12	192, 195, 204, 272	15:8	209, 211, 213, 217, 248, 250, 251, 256, 287, 309, 316, 331
14:13	192, 195, 196, 198, 231, 272, 275, 289, 327		
14:14–17	6, 197–200, 202, 204	16:1–9	7, 212–18, 229
		16:1	212–14, 217, 226, 236, 298
14:14	197–98, 199–201, 239, 293, 311	16:2	212, 213–14, 215, 217–19, 226, 229, 241, 283, 288, 297
14:15	197–201, 204, 210, 220, 226, 293		
14:16	197, 199, 201–2, 203, 204	16:3	212, 214, 216–18, 226, 277
14:17	197, 199–201, 204, 210, 226	16:4	212, 214, 215–16, 217, 218, 226, 241, 277, 318
14:18–20	6, 200–203, 204		
14:18	200–202, 217	16:5–7	11
14:19	201, 202, 204, 206, 210, 213, 279, 281	16:5–6	215
		16:5	212, 215, 217, 241, 253, 261, 276, 326, 333–34
14:20	201, 202, 216, 277, 279, 281, 312	16:6	212, 215, 216, 241, 261, 272, 277, 281–82
15:1—16:21	3, 7, 205–31		
15:1–4	7, 205–9, 230	16:7	212, 217, 223, 253, 261, 267, 273, 276, 279, 314
15:1	205–7, 210, 211, 217, 231, 248, 251, 308, 331	16:8	213, 217, 218, 226, 297
		16:9	213, 217–18, 219–20, 229–31, 250, 251, 271, 297, 315, 331, 327
15:2–4	11		
15:2	205–8, 245, 256, 315		
15:3–4	337	16:10–12	7, 218–20, 229
15:3	18n5, 205–6, 207, 208, 215, 217, 220, 223, 228, 230, 231, 241, 267, 273, 279, 314, 316	16:10–11	299
		16:10	218–20, 226, 229
		16:11	218, 219, 229–30, 231, 327
		16:12	218, 220, 222, 226

Scripture Index

16:13–16	7, 221–25, 230	17:8	240, 241, 242, 244, 256, 263, 265, 294, 295, 317, 337
16:13	221–22, 227, 228, 239, 250, 262, 281, 283	17:9–14	7, 242–46, 263
16:14	221, 222–23, 224, 225, 227, 230–31, 237, 250, 253, 279, 283, 291	17:9	242–45, 253
		17:10	242–44, 250, 263, 287
16:15	11, 221, 224–26, 247, 289, 324, 327	17:11	243–45
		17:12–13	250, 283
16:16	221, 224, 225, 281	17:12	243–45, 247, 248, 257, 263, 265
16:17–21	7, 225–29, 230	17:13	243, 245, 248, 263
16:17	225–27, 269, 299	17:14	243, 245, 248, 253, 263, 265, 273, 280, 283, 314, 315
16:18–21	300		
16:18	225, 227–29, 318	17:15–18	7, 246–48, 263
16:19	225–26, 227–30, 236, 237, 239, 240, 244, 248, 252	17:15	246–48, 253, 272, 298
		17:16	246–48, 250, 253, 256, 258, 263, 264, 273, 282
16:20	226, 228, 243, 293	17:17	246, 248, 252, 263, 273, 287
16:21	226, 228, 229, 231, 237, 297, 331	17:18	246, 248, 250, 257
17:1—21:8	2, 3, 7, 14, 233–304, 336	18:1–8	7, 249–54, 263
		18:1	249–51, 263, 281, 286, 315
17:1—18:24	3, 7, 235–65	18:2	249–51, 253, 263, 281, 286
17:1–5	7, 235–240, 264		
17:1–2	236	18:3	249, 251, 255, 257–59, 262, 268, 315, 318
17:1	2, 235–39, 241, 243, 246, 253, 261, 264, 268, 272, 287–88, 308, 336		
		18:4	249, 251, 252, 298, 331
17:2	235, 237–41, 243, 248, 250, 251, 255, 268, 315	18:5	249, 251–52, 294
		18:6	249, 252, 294
17:3–5	308	18:7–8	299
17:3	2, 18n2, 235, 238, 239, 241, 243, 246, 253, 275, 308, 309, 336	18:7	249, 252, 253, 256, 257
		18:8	249, 253, 256, 257, 261, 263, 264, 276, 331
17:4	236, 238, 239, 241, 250, 252, 257, 258, 268, 272, 297, 308, 309, 311–13, 316	18:9–19	8, 254–59
		18:9	254–57, 259, 263, 268, 315
17:5	236, 239, 241, 265, 276, 280, 297, 308, 316, 319	18:10	254, 256–58
		18:11	254, 257–59
17:6–8	7, 240–42, 263	18:12	254, 257, 258, 313
17:6	240–42, 247, 265, 272	18:13	254, 257
17:7	240, 241, 243, 244, 265	18:14	254–55, 257, 258, 318
		18:15–16	259

363

Scripture Index

18:15	255, 258, 259	19:13	275, 277–79, 288, 299, 302
18:16	255, 258, 272, 309, 312, 313	19:14	275, 283, 312
18:17	255, 258, 259	19:15	275, 278–79, 281, 284, 291, 302
18:18	255, 259, 263, 268	19:16	275, 279, 280, 314, 315
18:19	255, 259, 261, 264	19:17–21	8, 280–84, 302
18:20–24	8, 260–63, 264	19:17	280, 282, 284
18:20	260–62, 264, 268, 276, 288, 310, 327, 334	19:18	280, 282, 284
18:21–22	262	19:19	280, 283, 284, 291, 315
18:21	260–62, 265, 291	19:20–21	302
18:22	260, 262, 267	19:20	280–81, 283, 284, 287, 288, 291, 292, 295, 301
18:23	260, 262, 264, 267, 287, 315, 318	19:21	281, 284, 289, 291
18:24	260, 262, 272, 277	20:1–10	8, 285–92, 302
19:1—21:8	3, 8, 266–304	20:1	285–87, 291
19:1–8	11	20:2	285–87, 289–91
19:1–5	8, 266–69, 303	20:3	285, 287–92, 302, 318
19:1	266–71, 304, 315	20:4–5	295
19:2	18n5, 266–71, 273, 276, 277, 303	20:4	285, 287–90, 302, 303, 319
19:3	266, 268, 271	20:5	285, 289, 290
19:4	266–67, 269, 271, 273, 274, 299, 303	20:6	285, 289–91, 295, 301, 320, 327, 337
19:5	18n5, 267, 269, 270, 273, 283, 298, 303, 319, 333	20:7	285, 290
19:6–10	8, 270–75, 302	20:8	285–86, 290, 291, 302, 303, 318
19:6	270, 271, 279, 295, 302, 304, 314	20:9	286, 291, 293
19:7	216, 270–72, 295, 297, 302, 308, 315	20:10	286, 291, 292, 295, 301, 302
19:8	270, 272, 278, 295, 297, 302, 312, 318	20:11–15	8, 292–95, 302
19:9	270, 272, 273, 276, 281, 284, 289, 299, 327, 330, 331, 337	20:11	292–95, 298, 319
		20:12	292, 293–94, 295, 298, 337
19:10	12, 13, 29, 270, 273, 274, 323, 325, 330	20:13	293, 294, 297, 298, 302, 327
19:11–16	8, 275–80, 302	20:14–15	302
19:11	275, 276, 278, 279, 283, 293, 299, 303, 326, 334	20:14	293, 295, 299, 301, 317, 337
		20:15	293, 295, 301, 317, 337
		21:1–8	8, 296–301, 303
		21:1	296–99
19:12	275–77, 279	21:2	296–99, 308, 309, 312, 330

21:3	296, 298, 300, 301, 303, 304, 309	22:1–5	9, 317–20, 324
		22:1–2	320
21:4	296, 298–301, 304	22:1	317–21, 323, 324, 328, 330, 337
21:5	296, 299, 300, 303, 323		
21:6	216, 296, 300, 301, 304, 318, 327, 331, 337	22:2	216–18, 321, 328, 331, 337
21:7	296, 300, 301, 309, 318	22:3	18n5, 317, 319, 323
21:8	296–97, 301, 328, 331, 337	22:4	317, 319
		22:5	317, 319, 320, 321, 323
21:9—22:21	2, 3, 8, 14, 305–35, 336	22:6–21	3, 9, 11–14, 322–35
		22:6–9	9, 322–25, 334
21:9—22:5	3, 8, 307–21	22:6	13, 18n5, 19n6, 323–25, 330, 333, 334
21:9–14	8, 307–10, 320		
21:9–10	323	22:7	10, 322–27, 331, 332, 335
21:9	2, 307–11, 330, 331, 337		
		22:8–9	13
21:10	2, 18n2, 275, 307, 308–9, 311, 318, 320, 321, 337	22:8	10, 12, 29, 322–23, 324, 325, 330, 335
		22:9	323–26, 334
21:11	307, 309, 312, 313, 315	22:10–15	9, 325–28, 333
21:12–13	315, 320	22:10	10, 325, 326, 331, 335
21:12	307–8, 309–11, 313	22:11	325, 326, 328, 333
21:13	308, 310	22:12	13, 325, 327, 328, 330, 332, 334
21:14	308, 310–12		
21:15–22a	8, 310–13, 320	22:13	326, 327, 329
21:15	310–15, 320	22:14	13, 326–28, 330–31, 334, 337
21:16	310–12, 314, 320		
21:17	310, 312, 330	22:15	326, 328
21:18	310, 312–14, 320	22:16–21	9, 329–33, 334
21:19–20	313	22:16	13, 19n6, 329, 330–33, 335
21:19	310–11, 312, 314, 320		
21:20	311	22:17	13, 216, 329, 331, 332, 334, 337
21:21	311, 313–15, 318, 320		
21:22	311, 313–16, 318, 320, 321	22:18	10, 13, 329, 331–33, 335
21:22b–27	8, 313–20	22:19	10, 13, 329, 331, 337
21:23	314, 315, 319–21	22:20–21	337
22:24–26	333	22:20	13, 329, 332–35, 338
21:24	314–16, 318, 321, 337	22:21	329, 333–35, 337, 338
21:25	314, 315–16, 319, 320, 328		
21:26	314, 316, 318, 337		
21:27	314, 316–18, 328, 331, 337		

www.ingramcontent.com/pod-product-compliance
Lightning Source LLC
Chambersburg PA
CBHW021339300426
44114CB00012B/1008